DISCARDED

*A Dictionary of
Cinema Quotations from
Filmmakers and Critics*

A Dictionary of
Cinema Quotations from
Filmmakers and Critics

*Over 3400 Axioms, Criticisms,
Opinions and Witticisms from
100 Years of the Cinema*

Compiled and Edited by
STEPHEN M. RINGLER

McFarland & Company, Inc., Publishers
Jefferson, North Carolina, and London

Library of Congress Cataloguing-in-Publication Data

A dictionary of cinema quotations from filmmakers and critics : over 3400
axioms, criticisms, opinions and witticisms from 100 years of the cinema /
compiled and edited by Stephen M. Ringler.

     p.   cm.

   Includes bibliographical references and index.

   ISBN 0-7864-0849-9 (illustrated case binding : 50# alkaline paper) ∞

   1. Motion pictures — Quotations, maxims, etc.   I. Ringler, Stephen M.,
1944–

   PN1994.9.D53   2000

   791.43 — dc21   00-44219

British Library cataloguing data are available

Front cover: copyright © 2000 by Artville

Manufactured in the United States of America

McFarland & Company, Inc., Publishers
 Box 611, Jefferson, North Carolina 28640
  www.mcfarlandpub.com

Acknowledgments

My sincerest gratitude is extended to the many staff members of the research institutions I frequented in order to select and search the source material for the making of this book of 3,408 quotations. Hundreds of books, periodicals and clippings were read in the effort to discover relevant quotations.

This year-long task could not have been accomplished without the assistance and cooperation of the highly professional staff of these fine institutions, and the support of Darla McDavid, my expert word processor and quality-control guru.

A special thanks to: the Center for Motion Picture Study of the Academy of Motion Picture Arts and Sciences and the Academy Foundation, Beverly Hills, California; the American Film Institute, Louis B. Mayer Library, Hollywood, California; the University of California, Santa Barbara, Library, Film Studies Department; and the Santa Barbara Public Library.

Contents

Preface

It was Edison, Bell, Ford, and the Wrights who gave mankind better illumination, communication and transportation. But it was the Brothers Lumière who created a contraption that could illuminate, communicate and transport the human spirit. This dictionary of cinema quotations captures the history and spirit, the heart and soul of the movie entertainment industry, from the minds of the masters, the moguls, movie stars and magic makers, their very words of wisdom and witticisms, industry insight and entertaining enlightenment.

This book of quotations is the original voice of cinema history heard for over 100 years, from its silent beginning through its development in speech and song to the explosive evolution of color and special effects. The book's 31 chapters connect all of the dots of the filmmaking process and provide insight into the audience, testing, stardom, celebrity status, critics and reviews.

This work presents the best of what has been quoted from the multitude of moviemakers on the art, science and business of moviemaking for a century. This book of quotations is the ultimate reference source of relevant movie industry voices expressing their experiences and expertise in filmmaking, from its origin, to screenwriting, to production, directing, acting, musical scoring, editing and testing, to the roles, casting, genres, careers, stardom and awards of the players at all levels. These quotes are indeed the very essence of the world of cinema by and for its citizens, past, present and future. The camera peeks; the microphone eavesdrops; the film captures; the screen reveals; the audience responds; the critics critique — that's cinema.

Introduction

There are two types of motion picture fans. There is the common *movie* fan, whose simple attraction to movies begins and ends in the theater, with the possible exception of the occasional purchase of a movie magazine on the stars and coming attractions. Then there is the *film* fan, whose fascination is complex and probing, with unending questions like, "How did they do that?"

These two types of fans share a desire for pure cinematic entertainment — but there the similarity ends. The film fan wants *more* than entertainment. He or she yearns to know all about the filmmaking details, both behind and in front of the camera. The difference in the two fans is like the difference between a gourmand and a gourmet. The gourmand (movie fan) can enjoy his popcorn for what it is: popcorn. The gourmet (film fan) won't be fully satisfied until he learns how that tiny hard kernel became so large and supple, and why one tastes better than another. He will savor not only its taste, but its aesthetic.

This book was compiled with the film fan in mind, but certainly not to the exclusion of the movie fan. The only thing the book intentionally excludes is Hollywood gossip and tabloid kiss-and-tell tales.

What the book offers is thousands of kernels on filmmaking that were deemed "popworthy," exploded onto the page for the fan's consumption — revelations of the fundamentals of the art. There is more than enough to satisfy the appetites of all types of fans — as well as film students, motion picture professionals, film faculty and performing artists.

This book of film industry quotations is a ready reference distillation of thousands of wonderful books written on the world of cinema. Without such a work, the film student or advanced scholar would have little choice other than to read hundreds of books and articles in order to gain a broad overview of the industry's multifaceted makeup.

It is said that there are no better data than primary data, and no better communication than direct communication. That is the foundation for this dictionary, quoting directly from the masters, moguls, stars and critics.

I began my research and editing process by asking myself a question: If I were to form a film institute of learning, who would I want as my faculty? What better voice of experience to teach others wanting to learn about the motion picture industry than those very experts who created and built the film business themselves? What film student or enthusiast would not want to sit at the feet of the movie masters like John Ford, Charlie Chaplin, Frank Capra, Federico Fellini, Orson Welles, Irving Thalberg, George Cukor, John Huston, Alfred Hitchcock, Darryl Zanuck, Billy Wilder, Jean Renoir, Ingmar Bergman, David Lean, Woody Allen, Akira Kurosawa, Steven Spielberg, Haskell Wexler, Jack Warner, D. W. Griffith, Cecil B. DeMille, Otto Preminger, Howard Hawks, Martin Scorsese, Roger Corman, Walt Disney, François Truffaut, Richard Attenborough, John Sayles, Louis B. Mayer, Sidney Lumet, Stanley Kubrick and 1,850 more.

Some notable names within the industry,

past and present, have inevitably been omitted — not to slight them, but because some people did not have anything relevant to say within the context of this book. And of course, a good deal of quotable wisdom must have ridden off on the winds of time during the early years of no recording devices, limited reportage and lack of historical perspective. As they say in show business, "You go with what you've got."

These thousands of comments range from the witty to the wise, the sarcastic to the sagacious, the rude to the crude, the shallow to the profound. All are thought-provoking, which is the book's intent. And while being both entertained and enlightened by these quotes, the reader will also discover their many messengers to be the most creative and interesting cast of characters assembled within any industry in the world.

1

Cinema

1. I didn't invent cinema, but I did industrialize it.
Charles Pathé, circa 1950
Cited in *Business Week*, 1998

2. Cinema resembles so many other arts … (it) has literary characteristics … theatrical qualities; philosophical, painting, sculpture, musical. But cinema is, in the final analysis, cinema.
Akira Kurosawa, Director
Stated in his book, *Akira Kurosawa—*
Something Like an Autobiography, 1982

3. No such thing as a literary film or a figurative film exists. There exists only cinema, which incorporates the experience of all the other arts.
Míchelangelo Antonioni
Interview in *Film Culture*, 1962

4. Movies are rarely art … do you think bad art is still art?
Barbara Hershey, Actress
Interview in *Detour* magazine, 1997

5. Change is a long cultural process, and the cinema, art or literature, can only contribute to that process, not be responsible for it.
Kostantinos Costa-Gavras, Director
Interview in *Reel Conversations*, 1991

6. I don't think film has anything to do with theater … (or) to do with literature. It is borrowed from all these older art forms, but it is a qualified art form in itself.
Norman Jewison, Director
Interview in *Directors at Work*, 1970

7. People will go to the theater to see and hear a theatrical performance and to the cinema to see a cinematic one. The theater will be the theater precisely because it is theatrical.
Orson Welles
Cited in *Orson Welles:*
The Road to Xanadu, 1996

8. I come back to the theater for the words … whereas movies are about the visual.
Kevin Kline, Actor
Interview, *Playboy* magazine, March, 1998

9. Film is a religious experience … You commune in a darkened open room with mythological huge symbolic figures. There is — on an unconscious level — a religious experience going on…. Television is a minor experience.
Richard Dreyfuss, Actor
Interview in *Take 22: Moviemakers*
on Moviemaking, 1984

10. The cinema is not an eternal art. Its forms are not unchanging. Each of the aspects that it reveals is linked inevitably to the psychology of a period … its successive faces vanish … when new techniques make earlier ones marginal.
Alexandre Astruc
Cited in *On the History of Film Style*, 1997

11. (Cinema shows) us the process of the transformation of the world. The other arts can show us merely the end result of such transformation.
Jean Mitry, Author
From his book, *Esthétique et Psychologie de*
Cinéma, on the aesthetics
and psychology of the cinema, 1990

12. The (movie) medium will eventually take its place as art because there is no other medium of interest to so many people.
Irving Thalberg, 1929
Cited in *Mayer and Thalberg — The*
Make-Believe Saints, 1975

13. The cinematic institution is not just the cinema industry (which works to fill cinemas, not empty them), it is also the mental machinery … which spectators … have internalized historically and which has adapted them to the consumption of films.
Christian Metz, Writer
From his book, *The Imaginary Signifier*, 1992

14. The true "opium" of the audience is conformity; and the entire ... film world is dedicated to the propagation of this comfortable feeling, wrapped though it is at times in the insidious disguise of art.

Luis Buñuel, Director
Interview, *Show Business Illustrated*, April 1962

15. (With the motion picture camera) there has been fashioned a weapon of culture, and from this fact arises the duty of the creative film artist not to profane the rich art of the camera, but to use it in the services of true culture.

Günther Rittan, Director, 1929
Cited in *Cinematographers on the Art and Craft of Cinematography*, 1987

16. The cinema isn't a slice of life, it's a slice of cake.

Alfred Hitchcock, Director
Cited in *Movies and Society*, 1970

17. No one ever bought a ticket to watch technology ... content will determine the entertainment choices of the public....

Adolf Zukor
Formal statement in the 1953/54 Annual Report of the Motion Picture Export Association

18. In the theater there are 1,500 cameras rolling at the same time — in the cinema, there is only one.

Orson Welles, Actor-Director
Interview for *Interviews with Film Directors*, 1967

19. The film is a machine for seeing more than meets the eye.

I. Barry
Cited on the Internet Movie Database, 1998

20. A film is a petrified garden of thought.

Jean Cocteau
From his book, *Cocteau on the Film*, 1954

21. Film is the art of myriad and wonderful illusions.

Peter W. Englemeier
Translated from his German book, *Fashion in Film*, 1990

22. Through some wonderful alchemy of light, camera, recording medium and projection, we can be transported to innumerable worlds, real or imagined.

Richard Brestoff, Actor-Author
Stated in his book, *The Camera Smart Actor*, 1994

23. The art of the theater has become indistinguishable from the art of the camera.

Hilton Edwards
Cited in *Orson Welles: The Road to Xanadu*, 1996

24. A movie is an experience that happens to you for the first time and you react to it.

Burt Lancaster, Actor
Interview in *Take 22: Moviemakers on Moviemaking*, 1984

25. Movies are immortal art — the first new art ... since Greek drama.

Eric Johnston, Motion Picture Censor
Cited in *Inside Oscar, The Unofficial History of the Academy Awards*, 1946

26. I knew I was in the presence of a medium so powerful that it might change our whole attitude toward life, civilization, and established customs.

Father Daniel A. Lord
His impression upon viewing *The Birth of a Nation* (1915), as stated in his book, *Played By Ear*, 1955

27. Of all the arts, the cinema is the most important to us.

Lenin, circa 1925
On the Soviet Union, as cited in *A Film Editor's Story*, 1979

28. Perhaps Hollywood movies give us pleasure and a sense of identification simply because they enable us to recognize and adapt to the "acted" quality of everyday life....

James Naremore
From his book, *Acting in the Cinema*, 1988

29. Cinema is life, with the boring bits cut out.

Alfred Hitchcock
Cited in *Hollywood Cinema*, 1995

30. The cinema exists in the space between the audience and the screen.

Jean-Luc Godard
Cited in *Hollywood Cinema*, 1995

31. The cinema, having replaced the public executions and bare-knuckle fights of earlier ages, is the modern arena of peril, sadism and death.

David Densby, Writer
Writing in *The New Yorker*, April 6, 1998

32. The cinema ... is a total environment medium, and the wider the screen and the louder the sound, the more sense one has of being swallowed up in it.

I. C. Jarvie
From his book, *Movies and Society*, 1970

33. The one thing I want to say about cinéma-vérité is that it would be better to call it cinema-sincerity, if you like…. "This is what I saw. I didn't fake it."

Jean Rouch, Director
The father of cinéma vérité, cited in
Documentary Explorations, 1971

34. Everybody knows that movies promise more than they deliver.

John Waters, Director-Producer
Interview in *Directors at Work*, 1970

35. The motion picture is literally bound to the mental and moral level of its vast audience.

Board of Directors, AMPP
Formally stated by the Board of Directors
of the Association of Motion Picture
Producers to members of the Motion
Pictures Association of America, 1930

36. Film renders visible what we did not, or perhaps even could not, see before its advent.

Siegfried Kracauer
Cited in *Theory of Film*, 1971

37. The motion picture does not present the audience with tastes and manners and views and morals; it reflects those they already have.

Board of Directors, AMPP
Formally stated by the Board of Directors
of the Association of Motion Picture
Producers to members of the Motion
Pictures Association of America, 1930

38. The cinema, if it is to be worth anything at all, has to bear witness to the reality which surrounds us here and now.

J. A. Bardenn, Director
Interviewed in *Show Business Illustrated*,
April 1962

39. It was a world you created; it was not a world you went out and found.

Richard Sylbert
Cited in *American Cinema: One
Hundred Years of Filmmaking*, 1995

40. Film is for the "flow of life." Unlike photographs, film can show us reality in a time dimension.

Siegfried Kracauer
Cited in *Theory of Film*, 1971

41. Film is one of the three universal languages … the other two: mathematics and music.

Frank Capra, Producer-Director
Stated in his autobiography, *Frank Capra
— The Name Above the Title*, 1971

42. The visual dramatization is how (the audience) translates things. It's a whole language. Film is a language.

Richard Brooks, Writer-Director
Interview, *Directors at Work*, 1970

43. Film is the aesthetic means of communication in our society, in our world today.

Chris Evans, Special Effects Designer
Cited in *Moviemakers at Work*, 1987

44. The film is a language, very much like print, although not prose print, rather poetry print.

I. C. Jarvie
From his book, *Movies and Society*, 1970

45. The silent film was not only a vigorous popular art; it was a universal language — Esperanto for the eyes.

Kevin Brownlow, Writer
Stated in his co-authored book, *Hollywood —
The Pioneers*, with John Kobal, 1979

46. Cinema — the feel of the world.

Dziga Vertov, Cinematographer
Cited in *Film Makers on Film Making*, 1983

47. American cinema is international like the fairy tales were international.

Bernard Tavernier
Cited in *American Cinema: One
Hundred Years of Filmmaking*, 1995

48. (Movies are) one of the last bastions of community.

Laura Ziskin, Studio Head
Stated in the *Newsweek* 100 Best Movies
list from the American Film Institute, 1998

49. A film is like a short moment, just a thought, like a song or a speech, so I don't think a movie can change the world or country.

Konstantinos Costa-Gavras, Director
Interview in *Reel Conversations*, 1991

50. A film is the world in an hour and a half.

Jean-Luc Godard
Cited in *Hollywood Cinema*, 1995

51. Even the ritziest cinema is classless.

I. C. Jarvie
From his book, *Movies and Society*, 1970

52. It's true that watching (foreign) films is labor-intensive…. What they require, in short, is that you be in the mood.

Daphne Merkin, Writer
Writing in *The New Yorker*, May, 11, 1998

53. I just deplore classification of films into foreign or American and the automatic assumption is that the American films have to be inferior.

Robert Wise, Director
Interview in *Directors at Work*, 1970

54. You can take Hollywood for granted like I did, or you can dismiss it with the contempt we reserve for what we don't understand.

F. Scott Fitzgerald, Writer
Quoted from his book *The Last Tycoon*

55. Wherever motion pictures are shown — from Tokyo to Timbuctoo [sic] and from Nome to Buenos Aires — Hollywood is about as well-known as the sun and moon.

20th Century–Fox Film Corp.
Commenting on their industry in their
Annual Report to Stockholders, 1978

56. The very name Hollywood has colored the thought of this age. It has given to the world a new synonym for happiness....

Carl Milliken, Writer
Speech, "The Motion Picture as a Business," given
to the Motion Picture Association, April 1928

57. The moving picture is one of the greatest inventions of mankind. It makes mankind happy.

Dr. Hu Shih, Chinese Ambassador to the U.S.
Speaking at the Academy Awards, 1941

58. "Movies," like popcorn, are to be consumed.

James Monaco, Author-Scholar
From his book *How to Read a Film*, 1981

59. The only real Delta factor, the element which can truly alter your perspective on the movie-going experience, is this question, this factor alone: Do they have "Red Vines" or do they have "Twizzlers"?

Tom Hanks
Cited in *The New York Times Magazine*, 1987

60. The movies spoil us for life; nothing ever lives up to them.

Edmund White
Cited on the Internet Movie Database, 1998

61. Cinema should make you forget you're sitting in a theater.

Roman Polanski, Director
Cited on the Internet Movie Database, 1998

62. The cinema has no boundaries. It is a ribbon of dream.

Orson Welles, Actor-Director
Cited in *Orson Welles: The Road to Xanadu*, 1996

63. Forget acting, forget angst. The reason we go to the movies is to gaze with envy and adoration at the sublime genetic accidents up there on the screen.

Libby Gelman-Waxner, Writer
Stated in the *Newsweek*, "The 100 Best Movies"
list from the American Film Institute, 1998

64. I prefer cinema of lies, lies are much more interesting than truth.

Federico Fellini, Director
Quoted on the Internet Movie Database,
Ltd., "Film 100," 1998

65. The movies are our contemporaries — our buddies, our crushes, our lovers.

David Ansen, Writer
Stated in the *Newsweek*, "The 100 Best Movies" list
from the American Film Institute, 1998

66. Movie love puts people in touch with their own instincts and pleasures. Movies can lead to self-reconciliation....

David Densby, Writer
Written in *The New Yorker*, April 6, 1998

67. We are the movies and the movies are us.

David Ansen, Writer
Stated in the *Newsweek*, "The 100 Best Movies"
list from the American Film Institute, 1998

68. Art is man's quest to understand himself.

Danny Glover, Actor
Interview in *The Cable Guide*, September, 1990

69. Despite its promise of "escape" from the everyday world, Hollywood remains a social institution, and its movies describe recognizable social situations in their plots and themes.

Richard Maltby, Writer
Cited in *Hollywood Cinema*, 1995

70. Generally speaking, the original attraction of the theater was carnal rather than intellectual, and is still so today.

Josef von Sternberg
Writing in *Film Culture*, Winter 1955

71. Cinema is a melodramatic medium. We go to it to exercise our emotions rather than our thoughts.

David Mamet, Producer-Director
Interview in *Interview Magazine*, April 1998

72. (Cinema is) like a battleground: Love ... hate ... action ... violence ... death. In a word, emotion.

Samuel Fuller, Screenwriter
Interviewed in *Written By Magazine*, March 1998

73. Films can be thought of as dreams for people who are awake....
Chris Evans, Special Effects Designer
Cited in *Moviemakers at Work*, 1987

74. Movies are about emotions, not logic.
Billy Wilder
Cited in *American Cinema: One Hundred Years of Filmmaking*, 1995

75. (The cinema) has the same object as the other arts, the presentation of human thought, emotion, and experience, in terms of an appeal to the soul through the senses....
Production Code Preamble
As stated by the MPPDA, Motion Picture Producers, Directors Association, 1930

76. The cinema can achieve its greatest power of fascination over the viewer not simply because of its impression of reality, but more precisely because this impression of reality is intensified by the conditions of the dream.
Jean-Louis Bandry, Writer
Writing on cinema as a "dream-state," in his book *Apparatus*, 1981

77. It is a way of telling stories in American film in which simple emotional ideas are represented clearly.
Lawrence Kasdan
Cited in *American Cinema: One Hundred Years of Filmmaking*, 1995

78. The most beautiful thing we can experience is the mysterious. It is the source of all true art and science.
Albert Einstein
Spoken during the "What I Believe" Forum, October, 1930

79. The very nature and essence of movies is illusion which suggests that people attend expecting to be mentally manipulated, hence the references to "suspension of disbelief."
Bruce A. Austin
Stated in *Current Research in Film*, 1991

80. What is important to understand is that in movies there is nothing else — whatever is in the frame is all there is. There is nothing else. Everything else is fantasy....
Dusan Makavejev
Stated at the Film Forum, New York, 1985

81. We were struck by the great similarity between dreams and film: the power which they shared (however unequally) for representing an imaginary, fantasy world.
Jean Epstein
Cited in *Movies and Society*, 1970

82. The motion picture has more valuable points than people dream of who only want to be amused.
J. Stuart Blackton, Producer-Director
On the preservation of film, article, *Pearson's Magazine*, 1915

83. Maybe I'll get my masters in anthropology. That's what movies are about anyway. Cultural imprints.
George Lucas, Screenwriter-Director
Interview, *The Los Angeles Times Calendar*, June 5, 1977

84. Films do not involve people's imagination but present mythologies — true folk entertainment of our time.
I. C. Jarvie
From his book *Movies and Society*, 1970

85. Movies give us the myths we worship and the metaphors that simplify our existence.
Alexander Walker
Cited in *Chronicles of the Cinema*, 1995

86. The cinema (is) a somewhat dubious Muse in that it is incapable of waiting whilst all the other Muses wait, and should be painted and sculpted in waiting poses.
Jean Cocteau
From his book, *Cocteau on the Film*, 1954

87. Whatever ends up on that big, silvery screen will be more powerful than the words in a dusty, dog-eared novel.
Josh Young
Article in *George* magazine, March 1998

88. Something labeled "great" in Hollywood means in length.... "it is a great movie."
Unknown

89. No sequel is ever equal.
David McGillivray, Author
From his book *Anatomy of the Movies*, 1981

90. Not even the best sequel is a true substitute for the excitement of something genuinely new.
Janet Maslin, Author
As stated in *The New York Times*, June 26, 1983

91. Every great film should seem new every time you see it.

Roger Ebert, Film Critic
Quoted on the Internet Movie Database, Ltd.,
1998

92. Whatever the merits of a film, little is accomplished if it does not get seen.

William A. Bluem, Writer
From his co-authored book, *Movie Business:
American Film Industry Practice,* 1972

93. You have to block out of your mind the most awful thought of all – that the film could be running somewhere and there's no one in the theater.

Peter Weir, Director
Interview, *Premiere* magazine, July 1998

94. We will put into practice our firmly held belief that films, once preserved, must not be forever locked away in a remote vault....

James H. Billington, Librarian,
U.S. Library of Congress
Official statement within the National Film
Registry under the library's management, as
cited in *Chronicles of the Cinema,* 1995

95. My definition of a documentary film is a film that decides that you don't know enough about something, whatever it is....

Don Pennebaker, Director
Cited in *Documentary Explorations,*
by G. Roy Levin, 1971

96. I hate the word "documentary." I think it smells of dust and boredom. I think "realist" films much the best.

Alberto Cavalcanti
Cited in *The Rise and Fall of
British Documentary* by E. Sussex, 1975

97. I'm delighted with (television) because it used to be that films were the lowest form of art. Now we have something to look down to.

Billy Wilder, Director
Interview in *Newsweek,* April 26, 1993

98. In the year 2024 the most important single thing which the cinema will have helped in a large way to accomplish will be that of eliminating from the face of the civilized world all armed conflict.

D. W. Griffith, Producer-Director
Interview in *Collier's,* May 3, 1924

2

Filmmaking

99. Artists were too happy, so God invented film.

Sidney Meyers, Film Editor
Cited in *A Film Editor's Story*, 1979

100. A perfect movie is balanced between words, music and images.

Vittorio Storaro, Cinematographer
Cited in *Moviemaker* magazine, 1998

101. In everything you do, add a teaspoon of aesthetics.

Jeffrey Scott, Animation scriptwriter
Interview in *Animation* magazine, 1998

102. Film should be both literary and visual ... ideally you should do a combination of both.... Why should you have limitations?

Oliver Stone, Screenwriter-Director
Cited in *Reel Conversations*, 1991

103. Anything can be done in any way if that is how the filmmaker wants it done ... one's vision is all that matters.

Elena Oumano, Author
Stated in her *Film Forum*, 1985

104. In the cinema ... the camera has become a sort of god ... fixed on its tripod or crane ... like a heathen altar; about it are the high priests — the director, cameraman, assistants — who bring victims before the camera like burnt offerings, and cast them into the flames.

Jean Renoír, Director
Interviewed in *France Observateur*, 1958

105. Sensitivity, intuition, good taste and intelligence are the main (attributes required to make a worthwhile film) ... a little will yield very little ... a lot ... will make a masterpiece.

François Truffaut
Cited in *50 Major Film Makers*, 1975

106. [F]ilm is very sensitive. It just picks up a feeling, a vibration.

Bernardo Bertolucci
Cited in *Film Forum*, 1975

107. I can make an audience laugh, scream with terror, smile, believe in legends, become indignant, take offense, become enthusiastic, lower itself or yawn from boredom. I am, then, either a deceiver or — when the audience is aware of the fraud — an illusionist.

Ingmar Bergman
Stated in his 1956 *Cahiers du Cinéma*

108. Photography is truth, and film is truth twenty-four times a second.

Jean-Luc Godard, Director
Cited in *First Cut*, 1992

109. The ideal and disillusioning sides of theater are two faces of a single truth. Both represent man. I always like to show both sides....

Federico Fellini
Cited in *Fellini — A Life*, 1985

110. Every story visualized with the aid of the motion picture camera must be founded on a sincere desire to unfold some additional truth....

Douglas Fairbanks, Sr.,
Actor-Producer
Cited in *The Morning Telegraph*,
New York, 1922

111. It is the cameraman's duty to make it possible for us to see a spectacle, rather that the duty of the spectacle to take place for the benefit of the camera.

Jean Renoír, Director
Interviewed by André Bazin in
France Observateur, 1958,
on what is cinéma vérité

112. The first responsibility is to entertain. But

given the cost of a movie, if it can give you food for thought, so much the better.

Michael Douglas, Producer
Interview in Interview magazine, 1993

113. I don't think that any genuine artist has ever been oriented by some didactic point of view, even if he thought he was.

Stanley Kubrick, Director
Cited in the Santa Barbara
News-Press Scene, 1999

114. The minute you suspend disbelief you are in films.

Leonard Rosenman, Composer
Cited in Film Makers on
Film Making, 1983

115. Perfection in screen time takes a lot of money and a lot of time.

Alan Heim, Film Editor
Interview in First Cut, 1982

116. Your vision can never achieve perfection. If you want to be a movie-maker, you've got to say, "All right, I'll chop the dream down. I'll be very happy if I get 60 percent of my vision on the screen."

Mel Brooks, Screenwriter-Director

117. I don't think that writers or painters or filmmakers function because they have something they particularly want to say. They have something that they feel.

Stanley Kubrick, Director
Cited in the Santa Barbara
News-Press Scene, 1999

118. The task I'm trying to achieve is above all to make you see.

D. W. Griffith, Producer-Director
Cited in Novels Into Film, 1957

119. In a movie you don't tell people things, you show people things.

William Goldman, Writer
Stated in his 1983 Adventures
in the Screentrade

120. The images, for me, are the story.

Tim Burton, Director
On the feeling of a film, as stated in Inner
Views: Filmmakers in Conversation, 1992

121. Before we shoot the first frame, we have to shoot the poster. What is the image? What are we trying to sell here?

Arnold Schwarzenegger, Actor
Cited in Los Angeles Times Magazine, 1991

122. "Privileged moments" (are) intervals of beautiful imagery while nothing seems to be happening to develop the drama or advance the narrative (of the movie).

Andrew Sarris, Film Critic
Cited in Reel Conversations,
1991, elaborating on director
François Truffaut's quote

123. Words are no substitute for visual actions.... I'd feel much better about film as art if producers ... could really visualize what's down on paper.

Arthur Knight, Film Critic
Cited in The Reel Tinsel, 1970

124. Filmmaking is as simple as finding an association between two images and thereby telling a story.

Kathryn Bigelow, Writer-Director
Interview in People magazine, 1991

125. Chapters in a novel are not necessarily scenes in a film. Novelists live in every word on that page. Filmmakers live in a visual world.

Jude Pauline Eberhard, Screenwriter
Interview in ScrIpt magazine,
Vol. 4, No.2

126. The action is everything.... The picture itself is in many ways only action's by-product.

Joan Didion, Writer
Cited in The White Album, 1981

127. Talk is cheap and action is expensive.

Roger Corman, Producer-Director
On his preference for scripts with
more dialogue, as stated in his
1979 Movie World of Roger Corman

128. Movies should give pleasure, pleasure that encompasses sensibility and excitement.

Pauline Kael, Critic
Interview in Modern Maturity
magazine, 1998

129. I really prefer to make movies that tell a story by what you visualize and what you feel and what you sense.

Steven Spielberg, Director
As opposed to a lot of dialogue, as
stated in Take 22: Moviemakers
on Moviemaking, 1984

130. It must feel emotionally true.

Avi Lerner, Producer
On his definition of a good movie,
as cited in The New Yorker, 1988

131. If film is to be an oblique look at life, then you must be totally influenced by life.
Richard Lester, Director
Interview in *Directors at Work*, 1970

132. Give me a man looking at a woman and the woman looking back at the man, and I've got a story.
Jean Renoir, Director
Cited in *Premiere* magazine, 1988

133. I hate the idea of a woman's viewpoint ... a viewpoint is a viewpoint is a viewpoint. It's colored by more things than just what sex you are.
Joan Tewkesbury, Screenwriter-Director
On female sensibility in filmmaking,
as cited in *Reel Women:
Pioneers of the Cinema*, 1991

134. Whip me, beat me, but don't bore me.
Clint Eastwood
Cited in *Clint Eastwood
—A Biography*, 1996

135. There are no rules in filmmaking, only sins. And the cardinal sin is dullness.
Frank Capra, Producer-Director
Stated in his 1971 *Frank Capra*

136. It is easy to put a spectator in a state worse than the one he was in when he entered the theater; it is difficult to put him in a better state....
Ingmar Bergman
Stated in his 1956 *Cahiers du Cinéma*

137. A pie in the face represents a fine, wish-fulfilling, universal idea, especially in the face of authority ... it is an outrage to pumped-up dignity....
Mack Sennett, Director-Producer
On the custard pie as a comedic tool,
as cited in *Film Makers
on Film Making*, 1983

138. It is the task of the cinema to overcome the barriers of the commonplace.
Andrzej Wajda, Director
Cited in *Film and Filming* magazine, 1961

139. My films are not about cameras, they're about people.
Peter Bogdanovich, Writer-Director
Cited in *Inside Oscar*, 1996

140. (With movies) there's nothing small, nothing big. I am interested in the most complex things I know of— people ... in their relationships to each other.
Andre de Toth, Director
Interview in *Movie Maker* magazine, 1998

141. List all of the qualities you can discover in human beings and they all go to making a good picture.
John Huston
Cited in *The Hustons*, 1989

142. In order to be a storyteller you have to live a life. If your stories are not about life, you're just a very good craftsman.
François Truffaut
Cited in *Steven Spielberg— The
Unauthorized Biography*, 1996

143. The craft of making a movie is very important, but more important is expressing yourself and having something interesting to express.
Peter Bogdanovich, Writer-Director
Interview in *Take 22: Moviemakers
on Moviemaking*, 1984

144. The root of ... a film ... is the inner need to express something ... what makes it grow into a tree is the script; ... to bear flowers and fruit is the directing.
Akira Kurosawa, Director
Stated in his *Akira Kurosawa*, 1982

145. Story first, director second, actors last.
Michael Curtiz
The director's formula for good
pictures, as cited in *Bette and Joan
— The Divine Feud*, 1989

146. [I]t's the process, the examination of ideas and characters.... Reflection is less interesting to me than the pursuit.
Barry Levinson, Director
Interview in *A Cut Above*, 1988, on what he
looks for in his film projects

147. The story dictates its own style rather than the director's style dictating the story.
William Wyler, Director
Interview in *Directors at Work*, 1970

148. The power that matters is our ability to move people everywhere, to have them feel ... to laugh, to cry. That's what we do best, that is our reward.
Laura Ziskin, Studio President
Interview in *The Hollywood Reporter*, 1996

149. Everything's important. Mood and atmosphere are superimportant, but if you don't have a story, then you got diddly.

David Lynch, Screenwriter-Director
Interview in *Reel Conversations*, 1991

150. We try to tell a good story and develop a hefty plot. Themes emerge as we go along.

Alfred Hitchcock
Cited in *The Art of
Alfred Hitchcock*, 1976

151. A film is made while in progress; it is written right there on the spot, with the camera.

Míchelangelo Antonioni
Cited in *Film Culture*, 1962

152. There are directors who hate shooting because it's a compromise of their script.

Louis Malle, Director
Interview in *Film Buff*, 1976

153. People shouldn't assume that I think I'm doing something better by choosing to do Shakespeare.... All kinds of good work is out there. And good work is good work.

Kenneth Branagh, Actor-Director
Interview in *Creative
Screenwriting* magazine

154. For God's sake, just tell the story.

Billy Wilder, Director
Cited in *The Bright Side of Billy Wilder,
Primarily,* 1970, stating his basic
rule for making a movie

155. The film is the very type of work which demands a style. A film is not a spectacle, it is in the first place a style.

Robert Bresson, Director
Cited in *Great Film Directors
— A Critical Anthology*, 1978

156. I try to address each script in the cinematic fashion I think is right for that given script … there's no straight stylistic line in my work.

Robert Wise, Director
Stated in *Robert Wise, On His Films*, 1995

157. Every story imposes its form in a certain way.... Every movie is different. Every movie has its own right form.

Kostantinos Costa-Gavras, Director
Interview in *Reel Conversations*, 1991

158. A picture should end through the simple truism that each picture should have the ending which belongs to it, and if it rings true it will be accepted.

Fritz Lang, Director
Interview in *Penguin Film Review*, 1948

159. The film artist is noted for what he is able to make of his ideas, when he tries to transpose them into a partly non-verbal medium (the movies).

I. C. Jarvie, Author
Stated in his 1970 *Movies and Society*

160. What the eye sees is its own. What the heart can perceive is a very different matter.

Gordon Parks, Director
Interview in *KCET* magazine, 1988

161. Live theater is like literature. It deals primarily with words. Film is about photography. It's a very different thing.

Woody Allen, Writer-Director
Cited in *Woody Allen—
His Films and Career*, 1985

162. I don't want to make a film. I want to make a movie.

Steven Spielberg
Cited in *Steven Spielberg
— The Unauthorized Biography*, 1996

163. The creative act is not merely a mechanical manipulation of matter into form.

Bernard Beckerman,
Costume designer
Cited in *The Costume Designer's Handbook*,
1992, on creative form being
an emotional abstract as well

164. Film is a way of expressing something with light.

Federico Fellini
Cited in *Fellini—A Life*, 1986

165. The tragedy of the cinematography lies in its having to be successful immediately.... All arts can and must wait.

Jean Cocteau
Stated in his 1954 *Cocteau on the Film*

166. An entertainer wants to give you exactly what you want.... And an artist wants to give you what you don't know you want.

David Cronenberg, Director
Interview in *Inner Views:
Filmmakers in Conversation*, 1992

167. The degree to which films can be art, or considered artistic, is only to the extent that they succeed as forms of communication.

Kathryn Bigelow, Writer-Director
Interview in *Interview* magazine, 1990

168. My primary criteria, in an artistic sense, revolves around a movie's potential grosses. I don't … often put my material under the artistic glass.

Michael Backes, Screenwriter
Cited in *Beverly Hills* magazine, 1983

169. "Is the cinema an art?" My answer is, "What does it matter?"

Jean Renoír, Director
Stated in his 1974 *Jean Renoír —
My Life and Times*

170. I think in the end it's the painting, not the frame, that counts.

Peter Weir, Director
On the story being the key, not
the surrounds of the movie, as
cited in *Premiere* magazine, 1998

171. A picture is a whole; you cannot say this is the beginning, this is the end, and the middle. No.

Jean Renoír, French director
Cited in *Film Makers on
Film Making*, 1983

172. Every film of major importance must have one great sequence from the standpoint of the camera, in acting and story, in light and shadow, in sound and fury.

Laurence Stallings
Cited in *Mayer and Thalberg*, 1975

173. Movies are very fluid experiences. What turns out, finally … is very often at odds … than that which was intended….

Marlon Brando
Interview in *Conversations with Brando*, 1991

174. (The) "creative" process normally proceeds by trial and error, draft and revision. How things turn out, not the intrinsic inert of the original idea, is what counts.

I. C. Jarvie, Author
Stated in his 1970 *Movies and Society*

175. Failure is part of the creative process. If you're afraid of it, you can't really create.

Danny DeVito, Actor-Director
Interview in *The Los
Angeles Times Calendar*, 1997

176. When I'm making a film … I'm creating a new reality.

David Cronenberg, Director
Interview in *Inner Views: Filmmakers
in Conversation*, 1992

177. The role of the film creator is to observe, not extract fiction from it.

Cesare Zavattini, Screenwriter
Cited on the Internet
Movie Database, 1998

178. If we're not having a good time … if we're not being shocked and delighted, and we're not going "ooh" and "ah" and laughing at the funny bits — then the filmmaker … has not done his job.

David Mamet, Writer-Director
Interview in *Interview* magazine, 1998

179. The aesthetics of film is based on (a) psychological truth and need.

Jean Mitry, Author
Stated in his 1990 *Esthétique
et Psychologie de Cinéma*

180. The final fifteen minutes are the most important of any movie.

Paul Newman, Actor
Cited in *Adventures in
the Screen Trade*, 1983

181. Nothing matters but the final picture.

David O. Selznick, Producer
Cited in *Ingrid Bergman
— My Story*, 1980

182. Nobody has ever had the power a filmmaker has. No saint, no pope, no general, no sultan … the power to talk to hundreds of millions of people for two hours in the dark.

Frank Capra, Director
Interview in *Film Makers
on Film Making*, 1983

183. In filmmaking, you have limitless possibilities. You just have to open your mind and expand your thinking. It's the only way to keep the stories new and interesting for intelligent audiences who respond to the unusual, not the ordinary.

Don Burgess, Cinematographer
Interview in *Contemporary
Cinematographers: On Their Art*, 1998

184. If Hollywood is to remain atop the film

world … there must be more experimentation with out-of-the-way film subjects.

> Ida Lupino, Actress-Director
> Cited in *The Los Angeles Examiner*, 1950

185. Ideas come when you least expect them.… My subconscious often governs me much more than my conscious.

> Steven Spielberg, Director
> Interview in *Take 22:*
> *Moviemakers on Moviemaking*, 1984

186. I usually see the whole movie on the ceiling of my bedroom at night.

> Steven Spielberg, Director
> Cited on the Internet
> Movie Database, 1998

187. Make a film that reflects a community or creates mystery and fantasy, and the film will have an audience.

> Marcy De Veaux,
> Public Relations executive
> Cited in *The Los Angeles Times*, 1996

188. Black producers and directors, if they are to survive, must begin channeling their efforts into pictures that are universally acceptable.

> Gordon Parks, Director
> Interview in *The Los Angeles Times*, 1990

189. There's nothing more counterproductive than the notion of gender-specific filmmaking.

> Kathryn Bigelow, Writer-Director
> Interview in *Interview* magazine, 1995

190. To recapture the active response of the film-fan is the first step toward intelligent appreciation of most pictures.

> V. F. Perkins
> Stated in his 1972 *Film as Film*,
> "Understanding and
> Judging the Movies"

191. I don't want to work within a medium that is an incredible communicator to a mass audience and not reach a mass audience.

> Kathryn Bigelow, Writer-Director
> Interview in *Interview* magazine, 1990

192. I don't want to do a picture simply for the sake of doing a picture. I want an event.

> Arnold Schwarzenegger, Actor
> Interview in *GQ* magazine, 1992

193. In films, through the single eye of the camera, I could go anywhere I wanted and take the audience along.

> Busby Berkeley, Director
> Cited on the Internet
> Movie Database, 1998

194. My big problem: finding the new bad guys.

> Avi Lerner, Producer
> On movies having different antagonists,
> as stated in *The New Yorker*, 1998

195. Because the heroics of the movie hero are now reliant upon one-up-manship.… You have to constantly make your feats of daring so extraordinary. You can't save one person anymore. You have to save a nation.

> Sylvester Stallone, Actor
> Interview in *Esquire*, 1996

196. Filmmakers all over the world are united by a common bond: apprenticeship in the greatest of all art forms—film.

> Frank Capra, Producer-Director
> Stated in his 1971 *Frank Capra*

197. The filmmaking process is very social and public … it's a communal activity.…

> Chris Evans, Special Effects Designer
> Cited in *Moviemakers at Work*, 1987

198. In the film world, as in the "real" world, we are not living alone.

> John Woo, Director
> Interview in *A Cut Above*, 1998, on
> filmmakers learning from each other

199. In a way, you can compare filmmaking to the cultural role a cathedral had in the Middle Ages.

> Chris Evans, Special Effects Technician
> Cited in *Moviemakers at Work*, 1987

200. You have to treat people who are family members as a family member. Everyone has one goal. To make a good movie.

> Chow Yun-Fat, Actor
> On the movie cast and crew, as
> cited in *Premiere* magazine, 1998

201. I want my films to reflect a truly democratic spirit and I find myself siding with the lone minority.

> John Cassavetes, Producer-Director
> Cited in *Time*, 1997

202. The medium is terrific but those of us who use it are still pygmies.

> Frank Capra, Director
> Cited in *Inside Oscar*, 1996

203. (Filmmaking) … the only art form in which the artist cannot afford to buy his own tools.

> Charlton Heston
> Interview in *Film Makers*
> *on Film Making*, 1983

204. Making movies is a bit like having babies. It lasts nine months, and you go through morning sickness.

> Guy Hamilton, Director
> Interview in *Take 22: Moviemakers*
> *on Moviemaking*, 1984

205. (Filmmaking) is the idiocy of fabricating a tapeworm 8,000 feet long which will nourish itself on the life and mind of the actors, producers and creators.

> Ingmar Bergman
> Stated in his 1956 *Cahiers du Cinéma*

206. Filmmaking is easy and has no secrets.

> Luis Buñuel, Director
> Cited in *The Fierce Imagination*
> *of Luis Buñuel*, 1978

207. (Filmmaking) is waiting around … for your dynamic turn.

> John Cassavetes, Director
> Cited in *Time*, 1997

208. Filmmaking is a manual art, a craftsman's job.

> Jean Cocteau
> Stated in his 1954 *Cocteau on the Film*

209. Movies, in a way, are like Gothic cathedrals: a lot of meticulous labor goes into obscure corners of the structure.

> Alex Ross, Writer
> Stated in his 1998 "Scoring for Oscar," *The*
> *New Yorker*

210. The difference with film is that you can make love to a film, and you can't do that with television.

> Norman Lear,
> TV Producer-Director
> Interview in *Film Makers*
> *on Film Making*, 1983

211. Making a movie is a mathematical operation. It is like sending a missile to the moon.

> Federico Fellini, Director
> Cited on the Internet
> Movie Database, 1998

212. Only the actual invasion was possibly more complicated than this re-creation.

> Darryl F. Zanuck
> Cited in *American Cinema*, 1995,
> on *The Longest Day*, 1962

213. It takes a year writing and developing and then getting fucked over and going somewhere else and redeveloping, then finding a crew and shooting and editing….

> Amy Heckerling, Director
> On the moviemaking process, as cited in
> *Rolling Stone* magazine, 1998

214. [M]ovies are also like a circus … such an effort…. Even a bad movie is hard to make.

> Steve Martin, Actor
> Cited in *The Los Angeles Times*
> *Calendar*, 1994

215. We are the pigs. We are the ones who sniff out the truffles. You can put us on a leash, keep us under control. But we are the guys who dig out the gold.

> George Lucas
> On coming up with the money making film
> concepts, cited in *Steven Spielberg — The*
> *Unauthorized Biography*, 1996

216. Film is a language which can only be written down by several people working with a number of pieces of equipment … (it) is at least as important as the (director's) inspiration.

> I. C. Jarvie, Actor
> Stated in his 1970 *Movies and Society*

217. It's not really an auteur thing, it's an ensemble.

> Clint Eastwood
> On filmmaking, cited in
> *Clint Eastwood — A Biography*, 1996

218. The secret of great movies does not lie in just one artist.

> Garry Willis
> Stated in his 1997 *John Wayne's America*

219. The "auteur," the director's grand vision, which is often just ... a lot of accidents, a lot of moments you get forced into.
> Alan Heim, Film Editor
> Interview in *First Cut*, 1992

220. In art it is one man, one painting — one book — one film.
> Frank Capra, Director
> On his credo of "one man — one film,"
> stated in his 1971 *Frank Capra*

221. The auteur theory was not a theory. It was a policy.
> Andrew Sarris, Film Critic
> That the early studio director was the
> primary creative force behind a motion
> picture, as cited in *Reel Conversations*, 1991

222. The director overwrites with the camera. There isn't a word written on the page the meaning of which cannot be totally changed with the camera or in the editing and dubbing stages.
> Elliot Silverstein, Director
> Interview in *Directors at Work*, 1970

223. Only a few directors possess a conceptual talent — that is, a talent to crystallize every film they make into a cinematic concept ... a skill that goes far beyond mere photography of a script.
> Alexander Walker, Writer
> Cited in *Kubrick — Inside
> A Film Artist's Maze*, 1982

224. A filmmaker is someone who possesses and has total control over that means of expression and that art we call the cinema....
> Federico Fellini
> Cited in *Fellini — A Life*, 1986

225. From the commercial standpoint, producing is running the show ... his creativity is the cornerstone of the entire edifice.
> Roger Corman, Producer-Director
> Stated in his 1987 *Thinking in Pictures*

226. Great films are made in their every detail according to the vision of one man, not in buying part of what he has done.
> David O. Selznick, Producer
> Cited in *Ingrid Bergman — My Story*, 1980

227. What's important is to go back to film and create your own little universe there, like some folk artist.
> Martin Scorsese, Director
> Interview in *Reel Conversations*, 1991

228. You have to have something to come with, to give other people. Picture-making is some sort of responsibility.
> Ingmar Bergman, Director
> Interview in *Film Makers
> on Film Making*, 1983

229. A film should have a "raison d'être." If its reason is pure entertainment, then you're making a film for money.
> Norman Jewison, Director
> Interview in *Directors at Work*, 1970

230. It's my job to tell a story.... I hope people have a good time, but other than that, it's not my place to think what else they might bring away with them.
> David Mamet, Writer-Director
> Interview in *Interview* magazine, 1998

231. Everything in this film is a lie. Everything. Then we show it to an audience as if it is a true thing — an event that happened, a piece of history.
> Robert Altman, Director
> Interview in *Inner Views:
> Filmmakers in Conversation*,
> 1992, on the real life of a film

232. I don't think there's any great secret about capturing reality on film ... it's only when you get into capturing what life appears to be to you ... into that other world of the indicative and the impressionistic, that it becomes exciting.
> Norman Jewison, Director
> Interview in *Directors at Work*, 1970

233. To have what is known as an unhappy ending is to commit the unforgivable Hollywood sin called "being down-beat."
> Alfred Hitchcock
> Interview in *The Saturday
> Evening Post*, 1957

234. If you make a popular movie, you start to think where have I failed?
> Woody Allen, Writer-Director
> Cited in *Inside Oscar*, 1996

235. It's important not to get into that terrible syndrome where you're a creator of hits — then I think you're dead.
> Woody Allen
> Cited in *Woody Allen —
> His Films and Career*, 1985

236. What we know as the "nice little picture" will

become a thing of the past ... size and wallop preferred.

> Dore Schary
> Cited in *George Cukor—*
> *A Double Life*, 1991

237. Don't compromise ... only the valiant can create. Only the daring should make films.

> Frank Capra, Producer-Director
> Stated in his 1971 *Frank Capra*

238. We are in a very different time and age, and we need to ... do (Shakespeare) in very different ways. A lack of intimidation is ... sort of requirement for doing Shakespeare. Respect is total, intimidation, no.

> Kenneth Branagh, Actor-Director
> Interview in *Creative Screenwriting*,
> Vol. 5, No. 2

239. Making films is making decisions. If it hits you right off, it's good entertainment. If you have to think about it, forget it.

> Frank Capra, Producer-Director
> Stated in his 1971 *Frank Capra*

240. Every moment, every milligram of a movie is a choice ... the choices are very committed.

> Lina Wertmuller, Director
> Cited in *Film Forum*, 1985

241. Making up your mind is the hair-tearing part of film production — the decisions are mostly gut decisions.

> Frank Capra, Director
> Stated in his 1971 *Frank Capra*

242. When you create it and you write it and you're in it and you then say, "I'm going to direct it," you sort of say, "Hey, punch me!" It's a big "Kick me" sign on your back....

> Billy Crystal, All of the above
> Interview in *Box Office*, 1995

243. Filmmaking is a hot-eyed, hot-juiced, high-staked game of unrecallable hunches and gut decisions no computer can make for you.

> Frank Capra, Producer-Director
> Stated in his 1971 *Frank Capra*

244. We'd write 'em, shoot 'em and print 'em in a week.

> William Beaudine, Director
> Cited in *Newsweek*, 1970, recalling the
> "Silent Era"

245. Making motion pictures is compromise.

> Bill Varney, Sound Re-recordist
> Cited in *Moviemakers at Work*, 1987

246. Talk, talk, talk,— that's all I do. Get the writers together and talk the script. Get the actors together and talk acting. Get the camera crew together and talk production. I spend my life talking.

> Akira Kurosawa, Director
> Interview in *Show Business Illustrated*, 1962

247. Film is an aging art.... Not having confidence in their own stories or the way they tell them ... filmmakers in increasing numbers turn to the past for desperate inspiration.

> James Monaco, Author
> Stated in his 1979 *American Films Now*

248. Hollywood has it both ways by remaking old movies because it's the only way of getting reliability and novelty in the same package.

> Carrie Rickey, Author
> Interview in *The New York Times*, 1984

249. Filmmakers (are getting) their ideas not from life but from each other's pictures. We (are) creating within walls of mirrors.

> Frank Capra, Producer-Director
> On "Hollywood's Pattern
> of Sameness," 1946

250. Why this insistence on sequels? Have they so little imagination?

> Federico Fellini
> Cited in *Films and Filming*
> magazine, 1961

251. I think ... the relationship between a film script and the direction of the film ... is a relationship characterized by an apparent lack of fidelity.

> Jean Renoír, Director
> Stated in his 1974 *Jean Renoír
> — My Life and Times*

252. What is interesting about an adaptation (book to film) is not its resemblance to the original work but the way in which the filmmaker reacts to the original work.

> Jean Renoír, Director
> Stated in his 1974 *Jean Renoír
> — My Life and Times*

253. I just do my job, using cinematic means to narrate a story taken from a stage play.

> Alfred Hitchcock
> On *Dial M for Murder*, 1953, as cited in *The
> Art of Alfred Hitchcock*, 1976

254. We don't admire a painting for its fidelity to the model; all we want is for the model to stimulate the painters' imaginations.

Jean Renoír, Director
On adapting a novel for the screen,
as cited in his 1974 *Jean Renoír
— My Life and Times*

255. The use of "originality" per se as a criterion is kind of a twentieth-century phenomenon. But being inspired by what's gone before is a major part of the evolution of art and civilization.

Peter Bogdanovich, Writer-Director
Interview in *Take 22: Moviemakers on
Moviemaking*, 1984

256. Other sequels have stunk it up for the good ones ... so it kind of poisons the water when you want to do one.

Billy Crystal, Director
Cited in *Entertainment Weekly*, 1994

257. Cinéma vérité doesn't emphasize the poetic quality of material so much as the accumulation of real moments.

Geof Bartz, Film Editor
Interview in *First Cut*, 1992

258. The greatest danger for the filmmaker consists in the extraordinary means the medium provides in order to lie.

Míchelangelo Antonioni, Director
Cited in *Great Film Directors
— A Critical Anthology*, 1978

259. There is no such thing as historical accuracy. What is most important as a filmmaker is to get to the spirit of what you're trying to put on the screen.

Ken Russell, Director
Interview in *Reel Conversations*, 1991

260. Bad pictures get worse (with age) and good pictures get better.

King Vidor, Director
Interview in *Filmmakers
on Filmmaking*, 1983

261. If something is going to be flawed, why not have it be interestingly flawed, as opposed to boringly flawed?

Tim Burton, Director
Interview in *Inner Views:
Filmmakers in Conversation*, 1992

262. A bad film is like a poet without culture, content to tell a story in verse (with nothing of that which makes a poem a poem).

Jean Cocteau
Stated in his 1954 *Cocteau on the Film*

263. Murphy's Law reigns supreme in the picture business more than any other business.

Guy Hamilton, Director
Interview in *Take 22: Moviemakers on
Moviemaking*, 1984

264. I don't want to reach a stage (as a director) where everything is perfect. I would much rather catch life in a happy accident.

Richard Lester, Director
Interviews in *Directors at Work*, 1970

265. To lower the odds against a film being "quality" — there is no substitute for intensive attention to pre-production details.

Frank Capra
Stated in his 1971 *Frank Capra*

266. You can't rescue a bad screenplay. But you can rescue bad directing.

Sherman Alexie, Screenwriter
Interview in *Creative Screenwriting*
magazine, Vol. 5, No. 2

267. I'm really interested in embarrassing moments on film. I think there should be something embarrassing in every film.

David Lynch, Screenwriter-Director
Interview in *Reel Conversations*, 1991

268. If your name's going to be on the screen, you've got to live with your conscience.

David Puttnam, Producer
Cited in *Filmmakers on Filmmaking*, 1983

269. Louis Lumière was another Gutenberg. His invention has caused as many disasters as the dissemination of thought through books.

Jean Renoír, Director
On significance of the invention of the
motion picture camera by Lumière, stated
in his 1974 *Jean Renoír — My Life and Times*

270. The only thing you can tell from the dailies is whether it's in focus or not.... More people have bought their yachts on rushes and gone bankrupt on the premiere. Everything looks good in rushes....

Michael Caine, Actor
Interview in *Take 22: Moviemakers on
Moviemaking*, 1984

271. If you're going to take the raps, be prepared to take them for something that you're in love with.

Elliot Silverstein, Director
Interview in *Directors at Work*,
1970, on selecting your subject

272. (Movies are) a supremely pleasurable and dangerous art form.

Pauline Kael, Critic
Interview in *Modern Maturity*
magazine, 1998

273. The power of Hollywood to influence is formidable ... and, yes, there's the potential for both positive and negative.

Laura Ziskin, Studio President
Interview in *The Hollywood Reporter*, 1996

274. You have the power to say anything you want, so why not say something positive.

Frank Capra, Director
Interview in *Filmmakers*
on Filmmaking, 1983

275. All our fairy tales have some kind of violence — the good knight riding to kill the dragon, etc. Why do we have to show the knight spreading the serpent's guts all over the candy mountain?

John Wayne, Actor
Interview in *Playboy*, 1971

276. What is wrong is when young people are desensitized with films about endless destruction — Once somebody is desensitized, it's impossible for them to go back.

Laura Ziskin, Studio President
Interview in *The Hollywood Reporter*, 1996

277. It was very dangerous working with wild horses — they don't know about movies.

Eli Wallach, Actor
Interview in *Take 22: Moviemakers on*
Moviemaking, 1984, on *The Misfits*, 1960

278. There are more people taking care of animals on a set than people taking care of actors. If they took care of people the same way, we'd have a very developed society.

Walter Matthau, Actor
Cited in *Take 22: Moviemakers*
on Moviemaking, 1984

279. It's not a dirty word. We're not trying to hide what we're doing. If I'm making a B movie, I'm not making a C or D or Z movie. At least it comes right after "A."

Avi Lerner, Producer
Interview in *The New Yorker*, 1998

280. I think there are levels of filmmaking, just as there are levels of novel writing. We know the difference between Elmore Leonard and Saul Bellow. There's a big difference.

David Cronenberg, Director
Interview in *Inner Views:*
Filmmakers in Conversation, 1992

281. Nobody makes a film for an empty house, or purposely drives people out of the house.

Clint Eastwood, Director
Interview in *Inner Views: Filmmakers*
in Conversation, 1992

282. I'd rather make 'em laugh. It's not up to us to help anybody get their sex kicks.

William Beaudine, Director
On sex in the modern cinema,
as cited in *Ach'ow* magazine,
"60 Years in Film," 1969

283. Filmmaking is a neurotic job; it's abnormal to every creative process I know.

Ingmar Bergman, Director
Interview in *Filmmakers on*
Filmmaking, 1983

284. From the inside out ... there's a complex relationship between someone who makes films and his films.

David Cronenberg, Director
Interview in *Inner Views:*
Filmmakers in Conversation, 1992

285. I think you have to be slightly psychopathic to make movies.

David Cronenberg, Director
Interview in *Inner Views:*
Filmmakers in Conversation, 1992

286. I don't have any aesthetic. I just do what I like. I make a film in the same way that I cook what I like to eat.

Melvin van Peebles,
Screenwriter-Director
Cited in *The New York Times*, 1990

287. It takes a year or more to do a movie, so why on earth spend that much time doing something that means nothing to me, and has nothing to say to anybody?

Martha Coolidge, Director
Interview in *Beverly Hills* magazine, 1993

288. I love making movies. Because films are forever.

Norman Jewison, Director
Upon receiving the 1999 Irving Thalberg
Award from the Academy of
Motion Picture Arts and Sciences

3

Audience

289. Everyone's a fan. Everyone's a critic. All that time spent in the dark has shaped who we are. But are our dreams still safe in the hands of Hollywood?
David Ansen, Writer
Cited in *Adventure, Mystery and Romance*, 1976

290. (The audience) positively needs anxiety and uncertainty, thrives on confusion and risk, wants trouble, tension, jeopardy, novelty, mystery, would be lost without enemies.
Harry Berger, Jr., Writer
Cited in *Movies and Society*, 1970

291. Technically speaking, a film audience is a quasi-group; that is, a body of persons physically present to one another and united by one purpose only, lacking other ties, structures or traditions through time.
Douglas Ayer, Author
Stated in his co-authored, 1970
Wisconsin Law Review

292. Like the theatres, the cinema is a collective experience away from home; unlike the theatre it is not necessary to feel oneself on show....
I. C. Jarvie
Stated in his 1970 *Movies and Society*

293. Cinema replaces our gaze with a world in harmony with our desires.
Jean-Luc Godard, Director
Cited in *Time* magazine, 1997

294. Movie love is abiding throughout life. The movies have a fascination that our ordinary lives don't have.
Pauline Kael, Critic
Interview in *Modern Maturity*, 1998

295. Somewhere, in the primordial regions of our brains, we still retain our capacity for listening intently to a good story well told.
Nancy Hendrickson, Writer
Cited in *Creative Writing*

296. The cinematic institution is outside us and inside us, indistinctly collective and intimate, sociological and psychoanalytic.
Christian Metz, Writer
Stated in his 1982 *The Imaginary Signifier*

297. (The audience is) governed by a multiplicity of passions, prejudices, waves of intolerance and secret sympathies which influence and determine its behavior and which motivate its applause or its disapproval.
Vittorio De Sica, Director
Stated in his *De Sica—Miracle in Milan*, 1968

298. Man is the only animal that can laugh and has a soul. Are the two related?
Frank Capra, Producer-Director
Stated in his 1971 *Frank Capra
—The Name Above the Title*

299. Man remembers how things should be; when they are not, he laughs.
Frank Capra, Producer-Director
Stated in his 1971 *Frank Capra
—The Name Above the Title*

300. I'll never be convinced that the general public does not want serious entertainment rather than frivolous.
Lois Weber, Director
Interview in *Motion Picture* magazine, 1921

301. The world is a comedy to those who think and a tragedy to those who feel.
Horace Walpole
Unknown source

302. Movies don't create psychos. Movies make psychos more creative.
Kevin Williamson, Screenwriter of Horror Films
Cited in *Creative Screenwriting* magazine, 1998

303. I ... do not believe that you can tell if a

movie is "good" or "bad".... All you can be sure of is: Does it "work" or not? ... for audiences.

William Goldman, Author
Stated in his 1983 *Adventures in the Screentrade*

304. "Sensible" moviegoers (are) keenly interested in the craft of cinema without wanting to make a religion of it.

Judith Crist, Movie Critic
1984 interview in *Take 22: Moviemakers on Moviemaking*

305. Film lovers are sick people.

François Truffaut, Director
Cited on the Internet Movie Database, 1998

306. Why should people go out and pay money to see bad films, when they can stay at home and see bad television for free?

Sam Goldwyn, Studio Head
Cited in *Filmmakers and Financing*, 1994

307. Should the room in which you are viewing television be darkened to resemble a movie theater? Answer: Definitely Not!

Early ad for television
c. 1950, cited in *The Century*, 1998

308. People have asked me for years, "Who is your audience?" I've never known who it is.

Woody Allen
Cited in *The New York Times Magazine,* 1997

309. Your audience is always twenty-five and you're growing a year older; and it's Dorian Gray in reverse. And you slowly slip away wondering what's wrong with them — the audience.

Richard Lester, Director
Interview in *Directors at Work*, 1970

310. Don't forget that the audience is twelve years old. Tell them everything three times: before it happens, when it's happening and after it has happened.

Louis B. Mayer, Producer-MGM
Cited in *Fred Zinnemann — An Autobiography*, 1992

311. My audience is from six to sixty except that you would only get six to thirty admitting it, and thirty to sixty hide about it.

Jerry Lewis, Actor-Director
Interview in *Directors at Work*, 1970

312. You're seeing the films as an adult, but you sit and watch them as a child.

Clint Eastwood
Stated in his 1996 *Clint Eastwood — A Biography*

313. They tell me audiences are different (in the 1990s). Well, I don't think that audiences can be that immune to entertainment....

George Sidney, Director
Interview in *A Cut Above*, 1998

314. The spectator is a human being capable of reflection ... of imagination ... undevoured with curiosity.

Jean Renoír, Director
Stated in his 1974 *Jean Renoír — My Life and Times*

315. I don't care if my pictures don't make a dime, so long as everyone comes to see them.

Sam Goldwyn
Cited in *You Must Remember This*, 1975

316. Sundance audiences are not regular folk.

Rebecca Ascher-Walsh
Interview in *Entertainment Weekly*, 1998,
referring to the Sundance Film Festival

317. A Texas audience won't sit through four hours of complexes.

Jean-Paul Sartre
On the filming of "Freud," 1962,
as cited in *The Hustons*, 1989

318. It was a great picture, but nobody wanted to see it. In droves.

Sam Goldwyn
Cited in *The Hustons*, 1989

319. God instilled in me the desire to establish my (filmmaking) identity and proclaim it to an audience ... large or small, brilliant or lamentable, enthusiastic or scornful.

Jean Renoír, Director
Stated in his 1974 *Jean Renoír — My Life and Times*

320. All we're trying to do is get somebody's attention and make them concentrate.

Robert Altman
Cited in *American Cinema*, 1995

321. Get the audience by the throat. Don't let them escape. Don't wake them up. Don't let them stop and realize "this is only a movie."

Billy Wilder
Cited in *American Cinema*, 1995

322. I endeavor to cater to the masses as well as the classes, not forgetting the kids.

Roscoe "Fatty" Arbuckle, Actor, silent era
Cited in *The Great Movie Comedians*, 1978

323. I make a deal with my audience. My contract

is that there will be plenty of laughs. Some directors guarantee violence, others promise sex.

> Woody Allen, Writer-Director
> Cited in *Woody Allen—*
> *His Films and Career*, 1985

324. What do we "consume" when we go to the cinema? We consume a story, certainly, but not a story that can be … summarized in prose…. Our pleasure, in short, follows from our engagement in the film as process.

> Richard de Cordova
> Interview in *Picture Personalities*, 1990

325. "Box Office" means a combination of a star and a title that the public wants to see.

> Irving Thalberg
> Cited in *Mayer and Thalberg*
> *— The Make Believe Saints*, 1975

326. They'll go see anything! We can make money showing blank film.

> Nicholas Schenck, MGM
> About movie matinees during
> the Depression, as cited in
> *Mayer and Thalberg—*
> *The Make Believe Saints*, 1975

327. Audiences only see about ten percent of what's on the screen …

> Irving Thalberg
> Cited in *Mayer and Thalberg*
> *— The Make Believe Saints*, 1975

328. I would prefer my films to be popular. But I would never do anything to make them popular. You do what you do and just pray they like it. If they like it, great! And if they don't, you still do what you do.

> Woody Allen
> Interview in *The New York Times*, 1997

329. (Federico) Fellini doesn't think of the public. He makes a film only for himself, as a painter would paint a canvas.

> Serge Sevilloni
> Of the Italian Radio and Television Administration, as cited in *Fellini—A Life*, 1986

330. Pleasing the public is one of the most difficult tasks, because we don't really know ourselves what we really like and what we want.

> Walt Disney
> Cited in *Chronicle of the Cinema*, 1995

331. Audiences don't know what they want. They only know when they see it.

> Frank Capra
> Interview in *Film Makers on Film Making*, 1983

332. The public is a mysterious entity that bewilders me by its incongruous and unpredictable reactions.

> Vittorio De Sica, Director
> Stated in his 1968, *De Sica—*
> *Miracle in Milan*

333. One underlying factor why (people go) to a motion picture is to have their mood altered for two hours by having a voyeuristic, escapist experience through sharing in some way the lives of the people on the screen.

> Roger Ebert, Film Critic
> Interview in *Reel Conversations*, 1991

334. People should demand occasional surprise, because that's entertainment.

> Stanley Kramer, Producer-Director
> Interview in *Directors at Work*, 1970

335. The public … demands but one thing of the film: "I've paid … and, like a woman about to give birth, I want deliverance."

> Ingmar Bergman
> Interview in *Cahiers deu Cinéma*, 1956

336. Vicariously through this one embattled duck we live in dark theaters for a few magic moments the brave, liberty—loving lives we would like to live in the bright world outside—if only we dared.

> John Stanley, Writer
> Writing in *The Toledo Ohio Times*, 1937,
> "Introducing D. Duck—Fighting Professor," on Donald Duck symbolizing the anger of the post–Depression era audience

337. I've usually encountered a firm insistence from … the studios … that I attach a satisfactory ending. It may be that when (people) pay to go to a movie they feel they have bought the right to come out with a satisfied feeling.

> Alfred Hitchcock
> Interview in *The Saturday Evening Post*, 1957

338. Everybody has two businesses. Their own, and the movies.

> Unknown
> Cited in the 1995 *American Cinema*

339. "Please do not spit on the floor as it is very annoying and may spread disease."

> Notice to audience, projected
> on the screen prior to the movie
> c. 1910, cited in *Production Design*
> magazine, 1951

340. In the event of an air raid, customers not retaining their seat stubs will not be reseated when it is over.

> Sign in a Parisian movie theater, 1940
> Cited in *The Century*, 1998

341. The audience wanted to escape — not to a different galaxy; not to a different world — but to their own world as they might have wanted it to be.

> Joseph Mankiewicz
> On cinema "escapism," in
> *The American Cinema*, 1995

342. Entertainment is not, as we often think, a full-scale flight from our problems, not a means of forgetting them completely, but rather a rearrangement of our problems into shapes which tame them, which dispense them to the margins of our attention.

> Michael Wood, Writer
> In his 1975 *America in the Movies*

343. (People) go to the movies and they take what they're given, but people really want to see themselves more.

> Raul Julia, Actor
> Interview in *The Orange County
> Register — SHOW*, 1994

344. The most valuable thing you can cultivate (for the audience) is a kind of curiosity, a quality of observation about the world.

> Patrizia von Brandenstein,
> Production Designer
> Interview in *Moviemakers at Work*, 1987

345. People have a strong urge to find some magical place that will be the answer.

> Paul Mazursky, Director
> In a 1981 *New York Times*
> interview on "escapist" cinema

346. The (James Bond) pre-credit title sequences are always very important.... They say, "Children, sit down, leave your brains under the seat and come for a great big marvelous ride!"

> Guy Hamilton, Director
> Interview, 1984, in *Take 22:
> Moviemakers on Moviemaking*

347. We're leading the audience on a tour, and it's up to them to follow.

> Clint Eastwood, Director
> Interview in *Inner Views:
> Filmmakers in Conversation*, 1992

348. Audiences look around for where they are going to invest emotionally. They do this on a subconscious level ... you can't ask them to back the wrong horse....

> Sidney Poitier, Actor
> Interview in *American Film*, 1991

349. Audiences cannot both feel and think at the same time.

> Frank Capra, Producer-Director
> On not letting camera work become the
> story, as stated in his 1971
> *Frank Capra — The Name Above the Title*

350. No "think" gags. When the audience is thinking, they can't be laughing.

> Mack Sennett, Producer
> His caveat to his gag writers, as cited in
> *Frank Capra — The Name Above the Title*, 1971

351. The audience must be kept from thinking ... If they think of the actor, they cannot be carried along by the story, or be caught up by the suspense....

> Helen Klumph, Writer
> Interview in *Screen Acting*, 1922

352. Often it's better not to make things too clear, better to leave areas of mystery where an audience is tantalized or roused to thought and feelings of its own. All art is a shared experience.

> Elia Kazan, Director
> Interview in *Directors at Work*, 1970

353. I want to give the audience a hint of a scene. No more than that. Give them too much and they won't contribute anything themselves.

> Orson Welles
> Interview in *Collier's* magazine, 1938

354. An audience will not take something from a film or a book or of poetry if they do not give to it ... unless (they) have some corresponding depth, breadth of assimilation.

> Marlon Brando
> Interview in *Conversations with Brando*, 1991

355. Audiences don't want real, human emotion. They want the simplification of human emotion.

> Kevin Costner, Director-Actor
> Interview in *Details* magazine, 1993

356. The greater the expectation of manipulation (in movies), the greater the emotional response.

> Bruce A. Dustin and Thomas F. Gordon
> Stated in their 1991 *Current Research in Film*

357. The distance between your life and that in film was enormous; that was part of the success.

> Sydney Pollack
> Cited in *The American Cinema*, 1995

358. [N]o one wants ... to see a movie that reminds them of how oppressed they are.... They want to see things that … present an alternative or gives them kind of relief.

Keenan Ivory Wayans, Director
Interview in *A Cut Above*, 1998

359. We know … that a film will have a beginning, a middle and an end: reality, whatever it is, does not.

I. C. Jarvie
Stated in his 1970 *Movies and Society*

360. I have a theory: it is not to bore the audience.

William Wyler, Director
Interview in *Film Makers on Film Making*, 1983

361. The worst thing you can feel in a movie is manipulated.

Steve Martin, Actor
Interview in *The Los Angeles Times Calendar*, 1994

362. You play a piece of music or paint a painting and put it up on the wall, it's up to people to interpret it. It may not be the right way or your way of interpreting it, but at least they are participating.

Clint Eastwood, Director
Interview in *Inner Views: Filmmakers in Conversation*, 1992

363. Without any collaboration of the (audience) we have nothing. We must be in communion, the artist and the (audience).

Jean Renoir, French Director
Interview in *Film Makers on Film Making*, 1983

364. (There's) an experience as a filmgoer that I love — when you get that kind of almost musical communion with the image.

Peter Weir, Director
Interview in *Premiere*, 1998

365. I like the slow start, the start that goes under the audience's skin and involves them….

Stanley Kubrick, Director
Stated in *Kubrick — Inside a Film Artist's Maze*, 1982

366. I was discovering another axiom of entertainment; what interests people most is people.

Frank Capra, Director
Stated in his 1971 *Frank Capra — The Name Above the Title*

367. I think of the medium as a people-to-people medium…. You can only involve an audience with people.

Frank Capra, Director
Interview in *Film Makers on Film Making*, 1983

368. Expect the audience to bring something to the seat besides their asses.

Hugh Gray, Former UCLA professor
Cited in *Screenwriting 434*, 1993

369. Drama is not … just actors weeping and suffering…. It isn't drama unless the audiences are emotionally moved.

Frank Capra, Director
Stated in his 1971 *Frank Capra — The Name Above the Title*

370. An audience expects (screen) players to share "feelings" with them and feels cheated if this does not occur.

Brian Adams, Author
Stated in his 1986 *Screen Acting*

371. People are mature enough and emotionally stable enough that they can go through a long, emotional movie — it's not good to cut off an emotion.

Gena Rowlands, Actress
Interview in *Take 22: Moviemakers on Moviemaking*, 1984, on why her movies are over two hours

372. We have in pictures the most difficult, the most demanding audience of any medium…. Once you let them go, it's hard to get them back.

William Wyler, Director
Interview in *Directors at Work*, 1970, on captivating the viewers

373. The shallowness of movies can affect us as profoundly as their depths.

David Ansen, Writer
Cited in "The 100 Best Movies," *Newsweek Extra 2000*, 1998

374. If you go to see the film with ideologically limited glasses, you don't see it.

Federico Fellini
Cited in *Fellini — A Life*, 1986

375. The feel of the experience is the important thing, not the ability to verbalize or analyze it. Those who won't believe their eyes won't be able to appreciate this film.

Stanley Kubrick, Director
Cited in *Chronicle of the Cinema*, 1995, on his film *2001: A Space Odyssey*

376. There are plenty of filmmakers who say, "Man, if you have to ask, you'll never know."

Stanley Kramer, Producer-Director
Interview in *Directors at Work*, 1970

377. I think it's hysterical that an audience of intelligent people will discuss (James) Bond seriously.

Guy Hamilton, Director
Interview in *Take 22: Moviemakers on Moviemaking*, 1984

378. But as the level of proficiency in producing effects increases, the audience becomes more sophisticated and jaded and more demanding and discerning....

Jonathan Erland, Special Effects Technician
Interview in *Moviemakers at Work*, 1987

379. Ordinary folk may see films as a dream world, but when it pretends to be realism, they are ruthless in picking at it and undermining its pretence.

I. C. Jarvie
Stated in his 1970 *Movies and Society*

380. An audience really should just come in and look at a movie and either love it or hate it and go home.

Burt Lancaster, Actor
Interview in *Take 22: Moviemakers on Moviemaking*, 1984

381. If that's what you saw, that's what it's about.

Federico Fellini, Director
On individual audience interpretation on his films, stated in *Take 22: Moviemakers on Moviemaking*, 1984

382. I am not going to reform the audience. I am not going to better the audience. I just want the audience to drop the popcorn and listen.

Billy Wilder, Director
Cited in *The Bright Side of Billy Wilder, Primarily*, 1970

383. People want to laugh with their mouths, not their minds.

Moe Howard, Actor
Cited in *The Great Movie Comedians*, 1978

384. It is not my prerogative as an actress, to teach (the public) anything. They will teach me.

Mary Pickford, Actress-Producer
Cited in *Reel Women: Pioneers of the Cinema*, 1991

385. I'm not a social filmmaker.... The quickest way to turn me, as an audience off, is to say, "Look at that. Now do something about it because you've been shown the light...."

Joan Tewkesbury, Screenwriter-Director
Interview in *American Film*, 1979

386. The worst mistake you can make is to underestimate your audience. You have to look up to them.

Rouben Mamoulian, Director
Interview in *Film Makers on Film Making*, 1983

387. The public is the gauge of taste. If it doesn't like what you've done, in nine cases out of ten you've done the wrong thing.

Walt Disney
Cited in *The Magic Kingdom*, 1997

388. I don't think the audience is this dumb person lower than me. I am the audience.

Quentin Tarantino
Interview in *The New York Times Magazine*, 1997

389. I don't believe in playing down to children; either in life or in motion pictures. The American child is a highly intelligent human being ... (with a) healthy curiosity about the world in which he lives.

Walt Disney
Cited in *Deeds Rather Than Words*, 1962

390. Hollywood makes you pay attention to the pictorial world, not the means by which it brings it to you.

Richard Sylbert
Cited in *American Cinema*, 1995

391. Everybody in the world was once a child ... in every one of us something remains of our childhood.

Walt Disney
Cited in *The Magic Kingdom*, 1997

392. The audience is as smart as you challenge them to be.

Paul Mazursky, Director
Interview in *The Plain Dealer*, 1978

393. Teenagers ... that's the real movie audience ... it's the age when movies really count.

Amy Heckerling, Director
Interview in *Moviegoer* magazine, 1985

394. I don't think that people go to the movies seeking out the lowest common denominator.... They're in search of a unique experience.

Michael Cimino, Screenwriter-Director
Interview in *Reel Conversations*, 1991, on audiences being underestimated

395. Most of us do not consciously look at movies.

Roger Ebert, Film Critic
Cited in on the Internet Movie Database, 1998

396. Films have their own way of inviting the human imagination to fill in what is left out.

> I. C. Jarvie
> Stated in his 1970 *Movies and Society*

397. I think we don't demand enough of the audience. No subtlety, playing down to the lowest common denominator all the time, making films for an intelligence level of retarded twelve-year-olds.

> Spike Lee, Director
> Interview in *Inner Views: Filmmakers
> in Conversation*, 1992

398. Audiences will reach for quality but never stoop.

> Irving Thalberg, Studio Producer
> Cited in *Mayer and Thalberg*, 1975

399. Black movies have gone far beyond the confines of a sociological treatise on brotherhood and that the taste of American audiences has grown mature enough to accept a good movie whether or not it is "black."

> Melvin van Peebles, Screenwriter-Director
> Interview in *The Daily Breeze*, 1991

400. Boy, oh, boy, I wish I had a nickel for every time I was told, Mel, baby, there is no such thing as a Negro audience.

> Melvin van Peebles, Screenwriter-Director
> Interview in *The Los Angeles Times*, 1996

401. Sure, there are some tough crowds at my movie. That's because my movie is realistic and they can relate to it. We should try to improve their lives so that they can't.

> Mario van Peebles,
> Screenwriter-Director-Actor
> Interview in *The New York Times*, 1991

402. I never saw a more startled audience than that which saw the Lumière Cinématographe exhibited for the first time.

> Unknown Historian, Circa 1990
> Cited in the Internet Movie Database, 1998

403. (Silent movies) made everyone in the audience deaf mutes.

> Alfred Hitchcock
> Cited in *50 Major Film Makers*, 1975

404. This is a post-literate cinematic age, an age in which movie audiences, as in the silent era, can be fully satisfied by fresh, well-executed special effects and heroic myth.

> Kurt Andersen, Writer
> Interview in *The New Yorker*, 1998

405. A cinema … what better place to lose one's life than in a comfortable seat in a cinema....

> Roberto Rossellini, Director
> Going to a movie for shelter during a
> World War II bombing raid in Italy, circa
> 1944, told by Ingrid Bergman in her 1980
> *Ingrid Bergman — My Story*

406. As a kid I had puppet shows — I wanted people to like my puppet shows when I was eight years old.

> Steven Spielberg
> Cited in *Steven Spielberg—
> The Unauthorized Biography*, 1996

407. I get dressed up when I go out — because when people go see my movies I want to say thank you, not fuck you.

> Sharon Stone
> Interview in *The New York
> Times Magazine*, 1997

408. I'd rather see my daughter in a drive-in than parked in a dark alley somewhere.

> Richard Hollingshead
> Innovator of the drive-in theater, as cited
> on the Internet Movie Database, 1998

409. It tends to throw audience sympathy on the side of sin.

> *Tidings* magazine
> Official publication of the Archdiocese,
> disapproving of *Duel in the Sun*,
> 1946, as cited in *Inside Oscar*, 1996

410. Seventy percent of our American audiences are between the ages of sixteen and twenty-four. Do we want to scandalize them?

> A member of the Hays Censorship Office
> Referring to several "earthy" words
> in the 1942, *In Which We Serve*,
> as cited in *Inside Oscar*, 1996

411. When the monkey die, people gonna cry!

> Dino De Laurentis, Producer
> Cited in the Internet Movie Database,
> 1998, on director
> Willis O'Brien's *King Kong*

412. I was afraid of trees, clouds, the wind, the dark…. I liked being scared. It was very stimulating.

> Steven Spielberg
> Cited in Steven Spielberg
> *— The Unauthorized Biography*, 1996

413. I thought everybody saw every movie and everybody went to the movies.

> Kim Basinger, Actress
> Interviewed in *Interview* magazine,
> 1998, recalling when she first
> performed in the movies

414. The general decline of manners in society is reflected in the limited society called the movie theater.

> Gene Siskel, Film Critic
> In a June 1984 interview in
> *Playboy*, on "theater talkers"

415. The real responsibility for the spiritual stagnation of cinema lies with the amorphous mass, routinary and conformist, that makes up the audience. The producer limits himself merely to throwing to the beasts the food they demand of him.

> Luis Buñuel, Director
> Interview in *Show Business Illustrated*, 1962

4

Business

416. The biggest misconception about the movie business is that the movie is more important than the business. Many of us tend to think about filmmaking not as a business at all, but as an art form; in that case, it would be called "show art" instead of "show business."

Louise Levison, Author
Stated in *Filmmakers*
and Financing, 1994

417. The Hollywood mind remains the same, which, I suspect, is the way it will always be as long as the art remains a business.

Vincent Canby
Stated in *The New York Times*, 1977

418. I don't think that in the first place (movie-making) is a business. In the second place it's a business. I think first it's a creative enterprise. That's where it starts.

Blake Edwards, Writer-Director-Producer
Interview in *Take 22:*
Moviemakers on Moviemaking, 1984

419. We practice the art of the film business, not the business of the film art.

David Picker, Producer–Studio Head
Cited in *Motion Picture Marketing*
and Distribution, 1991

420. The trouble with movies as a business is that they're an art; the trouble with movies as an art is that they're a business.

Old Hollywood adage
Cited in *The American Cinema*, 1995

421. Being an artist and being in show business have nothing to do with each other. Show business is all about making a commotion so that people come and see you so that you can make some money.

Eddie Murphy, Actor
Interview in *US* magazine, 1993

422. We are a business concern and not patrons of the arts....

David O. Selznick, Selznick
International Pictures, 1938
Cited in *George Cukor—A Double Life*, 1991

423. A movie is a form of art, but a very expensive one.

Louise Levison, Author
Stated in her 1994 *Filmmakers and Financing*

424. The big tragedy of Hollywood today is that people here spend eighteen hours a day trying to get the best deal. No one spends time to get the best movie.

Billy Wilder, Actor
Stated in *The Bright Side of*
Billy Wilder, Primarily, 1970

425. There's nothing wrong with this business that a good picture won't cure.

Nicholas Schenck, MGM
Cited in *Mayer and Thalberg—*
The Make Believe Saints, 1975

426. As much as you keep reminding yourself with the mantra, "It's about the movies; it's about the movies," it's about the money.

Joe Roth, Chairman, Studio Film Division
Cited in a 1995 *Esquire* article,
"Brother, Can You Spare a Million?"

427. There is an old debate whether the motion picture business is controlled by finance capital or industrial capital. The issue may be quite moot. What matters ultimately is that the film business is controlled by capital.

Thomas Guback, Researcher, Film Economics
Cited in *Movies and Money*, 1982

428. Cinema is, above all, an organism whose medium is money.

John Baxter
Cited in *Steven Spielberg—*
The Unauthorized Biography, 1996

429. Hollywood ... has always had an Achilles pocketbook — money making is what it's about.
Melvin van Peebles, Screenwriter-Director
Interview in *The Daily Breeze*, 1991

430. In the name of competition and making a buck ... results are more important than methods.
McCormick Foundation
Study on the film industry, 1986

431. If the total of net (box office) receipts is large enough, a return on invested capital is assured to all who have participated. No other fact holds much meaning in the film business.
William A. Bluem, Writer
Stated in *Movie Business: American Film Industry Practice*, 1972

432. If you ever make a picture, forget the word "net." Never say it to yourself. Think of gross and you'll get rich.
Joseph E. Levine, Producer
Interview in *Film Makers on Film Making*, 1983

433. Success now breeds success, for the box office winners of today are providing and attracting the finance for producing the winners of tomorrow.
William Clayton, Assistant Secretary, Dept. of State
Stated in 1946

434. If I make a dollar profit, then I can go on to the next picture.
Woody Allen, Writer-Director
Cited in *Woody Allen — His Films and Career*, 1985

435. The length of a film has nothing to do with anything but economics. Every sacred cow in the business has to do with economics.
Gena Rowlands, Actress
Interview in *Take 22: Moviemakers on Moviemaking*, 1984

436. You need three things to succeed in the movie business — the intelligence and the financing and the guts to stay at the table and play.
Robert Daly
Cited in *Clint Eastwood — A Biography*, 1996

437. The most important thing to remember about a deal, and about negotiation is that it is all about appetite ... it's about how much you want it.
Dawn Steel
Cited in *Steven Spielberg — The Unauthorized Biography*, 1996

438. Hollywood is a company town, a deal-making society.
Faye Dunaway, Actress
Cited in *GQ* magazine, 1983

439. You make the deal, you shoot the deal, you edit the deal, and you release the deal.
Phil Messina, Independent Producer
Stated at the 1985 Film Forum, New York

440. There are so many kinds of deals out there — the official deal, the sealed deal, the vaulted deal, the safe deal and the producer's deal.
Arnold Schwarzenegger, Actor
Interview in *The Los Angeles Times Magazine*, 1991

441. Nobody will gamble on a movie. Everyone wants to gamble on the deal.
George Romero, Film Editor
Stated at the 1985 Film Forum, New York

442. I've learned about money. Money isn't money; it is a weapon, a tool, a way of people keeping you in your place.
Richard Dreyfuss
Interview in *Esquire*, 1978

443. Conviction is the key to success in this business ... the ability to stick to that conviction.
Lindsay Doran, Studio President
Interview in the *Hollywood Reporter*, 1996

444. If I'm right fifty-one percent of the time, I'm ahead of the game.
Jack Warner, Producer–Studio Head
Cited in *Clown Prince of Hollywood*, 1990

445. (A studio's movie has) a fifty percent chance of failing or succeeding, or working or not, and that's as good of a chance as you'll get on anything, and you're not going to do anything that's going to make it any better.
Tim Burton, Director
Interview in *Inner Views: Filmmakers in Conversation*, 1992

446. The (circus) tight-rope walker and the filmmaker are subject to the same inevitable risk: they can fall down and break their necks.
Ingmar Bergman
Interview in *50 Major Film Makers*, 1975

447. The tragedy with Hollywood today is that the great gamblers are dead.
Steven Spielberg
Cited in *Steven Spielberg — The Unauthorized Biography*, 1996

448. Logically, a hunch makes as much sense as, say, "All horses have tails; therefore, all tails have horses." [I]n the zany world of films you don't explain hunches — you just live and die by them.

Frank Capra, Director-Producer
Stated in his 1971 *Frank Capra — The Name Above the Title*, on taking chances

449. We, the so-called artists, are fools if we don't accept the fact that great sums of money are being risked when we're doing our own thing.

Paul Mazursky, Director
Interview in *The New York Times*, 1981

450. There has always been an intimate relationship between American movies and money. Indeed, Hollywood represents not only glamour, romance and adventure, but dollars and cents.

Janet Wasko, Author, Temple University
Stated in her 1982 *Movies and Money*

451. I don't think I've made a bad film. I think I've made films that have not performed in an equation that justifies their manufacture.

Robert Altman, Director
Interview in *Inner Views: Filmmakers in Conversation*, 1992

452. It was a manufacturing business, and the parts were the actors and actresses.

Richard Brandt
Cited in *The American Cinema*, 1995, on the early motion picture business

453. The fragile, intangible film world of creativity — a world of "no rules" — is built on and supported by a heavy industry that has rules and tangible costs.

Frank Capra, Director
Stated in his 1971 *Frank Capra — The Name Above the Title*

454. Cautious moviemakers might minimize their risks by emphasizing the familiar (remarks, sequels and series). More risk-oriented moviemakers, on the other hand, might emphasize the original.

Thomas Simonet
Stated in *Current Research in Film*, Vol. 3, 1991

455. It is sad but true that movies have always been an imitative — not innovative — industry. Miscalculation abounds.

Richard Lederer, Studio Executive
Cited in *Movie Business: American Film Industry Practice*, 1972

456. I work for the commercial film industry, which basically wants to take old formulas and make them with new actors. It's like Boeing — they have to make planes that will fly. They can't make one that flies on its side.

Francis Ford Coppola, Screenwriter-Director
Cited in *An Introduction to Film Studies*, 1996

457. The people who put up the (movie) money are loath to experiment because the experiment is unusually more perilous in show business than in chemistry ...

Elliot Silverstein, Director
Interview in *Directors at Work*, 1970

458. Making a sequel to anything is just a cheap corny trick.

Steven Spielberg
Stated at the San Francisco Film Festival, 1975

459. Hollywood never learns from its own failures, only other people's successes.

Robert Redford
Interview in *The New York Times Magazine*, 1997

460. There are no sure-fire commercial ideas anymore ... and there are no unbreakable rules....

William Goldman, Screenwriter
Cited in *Movie Business: American Film Industry Practice*, 1972

461. I had a monumental idea this morning, but I didn't like it.

Sam Goldwyn
Cited in *You Must Remember This*, 1975

462. There is no downside to success except, I guess, that you have to figure out something new to succeed at.

Sherry Lansing
Interview in *The Hollywood Reporter*, 1997

463. When you're dealing out of insecurity, it's hard to make good creative decisions.

Sue Mengers, Agent
Interview in *Film Makers on Film Making*, 1983, on studios' choices in movies

464. One of the best reasons to do a film is when everybody tells you you shouldn't do it.

Irwin Winkler, Producer
Interview in *Film Makers on Film Making*, 1983

465. Every film that was a breakthrough film — that changed the way films are made, and changed the way audiences see films ... has been an accident.

Robert Altman, Director
Interview in *Inner Views: Filmmakers in Conversation*, 1992

466. You can't explain anything in this business. It's a chain of accidents.

Clark Gable, Actor
Cited in the 1998 televised
A&E *Biography*, "Clark Gable"

467. You would not tell me a joke that you didn't think was funny on the off-chance that I might like it ... but that's the way they make movies.

Nicholas Meyer, Writer-Director
Interview in *Film Makers on Film Making*, 1983

468. (My theory is) that there are thousands of talented actors and hundreds of gifted directors walking around Hollywood but the ones you see making movies are the lucky ones.

Marshall Herskovitz, Screenwriter
Interview in *Movie Maker* magazine, 1998

469. The entertainment business is unfortunately a lot more entertaining than the entertainment it provides.

Todd Solondz, Director
Cited in the *Santa Barbara News-Press*, 1998

470. There was a time when they spoke of it as the motion picture "game." The word implied the elements of luck, chance, gamble, haphazard, hit or miss operation. Today ... (it is) a business that is coolly and calculatingly well planned.

John F. Barry
Interview in *Moving Picture World*

471. The trouble with a movie these days is that it is old before it is released. It is no accident that it comes in a can.

Orson Welles, Actor-Director
Cited in *Orson Welles: The Road to Xanadu*, 1996

472. Ideas are anyone's property in Hollywood until they actually become "properties."

Sammy Davis, Jr., Actor
Cited in *Hollywood in a Suitcase*

473. Each movie, while mass produced, is essentially a unique commodity.

Garth Jowett, Writer
Stated in his 1980 *Movies as Mass Communications*

474. A motion picture is the only commodity that does not carry an established price tag.

M.J.E. McCarthy, Movie Distributor
Cited in *Movie Business: American Film Industry Practice*, 1972

475. A film breaks even when its take reaches twice its cost.

Film Industry Axiom, 1948
Cited in *Frank Capra — The Name Above the Title*, 1971

476. If you can get one masterpiece (film) a year, do you have the right to expect more than that?

Quentin Tarantino
Commenting in *The New York Times Magazine* on the movie studio's excessive expectations, 1997

477. Hollywood ... it's an expedient town, and people deal with expediency only.

Blake Edwards, Writer-Producer-Director
Interview in *Take 22: Moviemakers on Moviemaking*, 1984

478. Between censorship, the vulgarity of the advertising, the stupidity of exhibitors, the mutilation, the inept dubbing into other languages — when I finish a picture it's best to forget I ever made it.

Federico Fellini
Cited in *Fellini — A Life*, 1986

479. Movies are, as one old-timer put it — not an industry, but a disease.

Richard Lederer, Studio Executive
Cited in *Movie Business: American Film Industry Practice*, 1972

480. I'm in the business of creating illusions.

Irving Thalberg
Cited in *Mayer and Thalberg — The Make Believe Saints*, 1975

481. We're supposed to be creative people. So let's make a creative deal.

Michael Eisner
To Tom Pollock, two studio chiefs, as cited in *American Cinema*, 1995

482. I have a nice gentleman's agreement with United Artists. I've traded the idea of making millions in return for artistic control.

Woody Allen, Writer-Director
Cited in *Woody Allen — His Films and Career*, 1985

483. It's one of the scriptures of show business: audiences attract dollars; stars attract audiences; characters attract stars.

David Geffner, Writer
Stated in *Movie Maker* magazine, 1998

484. Do not take any rejection personally, but allow rejection to fuel your drive to success. Be willing to serve before you rule.

Paula Wagner, Producer
Cited in *Power 50* magazine, 1995

485. The theater (business) is not the place for a man who bleeds easily.

> Sean O'Casey
> Cited in *Fred Zinnemann —
> An Autobiography*, 1992

486. If you want to be in movies, you'd better love them a lot, because it's going to break your heart.

> Richard Brooks, Writer-Director
> Interview in *Film Makers on Film Making*, 1983

487. (Making a movie pitch) is the most barbaric process in Hollywood.

> Amy Pascal, Columbia Pictures
> Interview in *Variety*, 1998

488. It's not a matter of "can you?" It's who is going to let you.

> Robert Aldrich, Director
> Interview in *Film Makers on Film Making*, 1983, on entry level filmmaking opportunities

489. You only need one person to say yes.

> Amy Heckerling, Screenwriter-Director
> Cited in *The Los Angeles Times*, 1989, on pitching a script

490. Trying to get a yes from a studio "exec" is about as easy as trying to get him to beg to be teargassed.

> Caldecot Chubb, Producer
> Cited in *Esquire*, 1992

491. "First Artists" get 25 percent of the gross.... They aren't, therefore, encouraged to make small, personal, noncommercial films for their enjoyment and therapy.

> Warner Bros.
> Commenting to the star owners of First Artist Production Co., as cited in *Going Hollywood*, 1978

492. Look at that ham up there — taking 90 percent of my money.

> Anonymous Agent
> Cited in *The Language of Show Biz*, viewing his actor-client on the screen

493. They respect you more when they pay you more.

> Barbra Streisand
> Cited in *Brentwood* magazine, 1997

494. What an interesting agent you have.... He takes ninety percent and you get ten percent.

> Friends of Ingrid Bergman
> Cited in *Ingrid Bergman — My Story*, 1980, on her studio producer renting her out to other studios for large sums

495. Agents don't have power in themselves. Their power is ceded to them by their clients.

> Rick Nicita
> Cited in *The American Cinema*, 1995

496. I could have been a multimillionaire but then I would have had to have been that kind of person.

> Marlon Brando, 1978
> Stated in *Conversations with Brando*, 1991

497. Show business is high school plus money.

> Hollywood saying
> Cited in *Steven Spielberg
> — The Unauthorized Biography*, 1996

498. Hollywood is no place for a grownup to work.

> Sidney Lumet, Director
> Stated at the 1985 *Film Forum*, New York

499. Shit, people are getting paid for this. This is kind of fun, you know....

> Clint Eastwood
> Cited in *Clint Eastwood — A Biography*, 1996

500. There are just two kinds of people in Hollywood: those trying to get contracts and those trying to get out of them.

> Walter Huston
> Cited in *The Hustons*, 1989

501. It's probably the only industry in the world where a contract just gives you the right to argue....

> Dennis Friedland, Attorney, Film Industry
> Cited in *Movie Business:
> American Film Industry Practice*, 1972

502. You're only as good as your last credit.

> Old Hollywood saying

503. A producer is only as good as what he's holding in his hand.

> Lawrence Godon
> Cited in *The New York Times Magazine*, 1997

504. Hollywood is a place where you are a hero today, gonif tomorrow.

> Jon Robin Baitz, Producer
> Cited in *The New Yorker*, 1998

505. If I'm going to make mistakes in my career, I want to make them, I don't want somebody else making them for me.

> Clint Eastwood
> Cited in *Clint Eastwood — A Biography*, 1996

506. The situation is utterly ridiculous ... we pay

George (Cukor) $4,250 weekly as a retainer for him to select what pictures ... he would like to make.

> David O. Selznick, 1938
> Cited in *George Cukor—A Double Life*, 1991

507. We look forward to a resurgent film industry ... and to the part the actor will play ... maybe someday you'll even let your daughter marry one.

> Charlton Heston, Actor,
> former president of SAG
> Cited in *Movie Business: American
> Film Industry Practice*, 1972

508. Every hairdresser in Beverly Hills has a brilliant idea for a movie.

> Bruce Feirstein
> Cited in *Fade In* magazine, Winter 1997/98

509. It was difficult for me to see my picture in terms of someone else's financial vision....

> Federico Fellini
> Cited in *Fellini—A Life*, 1986

510. Now I realize more than ever the secret of becoming a success in the business. No partners!

> Sam Goldwyn, MGM
> Cited in *You Must Remember This*, 1975

511. But bank presidents can't make moving pictures.

> Sidney R. Kent, Fox Film Corp. President
> Responding to criticism that Darryl F.
> Zanuck makes more money than bank
> presidents, as cited in *The Zanucks
> of Hollywood*, 1989

512. We have an agreement with the Bank of America: they don't make movies, we don't loan money.

> Jack Warner, Studio President
> Cited in *First Cut*, 1992, on not lending
> money to outside producers

513. Money is good only when you have judgment — otherwise every studio in town would be making a fortune.

> David Brown, Producer
> Interview in *Film Makers on Film Making*, 1983

514. The success of the American Film industry is based on its financial strength, which enables them to survive periods of bad management.

> William Clayton, Assistant Secretary,
> Dept. of State
> Stated in 1946

515. In the end ... the film ... is a synthesis of so many people ... it is impossible to remember who did what and when.

> Alan J. Pakula, Director
> Cited in *Film Makers on Film Making*, 1983

516. The people who give you the money to make pictures are very strange people.

> William Wyler, Director
> Interview in *Directors at Work*, 1969

517. (Hollywood) is like the game of "Life".... You pick a combination of points: money, power, love and fame.... If your choices don't get you around the game board, you have to switch priorities.

> Tom Pollock, Studio Head
> Cited in *Going Hollywood*, 1978

518. The pressure doesn't come from the dollars of it. It comes by way of the quality of the relationships of the people making the picture.

> Edward James Olmos, Actor
> Interview in the *Los Angeles Village View*, 1995

519. For creative differences.

> Everyone in Hollywood
> Cited in *Entertainment Weekly*, 1998,
> on the reason people fire others or get fired

520. All is forgiven when you have a good preview.

> John Stahl
> Cited in *Mayer and Thalberg
> — The Make Believe Saints*, 1975

521. The job expectancy of filmmakers (is) based on the age-old law of the marketplace — take in more than you spend or you're out.

> Frank Capra, Director
> Stated in *Frank Capra
> — The Name Above the Title*

522. Studio executives ... share one thing in common with baseball managers: they wake up every morning ... with the knowledge that sooner or later they're going to get fired.

> William Goldman, Author
> Stated in his *Adventures in the Screentrade*, 1983

523. The smiley-face hypocrisy of Hollywood: Nowhere else ... do people reveling in another person's flameout make such a show of earnest empathy while privately aching intensely for successful colleagues to fail.

> Kurt Andersen, Writer
> Stated in *The New Yorker*, 1998

524. No one in Hollywood wants anyone else's movie to succeed.

> Barry Sonnenfeld, Director
> Cited in *The Hollywood Reporter*, 1996

525. In Hollywood every person one does business with is a friend until shortly after the ink dries.

> Anonymous
> Cited in *Going Hollywood*, 1978, as
> a common Hollywood sentiment

526. I think Paramount's the only company I haven't sued. They all steal.

> Sean Connery, Actor
> Interview in *GQ* magazine, 1989

527. I know it's popular to mix (business) with sex in Hollywood, but not on this lot.

> Irving Thalberg
> Cited in *Mayer and Thalberg—The Make
> Believe Saints*, 1975, on the head of
> Universal-Hollywood, circa 1920

528. In spite of the money my films made I was not "commercial." It was worse than a label: it was like a tattoo mark on my forehead.

> Jean Renoir, French Director, in Hollywood
> Stated in his 1974 *Jean Renoir—
> My Life and Times*, referring to his
> Hollywood films versus his French films

529. Good taste is good business....

> Will Hays
> Stated in as head of the Academy's Self-Censor
> Board, 1930, as cited in *Inside Oscar*, 1996

530. Your whole job is about saying no. It's about introducing the ugly realities of money into a conversation about magic.

> Jodie Foster, Producer
> Interview in the *Santa Barbara
> News-Press*, 1998, on the job of a producer

531. The people who do well in the system are the people who do films that producers like to produce, not that people want to see.

> Orson Welles
> Cited in *Orson Welles: The Road to Xanadu*, 1996

532. If the creative wellspring for all movies is in the form of words committed to paper, the true source of any film is in the form of cash on the barrelhead.

> William A. Bluem, Writer
> Stated in his 1972 *Movie Business:
> American Film Industry Practice*

533. Actors are not worth a million dollars, the words are.

> Burt Reynolds, Actor-Director
> Interview in *Take 22: Moviemakers
> on Moviemaking*, 1984

534. Tell that (Sam) Harris I wouldn't shell out two hundred G's for the Second Coming!

> Harry Cohn, President of Columbia Pictures
> Just before paying that record price for *You
> Can't Take It with You*, 1938, cited in the
> 1971 Frank Capra autobiography

535. A story never looks as good as when someone else buys it and never looks as bad as when you do.

> Irving Thalberg
> Cited in *Mayer and Thalberg
> —The Make Believe Saints*, 1975

536. If you kill seventeen people but make an incredible movie, nobody looks at the seventeen bodies.

> Bruce Feirstein
> Cited in *Fade In* magazine, Winter 1997/98

537. The only morality that's ever been attached to Hollywood is: is there a profit that's going to be made.

> Todd Solondz, Director
> Cited in the *Santa Barbara News-Press*, 1998

538. In the old days, we had moguls—at least you knew whose behind to kiss.

> Billy Wilder, Writer-Director, 1987
> Cited in *Inside Oscar*, 1996

539. Power resides with the filmmakers. The people who make the movies, the writers, directors, and producers, they are the ones with power.

> Sherry Lansing, Chairman,
> Motion Picture Group
> Interview in *The Hollywood Reporter*, 1997

540. You really oughta bring "Batjac" back to Warner Brothers, Duke. You should be here, where you can be fucked by friends.

> Jack Warner, Studio Head
> To John Wayne on his production company
> filming at Warner Bros. again, as cited in
> *Clown Prince of Hollywood*, 1990

541. I love the idea of not being an independent filmmaker. I've liked working within the system.

> Steven Spielberg, Director
> Cited in *The Future of the Movies*, 1991

542. When you go to Hollywood they want to make a Hollywood movie, and that's the problem.
Elmore Leonard, Screenwriter
Interview in *Film Comment*, 1998

543. Studios always come up with reasons not to do a movie.
Mark Horowitz
Cited in *The New York Times Magazine*, 1997

544. In Hollywood, nobody wants to hear the simple truth if it's not negative.
Tim Burton, Producer-Director
Interview in *Variety Daily*, 1992

545. In this industry you can't afford to hate anybody for long.
Joseph E. Levine, Producer
Cited in *Sophia Loren—A Biography*, 1998

546. When business wins the day in our profession, it sets motion pictures back for at least a decade.
Frank Capra, Producer-Director
Stated in his 1971 *Frank Capra
— The Name Above the Title*

547. The truth is that running a studio is a bit like being president of Zaire—the perks are great, but it's basically a lonely, miserable, maximum-stress job.
Unknown
Los Angeles magazine, March 1997

548. Having the green light means you have nowhere to hide.
Unknown
Los Angeles magazine

549. What does it say around the lion's head on the MGM trademark? "Ars gratia artis," Latin for "art for art's sake," a motto the studio, of course, has scrupulously observed over the years.
Roger Ebert
Stated in his 1997
Questions for the Movie Answer Man

550. MGM = Mayers-Ganza-Mishpaka.
MGM
The rumored hidden meaning of MGM,
"Mayer's-Whole-Family," as cited in *Mayer and
Thalberg—The Make Believe Saints*, 1975

551. For God's sake, you play like this game was played in the nineteenth century!
Fortune, December 1935
Cited in *The Zanucks of Hollywood*, 1989,
to Sam Engel, his new movie studio partner,

after their polo ponies collided, inspiring the "Twentieth Century" company name, 1924

552. Every Friday, the front door of this studio opens and I spit a movie out onto Gower Street.... If that door opens and I spit and nothing comes out, it means a lot of people are out of work....
Harry Cohn, President, Columbia Studios
Upon the "Twentieth Century"
merger with "Fox"

553. We're being paid on the theory that we might be in touch with a public for a certain length of time.
Richard Lester, Director
Cited in *Growing Up in Hollywood*, 1976

554. We always get paid. If the checks come from an empty lot, who cares? They come.
Sam Cohn, Head of Paramount
Interview in *Directors at Work*, 1970

555. When it comes to spending money, studios are as reactive to trends as the mercurial fashion industry.
Dan Cox, Hollywood Writer
Cited in *Going Hollywood*, 1978

556. Don't fuck with the mouse.
Warning at Disney Studios
to all incoming executives
Stated in *Movie Maker* magazine, 1998

557. I do not feel, as many do, that it is out of pure racial malice that the studios goof up. After all, no one intentionally sets fire to his or her wallet.
Melvin van Peebles, Screenwriter-Director
Cited in *Steven Spielberg
— The Unauthorized Biography*, 1996

558. It's sad to realize that cinema has been going on for 60 years and until now we've been frozen out.
Melvin van Peebles
Cited in *The Los Angeles Times*, 1996

559. Hollywood isn't as much black and white as it is ultra-green.
Melvin van Peebles
Referring to black producers and directors
in a 1968 *The Hollywood Reporter* interview

560. You ask me "Is it difficult to be a woman director?" I'd say it is difficult to be a director period.... It is difficult not to be drowned in the system.
Agnes Varda
Interview in *The Daily Breeze*, 1991

561. If you want to play in this business, you play like a man, or you're out. And if you happen to be a woman, better not mention it to anybody.
Lois Weber, Director, circa 1920
Cited in *Reel Women:*
Pioneers of the Cinema, 1991

562. If you're lucky enough to have a hit then you're allowed four failures, they say. But I don't know if that applies to women. And I don't wish to find out.
Penny Marshall, Director
Cited in *Reel Women:*
Pioneers of the Cinema, 1991

563. We can be like anyone else and bid for the existing "real estate" (movie material) or ... be architects and builders ourselves. I think we can create some very valuable real estate on our own.
Laura Ziskin, Studio President
Interview in *The Hollywood Reporter*, 1992

564. For years people said, "Oh, we can't make that movie because it's a woman's movie." What's wrong with that? Can't they count the population?
Laura Ziskin, Executive Producer
Interview in *The Wall Street Journal*, 1994

565. You need to have women in the creative process because they are going to be in touch with the taste of that gender.
Laura Ziskin, Studio President
Interview in *Los Angeles Style*, 1991

566. Sometimes I wonder how men can be producers. A large part of it is being a mother.
Laura Ziskin, Executive Producer
Interview in *The Hollywood Reporter*, 1995

567. I look forward to the day when the measure of success focuses on a skill set and work ethic rather than gender.
Kathleen Kennedy, Studio Executive
Interview in *Los Angeles Style*, 1991

568. Men's salaries are preposterous. If actresses had parity, you couldn't make a movie. Men pay men more, period.
Meryl Streep, Actress
Interview in *The Hollywood Reporter*, 1996

569. I wonder what Harry Cohn and Jack Warner would say if they came back and saw all the "skirts" near the top.
Lucy Fisher, Studio Vice-Chairman, 1997
Cited in *Behind the Oscar*, 1993

570. (American Films) dominate world screens —
not because of armies, bayonets or nuclear bombs, but because what we are exhibiting on foreign screens the people of those countries want to see.
Louis Althusser
Interview in *The Hollywood Reporter*, 1997

571. The French invented cinema, and they hardly ever get nominated, but do you hear them complaining? Mais non!
Roger Ebert
Stated in his 1970 *For Marx*

572. In the thirties, to be a film director in London ... was like wanting to run a brothel.
Guy Hamilton, Director
Stated in his 1997 *Questions*
for the Movie Answer Man

573. The propaganda arm of the American Dream machine, Hollywood.
Molly Haskell
Interview in *Take 22:*
Moviemakers on Moviemaking, 1984

574. What scares (studio) marketing people to death: they want to be the only movie that everybody wants to see.
Tom Hanks

575. Today Hollywood rules over a divided audience, and its energies are focused more on selling than on what it sells.
David Ansen, Writer
Cited in *Webster's Dictionary*
of Quotations, 1998

576. The promotional system rarely sells the particular qualities of a given movie — the tone, the temper, the body. It just sells, period.
David Densby, Writer
Interview in *The New York Times*
Magazine, 1997

577. You can only do so much with advertising. After a while, they don't believe all the lies we tell them. You have to have a film to back it up.
Joseph E. Levine
Stated in his "The 100 Best Movies,"
Newsweek Extra 2000, 1998

578. You can fool all of the people all of the time if the advertising is right and the budget is big enough.
Joseph E. Levine, Producer
Stated in *The New Yorker*, 1998

579. In the new Hollywood "system," anything

goes as long as it makes sense, and, of course, its money back....

Rick Setlowe, Studio Creative Executive
Interview in Film Makers on Film Making, 1983

580. The Oscar is the most valuable, but least expensive, item of worldwide public relations ever invented by any industry.

Frank Capra
Cited in Sophia Loren—A Biography, 1998

581. A theater never makes up its loss when a picture plays to an empty seat.

Anonymous
Stated in 1970 as cited in Movie Business:
American Film Industry Practice, 1972

582. (Movie) theaters are the stores where customers buy entertainment ... then ... leaves with only the memory of it.

Samuel Marx
Cited in Inside Oscar, 1996

583. Where there's a hit, there's a writ.

Hollywood studio saying
Movie industry saying, cited in Mayer and
Thalberg—The Make Believe Saints, 1975

584. This business is not founded on ethics.

McCormick Study
Cited in Mayer and Thalberg
—The Make Believe Saints, 1975

585. There are no ethical decisions in the movie business, just the decision of how far to go and get away with it.

McCormick Study
Cited in Steven Spielberg
—The Unauthorized Biography, 1996

586. In a word, the profit motive renders ethics irrelevant.

McCormick Study
Ethical issues study on the film industry, 1986

587. You could stuff all the integrity in Hollywood into a gnat's naval and still have enough room for the heart of an agent.

Fred Allen
Ethical issues study on the film industry, 1986

588. Today's film industry is not just dog-eat-dog. It's pit bull–eat–pit bull.

Fade In magazine
Ethical issues study on the film industry, 1986

589. The name of the game (in pictures) is power.

In terms of ethics, this translates into selling people out.

McCormick Study
Cited in The Language of Show Biz

590. As long as success, personal gain, and competing with one's neighbor and corporations are the rules, ethics will never find a place.

McCormick Study
"How the Hell Do You Survive in
Hollywood?" Winter 1997/98

591. In the movie business ... there is lying, cheating, stealing, bribes, payoffs, kickbacks, and just plain old double-dealings.

Advertising Manager
Ethical issues study on the film industry, 1986

592. "We Make The Money, You Try and Find It."

Mel Brooks, Screenwriter-Director
Ethical issues study on the film industry, 1986

593. I'm working for myself now, and it's my own money, and I'm not cheating me.

Michael Curtiz, Producer-Director
Of a regional chain (133 theaters) with 35 years
experience, reporting to the McCormick Foun-
dation for their 1986 Ethical Issues Study

594. It is well known what a middleman is: he is the man who bamboozles one party and plunders the other.

Benjamin Disraeli
Interview in Playboy, February 1975,
on what he believed the motto
of Avco Embassy studios was

595. Granted the big guys push us around.... What worries me is that we push the little guys around ... the powerful take advantage of the lesser ... not just in the name of profit but for the hell of it....

McCormick Study
Interview in Liberty magazine, 1948

596. (L. B. Mayer's) hand on your shoulder meant it was closer to your throat.

Jules Dassin, Director
Speech at Maynooth, England, April 11, 1845,
as cited in Filmmakers and Financing, 1994

597. In a sense, the (movie) industry lives on honor; mostly it works, sometimes it doesn't....

Saul Rittenberg, Studio Attorney
Movie director on "Ethical Issues," in the
1986 study of the film industry

598. The key to this business is sincerity. Once you can fake that, you've got it made.

Unknown
Cited in *Bette and Joan
— The Divine Feud*, 1989

599. Look-a my face. The guarantee I give you is my face. I am what you see.

Dino De Laurentiis, Producer

Cited in *Movie Business: American Film
Industry Practice*, 1972

600. The noblest of all titles: an honest man.

Frank Capra, Producer-Director
Cited in *Script* magazine, Vol. 4, No. 2, on
an old Hollywood saying

5

Budget

601. The budget must be considered in light of the screenplay it represents, and in proportion to the projected commercial strength of the picture.

> William A. Bluem, Writer
> Stated in his *Movie Business:*
> *American Film Industry Practice*, 1972

602. The amount the Americans are prepared to spend on making their films is in a way a sign of respect for the audience.

> Andrzej Wajda
> Stated in *Dreams for Sale*, 1989

603. Inexpensive moviemaking comes down to one thing: the passion of the director, which translates into careful planning and attention to detail.

> Jonathan D. Krane, Producer
> Interview in *The Los Angeles Times*, 1989

604. You have to be incredibly precise, incredibly prepared, and find people who are willing to be incredibly taken advantage of.

> Gale Anne Hurd, Producer
> Interview in *Movieline* magazine,
> 1998, on getting the "biggest bang
> for your buck" film production

605. It's not a matter of cutting a budget down to a given figure, but rather, an attempt to come up with an intelligent plan which ... will produce a good product.

> Marshall Green, Executive Production Manager
> Cited in *Movie Business:*
> *American Film Industry Practice*, 1972

606. When your alternatives are limited, it produces combustion that is creative.

> Warren Beatty, Producer-Director
> Interview in *American Premiere*, 1992, on
> filming under financial constraints

607. What budget? I've got to do this shot.

> David Lean, Director
> Cited in *David Lean — A Biography*, 1996, while
> filming *The Bridge on the River Kwai*, 1957

608. Never mind about the cost. If it's a good picture, we'll make it.

> Sam Goldwyn
> When a director complained that
> the script was too "caustic," as cited
> in *You Must Remember This*, 1975

609. "What did it cost?" was the wrong question. One should ask, "Is it worth $7.00?", the price of a cinema seat.

> Steven Spielberg
> Cited in *Steven Spielberg*
> *— The Unauthorized Biography*, 1996

610. If it's a thrilling spectacle, $12 million is a drop in the bucket. If not, $12 million was too much.

> Kirk Douglas, Actor
> On *Spartacus,* cited in
> *Chronicle of the Cinema*, 1995

611. It costs money to achieve style.

> Polly Platt, Production Designer
> Interview in *Film Makers on Film Making*, 1983

612. The budget is the aesthetic.

> James Schamus
> Quoted in the "Robert Leedham"
> column, *Guardian*, 1991

613. The quality will be remembered long after the cost is forgotten.

> Anonymous Director
> Cited in *What an Art Director Does*, 1994

614. The cost will be remembered long after the quality is forgotten.

> Hal Herman, Production Manager
> Cited in *What an Art Director Does*, 1994

615. To go over budget gets you a bad reputation — unless you get an Oscar.

> Polly Platt, Costume Designer
> Interview in *Film Makers*
> *on Film Making*, 1983

616. The bigger the budget, the less freedom the director has.

Francis Ford Coppola, Screenwriter-Director
Interview in *Reel Conversations*, 1991

617. Shooting a feature film is hard work. Shooting a low budget feature film is insane.

Mark Petersen, Cinematographer
Cited in *Movie Maker* magazine, 1998

618. Economics is probably the most inhibiting factor for a director making a film.... Every time the director says, "Let's try it this way," and not, "Let's do it this way," he is spending money at enormous rates ...

Sydney Pollack, Director
Cited in *Movie Business: American
Film Industry Practice*, 1972

619. I do not believe in wasting money. On the other hand, nobody is going to go and see a picture simply because it came under budget.

Billy Wilder, Producer-Director
Cited in *The Bright Side of
Billy Wilder, Primarily*, 1970

620. Laughs are the only things that can compete with big-budget special effects. Money is the enemy of comedy. Too much money and you fuck up the job.

Bob Simonds, Producer
Interview in *Los Angeles* magazine, 1997

621. The only thing you can make with a big budget is a big, dishonest, impersonal movie.

Dennis Hopper, Actor-Director
Cited in the Internet Movie Database, 1998

622. Begin with a low budget and obey it.

Avi Lerner, Producer
Interview in *The New Yorker*, 1998,
on how to turn a profit in films

623. I don't want to appear self-righteous, but I do certainly find it hard to understand why a film should go over budget.... It's self-defeating.

Paul Mazursky, Director
Interview in *Screen International*, 1980

624. The one who takes money from the other has to prove, in a sense, that he is not a thief.

Federico Fellini
Cited in *Fellini—A Life*, 1986

625. It doesn't matter that you are $4,000 under

budget ... it only matters that you are $3,000 over budget....

Polly Platt, Production Designer
Interview in *Film Makers on Film Making*, 1983

626. The film was put in the can for $20,000.... To it's credit, some people say that it looks like we spent at least $21,000 or $22,000 on it.

Ash, Director
Interview in *Movie Maker* magazine, 1998

627. To paint, a man needs some canvas and some paint. To write ... paper and pencil. To sculpture, ... a block of granite.... To make a picture, you need a million dollars right away.

William Wyler, Director
Interview in *Directors at Work*, 1970

628. If you go into overtime, then I would rather be an actor instead of president of the company, because that's where the money is.

Jack Warner, Studio Head
Referring to actors' generous contracts,
cited in *Clown Prince of Hollywood*, 1990

629. Shooting a film can be quite exorbitant.... After eight hours, you go into overtime, golden time, and platinum time.

Paul Mazursky, Director
Cited in *The Plain Dealer*, 1978

630. Making a big budget movie is the biggest electric train set a kid can have.

Orson Welles
Cited in *The New York Times Magazine*, 1997

631. *War and Peace* cost nine million dollars — that's more than the real war cost.

Jerry Lewis, Actor-Director
Comment at the 1956 Academy Awards

632. With Francis Ford Coppola's budget, I could have invaded a country.

Clint Eastwood
Stated in *Clint Eastwood—A Biography*,
1996, referring to *Apocalypse Now*

633. Do you realize I can feed half the Navajo nation on what a film will cost in this country....

Norman Jewison, Director
Referring to the U.S.A., 1971,
as cited in *Directors at Work*

634. You know you've entered new territory when you realize your outfit cost more than your film.

Jessica Wu, Director
From her Academy Award
acceptance speech upon winning
for Best Documentary Short, 1998

635. Today, a million dollars is what you pay a star you don't want.

William Goldman, Author
Stated in his *Adventures in the Screentrade*, 1982

636. Audiences want bigger, better, faster and more.

Paula Wagner, Producer
Cited in *The Hollywood Reporter*, 1996, on what is driving movie costs up

6

Genre

637. I believe that a picture is a state of mind.
Jean Renoir, French Director
Interview in *Film Makers on Film Making*, 1983

638. Genre in film, if it is to have meaning, must have a limited scope, a limited definition.
Stuart A. Kaminsky, Writer
Stated in his 1984 *American Film Genres*

639. Genre films are created on the intense, nervous playground where America's most sacred beliefs and fantasies confront what is most unthinkable, most unspeakable in the dominant culture.
Gerald C. Wood, Writer
Cited in the *Handbook of American Film Genres*, 1988

640. (Genres have) conventions of narrative structure, characterization, theme, and visual design.
Foster Hirsch, Writer
Stated in his 1981 *The Dark Side of the Screen: Film Noir*

641. Although plot/story and genre are conceptually distinct variables, in practice the two are not mutually exclusive and appear to be virtually synonymous ... "a western which is about ..."
Variety
1981

642. A picture is rarely entirely "western" or "mystery" or "comedy" in nature.
Leo Handel, Motion Picture Research
Stated in the 1947 *Journal of Marketing*

643. The major genres traditionally give the audience a peek at discomforting images but then quickly draw a curtain over the troubling sites.
Gerald C. Wood, Writer
Cited in the *Handbook of American Film Genres*, 1988

644. Ultimately, our familiarity with any genre seems to depend less on recognizing a specific setting than on recognizing certain dramatic conflicts that we associate with specific patterns of action and character relationships.
Thomas Schatz, Author
Stated in his 1981 *Hollywood Genres*

645. There are basically only two ways of treating a fictional film subject: either dramatically or comically.
The British Film Industry
Stated in their 1952 "Political and Economic Planning, London"

646. Really, the ultimate film story is nothing more than good over evil.
Bruce Joel Rubin, Screenwriter
Interview in *Screenwriters on Screenwriting*, 1995

647. Confront a man in his office with a nuclear alarm, and you have a documentary. If the news reaches him in his living room, you have a drama. If it catches him in the lavatory, the result is a comedy.
Stanley Kubrick, Director
Cited in *Kubrick— Inside a Film Artist's Maze*, 1982

648. Hollywood knows it's got us. Of all the genres in film history — film noir, screwball, alien invasion, kung fu — there is perhaps none more constant than the tear-jerker.
Jack Kroll, Writer
Cited in *Newsweek Extra 2000*, "The 100 Best Movies," 1988

649. I would like to make ... a contemporary story that really gave a feeling of the times, psychologically, sexually, politically, personally ... it would be the hardest film to make.
Stanley Kubrick, Director
Cited in *Kubrick— Inside A Film Artist's Maze*, 1982

650. [N]o matter what the language or nation of origin, as long as persons have the deep-felt need to express themselves, the art cinema will crop up in some form.

> William C. Siska, Writer
> Cited in the *Handbook of American Film Genres*

651. You can make classy movies in any genre. You don't have to always say "thou" or "forsooth."

> Lindsay Doran, Studio Resident
> Cited in *The Los Angeles Times*, 1997

652. The death of a beautiful woman is always a poetic subject.

> Robert Evans, Paramount Executive
> Cited in *Chronicle of the Cinema*,
> 1995, on *Love Story*, 1970

653. Reading about people's foibles and the human condition ... we're very interested in them as movies.

> David Vogel, President,
> Hollywood Pictures, Disney Pictures
> Cited in *Variety*, 1998

654. Contemporary Americana is your blue-plate special.

> Frank Capra, Producer-Director
> Describing his time-tested successful film genre
> in his 1971 autobiography, *Frank Capra*

655. What's wrong with pictures about people who have problems?

> Stanley Kramer, Director
> Cited in *Handbook of American Film Genres*,
> 1988, defending social problem films

656. The Swedes, being neutral, couldn't blame anybody. So they just threw away the plot and dared you to understand their films. The critics couldn't understand them either so they called them "art."

> Frank Capra, Producer-Director
> Stated in his 1971 *Frank Capra*

657. Films about Lincoln, about saints, about Christ, are dangerous. Actors begin wearing halos long before they've earned them.

> Frank Capra, Producer-Director
> Stated in his 1971 *Frank Capra*

658. Genre films depict familiar, basically one-dimensional characters enacting a predictable story line within a familiar social setting.

> J. Allen
> Stated in the 1980 *Quarterly Review of Film
> Studies*, "The Film Viewer as Consumer"

659. The joy in genre is to see what can be dared

in the creation of a new form or the creative complication of an old one.

> Leo Braudy
> Stated in his 1976 *The Word in a Frame*

660. Hits create genres.... And since the public creates hits, they also create genres.... If something is successful, they will say get five of those. It's like the dress business....

> Andrew Bergman, Writer
> Cited in *American Cinema*, 1995

661. Genres are not dead as long as they are treated with sophistication.

> Kevin Costner, Producer-Director-Actor
> Cited in *Behind the Oscar*, 1993

662. Man, according to Hollywood, is either completely good, or bad.... The villain is a black-eyed sinner ... while the hero is a glamorous being....

> Hortense Powdermaker, Anthropologist
> Stated in her 1950 *Hollywood:
> The Dream Factory*

663. Melodrama is the most highly colored form of storytelling ... usually played heavy-handedly and bumblefootedly.

> Alfred Hitchcock
> Cited in *Hitchcock*, 1983

664. If we always wanted works of complexity and depth we wouldn't be going to movies about glamorous thieves and seductive women who sing in cheap cafes.

> Pauline Kael, Film Critic
> Stated in her 1970 *Going Steady*

665. That's the great thing about icons — they're durable. They blossom from reinterpretation.

> Akiva Goldsman, Producer-Writer
> Interview in *Entertainment Weekly*, 1998

666. A hero is one who looks like a hero.

> Robert Warshaw, Writer
> Stated in his 1985 "Movie Chronicle: The
> Westerner," *Film Theory and Criticism*

667. (A true film noir must leave a) continuing, persistent malaise in its wake ... a film noir cannot have a conventional happy ending and still be considered film noir.

> Jon Tuska, Writer
> Stated in his 1984 *Dark Cinema*

668. At the film noir film, you're dealing almost with a very simple, fundamental notion of morality, of what is good and evil … there's really no gray scale of behavior; things stand in very bold relief.

John Bailey, Writer
Cited in *American Cinema*, 1995

669. (Film) noir showed its audiences that the world is malevolent and to be too ambitious for money or sex or power leads to violence and death. The only logical alternative was to seek a life of total safety.

Jack Nachbar, Writer
Cited in *Handbook of
American Film Genres*, 1988

670. If film noir males are destroyed or nearly destroyed by fate, the noir woman is fate's emissary, a siren leading the man to ruination.

Jack Nachbar, Writer
Cited in *Handbook of
American Film Genres*, 1988

671. Film noir has to be alone at night. Otherwise it's not film noir.

John Bailey
Cited in *American Cinema*, 1995

672. A world gone wrong.… The law was something to be manipulated for profit and power. The streets were dark with something more than night.

Raymond Chandler
His description of film noir, as
cited in *American Cinema*, 1995

673. What is drama but life with the dull bits cut out.

Alfred Hitchcock
Cited in *The Art of Alfred Hitchcock*, 1976

674. Tragedy (drama) is frustration, failure, despair: the evil in man prevails; there is no mourning.

Frank Capra, Producer-Director
Stated in his 1971 *Frank Capra*

675. Murder, crime, betrayal, lust — there's nothing like the pleasure of being drawn into a story of people who've broken the rules and crossed the usual boundaries of emotion.

Curtis Hanson, Writer
Cited in *Newsweek Extra 2000*, "The 100
Best Movies," on the "dark side" of cinema

676. The most powerful (film suspense stories are) — stories full of fear, guilt and loneliness, breakdown and despair, and a sense that the world is controlled by malignant forces preying on us.

Francis M. Nevins, Jr., Writer
On pulp film noir, as cited in *The Black
Path of Fear*, 1982

677. The effect of the gangster film is to embody this dilemma in the person of the gangster and resolve it by his death … not ours.

Robert Warshaw, Writer
Stated in his 1970 *The Gangster as Tragic Hero*

678. The purpose of this film is to depict an environment, rather than glorify the criminal.

Preface to *The Public Enemy*, 1931
On the gangster film

679. (The gangster film) shows a certain section of America to itself.

Jay Leyda, Writer
Stated in *Post-War American Films:
The Gangster Film*

680. Crime never paid in our pictures.

Hal Wallis, Producer
Cited in *Film Makers on Film Making*, 1983

681. The key to a successful action movie today is righteous violence. Audiences cannot simply partake in gruesome barbarism; they must feel redeemed by it.

Fareed Zakaria
Cited in *The New York Times Magazine*, 1997

682. The action film is no longer the action film. It's the ultraviolence film.…

Sylvester Stallone, Actor
Interview in *Esquire* magazine, 1996

683. The violence in my pictures … is lusty and a little bit humorous, because I believe humor nullifies violence.

John Wayne, Actor
Interview in *Playboy*, May, 1971

684. The violence, when the characters are violent, is not gratuitous violence. The violence is there because it's the truth of those characters.

Kathryn Bigelow, Writer-Director
in the *Village View*, 1990, on her action films

685. Art imitates life and you have to be unflinching to be faithful to the truth. Films don't make violence, there is violence in society.

Kathryn Bigelow, Writer-Director
Interview in *The Independent
on Sunday*, London, 1996

686. Real violence (in movies) has nothing to do with hardware, blowing up buildings. Real violence is from within — the violence of people.…

Andre de Toth, Director
Interview in *Movie Maker* magazine, 1998

687. I think … films … that merely celebrates the

violent, destructive side of human nature is generally worthless. Why celebrate it?

Kevin Kline
Interview in *Playboy*, March, 1998

688. I don't think we should glamorize or glorify violence (in movies). We should show it has consequences.

Sherry Lansing, Chairman, Motion Picture Group
Interview in *The Hollywood Reporter*, 1996

689. I personally do not find much difference between violence and comedy. An event can be regarded as violence by a participant, but for the spectator it can be comedy.

Takeshi Kitano, Actor-Director
Interview in *Film Comment*, 1998

690. Tragedy is life in close-up and comedy is life in long-shot.

Charlie Chaplin, Actor-Director
Cited in *Chaplin*, 1974

691. If there ever was a purely masculine genre, it is surely the war film.

Tania Modleski
Cited in *The New American Cinema*, 1998

692. Every war movie, good or bad, is an anti-war movie.

Steven Spielberg, Director
Cited in *Newsweek Extra 2000*,
"The 100 Best Movies," 1998

693. Gentlemen, if I ever make anything other than an anti-war film, I hope you take me out and shoot me.

John Huston
Cited in *The Hustons*, 1989, to his
commanding officer's reaction to his
WWII war zone documentary, c. 1942

694. Making an anti-war film's like making an anti-rain film.

John Milius, Director
Interview in *Reel Conversations*, 1991

695. Forget it, Louie. No civil war picture ever made a nickel.

Irving Thalberg, Producer
To MGM studio chief, Louis B. Mayer, on
Gone with the Wind, c. 1939, as cited on
the Internet Movie Database, 1998

696. The West was the American dream space, the landscape of our national desire, the testing ground for the face-off between the urge for free-ranging individualism and the need for social order.

Jack Kroll, Writer
Cited in *Newsweek Extra 2000*, "The 100
Best Movies," 1998

697. The cowboy movie was typically the vehicle America used to explain itself to itself. Who makes the laws? What is the order…? Why is it that a man's gotta do what a man's gotta do — and how does he do it?

J. Hoberman
Stated in his 1994 *They Went Thataway*

698. The "Western" is the only genre whose origins are almost identical with those of the cinema itself …

Andre Bazin, Writer
Stated in his 1971 "The Western: or
The American Film Par Excellence,"
What Is Cinema

699. The Westerner is the last gentleman, and the movies which over and over again tell his story are probably the last art form in which the concept of honor retains its strength….

Robert Warshaw, Writer
Stated in his "Movie Chronicle: The Westerner," *Film Theory and Criticism*, 1985

700. A little song, a little riding, a little shooting, and a girl to be saved from hazard.

Roy Rogers, Actor
Summarizing his film formula of the Western, as cited in *Entertainment '99 Yearbook*

701. We know that people like legends. I think people like legends more than they like truth. I think there is a fascination with the Western hero, because the West is a great myth.

Lindsay Anderson
Cited in *American Cinema*, 1995

702. The Western is a universal frame within which it is possible to comment on today.

Sam Peckinpah, Director
Interview in *Directors in Action*, 1968

703. The West was made by violent, uncomplicated men, and it's that strength and simplicity I want to recapture.

Sergio Leone, Director
Cited in *Clint Eastwood — A Biography*, 1996

704. The Western, like water, gains flavor from its impurities….

Andrew Sarris
Cited in *Clint Eastwood — A Biography*, 1996

705. You've got fellows with guns, and one of them's a sheriff.

> Howard Hawks, Director
> Stated in his 1972 *Hawks on Hawks*,
> on his description of a Western

706. (Western heroes were) an outsider or principled loner face to face with outlaws or sadists, prodded into a final showdown.

> Michael Wilmington
> Cited in *They Went Thataway*

707. The vision retained of (the screen Western hero) is of a man … riding off alone into the high country toward some confrontation — not only with the villain but with his own driving obsessions.

> Richard Schickel
> Stated in his 1982 *Heroes of the Silver Screen*

708. Westerns meant "smile when you say that, pardner."

> Jeanine Basinger, Writer
> Stated in her 1995 *American Cinema*

709. People ride in, ride out. With physical action. It's almost pure cinema.

> Arthur Penn, Writer
> Cited in *American Cinema*,
> 1995, on the "Western"

710. The Western is the simplest form of drama — a gun, death.

> Howard Hawks, Director
> Stated in his 1972 *Hawks on Hawks*

711. I've killed more Indians than Custer.

> John Ford, Director
> On the scores of Westerns he's filmed,
> as cited in *John Ford*, 1968

712. Nothing society has taught you about Indians is true. Nothing.

> Sherman Alexie, Screenwriter
> A Spokane/Coeur d'Alene Indian, 1988, as
> cited in *Creative Screenwriting* magazine, 1998

713. All you gotta have in a John Wayne picture is a hoity-toity dame with big tits that Duke can throw over his knee and spank.

> Jimmy Grant, Screenwriter for Wayne movies
> Cited in *John Wayne's America*, 1997

714. They used to go see a "John Wayne movie." Now they don't go to see anybody anymore.

> James Caan, Actor
> Cited in the Internet Movie Database, 1998

715. What is a Clint Eastwood movie? To me, a Clint Eastwood picture is one I'm in.

> Clint Eastwood
> Cited in *Paul Newman*, 1989

716. All is ridiculous!

> Mack Sennett, Producer-
> Director of comedy films
> On his subject matter,
> as cited in *Frank Capra*, 1971

717. Through humor, we see in what seems rational, the irrational; in what seems important, the unimportant. It also heightens our sense of survival and preserves our sanity.

> Charlie Chaplin
> Cited in *The Great Movie Comedians*, 1978

718. Comedy is a fulfillment, accomplishment, overcoming. It is victory over odds, a triumph of good over evil.

> Frank Capra, Producer-Director
> Stated in his 1971 *Frank Capra*

719. Comedy is a complete surrender of one's defenses.

> Frank Capra
> Stated in his 1971 *Frank Capra*

720. Our society was exasperated dignity and the discombobulation of authority.

> Mack Sennett, Keystone Comedy Film Co.
> On content and culture of their
> silent films, as cited in *Chaplin*, 1974

721. In (Mack) Sennett's world all lawyers were shysters, all pious people hypocrites, all sheriffs both stupid and venal, and in that world everybody was caught with their pants down.

> Richard Griffith, Author *The Movies*
> Cited in *Frank Capra*, 1971

722. The form must be pure, either slapstick or drama; you cannot mix them, otherwise one element of your story will fail.

> Charlie Chaplin, Director
> Cited in *The Great Movie Comedians*, 1978

723. A comedy (film), for me, has the quality of being a little dessert, a diversion…. The real meat and potatoes are serious films.

> Woody Allen
> Cited in *Woody Allen —
> His Films and Career*, 1985

724. With comedy you can buy yourself out of the problems of life and diffuse them. In tragedy, you must confront them and it is painful….

> Woody Allen, Writer-Director
> Cited in *Woody Allen
> — His Films and Career*, 1985

725. I think drama is safer than comedy ... in a comedy, if the audience is quiet, you've failed.... There's a clear cut line between success and failure. You can hear it!

> Sally Field, Actress
> Interview in *Drama-Logue*, 1991

726. A man slips on a banana peel and it is funny. However, there is another point of view that could make it terribly sad.

> Elliot Silverstein, Director
> Interview in *Directors at Work*, 1970, on
> what is comedy and what is drama

727. At its most fundamental, black humor is a genre of comic irreverence which flippantly attacks what are normally society's most sacred serious subjects — especially that of death.

> Wes D. Gehring, Writer
> Stated in his 1998 *Handbook*
> *of American Film Genres*, 1988

728. Black humor is the midnight world of the comic antihero, the foundation for the screwball comedy genre.

> Wes D. Gehring, Writer
> Stated in his 1998 *Handbook*
> *of American Film Genres*, 1988

729. (The screwball is) a pitch with a particular spin that sort of flutters and drops and goes in very unexpected manners ... screwball comedy was unconventional and went in unexpected directions.

> Andrew Bergman
> Cited in *American Cinema*, 1995

730. You introduced the man and the woman — and then you complicate it.

> Susan Seidelman
> Cited in *American Cinema*, 1995, on the
> formula for a romantic "screwball comedy"

731. "They're at each other's throats — when they're not in each other's arms!"

> Advertisement for *His Girl Friday*, 1931
> A screwball comedy, as
> cited in *American Cinema*, 1995

732. My comedy is midnight blue. Not black comedy — I like people too much.

> Mel Brooks, Screenwriter-Director
> Interview in *Playboy*, February, 1975

733. It's okay to have them laugh at you, but they have to laugh with you, too.

> George S. Kaufman
> On motion picture comedy, as
> cited in *Mayer and Thalberg*, 1975

734. A half-laugh is worse than none at all.

> Anita Loos, Writer — MGM
> Stated in *Anita Loos — Cast of Thousands*, 1977

735. Comedy is the most serious study in the world. I start out to find my characters in real life....

> Charlie Chaplin
> Cited in *Chaplin*, 1974

736. Love! Comedians must be loved to get laughs.

> Frank Capra, Director
> Stated in his 1971 *Frank Capra*

737. I'm not saying that until they laugh.

> Dustin Hoffman, Actor
> Interview in *The Sunday Times*, London, 1993,
> when asked if his new film was a comedy

738. All I know is that I learned how to get laughs, and that's all I know about it. You have to learn what people will laugh at, then proceed accordingly.

> Stan Laurel
> Cited in *The Great Movie Comedians*,
> 1978, when asked, "What is comedy?"

739. (Laurel and Hardy) are perhaps the Civil Servants of comedy. There is no wonder the life they lead goes to the heart of the multitude.

> John Grierson
> Cited in *American Cinema*, 1995, on
> comedians Stan Laurel and Oliver Hardy

740. Mack Sennett comics just ran faster than anybody.

> Frank Capra, Screenwriter-Director
> Cited on the Internet Movie Database, 1998

741. If I'm going to (make) a dumb comedy ... I want a smart dumb comedy.

> Amy Pascal, Studio Production Executive
> Cited in *The Los Angeles Times*, 1995

742. If you're working on comedy, you really have to keep moving, or it just lies there.

> Woody Allen
> Cited in *Woody Allen*
> *— His Films and Career*, 1985

743. If you're going to do a comedy ... make it a visual comedy, and the best way is to give it some size, inject it with special effects.

> Mark Horowitz
> Cited in *The New York Times Magazine*, 1997

744. Comedy films are unlike other films: What's

important in a comedy is the content of the shot, not the shot itself.

> Woody Allen
> Cited in *Woody Allen*
> *— His Films and Career*, 1985

745. Comedy is like bass fishing. Everyone is an expert, the fish is smarter than all of them, and the flashiest, shiniest lures never work.

> Cameron Crowe, Director
> Cited in *Newsweek Extra 2000*,
> "The 100 Best Movies," 1998

746. I suppose we could talk about the varieties of comedy as found in Aristotle, but really, this movie is just a big yuk.

> Richard Dreyfuss, Actor
> Cited in *Entertainment Weekly*, 1998, on
> not trying to analyze his new comedy film

747. When you do comedy, you're not sitting at the grownup's table, you're sitting at the children's table.

> Woody Allen, Writer-Director
> Cited in *Woody Allen*
> *— His Films and Career*, 1985

748. Fantasy film continues to make clear in how many directions one may travel down the Yellow Brick Road and with what joy one may make that journey.

> Wade Jennings, Writer
> Cited in *Handbook of*
> *American Film Genres*, 1988

749. All fantasy (films) begin with a very simple question: "What if...?"

> Wade Jennings, Writer
> Cited in *Handbook of*
> *American Film Genres*, 1988

750. The classic art films focus on the problem of the self in a universe where God is silent and technology has irremediably altered the individual's relationship to time, space and other people.

> William C. Siska, Writer
> Cited in *Handbook of*
> *American Film Genres*, 1988

751. Most musicals are silly damned things....

> George Cukor
> Cited in *George Cukor — A Double Life*, 1991

752. Any musical fantasizes to begin with; you fight realism right away.

> Gene Kelly, Actor-Director
> Cited in *Entertainment World*, 1970

753. We've lost the vocabulary for musicals.... It's

such an abstract art. The only flame of expressionism and surrealism Hollywood kept alive is in musicals.

> Antonio Banderas, Actor
> Interview in *Movieline*, 1998

754. The movie musical — there's always a resuscitation of the poor creature that seems desiccated and dying ... the musical has always had it pretty tough....

> Gene Kelly, Actor-Director
> Cited in *Entertainment World*, 1970

755. We're lost if we don't convince the audience in the first five minutes that this is a world where people sing instead of talk.

> Alan Parker, Director
> On musicals, as stated in
> *Movieline* magazine, 1998

756. I am interested in the Bible as a universal myth and support the idea of multiple legends.

> Dino De Laurentiis, Film producer of *The Bible*
> Cited in *The Hustons*, 1989

757. (Walt Disney) villains (are) animals, and animals don't go to the movies, or else Disney would have been picketed by the "Wolf's Protective League."

> Frank Capra, Producer-Director
> Stated in his 1971 *Frank Capra*

758. A literary eat-your-spinach-it's-good-for-you movie.

> Sydney Pollack, Producer-Director
> Cited in *Screen International*,
> 1996, on literary movies

759. The mighty man of American myth ... (like Johnny Appleseed, John Henry, Pecos Bill, and Paul Bunyan) ... they are worth looking at soberly and in fun ...

> Walt Disney
> Stated in Hedda Hopper's column,
> 1948, *Chicago Tribune*, on his history
> movies of American folk heroes

760. The science fiction film gives concrete narrative shape and visible form to our changing historical imagination of social progress and disaster....

> Vivian Sobchack, Writer
> Cited in *Handbook of*
> *American Film Genres*, 1988

761. Science fiction reflects the views of fictionists, not scientists.

> David Gates, Writer
> Cited in *Newsweek Extra 2000*,
> "The 100 Best Movies," 1998

762. Big action films ... work with an illiterate or subliterate audience.

Pauline Kael, Critic
Interview in *Modern Maturity* magazine, 1998

763. The ideas children get fed are important, so to me *Superman*'s an important movie.

Nicolas Cage, Actor
Interview in *The Los Angeles Times*, 1997

764. ("Batman" type movies) I think of as a comic book opera ... things flying around ... whacked-out perspectives and colors ... a comic book extravaganza.

Elliot Goldenthal, Film Composer
Interview in *Film Score Monthly*, 1997

765. The last couple of years, I thought that a large proportion of the American public wanted to see blood and breasts. Now I think they want to see cars.

Roger Corman, Director
Cited in a James Hillier column, 1977

766. One of the rules with the Bond pictures is that you're not allowed to have a leading lady who can act.... People go to see the hardware and James Bond.

Guy Hamilton, Director
Interview in *Take 22: Moviemakers on Moviemaking*, 1984

767. *Jaws* is a disaster movie only if it doesn't make money. Then it's a disaster.

Steven Spielberg
Cited in *The New York Post*

768. *Billy Jack* is more than a movie. It makes the individual feel like he can go out and do something about corruption. *Billy Jack* is a philosophy of life.

Tom Laughlin, Creator-Producer-
Actor of *Billy Jack*, 1973
Cited in *Going Hollywood*, 1978

769. I'm disappointed when women make generic films. There are enough men around to do that.

Susan Seidelman, Director
Cited in *The Devil and Susan Seidelman*, 1990

770. A movie without sex would be like a candy bar without nuts.

Earl Wilson
Stated in his column

771. Nudity hurts laughs ... if you're watching somebody's boobs, you're not listening to the dialogue.

I.A.L. Diamond, Screenwriter
Interview in *Film Makers on Film Making*, 1983

772. The nudity was boring and so ever present that you were left almost crying out for people to put on their clothes.

Joe Eszterhaus, Screenwriter
Interview in *Playboy*, 1998,
on his film *Showgirls*, 1997

773. At the heart of pornography is sexuality haunted by its own disappearance.

Jean Baudrillard
Stated in her 1994 *Overtones and Undertones*

774. The basic formula of the horror film is that normality is threatened by the Monster.

R. Wood
Interview in *Film Comment*, 1978

775. All monster movies are basically one story. It's *Beauty and the Beast*.

Tim Burton, Director
Interview in *Inner Views:
Filmmakers in Conversation*, 1992

776. The horror genre is a way for humans to revisit that primal fear, to turn it into pleasure, the pleasure of being safely scared.

Jack Kroll, Writer
Cited in *Newsweek Extra 2000*,
"The 100 Best Movies," 1998

777. I aim to provide the public with beneficial shocks. Civilization has become so protective that we're no longer able to get our goose bumps instinctively. The best way to achieve that ... is through a movie.

Alfred Hitchcock, Director
Cited in *The Art of Alfred Hitchcock*,
1976, on horror films

778. "Psycho" is a film made with quite a sense of amusement ... it's a fun picture.

Alfred Hitchcock
Cited in *The Art of Alfred Hitchcock*, 1976

779. I didn't get PMS for six months because of that movie.

Drew Barrymore, Actress
Interview in *Movieline* magazine,
1998, on her role in *Scream*, 1997

780. I hadn't the foggiest idea of how to make a

documentary film. To me, documentaries were ash-can films made by kooks with long hair.

> Major Frank Capra, Producer-Director
> Upon entering the Army, 1941, WWII, in
> charge of orientation documentaries, as
> stated in his 1971 *Frank Capra*

781. We must persuade and convince, not by rage but by reason.

> Colonel Frank Capra, Producer-Director
> Stated in his 1971 *Frank Capra*,
> on documentaries

782. Who wants to see a documentary about how to become a nun?

> Warner Bros.
> Cited in *Inside Oscar*, 1996, to director Fred
> Zinnemann on *The Nun's Story*, later
> nominated for Best Picture, 1959

783. Irving, the public won't buy pictures about American farmers and you want to give them Chinese farmers?

> Louis B. Mayer, Producer
> Arguing with Irving Thalberg at MGM,
> about to make Pearl Buck's *The Good
> Earth*, 1938, as cited in *Inside Oscar*, 1996

784. (Alfred) Hitchcock films (are) made up of three elements: fear, sex and death.

> François Truffaut, Director
> Stated in *50 Major Film Makers*, 1975

785. It has been said of me that if I made *Cinderella*, the audience would start looking for a body in the pumpkin coach.

> Alfred Hitchcock
> Interview in *The Saturday Evening Post*, 1957

786. Mystery is mystifying: it is an intellectual thing. Suspense is an emotional thing.

> Alfred Hitchcock, Director
> Interview in *Directors in Action*, 1968

787. The Alfred Hitchcock genre was: melodrama, layered with light comedy....

> Sidney Lumet, Director
> Stated in his 1995 *Making Movies*

788. My chief aim was ... to make films — to express the common humanity of men.

> Jean Renoir, Director
> Stated in his 1974 *Jean Renoir
> — My Life and Times*

789. No filmmaker has been so autobiographical (as Woody Allen).

> Bob Abel, Writer
> Cited in *Woody Allen
> — His Films and Career*, 1985

790. Call me a guerilla historian.

> Oliver Stone, Director
> On his often controversial film
> retrospectives, i.e., *JFK, Nixon*,
> as cited in *Inside Oscar*, 1996

791. I don't make movies that bring people together. I make movies that split people apart.

> Quentin Tarantino, Screenwriter-Director
> Cited in *Inside Oscar*, 1996

792. I must make my films simply to participate in the development of the society in which I live.

> Francesco Rosi
> Stated in *50 Major Film Makers*, 1975

793. (Sergio) Leone's films always had the strange look and displaced sound of an unmistakably Italian director's dream of what Hollywood movies should be like, but aren't.

> Vincent Canby
> Cited in *The New York Times*

794. Well, it's about two hours long.

> Howard Hawks, Director
> When asked what his next movie was
> about, as cited in *Going Hollywood*, 1978

7

Screenwriting

795. As a (screen) writer, you have two hours to talk to the world; what do you want to tell them? This is an extraordinarily privileged opportunity.

Bruce Joel Rubin, Screenwriter
Interview in *Screenwriters on Screenwriting*, 1995

796. Radio didn't kill theater and records didn't kill live concerts. It's not the technique which is going to attract the people to the movies; it will always be the story.

Milos Forman
Cited in *Lew Hunter's Screenwriting 434*

797. Today, aspiring writers think that they must write a screenplay rather than focus on the story itself. But the story is where it all begins.

Francis Ford Coppola, Writer-Director
Interview in *Attaché* magazine, 1997,
encouraging the writing of a short story first

798. A story starts at one place and goes on to another place; as a result of incidents people are affected. That is storytelling.

Richard Brooks, Writer-Director
Interview in *Directors at Work*, 1970

799. But at the end of the day, it comes down to the story ... a concept you feel is a film.

Marc Platt, Universal
Cited in *Variety*, 1998

800. Nobody ever tells a story quite like anyone else ... no two writers will literally agree on what constitutes a story.

Paddy Chayefsky, Screenwriter
Stated in *The Collected Works of Paddy Chayefsky*, 1995

801. The rules of screenwriting were not carved in stone by the hand of God. They were merely extrapolated from commonalities detected in a sampling of successful films.

Nancy Hendrickson, Writer
Interview in *Creative Screenwriting* magazine, 5/1

802. The only hard and fast rule of screenwriting: keep the audience interested.

Nancy Hendrickson, Writer
Interview in *Creative Screenwriting* magazine, 5/1

803. Everything and everybody must serve the "Thou shalt not be dull" commandment.

Lew Hunter
Stated in his 1993 *Lew Hunter's Screenwriting 434*

804. The most important thing in your script—and if you don't find it, your script, frankly, is going to be dead—is the voice....

Whit Stillman, Screenwriter
Interview in *Movie Maker* magazine, 1998

805. When (Charlie Chaplin) found a voice to say what was on his mind, he was like a child of eight writing lyrics for Beethoven's Ninth.

Billy Wilder
Referring to the new "talkies" of film,
as cited in *The Bright Side of Billy Wilder, Primarily*, 1970

806. The main thing about telling a story ... is finding out why you should tell a story—what makes the story worth telling? That is always the human way.

Randell Wallace, Screenwriter
Cited in *ScrIpt* magazine, 4/2

807. Good stories write themselves. Bad ones have to be written.

F. Scott Fitzgerald
Cited in his 1993 *Lew Hunter's Screenwriting 434*, 1993

808. What a screenwriter must accomplish ... it's this: to create a source of life, to find the bedrock in a given idea, to prevent most of the work from evaporating.

Robert Towne
Interview in *Written By*, 1997

809. The simpler the story, the better…A child always wants to know what happens next. That's the magic of movies — what happens next?
Richard Brooks, Writer-Director
Interview in *Directors at Work*, 1970

810. If the essential subject of a story is of interest to everyone … then all you need are the circumstances….
Katharine Hepburn
Cited in *David Lean — A Biography*, 1996

811. I have only one (absolute) rule: a drama can have only one story…one leading character; all others are used…only as they facilitate the main story.
Paddy Chayefsky, Screenwriter
Stated in *The Collected Works of Paddy Chayefsky*, 1995

812. I tried to write dialogue as if it had been wire-tapped … as if cameras had … focused upon the unsuspecting characters … in an untouched moment of life.
Paddy Chayefsky, Screenwriter
Interview in *Creative Screenwriting* magazine

813. Tell the story in terms of action as much as possible. Try to sandwich it in with action, action, action and more action.
John T. Kelley
Cited in *Lew Hunter's Screenwriting 434*, 1993

814. A great action scene has the qualities of a great action movie as a whole: with ingenuity, surprise and pleasing complication instead of just a bigger and better fireball.
Stephen Farber, Writer
Interview in *Movieline* magazine, 1998

815. A mass of ideas, however good they are, is not sufficient to create a successful picture.
Alfred Hitchcock
Cited in *The Art of Alfred Hitchcock*, 1975

816. The so-called happy ending of a high comedy should have a sardonic overtone … because there is no such thing as a happy ending for an intelligent writer.
Samson Raphaelson
Cited in *Ernst Lubitsch: A Critical Study*

817. The ending becomes the culmination of the spectator's absorption, as all the causal gaps get filled.
Barrett C. Kiesling, Writer
Stated in his 1937 *Talking Pictures*

818. [T]he key to effective suspense is believability. The simpler and more homely the peril, the more real the peril.
Alfred Hitchcock
Interview in *The Saturday Evening Post*, 1957

819. I read a script and can tell by page five if it's a story or not worth telling….
Kevin Kline, Actor
Interview in *Playboy*, March, 1998

820. A bad script is a bad script and a good script is a diamond.
Mark Petersen, Cinematographer
Cited in *Movie Maker* magazine, 1998

821. If you make a good movie with an absorbing story line, you have to trust that people will come. If that isn't the case, then I'm in the wrong business.
Gregory Hoblit
Interview in *The New York Times*, 1998

822. Until the lump of clay is on the table, you can't shape it. So the first job is to get it there. Then you go back and … make it into what it's supposed to be.
Bruce Joel Rubin, Screenwriter
Interview in *Creative Screenwriting*, 1998, on getting started with a screenplay

823. Behold the child who plays with imaginary friends in a make-believe world. For he or she may one day become a screenwriter.
Stephen M. Ringler

824. All creative writers need a certain amount of time when they're creating something where nobody should criticize them at all — at all. Because at a certain point you have to make it your own — not the world's.
Gena Rowlands, Actress
Interview in *Take 22: Moviemakers on Moviemaking*, 1984

825. Screenwriting has two levels … initially working on the script … in isolation. Then you … bring it into … the real phony world which is the movie world. You've got to be schizophrenic about it.
Robert Towne
Interview in *Film Makers on Film Making*, 1983

826. We just stare at each other.
Billy Wilder
On how he and co-writer I.A.L. Diamond work together, as stated in *Film Makers on Film Making*, 1983

827. I can sit in a little room and play God and make up stories and characters out of my guts and heart and head....

> Joe Eszterhaus, Screenwriter
> Interview in *Playboy*, April, 1998

828. As you start the process of writing a screenplay...you're dreaming a dream. The job is to make the dream come true.

> Robert Towne, Screenwriter
> Cited in *Screenwriters on Screenwriting*, 1995

829. That's really what the lifeblood of this whole thing is; there is nothing more valuable than a good idea.

> Tom Hanks
> Interview in *The New York Times Magazine,* 1997

830. Imagining is creating and illusions are its most rewarding product.

> Sol Saks, Writer
> Stated in his 1985 *Funny Business:*
> *The Craft of Comedy Writing*

831. Take the obvious and turn it 180 degrees.

> Phil Saltzman
> Cited in *Lew Hunter's Screenwriting 434*

832. One has to invent and have something to say.

> Federico Fellini
> Cited in *Fellini — A Life*, 1986

833. It's okay to just try to entertain ... to just create mayhem and spectacle. But you can do more, you can say something. You can have a point of view.

> Bruce Joel Rubin, Screenwriter
> Interview in *Creative Screenwriting*, 1998,
> on his responsibility to his audience

834. The important thing is, does anybody have anything to say?

> Paul Mazursky, Director
> Interview in *Rolling Stone* magazine, 1982

835. Filmmakers are once again understanding that your competition is really your creative vision.

> Arthur Chang, Producer, 1998
> Interview in *Scr(i)pt* magazine, 1998

836. You can't wait for inspiration. You have to go after it with a club.

> Jack London
> Cited in *Lew Hunter's Screenwriting 434*, 1993

837. Everything is a cliché. You're born, you live, die, all clichés. It's what you do with the clichés that's important.

> A.I. Bezzerides, Screenwriter
> Interview in *Screenwriters on Screenwriting*, 1995

838. The human imagination is dangerously limited. It tends to resort to nothing but clichés.

> Jean Renoír, Director
> Stated in his 1974 *Jean Renoír*
> *— My Life and Times*

839. What is writing but trying to order reality? Trying to make order out of chaos.... To create your own reality.

> David Cronenberg, Director
> Interview in *Inner Views: Filmmakers*
> *in Conversation*, 1992

840. The main thing is to make (the screenplay) credible so people can believe in the fantasy.

> Marlon Brando
> Stated in *Conversations with Brando*, 1991

841. We must all start with the believable. That is the essence of our craft.

> Chuck Jones
> Cited in *Steven Spielberg*
> *— The Unauthorized Biography*, 1996

842. Drama is the resolution of conflict. Characters go through conflict and must resolve it to uplift the human spirit in some way.

> Danny Glover, Actor
> Interview in the *Village View*, 1991

843. The fewer options you've got, the more drama there is.

> Sean Penn, Actor-Director
> Interview in *Interview* magazine,
> 1995, on story development

844. I've never used the whodunit technique, since it is concerned altogether with mystification, which diffuses and unfocuses suspense .... I believe in giving the audience all the facts as early as possible.

> Alfred Hitchcock
> Interview in *The Saturday Evening Post*, 1957

845. You can't be smug when you do a screenplay. Now it's your subject. Now you have the responsibility to find the truth.

> James L. Brooks, Screenwriter-Director
> Interview in *Written By*, 1998

846. John Huston taught me to challenge the lie until I found the truth.

> Richard Brooks, Screenwriter
> Cited in *The Hustons*, 1989

847. Truth is best served through fiction.

> Ernest Hemingway
> Cited in *Lew Hunter's Screenwriting 434*, 1993

848. In politics, you can get to an even deeper level of truth when you fictionalize, and on film you can alter the truth forever.

Jeremy Larner, Screenwriter
Interview in *George* magazine, 1998

849. Truth is the big thing. The characters have gotta be true to themselves … a character can't do anything good or bad, they can only do something that's true or not.

Quentin Tarantino, Screenwriter-Director
Interview in *Creative Screenwriting*, 5/1

850. Throw it all away — it can only cripple the fine spirit of invention.

Orson Welles, Director
On researching for a screenplay, as cited in
Orson Welles: The Road to Xanadu, 1996

851. Every film should be summarized in one word.

François Truffaut, Director,
"Truffaut's dictum," cited in
Films and Filming magazine, 1962

852. Every once in a while, there is a film that has a chance of being different….

Jennifer Leitzes
Cited in *Premiere* magazine, 1998

853. The film seeks to realize the experience which is the most basic for opening up any social project: the joint experience between man and man … the profound link between one person and the next.

Federico Fellini
Recited in *Fellini — A Life*, 1986,
from his letter to
Il Contemporaneo newspaper, Rome, Italy

854. We're all different, we're all alike. We are rivers. Broad, narrow, warm, cold, shallow, deep.

The "Tolstoy Filter"
Cited in *Lew Hunter's Screenwriting 434*, 1993

855. I see myself making an effort to find the dignity in the trivial of our daily life … and the validity of each individual's emotion.

Thornton Wilder
Cited in *Lew Hunter's Screenwriting 434*, 1993

856. What draws me to … biography … is that it's real. It's always more interesting than anything you dreamed up…. You try and get into the essence of them … you're interviewing their lives.

John Milius, Screenwriter-Director
In *Written By* magazine, 1998

857. Male heroes have been done to death, whereas with women you can be like Lewis and Clark.

Gale Anne Hurd, Producer
Cited in *Ms.* magazine, 1989

858. Fundamentally, it (is) the story line, the construction. The construction is the most important goddamned thing.

Charles Bennett, Screenwriter
Interview in *Screenwriters on Screenwriting*, 1995

859. The construction of a screenplay happens to follow the ancient rules of Greek drama: the three unities of time, space and action.

Fred Zinnemann, Director
Stated in his 1992 *Fred Zinnemann
— An Autobiography*

860. A good structure for a screenplay is that of a symphony, with its three or four movements and differing tempos.

Akira Kurosawa, Director
Stated in his 1982 *Akira Kurosawa*

861. The main work in writing a script is in making up the outline…. When one knows the outline, the movie's done.

David Mamet, Writer-Director
Interview in *Interview* magazine, 1998

862. The writer has to lay down pipe in the first two acts or else who cares about what happens to the character in the end?

Max Wong, Production Executive
Interview in *Movie Maker* magazine, 1998

863. Screenplays have this expectation of rhythm and rhyme, and meter and structure, the same as a sonnet.

Sherman Alexie, Screenwriter
Interview in *Creative
Screenwriting* magazine, 1998

864. In order to write scripts, you must first study the great novels and dramas of the world. You must consider why they are great.

Akira Kurosawa, Director
Stated in his 1982 *Akira Kurosawa*

865. Just have good characters and good scenes and something that plays.

Billy Wilder
Stated in *Film Makers on Film Making*,
1983, on good screenwriting

866. Just take a piece of ivory and cut away everything that isn't walrus.

Sol Saks, Writer
Stated in his 1985 *Funny Business:
The Craft of Comedy Writing*

867. A scene between two people who agree is a waste of time.

Jack Sowards, Screenwriter
Cited in *Written By* magazine, 1997

868. There are two kinds of scenes: the Pet the Dog scene and the Kick the Dog scene.

Paddy Chayefsky, Screenwriter
Cited in *Making Movies*, 1995

869. Show, don't tell. You're writing movies. Make them move.

Lew Hunter
Stated in his 1993, *Lew Hunter's Screenwriting 434*

870. I've always equated the writing process with ... editing the movie, that's like my last draft of the screenplay.

Quentin Tarantino, Screenwriter-Director
Interview in *Creative Screenwriting*, 5/1

871. (Words are) not the primary means of communication in film. The words are really supportive — and it's only because of our own lack of imagination that we rely so strongly on the words anyway....

Sydney Pollack, Director
Interview in *Take 22: Moviemakers on Moviemaking*, 1984

872. Proper words in proper places make a true definition of style.

Jonathan Swift, Writer
Cited in *Funny Business: The Craft of Comedy Writing*, 1985

873. The meaning of life is beyond me. The best I can do is deal with it one word at a time.

Larry Gelbart
Stated in his 1998 *Laughing Matters*

874. Words make me tick. In my case, words are in fact a tic.

Larry Gelbart
Stated in his 1998 *Laughing Matters*

875. Movies have been the literature of my life.... I think it's time to renew our romance with the word.

Steven Spielberg
Cited in *Steven Spielberg — The Unauthorized Biography*, 1996, from his acceptance speech of the Thalberg Memorial Award, 1987

876. There is no word that should stay in word jail, every word is completely free.... It's all language, it's all communication.

Quentin Tarantino, Screenwriter-Director
Interview in *Creative Screenwriting*, 5/1

877. Complete sentences.

Paul Thomas Anderson, Writer-Director
Interview in *Creative Screenwriting* magazine, on the most common mistake in written dialogue

878. Suggestion is every bit as good as statement....

Jose Ferrer, Actor
Cited in *The Hustons*, 1989

879. Adding explanation to the description passages of a screenplay is the most dangerous trap you can fall into.

Akira Kurosawa, Director
Stated in his 1982 *Akira Kurosawa*

880. In film, thanks to the close-up, so much (language) explicitness is unnecessary.

Jean Renoir, Director
Stated in his 1974 *Jean Renoir — My Life and Times*

881. A story is a story is a story ... but without realistic, compelling, well-developed characters, there is no story worth telling.

Sally B. Merlin, Writer
Interview in *ScRIpt* magazine, 4/1

882. A lot of movies you see coming out are paint-by-numbers, too gimmicky or concepty ... when it's character driven, it has something to say.

Stacy Attanasio, Production Executive
Cited in *Movie Maker* magazine, 1998

883. The rules are not rules. They're just something you feel. You intuit your way into the process of writing. You tell the story from inside the character.

Bruce Joel Rubin, Screenwriter
Interview in *Screenwriters on Screenwriting*, 1995

884. If you can do characters, you can forget about the plot.... Let them tell the story for you. Movements come from characterization.

Howard Hawks, Director
Stated in his 1972 *Hawks on Hawks*

885. Plot is secondary, not that important to me. Once I know my characters I'm confident a plot will come out of them.

Elmore Leonard
Interview in *Film Comment*, 1998

886. If we wish to know the structure of conflict, we must first know character.

Lajos Egri
Cited in *Lew Hunter's Screenwriting 434,* 1993

887. Actions become complications. Complications cause conflict, and conflict is born in character.

> Lew Hunter
> Stated in his 1993
> *Lew Hunter's Screenwriting 434*

888. Movies to me are only about wanting something, a character wanting something that ... the audience desperately wants him to have.

> Bruce Joel Rubin, Screenwriter
> Interview in *Screenwriters*
> *on Screenwriting*, 1995

889. The power of the rooting interest ... is the essence of moviedom. It's everything.... A film works when ... the audience wants something for a character as much as he wants it for himself.

> Bruce Joel Rubin, Screenwriter
> Interview in *Screenwriters*
> *on Screenwriting*, 1995

890. There's a certain excitement to live in your head as each of the characters. You're everyone.

> Jude Pauline Eberhard, Screenwriter
> Interview in *ScrIpt* magazine, 4/2

891. (Film) dialogue is a part of the theme and reveals character. For the real theme is the person, whom dialogue, picture, situation, setting ... lighting ... combine together to depict.

> Jean Renoir, Director
> Stated in his 1974 *Jean Renoir*
> *— My Life and Times*

892. I ask the filmmaker what the holes in the script are, then I play a character who's designed to plug them up.

> Samuel Fuller, Screenwriter
> Interview in *Written By* magazine,
> 1998, on the script doctoring process

893. Thou shalt have an active protagonist.

> Cardinal Rule of Screenwriting
> Cited in *Creative Screenwriting* magazine, 5/1

894. In order for the dialogue to be stereotypical, the drawing of the character has to be stereotypical. One gives rise to the other.

> Sidney Poitier, Actor
> Interview in *American Film* magazine, 1991

895. If you are writing about people who are still living, you hope you get it right.

> Cynthia Whitcomb, Screenwriter
> Cited in *Written By*, 1998

896. I've always tried to avoid heroes and villains, but I haven't always successfully avoided fools.

> Michael Chekhov
> Interview in *Playboy*, March, 1998

897. To require a white person to write only for whites is stupid. To require me to write only for blacks is also stupid.

> Sidney Poitier, Actor
> Interview in *American Film*, 1991

898. ... People are people.... If I can't write about gay people because I'm straight, about Christian people because I'm Jewish, about women because I'm a man, I'm going to end up writing about my shoes.

> Sean Penn, Writer-Director-Actor
> Interview in *Interview* magazine, 1995

899. If writers thought beforehand of all the revisions they'd need to do to complete a project, we'd be crippled before we started.

> Richard Krevalin, Screenwriter
> In his opening to *The Adventures*
> *of Huckleberry Finn*

900. There's this theory about screenwriting, you gotta be terse. "Underwritten is king." And I always love if you can pull off speeches. God knows, you yank a lot out if you direct 'em, so put 'em in there.

> James L. Brooks, Screenwriter-Director
> Interview in *Written By*, 1998

901. With a good script, you get impressed by what they didn't write.

> Jack Lemmon, Actor
> On the economy of words, as cited in *The*
> *Bright Side of Billy Wilder, Primarily*, 1970

902. A lot of times, good dialogue means not talking. Subtext.

> Carrie Fisher, Screenwriter
> Interview in *Creative Screenwriting*, 1998

903. One scene a night for three months, and you'll have a movie ....

> Bruce Joel Rubin, Screenwriter
> Response to those who claim they don't
> have time to write a movie, as stated in
> *Screenwriters on Screenwriting*, 1995

904. Never stop writing. Do a page a day, everyday for the rest of your life.

> Ron Suppa, Writer
> Cited in *Creative Screenwriting*, 1998

905. Don't write like a great man, just write.

> Unknown
> Cited in *Inner Views*, 1992

906. I would write a version…. Then I would cry for a while and then go back to work. And that's how it was for three years.

Emma Thompson
Interview in *Movieline* magazine, 1998,
screenwriter of *Sense and Sensibility*

907. Screenwriting life is a game show. We escalate from plateau to plateau, thinking and answering until the ecstatic conclusion.

Lew Hunter
Stated in his 1993 *Lew Hunter's
Screenwriting 434*

908. It doesn't seem to impress anybody when writers boast they've turned out a draft in two weeks. It simply means they can type fast.

Max Wong, Production Executive
Interview in *Movie Maker* magazine, 1998

909. All of your personal stories are already written. They're already in the drawer. It's just a matter of sitting at your desk: some days the drawer is open, some days the drawer is closed.

Anthony Minghella, Screenwriter
Stated at the 1997 Santa Barbara
Film Festival Screenwriters Panel

910. The only goal of a first draft is to finish it.

Todd Sussman, Screenwriter
Cited in *ScRipt* magazine, 4/2

911. As soon as you have chosen and decided upon an idea for a subject, you have already made a success or a failure.

Billy Wilder, Screenwriter-Director
Stated in *Film Makers on Film Making*,
1983, on initiating the screenplay

912. The secret to writing is writing.

Jeff Gordon, Screenwriter
Cited in *Movie Maker* magazine, 1998

913. Just write the scene. Just sitting down and trying to write — it doesn't have to be the beginning or the end of the film, but just getting in there.

Whit Stillman, Screenwriter
Interview in *Movie Maker* magazine, 1998

914. I submerge myself, as in water, and the writing is automatic.

Zoë Akins, Screenwriter
Cited in *George Cukor — A Double Life*, 1991

915. I sit at a desk, I face the wall. If you sit facing the wall, the only way out is through the sentences.

E. L. Doctorow, Screenwriter
Cited in the *Santa Barbara News-Press*, 1998

916. Write what you, yourself, would want to watch or read if someone else wrote it.

Burt Prelutsky, Screenwriter
Cited in *Written By* magazine, 1998

917. The worst thing you write is better than the best thing you didn't write.

Sol Saks, Comedy Writer
Stated in his 1985 *Funny Business:
The Craft of Comedy Writing*

918. (Like) phone calls from nowhere.

Stephen King, Author-Screenwriter
On where his ideas come from,
as cited in *People* magazine, 1999

919. It's such a lonely activity … sitting around making stuff up … and (when) the audience responds to it, all that loneliness goes away.

Herb Gardner, Screenwriter
Interview in *Creative
Screenwriting* magazine, 1998

920. They just stack up like planes over an airport, and sometimes they crash before they ever land.

Ted Tally, Screenwriter
Cited in *Creative Screenwriting*, 1998, on
the number of screenplays he's written

921. It's a scary world, and fiction is the comforting thing.

Stephen King, Author-Screenwriter
On his fear of "real life,"
as cited in *People* magazine, 1999

922. (Eliminating violence from film) would be like eliminating one of the primary colors from the palette of the painter.

Arthur Penn, Screenwriter
Cited in *The Encyclopedia of Film*, 1991

923. What takes the place of good writing is violence — the Esperanto of the modern media world.

Fareed Zakaria
Cited in *The New York Times Magazine*, 1997

924. We have made a conscious decision to not write anything with violence. That decision is based on our high moral principles and our complete inability to write the stuff.

Arlene Sarner, Screenwriter
— with Jerry Leichthling
Interview in *Written By* magazine, 1998

925. You've got to be willing to kill your darlings.

William Goldman, Screenwriter
On the writer sacrificing his favorite characters,
as cited in *Creative Screenwriting*, 1998

926. Wit is crucial to action movies because they all flirt with absurdity.

Stephen Farber, Writer
Interview in *Movieline* magazine, 1998

927. If the film author tried to oversee what happens to his work, he would quickly die of a broken heart.

Federico Fellini
Cited in *Fellini — A Life*, 1986

928. When you sell a script, it's theirs. You've got to accept what happens to it.

J. F. Lawton, Screenwriter
Cited in *Inside Oscar*, 1996, on his script *3000*,
changed to *Pretty Woman*, 1990

929. If you take the money, you got nothing to say. You've made your deal with the devil, so accept it.

Sherman Alexie, Screenwriter
On selling your script to a producer, as stated
in *Creative Screenwriting* magazine, 1998

930. When you are writing a screenplay, one of the things you are doing, in a sense, is writing a prospectus for a stock offering.

Howard Rodman, Screenwriter
Cited in *Naked Hollywood*, 1991

931. It all starts with the screenplay, not the bottom line.

Tracey Jacobs, Agent
Cited in *Biography* magazine, 1998, on
client Johnny Depp's career role choices

932. I mean, if it's movies, the first draft tends to be yours, the second draft tends to be everybody's … the third draft, everybody's and their hairdressers.

Larry Gelbart
Interview in *Written By* magazine, 1997

933. My feeling … is like a guy who sends his daughter off to college. You hope she'll do well. You hope she won't be raped at a fraternity party.

Stephen King, Author
Unknown source

934. (The studio is) going to force you to cut something. So give them something to cut (from the script) that doesn't cost anything.

Bruce Joel Rubin, Screenwriter
Interview in *Screenwriters on Screenwriting*,
1995, on how the game is played

935. With unproduced scripts, there's one enormous consolation: they haven't been ruined.

Nick Kazan
Cited in *Fade In* magazine, 1998

936. Irving (Thalberg had) a theory that writers never write the story they intended to write. So he fixes them.

Charlie MacArthur, MGM
Cited in *Mayer and Thalberg*, 1975

937. (Darryl) Zanuck loved my screenplay. He wants to rewrite it.

Anonymous Writer
Cited in *The Zanucks of Hollywood*, 1989

938. The screenplay is just a blueprint. It's a fantasy. No matter how good … it's going to be rewritten.

Robert Towne
Interview in *Film Makers
on Film Making*, Vol. II, 1983

939. All scripts are rewritten…. It's just a question of whether or not it's going to be rewritten well.

Robert Towne
Interview in *Film Makers
on Film Making*, Vol. II, 1983

940. Almost everyone unconsciously feels he knows as much about writing as a writer.

Ernest Lehman, Screenwriter
Interview in *Film Makers on Film Making*, 1983

941. The screenplay compared to a novel is like a comic strip. But I don't use the term pejoratively….

Thomas Keneally
Cited in *Steven Spielberg
— The Unauthorized Biography*, 1996

942. The novel which is mainly concerned with the inner life of its characters will give the (screen) adapter an absolute compass bearing….

Stanley Kubrick, Director
On "the perfect novel" for screen
development, as cited in *Kubrick
— Inside a Film Artist's Maze*, 1982

943. I think it takes more courage, more stupidity … to deal with original material.

Robert Towne
As opposed to adaptation, as stated in *Film
Makers on Film Making*, Vol. II, 1983

944. I don't like to do books or plays. I prefer to take a short story and expand it, rather than take a novel and condense it.

John Ford, Director
Cited in *John Ford*, 1968

945. Writing novels, you're the boss, you're the studio.
Mario Puzo, Writer
Interview in *Film Makers on Film Making*, 1983

946. It's easier to adapt a bad book because you feel freer to make changes. Every filmmaker dreads the epitaph: "I preferred the book."
Peter Weir, Director
Interview in *Movieline*, 1998

947. Rewrites are supposed to be a creative activity, not a regurgitation of other people's notes.
Judith Weston, Author
Cited in *Movie Maker* magazine, 1998

948. A work written by one man and then transposed onto the screen by another is no more than a translation....
Jean Cocteau
Stated in his 1954 *Cocteau on the Film*

949. You know the three biggest lies? I love you, one size fits all, and just a two-week polish.
Carrie Fisher, Screenwriter — Script Doctor
On quick rewrites for director, as stated in
Creative Screenwriting magazine, 1998

950. When you're adapting a book or a novel, you really have to ask the question, "What's the book about?" Then you have to discard everything else....
John Milius, Screenwriter-Director
Interview in *Written By* magazine, 1998

951. You'd rather work on somebody else's mediocre material than on your own mediocre material.
Robert Towne
Doing adaptations instead of
original scripts, as stated in *Film Makers
on Film Making*, Vol. II, 1983

952. We are making a motion picture, we are not photographing Hemingway's book like slaves.
David O. Selznick
Producer of *A Farewell to Arms*,
1957, as cited in *The Hustons*, 1989

953. "Written by William Shakespeare, additional dialogue by Sam Taylor."
Screenplay Credit
For *The Taming of the Shrew*,
1929, as cited in *Inside Oscar*, 1996

954. If a guy says, "I'm inspired by Shakespeare," people say he's a schmuck.
Paul Mazursky, Director
Interview in *Rolling Stone* magazine, 1982

955. Nobody can be the sole author of a movie. Not even the director.
Robert Towne
Interview in *Film Makers on
Film Making*, Vol. II, 1983

956. This is indeed a crazy business where I am being sued for plagiarism on one hand and given the (Oscar) statuette for originality on the other.
John Monk Saunders
Author, *The Dawn Patrol*, 1931,
as cited in *Inside Oscar*, 1996

957. Material is, finally, Hollywood's Holy Grail....
Nancy Griffin and Holly Sorenson
Interview in *Los Angeles* magazine, 1997

958. Among a number of realities which affect the economics of moviemaking, the most insistent is a fundamental and pervasive dependence upon the screenplay.
William A. Bluem, Writer
Stated in his co-authored *Movie Business:
American Film Industry Practice*, 1972

959. All of (Alfred) Hitchcock's successes are primarily writers' films — expertly directed, but overwhelmingly dependent on their scripts.
Stanley Kauffmann
Stated in his 1971 *Living Images*

960. Hollywood is too comfortable, too luxurious for mental stimulus.
Moss Hart, Screenwriter
Cited in *Inside Oscar*, 1996

961. Never allow a studio to tie you down to a time you can write. No, no.
Charles Bennett, Screenwriter
Interview in *Screenwriters on Screenwriting*, 1995

962. They're all "the best script they've (studios) ever read" ... but you know when they mean it is when they pay you.
Bruce Joel Rubin, Screenwriter
Interview in *Screenwriters on Screenwriting*, 1995

963. When Steven Spielberg hires you, all the people who wouldn't even read your scripts find them brilliant.
Mick Garris
Cited in *Steven Spielberg
— The Unauthorized Biography*, 1996

964. Be careful. Don't let them push your salary

too high. Because, if you reach a certain stage, you are to blame when the picture's a flop.
W. P. Lipscomb, Screenwriter
His advice to new studio contract
screenwriters, as cited in *Screenwriters
on Screenwriting*, 1995

965. There's no shortage of good stories, only people who recognize them.
Irving Thalberg
Cited in *Mayer and Thalberg*, 1975

966. People at studios can't, or won't read.
David Lean
Cited in *Steven Spielberg
— The Unauthorized Biography*, 1996

967. Highly paid writers fall into two categories: whores — people who do what other people want them to do ... and people who care passionately about their work and fight tooth and nail.
Nichola Kazan, Screenwriter
Interview in *ScrIpt*, 4/2

968. If you're going to spend months writing a screenplay, at least take the time to find the right person to send it to.
Judd Payne
Cited in *Movie Maker* magazine, 1998

969. What really gets my goat is that these people expect to make a million dollars off their screenplay and they won't even spell check!
Marcie Wright, Agent
Cited in *Movie Maker* magazine, 1998

970. The worst thing that writers do today is sit there and say, "What's going to sell? What's commercial?"
John Milius, Screenwriter-Director
Interview in *Written By*, 1998

971. If you're thinking about what they want, it's sort of the first road to artistic ruin.
Steve Martin, Actor
Cited in *Life* magazine, 1992

972. It's a reaction to the success at the box office.... When the writers start trying to write what they think the studios are going to buy, the scripts lose their souls.
Stacy Attanasio, Production Executive
Cited in *Movie Maker* magazine, 1998

973. Writers! Do not discuss embryo ideas! You'll get envy and you'll get stealing.
Mel Brooks, Actor-Writer-Director
Interview in *Film Makers on Film Making*, 1983

974. The writer has always been screwed in Hollywood. Always.
Martin Scorsese
Cited in *Fade In* magazine, 1997

975. (MGM has) more members of the literati than it took to produce the King James Version of the Bible.
Fortune magazine
Referring to their large staff
of screenwriters, May 1930

976. Damn it! I can keep tabs on everybody else in the studio.... But I can never tell what's going on in those so-called brains of yours.
Irving Thalberg
MGM, to his screenwriters, as
cited in *Mayer and Thalberg*, 1975

977. If my books had been any worse, I should not have been invited to Hollywood. If they had been any better, I should not have come.
Raymond Chandler
Stated in *Raymond Chandler in Hollywood*, 1983

978. Ever since that dreaded moment when Al Jolson said "You ain't heard nothing yet" — it's been a writer's medium.
Gore Vidal, Writer
Cited in *Film Makers on Film Making*, 1983

979. Most (screen) writers, when they are at work on a project ... become interested, and then involved, and then obsessed.
William Goldman, Screenwriter
Stated in his 1983 *Adventures in the Screen Trade*

980. If actors are the roses on the film bush, writers are its roots.
Frank Capra, Producer-Director
Stated in his 1971 *Frank Capra
— The Name Above the Title*

981. Writers do not have the advantage of multiple takes, good cinematographers and film editors to protect them. A writer's work lays naked on the page.
Sam A. Scribner, Writer
Interview in *Movie Maker* magazine, 1998

982. No one said something has to be good to be creative, it only has to be brought into existence.
Jeffrey Scott, Animation script writer
Cited in *Animation* magazine, 1998

983. Where were you when the paper was blank?
Anonymous Scriptwriter
To actor complaining that the

writer gets to watch and do nothing,
as cited in *The Language of Show Business*

984. I am not a defiler of a pristine white page at a typewriter.

Richard Lester, Director
On not originating a screenplay,
as stated in *Directors at Work*, 1970

985. I tend to write a more literary type of screenplay than is proper for the medium.

Paddy Chayefsky, Screenwriter
Interview in *Creative Screenplay* magazine

986. I think there's nothing you can't do on paper. I'm making my movies first here on the page.

Quentin Tarantino, Screenwriter-Director
Interview in *Creative Screenplay* magazine, 5/1

987. No one should ever submit a first draft … submit a fourth or fifth draft and call it your first.

Steven de Souza, Screenwriter
Cited in *ScrIpt* magazine, 4/1

988. We're dealing with a generation of screenwriters who don't read and who are just recycling.

Michael De Luca, Newline Cinema Exec.
Cited in *Los Angeles* magazine, 1997

989. Rewriting is for pussies! Send it out, zits and all, is my feeling.

Paul Thomas Anderson, Writer-Director
Interview in *Creative
Screenwriting* magazine, 1998

990. I have enormous sympathy for screenwriters. They're the most abused people on the food chain.

Kenneth Branagh, Actor-Director
Cited in *Creative Screenwriting* magazine

991. I'm one of life's great self-haters. I figure you've got to hate yourself if you've got any integrity at all.

Woody Allen, Writer-Director
On always being his own target in
his films, as cited in *Woody Allen
— His Films and Career*, 1985

992. It's a need to work, to write. I'm driven to it. If I don't write every free minute, I have this terrible guilt … like — if I don't write, I'll be sorry someday.

Woody Allen, Screenwriter-Director, 1970
Cited in *Woody Allen
— His Films and Career*, 1985

993. I don't care if there is life after death, I hope there's writing after death.…

Larry Gelbart
Stated in his 1998 *Laughing Matters*

994. What's my favorite failure? I'm hoping to still write that.

Larry Gelbart
Stated in his 1998 *Laughing Matters*

995. Idiocy is all right in its own way, but you can't make it the foundation of a career.

Herman J. Mankiewicz
Cited in *Orson Welles:
The Road to Xanadu*, 1996

996. I'm a director trapped in a screenwriter's body.

Brian Helgeland
Cited in *Los Angeles* magazine, 1997

997. If he wants to write for the theater, the best way is for him to be around the theater.

Eugene O'Neill, Writer
Cited in *The Hustons*, 1989, with advice to
actor Walter Huston for his son, John

998. I come from the theater. There, the writer's work is sacred.

Sidney Lumet, Movie Director
Stated in his 1995 *Making Movies*

999. (Writing for the screen), that's where the money is.

Irving Thalberg
Speech to the USC students, 1929, as cited
in *Anita Loos — Cast of Thousands*, 1977

1000. If you know how to make pictures without writers, tell me how!

Irving Thalberg, MGM
Cited in *Mayer and Thalberg*, 1975

1001. The best screenwriters have an eye and an ear.

Robert Towne, Writer-Director
Stated on a 1998 televised interview

1002. All directors look alike, but writers look different … directors all seem to be satisfied with what they are doing. Writers don't.

Lu Capra
Wife of director Frank Capra, cited in his
1971 autobiography, *Frank Capra*

1003. Oh, damn! This isn't a pencil, it's a cigarette!

F. Scott Fitzgerald
Cited in *Mayer and Thalberg*, 1975,
as overheard by Louis B. Mayer

1004. I want to write for Mickey Mouse.

William Faulkner
To reporters upon arriving in
Hollywood as a new screenwriter,
as cited in *Mayer and Thalberg*, 1975

1005. While the script may not be everything, everything else is worthless without it.

Joel Engel, Author
Stated in his 1995 *Screenwriters on Screenwriting*

1006. (Some screenwriters say they're) there to serve the director's vision. I disagree. The vision belongs to the writer. Realizing the vision onscreen is what the director does.

Joe Eszterhaus, Screenwriter
Interview in *Playboy*, April 1998

1007. "Well, the picture is finished."

Alfred Hitchcock, Director
What he always said when the writing of the script was finished, as cited in *Screenwriters on Screenwriting*, 1995

1008. If it reads good, it won't play good.

Howard Hawks, Director
Stated in *Hawks on Hawks*, 1992, referring to the "spoken" word on the set differing from the novelized word

1009. Every scene's been done. Now, your job is to do 'em a little differently. To get mad a little differently. To steal a little differently.

Howard Hawks, Director
Stated in *Hawks on Hawks*, 1972, on writing and performing with a creative edge

1010. I don't want the script to be too complete, otherwise the picture will be dead. I'd feel that the (film) had already been accomplished in the writing.

Federico Fellini
Cited in *Fellini — A Life*, 1986

1011. If you see a man coming through a doorway, it means nothing. If you see him coming through a window, that is at once interesting.

Billy Wilder
Cited in *Lew Hunter's Screenwriting 434*, 1993

1012. A good director can make a good script slightly better but he can never make a bad script good.

Marvin Chomsky
Cited in *DGA* magazine, 1997

1013. I know screenwriters like to think that the script is the script. But, boy, different directors will make remarkable different films out of the same basic story material.

Ron Bass
Interview in *Variety*, 1998

1014. I never wrote a picture that I did not mentally direct. Every situation was as clear in my mind as though the film was already photographed.

Marguerite Bertsch,
Screenwriter-Director, 1916
Cited in *Early Women Directors*, 1977

1015. If a director can get eighty-five percent of the writer's intention on the screen, the writer should consider himself fortunate.

Alfred Hitchcock, Director
Cited in *Screenwriters on Screenwriting*, 1995

1016. The movies are very strange; it's the director's medium, not the writer's. The camera makes everything concrete....

Arthur Miller, Author-Screenwriter
Cited in *The Hustons*, 1989

1017. The biggest piece of action is trying to pass the port.

John Huston
Cited in *The Hustons*, 1989, on criticizing a screenplay's story-line

1018. Design is an extension of writing — writing is an extension of design....

Polly Platt, Production Designer
Cited in *Film Makers on Film Making*, 1983

1019. Now I write plays and I call them movies. They're still plays.

Paddy Chayefsky, Screenwriter
Interview in *Creative Screenwriting* magazine, 1998

1020. It was the reason I became a director.

Woody Allen, Writer-Director
On wanting to protect his "words" as a screenwriter, as cited in *Woody Allen — His Films and Career*, 1985

1021. Why bother writing good lines ... if they'll only be mistranslated?

David Kipen
Cited in *The New York Times*, 1997

1022. I always thought the actors were hired to ruin the writer's lives.

Robert Benton
Cited in *Inside Oscar*, 1996

1023. When you're writing for actors, you don't have to make it too cerebral.

Robert Duvall, Writer-Director-Actor
Interview in *ScrIpt* magazine, 4/1

1024. What were these words I had written going

to sound like from the mouths of strangers? It was a defining moment.

> Jude Pauline Eberhard, Screenwriter
> Interview in *ScrIpt* magazine, 4/2,
> on hearing actors perform her
> screenplay for the first time

1025. If an actor is working with me and something comes out that's better than what I've written, I'm going to go with it … what I write is not deathless prose.

> Cliff Robertson, Actor-Writer
> Interview in *Take 22: Moviemakers
> on Moviemaking*, 1984

1026. (If actors) get to a scene they've honestly tried to do — and if they still can't get it, then there's something wrong with the writing.

> Gena Rowlands, Actress
> Interview in *Take 22: Moviemakers
> on Moviemaking*, 1984

1027. Joanne (Woodward), if I didn't know I'd written this play about my mama, I would've thought I'd written it about yours.

> Tennessee Williams
> To his actress, filming *The Glass Menagerie*

1028. Whenever I have to deliver exposition, I hope they put two camels behind me fucking so the audience'll have something interesting to look at.

> Humphrey Bogart
> Cited in *Lew Hunter's Screenwriting 434*,
> 1993, on his dislike of lengthy dialogue

1029. Every humorous anecdote, every two-line job, is a story and follows the three-act construction — situation, development, resolution.

> Sol Saks
> Stated in *Funny Business:
> The Craft of Comedy Writing*, 1985

1030. Through humour we see in what seems rational, the irrational; in what seems important, the unimportant….

> Charlie Chaplin
> Cited in *Chaplin*, 1974

1031. It's not what you say, not how you say it. If you have an unfunny line, it doesn't matter how it looks; it won't make any difference.

> Woody Allen
> Cited in *The Great Movie Comedians*,
> 1978, on screen comedy

1032. The more serious the situation, the funnier the comedy can be. Comedy is a red rubber ball

and if you throw it against a soft, funny wall, it will not come back.

> Mel Brooks, Screenwriter-Director
> Interview in *Playboy*, February, 1975

1033. Stop dying. Am trying to write a comedy.

> Wilson Mizner, Screenwriter
> His telegram reply to his brother upon
> hearing of his pending death, as cited in
> *Clown Prince of Hollywood*, 1985

1034. Listening to (Arthur Ripley) ramble on about a theme was like listening to Chopin played backward, or sometimes, Wagner.

> Frank Capra, Director
> On the agony of analyzing a story, as
> recited in his 1971 *Frank Capra
> — The Name Above the Title*

1035. When I want to send a message I use Western Union.

> Howard Hughes, Filmmaker
> To critics claiming his movies had no
> message, as cited in *Frank Capra
> — The Name Above the Title*, 1971

1036. [A]nytime you try to have a message in a movie, you sound like you're on C-SPAN…. The intention is always to entertain.

> Warren Beatty
> Cited in *The New York Times Magazine*, 1998

1037. Who knows what's good? I mean, I know what's bad….

> Sue Mengers, Agent
> Cited in *Film Makers on Film Making*, 1983

1038. I do not feel I have a copyright on hoop skirts or hot-blooded Southerners.

> Margaret Mitchell, Author
> *Gone with the Wind* being
> compared to the later *Jezebel*, 1938

1039. A Queen is not a lady.

> Bette Davis, Actress
> Cited in Warner Bros., 1975, on a proposed
> title change to *The Lady and the Knight*

1040. It's a good picture. It's meaty and down to earth. But I think it needs a happier ending.

> Darryl F. Zanuck, Producer-Studio Chief
> Cited on the Internet Movie Database,
> 1998, on *The Grapes of Wrath*, 1940

1041. If this isn't the best screenplay you've read, don't see me.

> Bob Aldrich, Producer-Director
> Upon sending the script to Bette Davis for

Whatever Happened to Baby Jane, 1962, as cited
in *Bette and Joan — The Divine Feud*, 1989

1042. What we want is a story that starts with an earthquake and works its way up to a climax.

Sam Goldwyn, Studio Head
Cited in *You Must Remember This*, 1975

1043. If he had a mother, she'd bark.

Billy Wilder

Reciting an early film censor's preferred version of "son of a bitch," stated in *Film Makers on Film Making*, 1983

1044. There's a reason there's a wall around a studio. It's to keep all you people out.

Mark Norman
Screenwriter
Stated to the audience of screenwriters
at the 1999 Santa Barbara Film Festival

8

Directing

1045. If not a director I would've been an actor, a singer, a painter, a circus performer, a musician, a writer, and a doctor in a mental hospital. I am very fortunate. As a director I can be all of these.

> Federico Fellini, CNN interview
> Cited in *Fellini—A Life*, 1986

1046. The director is simultaneously an architect, a poet, a painter, a composer but above all, a film artist ... thinking synthetically, an artist-innovator....

> Sergei Yutkevich
> On how Sergei Eisenstein
> imagines a director to be,
> cited in *Lessons with Eisenstein*, 1962

1047. In the beginning (of silent films) there weren't any good directors, and there weren't any bad directors. It was a question of "What's a director?"

> Allan Dwan, Director
> Cited in *Hollywood—The Pioneers*, 1979

1048. A director must be a policeman, a midwife, a psychoanalyst, a sycophant and a bastard.

> Billy Wilder, Director
> Stated in *The Bright Side of
> Billy Wilder, Primarily,* 1970

1049. [A] director's function is interpretive, that a director has to be able to project himself into Shakespearean England, or outer space.

> Edward Zwick, Director
> Interview in *A Cut Above*, 1998

1050. The great directors are exploiters.

> Robert Towne
> Cited in *Film Makers on Film Making*, 1983

1051. Sadism.

> John Huston
> Commenting on what the best
> part of being a director was, as
> cited in *The Hustons*, 1989

1052. I've tried directing.... It is lovin' everybody without getting a chance to screw anybody.

> James Earl Jones, Actor
> Cited in the *Village View*, 1990

1053. My only instrument in my profession is my intuition.

> Ingmar Bergman, Director
> Interview in *Film Makers on Film Making*, 1983

1054. Directing is an instinct. If you don't find it very quickly, you go under very fast.

> Gordon Parks, Director
> Cited in *Suddenly Doors Open Up*

1055. Men think analytically. Women rely on what they call intuition and emotion ... but those qualities do not help any one in directing. A director must be able to reason things out in logical sequence.

> Dorothy Arzner, Director
> Cited in "Feminine Director Depends on Reason, Discards Intuition," *New York Herald*, 1932

1056. Every painter has his own palette, every writer his personal vocabulary and style. What does the method of working matter as long as the result obtained is both poetic and true.

> Vittorio De Sica, Director
> Stated in his 1968, *De Sica—Miracle in Milan*

1057. Making films is about solving problems.

> Felix Enrique Alcola,
> Director-Cinematographer
> Cited in *Movie Maker* magazine, 1998

1058. People are incorrect to compare a director to an author. If he's a creator, he's more like an architect. And an architect conceives his plans according to precise circumstances.

> John Ford
> Cited in *John Ford*, 1975

1059. If your heart's in it, then you can do a good

movie. If your heart isn't — who knows? Then you'd better have a good script and a good cast.
> John Milius, Director
> Interview in *Reel Conversations*, 1991

1060. (Directing) is getting people to do what I want them to do!
> Jon Peters, Director
> Cited in *The New York Times*, 1975

1061. Of course I want utter and complete control over every product I do! The audience buys my work because I do control it.
> Barbra Streisand
> Cited in *Brentwood* magazine, 1997

1062. There is no magic wand to directing. It is … thorough knowledge of your craft and of your subject and, if possible, a passion for both.
> William Wyler, Director
> Cited in *David Lean — A Biography*, 1996

1063. The quality of direction is proportional to how interested you are in a subject and how open you are to the opinions of others whom you trust....
> Warren Beatty, Director
> Cited in *American Premiere*, 1992

1064. I've … found one disturbing thing: the more fun I have as a director, the less the quality of the directorial work.
> Warren Beatty, Actor-Director
> Cited in *Rolling Stone* magazine, 1992

1065. To be a director, all you need is a hide like a rhinoceros — and strong legs, and the ability to think on your feet … talent is something else.
> Guy Hamilton, Director
> Interview in *Take 22: Moviemakers on Moviemaking*, 1984

1066. The most important thing for a director is to have a good pair of shoes. It's murder on your feet.
> Martha Coolidge, Director
> Cited in "Dialogue On Film — Martha Coolidge," *American Film*, 1988

1067. Wear comfortable shoes to work!
> Steven Spielberg, Director
> Interview in *The Future of Movies*, 1991, on his only advice to director Bob Zemeckis before his first feature film job

1068. Always sit down when there's a scene (being shot) … you are trying to conserve energy, because you've got to have more than anyone else.
> John Huston
> Advice to future director, John Milius, as cited in *The Hustons*, 1989

1069. [T]o be in good physical shape.
> Sydney Pollack, Director
> On the most important thing about directing, as stated in *Film Makers on Film Making*, 1983

1070. When you're a director, you feel like you're this one locomotive, trying to pull this big train.
> Paul Verhoeven, Director
> Cited in *The Los Angeles Times Magazine*, 1996

1071. Every night at 3 a.m. the film is run in the projection room inside (the director's) skull.
> Charlton Heston
> Interview in *Film Makers on Film Making*, 1983

1072. That's my test. If a film (I'm shooting) keeps me awake nights, there is generally something wrong.
> Richard Thorpe, Director
> Cited in *The Los Angeles Times*, 1991

1073. [Y]ou (may) try something that doesn't quite work. It's only film … there's always that possibility that we may discover a great moment.
> Barry Levinson, Director
> Interview in *A Cut Above*, 1998, on directing actors who are adventurous

1074. Directors, too, are insecure. You have to pat them on the back, just like anyone else.
> Edward Dmytryk, Paramount Editor
> Cited in *George Cukor — A Double Life*, 1991

1075. I don't wear make-up (to work) — you don't have to when you're a director. You've just got to be clean.
> Penny Marshall, Director
> Interview in *Harper's Bazaar*, 1996

1076. Directing is preventing the bad picture from happening, rather than making the good movie.
> James L. Brooks
> Cited in *Premiere* magazine, 1998

1077. (The director) is the only one who can shape the film by kneading its different elements in the way that a sculptor kneads clay.
> Jean Renoir, Director
> Stated in his 1974 *Jean Renoir — My Life and Times*

1078. Walk on the set, look at the set, look at the locations.... That's all there is to it.
> John Ford, Director
> Cited in *John Ford*, 1975, on how he plans shots

1079. "A fish stinks first from the head," and in films the director is the head.
> Frank Capra, Producer-Director
> Stated in his 1971 *Frank Capra*, on who is ultimately responsible

1080. You're just a platoon leader with a backpack on your back the same as everyone else. You just get to point the direction we're going, whether it's east or west.

> Clint Eastwood
> On being a director, as cited in
> *Clint Eastwood — A Biography*, 1996

1081. You're not in control as a director. You're the chairman of the selection committee. You make a lot of choices. And then, you jump out of the plane with those people, and hope everyone lands safely.

> Sean Penn, Actor-Director
> Interview in *L.A. Style*, 1991

1082. Most directors in the motion picture business are traffic cops.

> Anthony Quinn
> Cited in *Film Makers on Film Making*, 1983

1083. We are, simply, midwives.

> Jean Renoir, French director
> Interview in *Film Makers on Film Making*, 1983

1084. I try not to be (arty). But you do commit that sin a lot of the time.

> Martin Scorsese
> Interview in *Fade In* magazine, 1997

1085. Make sure the crew and the cast believe in what you are doing, even if you don't know what you are doing.

> Henry Hathaway
> Cited in *Steven Spielberg
> — The Unauthorized Biography*, 1996

1086. The director is the only guy who doesn't have a job on the set.

> Robert Towne, Writer-Director
> Stated in a 1999 televised cable interview

1087. Directing is 80 percent communication and 20 percent know-how.

> Steven Spielberg
> Cited in *Steven Spielberg
> — The Unauthorized Biography*, 1996

1088. I know now that I want to be listened to.

> Diane Keaton, Actress
> On becoming a director,
> as cited in *Premiere* magazine, 1998

1089. Film is primarily a director's medium.

> Charlton Heston
> Interview in *Film Makers on Film Making*, 1983

1090. My philosophy is that to be a director you cannot be subject to anyone, even the head of the studio.

> Dorothy Arzner, Director
> Commenting in the 1979 *Directors Guild of
> American News*, on becoming the first
> woman member of the Directors Guild

1091. The captain of the ship would never stand for the (ship) owner ... to be around while he was on the bridge or quarterdeck.

> Raoul Walsh, Director
> Interview in *Directing — Learn
> from the Masters*, 1996, on not
> allowing writers or producers on the set

1092. Film directors are the filmmakers; no two work alike.

> Frank Capra, Producer-Director
> Stated in his 1971 *Frank Capra*

1093. If you can't do it my way, fake it.

> Alfred Hitchcock, Director
> Cited in *Ingrid Bergman — My Story*, 1980

1094. I think that's like a woman watching another woman giving birth, it's just not the same thing.

> Steven Soderbergh, Director
> Interview in *A Cut Above*, 1998, on the
> suggestion that you can learn to
> direct by watching films

1095. The "auteur" theory came out of France, where the director was the "author" of the film. It sure as shit isn't true in Hollywood.

> William Goldman, Author
> Stated in his 1983 *Adventures in the Screentrade*

1096. Not all directors are "auteurs." Indeed, most directors are virtually anonymous.

> Andrew Sarris, Writer
> Cited in *Screenwriters on Screenwriting*, 1995

1097. Right or wrong, you must have a point of view. Good or bad, you've got to know what you want. It's authority.

> Lucille Ball
> On what makes a good director, as stated
> in *Film Makers on Film Making*, 1983

1098. Very interesting suggestions. If you were directing the picture, you would use them. As I am directing the picture, I shan't use them.

> Otto Preminger
> Rebuffing one of his actors,
> as cited in *Paul Newman*, 1989

1099. In self-defense. Basically, I'm a writer. I'm

the proprietor of the vision. So, if you have a valuable idea, the only way to protect it is to direct it.
Mel Brooks, Screenwriter-Director
Interview in *Playboy*, February,
1975, on why he chose to direct

1100. Yes, if I can reshoot it with different actors and a different script.
Leonard Rosenman
When asked by a studio if he could "save" a
film production for them, as cited
in *Film Makers on Film Making*, 1983

1101. To me, a script is simply a vehicle to be modified as one draws nearer to the (filmmaker's) real intention, which must not change.
Jean Renoir, Director
Stated in his 1974 *Jean Renoir
— My Life and Times*

1102. A phrase addressed to the camera placed above the actor doesn't have the same meaning it would if the camera were placed below him.
Michelangelo Antonioni
Interview in *Film Culture* magazine, 1961

1103. ... It is always dangerous to fall in love with ... formulated images ...
Michelangelo Antonioni
Interview in *Film Culture* magazine, 1962

1104. If the design image I have in mind interferes with the acting, the reality of human behavior, I drop the design image.
Alan J. Pakula, Director
Cited in the *Santa Barbara News-Press*, 1998

1105. The ideal method of directing ... which consists in shooting a film as one writes a novel. The elements by which the author (director) is surrounded inspire him ... absorbs them ... working to achieve the realization of ideas....
Jean Renoir, Director
Stated in his 1974 *Jean Renoir
— My Life and Times*

1106. I expect the scene, the place, and the actors to inspire me.... You must allow yourself to be bombarded by many different things.
Norman Jewison, Director
Interview in *Directors at Work*, 1970

1107. I believe the best (filming) results are obtained by the "collision" that takes place between the environment (set) and my own particular state of mind at that specific moment ... to enter into a rapport with (it).
Michelangelo Antonioni
Interview in *Film Culture* magazine, 1962

1108. Every director, except (D.W.) Griffith, has been inspired or influenced by or has simply stolen from other directors.
Peter Bogdanovich, Writer-Director
Interview in *Take 22: Moviemakers
on Moviemaking*, 1984

1109. I like to make things look like they feel....
Sean Penn, Director
Interview in *Interview* magazine,
1995, on choosing images

1110. The slightest things gave me ideas.
George Cukor
Cited in *George Cukor — A Double Life*, 1991

1111. My job on the set is to materialize what I've imagined.
Federico Fellini
Cited in *Fellini — A Life*, 1986

1112. To work with Fellini one must understand that it is necessary for him to transform. (Fellini) has to transform everything with his imagination.
Bernardino Zapponi
Cited in *Fellini — A Life*, 1986

1113. In the center of my story is where I feel the center of my existence. That is the reason for which I exist — doing what is really the reason of your destiny.
Federico Fellini
Cited in *Fellini — A Life*, 1986

1114. Contrasts establish a counterpart. They elevate the commonplace in life to a higher level.
Alfred Hitchcock
Cited in *The Art of Alfred Hitchcock*, 1976

1115. We (want) to get into the conflict within the character. It (is) our way of best serving a movie, a story.
Emmanuel Lubezlei, Cinematographer
Cited in *Contemporary Cinematographers:
On Their Art*, 1998

1116. Sometimes it is the picture that directs you when you work in an open and honest way.
Federico Fellini, Director
Cited in *Film Makers on Film Making*, 1983

1117. The films take me where they're going ... It controls you ... pick up your feet at the right moment and coast with it, and make the accidents work for you....
Richard Lester, Director
Interview in *Directors at Work*, 1970

1118. The fact that I have no contact with the

audience during the execution of the film work fills me with daring.

Jean Renoir, Director
Stated in his 1974 *Jean Renoir—My Life and Times*

1119. If a scene seems exciting to you ... you assume the audience will agree, because that is whom you've been working for since the beginning.

Mike Nichols, Writer-Director
Interview in *Interview* magazine, 1998

1120. Don't figure it—feel it. An appeal to the senses ... in which you create excitement.

Stanley Kramer, Producer-Director
Cited in *Directors at Work*, 1970

1121. I gotta hear it. I gotta know.

Penny Marshall, Director
Cited in *The Hollywood Reporter*, 1995

1122. I try to have times where nothing is being said, but everything is being said.

John Singleton, Director
On silence as a narrative tool, as
cited in *Venice* magazine, 1991

1123. I never approach a movie intellectually. I approach it practically.... It is profoundly intuitive in my case.

Peter Weir, Director
Cited in *Premiere* magazine, 1998

1124. Some directors work with fear, others with intellect and analyzation. Begging is our approach. We beg.

Garry Marshall, Director
Cited in *Playboy*, January, 1991, on himself
and sister, director Penny Marshall

1125. You don't want to get paralysis from analysis.

Don Siegel
Cited in *Clint Eastwood—A Biography*, 1996

1126. You do tend to lose objectivity when you work for two years on (a film); you tend to want to overclarify. You get worried that people won't get it.

Sydney Pollack, Director
Interview in *Take 22: Moviemakers
on Moviemaking*, 1984

1127. I don't allow any dull moments to develop in my films. I was always afraid that the audience might get ahead of me and say to themselves, "That guy is going to get killed in a minute." Therefore, I had to go faster than them.

Raoul Walsh
Stated at the *Edinburg Film Festival*, 1974

1128. If you have no limits, it does become more difficult, because there are so many options. Now you can virtually do what you want to do and it becomes more of an aesthetic decision.

Martin Scorsese, Director
Interview in *The New York Times Magazine*,
1997, on movie ratings and no censorship

1129. In film you've always got to make an inspired guess, because you often shoot the last scene first and the first scene last. Everything in between is like a jigsaw puzzle.

Ken Russell, Director
Interview in *Reel Conversations*, 1991

1130. I don't do satisfactory endings because I don't think anything stops. The only ending I know about is death.

Robert Altman, Director
Interview in *Inner Views: Filmmakers in
Conversation*, 1992, on endings to his movies

1131. Trust your swing. You've got to trust that the audience is going to come with you.

Clint Eastwood, Director
Interview in *Inner Views: Filmmakers in
Conversation*, 1992, on trusting
your directorial judgment

1132. I've wanted to try to involve the audience as much as I can so they no longer think they're sitting in an audience.

Steven Spielberg
Cited in *Steven Spielberg
—The Unauthorized Biography*, 1996

1133. There is probably no moment in picture-making that is more acutely essential to a director's success than the instant of his choice of story material. For the director, that is the moment of conception.

Raoul Walsh, Director
Interview in *Directing
—Learn from the Masters*, 1996

1134. Directors are storytellers ... you're not trying to photograph a budget or a cost sheet. You're trying to make a scene.

Howard Hawks, Director
Stated in his 1972 *Hawks on Hawks*

1135. A sunset is a sunset. Story, story, what's the story?

Billy Wilder, Writer-Director
Interview in *Film Makers on Film Making*, 1983

1136. My first obligation is not to the author. My first obligation is to the film.

> Norman Jewison, Director
> Interview in *Directors at Work*, 1970

1137. A film director has to convince a great number of people to follow him ... the script is the battle flag and the director is the commander....

> Akira Kurosawa, Director
> Stated in his 1982 *Akira Kurosawa
> — Something Like an Autobiography*

1138. I try more and more in my films to suppress what people call plot. Plot is a novelist's trick.

> Robert Bresson, Director
> Cited in *Great Film Directors*, 1978

1139. The camera is a tool to express the story visually, but it should not be a substitute for handling the story.

> Milton Katselas, Director
> Cited in *Film Makers on Film Making*, 1983

1140. I always wanted the camera to serve the piece.... I wanted the (camera) to be buried in the material.

> Barry Levinson, Director
> Interview in *A Cut Above*, 1998, on the
> camera not being the star of his film

1141. I love to be simply the translator and not necessarily put my stamp on it.... I like to be just a conduit.

> Kathryn Bigelow, Director
> On directing a script she didn't write, as
> stated in *Interview* magazine, 1989

1142. In all the movies I've made, if a day goes by when I don't think of something that wasn't in the script, I feel I've let that day down, I haven't contributed as a director.

> Steven Spielberg, Director
> Interview in *Take 22:
> Moviemakers on Moviemaking*, 1984

1143. English people behave towards each other in a very polite manner.... In the (screenplay) the characters are constantly apologizing to one another.... I lost twenty minutes just by crossing out all the apologies.

> John Badham, Director
> Cited in *Take 22:
> Moviemakers on Moviemaking*, 1984

1144. Directing is an extension of writing, except you're writing with film.

> Richard Brooks, Writer-Director
> Cited in *Directors at Work*, 1970

1145. So, when you ask me if the director writes, say from the first time the camera rolls, he's dipped his pen into the inkwell.

> Elliot Silverstein, Director
> Interview in *Directors at Work*, 1970

1146. The director writes in film.

> André Bazin
> Stated in *What Is Cinema?* 1971

1147. This new age of cinema (is) the age of "caméra-stylo (camera-pen)."

> Alexandre Astruc
> Cited in *The New Wave*, 1968

1148. Who has the bravery and talent to photograph a dream? People who direct musicals are the screen's poets.

> Antonio Banderas, Director-Actor
> Interview in *Movieline* magazine, 1998

1149. I don't have anything to say. I'm saying what other people have to say ... the way it appears to me. It's like a painting. I'm not going to make up a sunset. I'm going to paint a sunset.

> Robert Altman, Director
> Interview in *Inner Views:
> Filmmakers in Conversation*, 1992

1150. (Directing) ... it's like doing a living mural.

> Robert Altman, Director
> Interview in *Inner Views:
> Filmmakers in Conversation*, 1992

1151. I want to be the painter. I'm tired of being the paint.

> Jada Pinkett, Actress-Director
> Cited in *Los Angeles* magazine, 1997

1152. My job is to care about and be responsible for every frame of every movie I make.

> Sidney Lumet, Director
> Stated in his 1995 *Making Movies*

1153. Directing is the art of framing things in such a way that a surprise is always possible.

> Benoit Jacquot, Director
> Cited in *Women Film Directors*, 1995

1154. I have to worry about what goes on each one of those frames as they move through the camera.

> Gordon Parks, Director
> Cited in *Suddenly Doors Open Up*

1155. [I]n film ... to have parallel action outside the frame and in the frame — it's the combination of the two that produces cinematic effect.

> André Techine, Cinematographer
> Cited in *Film Forum*, 1985

1156. Every fucking moment of your movie should be a big deal, and if it's not cohesively part of one person's heart, it's shit.... You use your heart as a barometer for your movie's completeness.

Sean Penn, Director
Interview in *Interview* magazine, 1995

1157. I make my pictures by hand.

Martin Scorsese
Interview in *Fade In* magazine, 1997

1158. Shoot each scene as if it was the most important scene in the film.

Henry Blanke
Advice to John Huston, directing his first
film, as cited in *The Hustons*, 1989

1159. Give it scope, a spectacular look, but at the same time focus totally on the intimate side of the story.

Wolfgang Petersen
Cited in *Clint Eastwood—A Biography*, 1996

1160. Filming a scene can be like writing a story. If you want to get certain rhythms, you must select the words you want to use, perhaps certain adjectives. In filmmaking, this is replaced by camera angles or movements....

Kostantinos Costa-Gavras, Director
Interview in *Reel Conversations*, 1991

1161. I (maintain) the rule of varying the size of the image in relation to its emotional importance within a given episode.

Alfred Hitchcock
Cited in *The Art of Alfred Hitchcock*, 1976

1162. It's so easy to manipulate—with a line, a face, an angle, a look. It's quite terrifying how easy it is sometimes.

Kostantinos Costa-Gavras, Director
Interview in *Reel Conversations*, 1991

1163. With a good actor, some dialogue is redundant. There are looks on his face (with which) you can just cut five lines out immediately.

Herb Gardner, Screenwriter
Cited in *Creative Screenwriting* magazine, 1998

1164. I'd do anything to get a performance, short of malice.

Sean Penn, Director
Interview in *Interview* magazine,
1995, on directing screen actors

1165. You have to demand that (actors) do things that are going to make them uncomfortable.

Laurence Fishburne, Actor-Director
Interview in the *Los Angeles Village View*, 1994

1166. I never said that actors were cattle—I said that they should be treated like cattle.

Otto Preminger, Producer
Cited in *Detour* magazine, 1995

1167. The director's role is almost like a critic's. You're there sitting and judging as an audience responding to what the actors are giving you.

Robert Wise, Director
Stated in his 1995 *Robert Wise: On His Films*

1168. When I see a (filming) scene I just close my eyes and listen, because if it sounds right, it also looks right.

Ingmar Bergman, Director
Interview in *Film Makers on Film Making*, 1983

1169. The best that I can get out of a scene is when it stops being something that you're looking at and becomes an experience.

John Huston
Cited in *The Hustons*, 1989

1170. Every living piece (of film) that is to carry a shock of recognition must contain something about which people say, "Can you do that? I don't think you can do that!"

Mike Nichols, Writer-Director
Interview in *Interview* magazine, 1998

1171. The set is nothing but the set. To me, it is completely wrong to photograph it just because it's lavish.

Henry King, Director
Cited in *The Parade's Gone By*, 1968

1172. The audience must never become aware that there is a camera within a thousand miles of the screen.

Frank Capra, Producer-Director
Stated in his 1971 *Frank Capra*

1173. Technique should be something you have in your back pocket. You rely on it, but you don't force it out and say, "Look how good my technique is."

George Sidney, Director
Interview in *A Cut Above*, 1998

1174. The crucial thing in a movie—the acting. If the audience is watching the camera, it's either a strange audience or you've made a bad picture.

Peter Bogdanovich, Writer-Director
Interview in *Take 22:
Moviemakers on Moviemaking*, 1984

1175. The intelligent director works creatively

with his cameraman, never treating him as a mere photographer.

> Hal Mohr, Director of Photography
> Cited in *The Reel Tinsel*, 1970

1176. Literally, you make a thousand setups in a film; I'd say that fifty of them are good ... about fifty out of a thousand are perfect.

> Richard Lester, Director
> Interview in *Directors at Work*, 1970

1177. (In movies) somehow, psychologically, everybody knows that ... finally something is going to happen — but what it is and when it is, that's up to me. That's what makes it fun to make movies: I know and you don't.

> Steven Spielberg, Director
> Interview in *Take 22:*
> *Moviemakers on Moviemaking*, 1984

1178. It's anticipation. In my mind, anticipation in a motion picture is the most exciting part of it.

> Burt Reynolds, Actor-Director
> Cited in *Take 22: Moviemakers*
> *on Moviemaking*, 1984

1179. The rhythm of life is not made up of one steady beat ... and I believe all this should go into the making of a film.

> Michelangelo Antonioni
> Interview in *Film Culture* magazine, 1962

1180. Every scene has its own particular rhythms, and the rhythms give it variety, and the interest and the colors.

> Ted Post
> Cited in *Clint Eastwood — A Biography*, 1996

1181. It's not always a matter of tempo. It's a matter of interest. This is not always done with tempo. Sometimes things can be very slow and very interesting.

> William Wyler, Director
> Interview in *Directors at Work*, 1970

1182. A cardinal rule: each time-increment of a film (however short) is as necessary and important as any other time-increment (however long).

> Frank Capra, Producer-Director
> Stated in his 1971 *Frank Capra*

1183. Time, though invisible and abstract, has many concrete ways of assisting or damaging the motion picture narration.

> Eugene Vale, Screenwriter
> Stated in *The Technique of*
> *Screenplay Writing*, 1973

1184. If a scene seems a trifle slow on the set, it will be twice as slow in the projection room.

> Robert Wise, Director
> Stated in his 1995, *Robert Wise: On His Films*

1185. He understood that silence itself was a meaningful dimension.

> Richard Stromgren
> Cited in the Internet Movie Database,
> 1998, on screenwriter Fritz Lang

1186. My instinct is to let that silence sit like a painting.

> Paul Newman, Actor
> Cited in *Paul Newman*, 1989

1187. The hardest thing to do is genuine simplicity.

> Martin Scorsese
> Interview in *Fade In* magazine, 1997

1188. Choosing a setting forces me to bring into being an indistinct world, to deal with real possibilities ... that is why I am tremendously afraid of that moment.

> Federico Fellini
> Cited in *Fellini — A Life*, 1986

1189. Understatement is important to me.

> Alfred Hitchcock
> Cited in *The Art of Alfred Hitchcock*, 1976

1190. If one works on the stage, you're able to stage, you move the actors around. If you work in films, you tend ... to move the audience around.

> Elliot Silverstein, Director
> Interview in *Directors at Work*, 1970

1191. To me theatricalism means dramatic embellishment ... if treated sensitively and with discretion, they are the poetry of theater.

> Charlie Chaplin
> Cited in *Chaplin*, 1974

1192. Desire is the key, not fulfillment. The chase, not the catch.

> Frank Capra, Producer-Director
> Stated in his 1971 *Frank Capra*

1193. It's very easy to scare people with noise, to lift you from your chair with a loud sound ... another interesting way is to let the assault come for your eyes.

> Steven Spielberg, Director
> Interview in *Take 22:*
> *Moviemakers on Moviemaking*, 1984

1194. If you're going to surprise an audience, first you must nearly bore them to death.

William Wyler, Director
Interview in *Directors at Work*, 1970

1195. It's like the old story that Lubitsch could do more with a closed door than another director could do with an open fly.

Martin Scorsese
Interview in *The New York Times Magazine*, 1997

1196. (Ernst Lubitsch) didn't give a hoot about the wedding night. He skipped it entirely. He photographed the lovers having breakfast.

Billy Wilder, Director
Stated in *The Bright Side of Billy Wilder, Primarily*, 1970

1197. The next time you make a movie, take a point of view. You may be wrong, but at least do it.

Michael Caine, Actor
Interview in *Take 22: Moviemakers on Moviemaking*, 1984

1198. You have to be honest ... and as truthful as possible to the subject. You may run the risk of offending people, but you have to take it.

Martin Scorsese
Interview in *Fade In* magazine, 1997

1199. I'm a director, not a politician. I just wanted people seeing my film to feel a little ashamed....

Federico Fellini
Cited in *Fellini — A Life*, 1986

1200. Between truth and entertainment, I will always bend slightly toward the entertaining. I have a vast and terrible drive never to bore.

Billy Wilder, Director
Stated in *The Bright Side of Billy Wilder, Primarily*, 1970

1201. The job of the director is really to synthesize everybody's best work ...

Alan Heim, Film Editor
Cited in *First Cut*, 1992

1202. A good cameraman can function only with a good director.

Roman Polanski, Director
Interview in *Film Makers on Film Making*, 1983

1203. I'm sort of from the haphazard school of filmmaking.... I don't quite tell the d.p. what we're doing ... keeps them on their toes.

Penny Marshall, Director
Interview in *Variety Daily*, 1991

1204. When a cameraman has free rein, he becomes the director and the director becomes the apprentice.

Steven Spielberg
Cited in *Steven Spielberg — The Unauthorized Biography*, 1996

1205. I have to go into the cage ... and he's outside.

Billy Wilder, Director
The relationship on the set between director and screenwriter, as stated in *Film Makers on Film Making*, 1983

1206. The job as a screenwriter or director is that you're sitting there with a blank piece of paper and saying, "OK, what's a cool idea here?" ... it frees me up from just depending on the marketplace for my inspiration.

Tom Hanks, Actor-Director
Cited in *The Los Angeles Times Calendar*, 1998

1207. It's simple. I told (Katharine) Hepburn she could rule the set from eight a.m. to one; and Ginger (Rogers) could take over after lunch.

Pandro Berman, Producer
On assuring that the two co-stars would get along, as cited in *Bette and Joan — The Divine Feud*, 1989

1208. When you raised your voice, I never listened. It's why we got on.

Katharine Hepburn
To director George Cukor, as cited in *Los Angeles* magazine, 1997

1209. You'll never find a bull-horn on a (Clint) Eastwood set.

Lloyd Nelson
Cited in *Clint Eastwood — A Biography*, 1996

1210. He's the only director I've worked with who's still trying to get over the impact of the talkies.

John Cleese, Writer-Actor
On his director, Charles Crichton, 1988, as cited in *Inside Oscar*, 1996

1211. Please do it this way, I have a headache and I'm going to throw up.

Penny Marshall, Director
To actors in her movie, *Awakenings*, as cited in *Movieline* magazine, 1998

1212. Go from here to there and say this and then that while you're doing it.

Penny Marshall, Director
Interview in *Playboy*, January 1991, on directing

1213. You didn't get it right. Think about that when you go to bed.

> Steven Spielberg
> Comment to an actor on the set, as
> cited in *Steven Spielberg
> — The Unauthorized Biography*, 1996

1214. We shoot. But we don't eat.

> Billy Wilder, Director
> On being criticized for filming on the Holy
> Day, Yom Kippur, as cited in *The Bright
> Side of Billy Wilder, Primarily*, 1970

1215. My work as a director starts with the actor. He is what the public sees and hears, and it is he who will determine our success or failure.

> Jean Renoír, Director
> Stated in his 1974 *Jean Renoír
> — My Life and Times*

1216. A director's function is to use an actor's strengths and cover up his weaknesses.

> Guy Hamilton, Director
> Interview in *Take 22:
> Moviemakers on Moviemaking*, 1984

1217. I want to involve my actors in the choreography of the scene. Why manipulate them like puppets when I've hired them because they're wonderful actors.... They're like dancers.

> David Cronenberg, Director
> Interview in *Inner Views:
> Filmmakers in Conversation*, 1992

1218. Always give an actor the maximum he can possibly handle, something that taxes him and calls on his capacities. Because if he's good, he'll respond by giving you much more.

> George Cukor, Director
> Cited in *Movie Maker* magazine, 1998

1219. When I cast a film, I think, looking at the actor, I'm giving you the script, the story, the role — what are you going to give me?

> King Vidor, Director
> Interview in *Directing
> — Learn from the Masters*, 1996

1220. Every good director has been, or somewhere inside him is, an actor.

> Peter Bogdanovich, Writer-Director
> Interview in *Take 22:
> Moviemakers on Moviemaking*, 1984

1221. I want to be one of the artists of the cathedral that stands above the plains. I want to occupy myself making from stone a dragon's head, an angel or a devil, or perhaps a saint....

> Ingmar Bergman, Director
> On the goals of his films, as stated
> in his 1956 *Cahiers du Cinéma*

1222. I may privately think that I did it all, but if I do I'm kidding myself, because I am the channel of other people's talents.

> Alexander MacKendrick, Director
> Cited in *Film Makers on Film Making*, 1983

1223. (As a director) I try to walk in the same shoes (the actor's) in.... You, hopefully, just try to aid them to step where their spirit is trying to step anyway.

> Forest Whitaker, Actor-Director
> Interview in *Venice* magazine, 1998

1224. The best of film for me, and the worst of film, is that it is such a collaborative process.

> Alan J. Pakula, Director
> Cited in *Film Makers on Film Making*, 1983

1225. I took my clothes off. Not all of them, of course. I didn't want to make them ill. But it helps build camaraderie once you've seen each other's bums.

> Peter Cattaneo, Director
> On preparing his male actors in *The Full
> Monty* for their strip scene, 1997, as stated
> in *Entertainment Weekly*, 1998

1226. I am afraid of violence and I find it highly convenient to send actors to suffer in my place.

> Jean Renoír, Director
> Stated in his 1974 *Jean Renoír
> — My Life and Times*

1227. The greatest directors are the ones who want to learn something new — from their actors, their writers, their cinematographers.

> James Woods, Actor
> Interview in *Film Comment* magazine, 1997

1228. (Actors want to show directors) their strings, hope that you will take them and move them gently, gracefully, politely and importantly.

> Jerry Lewis, Actor-Director
> Interview in *Directors at Work*, 1970

1229. He pulled gently on the reins. And before I knew it, I was performing dressage.

> Anjelica Huston
> On being directed by her father,
> John, as cited in *The Hustons*, 1989

1230. It's so wonderful to have a director who is a perfect mirror.

> Sophia Loren
> Stated in *Sophia Loren — A Biography*,
> 1998, about Vittorio De Sica,
> responding to her acting

1231. People are basically characters. What you

want to do is try to get that up there on the screen. There really is no more to it.

John Milius
Cited in *The Hustons*, 1989

1232. Let them know you don't know.... That's how you build confidence with an actor.

Elia Kazan, Director
Interview in *Film Makers on Film Making*, 1983

1233. You've got to give them the feeling that they're in control and utilize whatever sensitivity and temperament they have to extract the values that the scene calls for.

Ted Post
Cited in *Clint Eastwood
—A Biography*, 1996, on actors

1234. It sure is tough to (be in a shoot) where (Bette Davis) is the whole band; the music and all the instruments, including the bazooka.

Frank Mattison, Production Manager
On wanting total control of the filmmak-
ing, as cited in *Bette and Joan
—The Divine Feud*, 1989

1235. He (Roman Polanski) comes from that school of directors that thinks the less secure the actor feels, the better.

Sigourney Weaver, Actress
Cited in *Premiere* magazine, 1998

1236. You're just a chess piece on my board on my set.

Roman Polanski
To actress Faye Dunaway, *Chinatown*, 1974, as
cited in *Jack Nicholson—A Biography*, 1994

1237. (The) rehearsal (is) now on its way to becoming a lost art ... that there is no time for rehearsal is a cover-up for the simple fact that directors don't know how to rehearse.

Judith Weston, Director
Interview in *Movie Maker* magazine, 1998

1238. Actually, "rehearsal" is a bad name for it, because it makes it sound like just what it isn't — a repetition.... Perhaps instead it should be called "exploration" or "preparing to work."

Judith Weston, Director
Interview in *Movie Maker* magazine, 1998

1239. One of the most important functions of rehearsal is a chance for actors to make "connection." "Getting connected" is sometimes called "getting comfortable."

Judith Weston, Director
Interview in *Movie Maker* magazine, 1998

1240. My fantasy of making the perfect movie is very simple. You have an idea, you work with a screenwriter or a playwright, get a marvelously inventive director, cast it a certain way, have four incredible weeks of rehearsal, then you shut it down. And no one ever sees it. That would be a marvelous movie.

Paul Newman
Cited in *Paul Newman*, 1989

1241. Improvisation can work well as long as you have the structure, as long as the tune is playing.

Clint Eastwood, Director
Interview in *Inner Views:
Filmmakers in Conversation*, 1992

1242. I love to improvise; something lucky and unexpected in one scene opens the door to another and another.

Federico Fellini
Cited in *Fellini—A Life*, 1986

1243. If you have really great players, great things happen by accident.

Clint Eastwood, Director
Interview in *Inner Views:
Filmmakers in Conversation*, 1992

1244. "Improvisation." That's one of the silliest words that's used in the motion picture industry. What the hell do they think a director does? ... I must change to fit the action because, after all, it's a motion picture.

Howard Hawks, Director
Stated in his 1972 *Hawks on Hawks*

1245. First class directors have no fear about what would be termed an actor's interference.

Burt Lancaster, Actor
Cited in *Take 22:
Moviemakers on Moviemaking*, 1984

1246. I'm not as possessive of the words. A lot of times once an actor puts in his own words, it's better.

Spike Lee, Director
Interview in *Inner Views:
Filmmakers in Conversation*, 1992

1247. I prefer that ... ideas remain fluid, believing set formulations, rules and rigid procedures to be ... the deadly enemy of creativeness.

Fritz Lang, Director
Interview in *Penguin Film Review*, 1948

1248. An actor is always a creative human being ... (you have to) free the creative power.

Ingmar Bergman
Interview in *Film Makers on Film Making*, 1983

1249. A director should create a climate in which people can make fools of themselves with freedom.
George Cukor, Director
Interview in *Film Makers on
Film Making*, Vol. II, 1983

1250. It did no good to learn a line. He would talk to you, look at you, and somehow he made you understand what you had to do.
Norma West
On Federico Fellini, as stated in
Fellini — A Life, 1986

1251. I explain to actors what I want, but not how to do it.
Fred Zinnemann, Director
Stated in his 1992 autobiography,
Fred Zinnemann

1252. There is no way you can direct an actor to look at a painting.
Billy Wilder, Director
Cited in *Moviemakers at Work*, 1987

1253. The more one directs, the more there is a tendency to monotony ... telling each person what to do, one ends up with a host of little replicas of oneself.
John Huston, Director
Cited in *The Hustons*, 1989

1254. I am not an intuitive actor. I direct myself, which I suppose in the long run makes me more of a director than an actor.
Paul Newman
Cited in *Paul Newman*, 1989

1255. When he wants to realize a scene, it's not work. We just dream together.
Marcello Mastroianni
On Federico Fellini, as cited
in *Fellini — A Life*, 1986

1256. When I can, I have one take; I like to be a slave of my decision.
Jean Renoir, French Director
Interview in *Film Makers
on Film Making*, 1983

1257. If it works immediately, you've got to have enough wherewithal to say, "That's it. That's good, that's what I want." Because you have to have the picture in your mind before you make it. If you don't you're not a director, you're just a guesser.
Clint Eastwood
Cited in *Clint Eastwood
— A Biography*, 1996

1258. I believe in doing most of the work before the camera is called into action. It should never be necessary, except in the case of accident, to retake a scene.
Cleo Madison, Actress-Director
Interview in *Moving Picture Weekly*, "The
Dual Personality of Cleo Madison," 1916

1259. I do make an attempt to always get that first take ... but you've got to be like stepping up to bat. You're not stepping up to bunt. You're stepping up to hit the damn thing.
Clint Eastwood, Director
Interview in *Inner Views:
Filmmakers in Conversation*, 1992

1260. The fact (is) that film (is) the cheapest single thing that (goes) into a movie and never be stingy with it.
Robert Wise, Director
Cited in *Directors at Work*, 1970

1261. We are free to manipulate as we please a world in which nothing seems to permit man to overcome his limitations.
Jean Cocteau, Director
Stated in his 1954 *Cocteau
on the Film*, referring to directors

1262. That's not me being a good director, that's me being a bad babysitter.
Steven Spielberg, Director
Interview in *Take 22: Moviemakers on
Moviemaking*, 1984, on getting
an on-camera baby to cry on cue

1263. The film's emotional moments must feel captured, as opposed to set up and driven into the ground.
Meryl Streep, Actress
Cited in *Clint Eastwood — A Biography*, 1996

1264. I divide directors into two categories. One ... whose work starts with the camera ... (the second) with the actors.
Jean Renoir, French director
Interview in *Film Makers on Film Making*, 1983

1265. I always had my shots set up and I'd just plug my actors in.
Sergio Leone
Cited in *Film Comment* magazine, 1997

1266. If my movie has two stars in it, I always know it really has three. The third star is the camera.
Sidney Lumet, Director
Stated in his 1995 *Making Movies*

1267. To think of the camera first is like tailoring a suit ... then looking for a person who will fit it.

Roman Polanski, Director
Interview in *Film Makers on Film Making*, 1983

1268. Most directors ... use the camera like a machine gun. John Huston used it like a sniper.

Michael Caine
Cited in *The Hustons*, 1989

1269. Action! Cut!

J. Stuart Blackton,
Producer-Director, Founder of Vitagraph
The notorious first studio, and first to cry
out those words on set, as cited
in *Biography* magazine, 1998

1270. I say "Action" and sit in my chair just like the audience. If the scene rings true, I say "Print it" and not before.

Mervyn LeRoy, Director
Cited in *Films of the Golden Age* magazine, 1998

1271. Saying "print" is my biggest responsibility.

Sidney Lumet, Director
Stated in his 1995, *Making Movies*

1272. Any director will say print when the subjective factors all are reasonably satisfied and his objective judgment is that the subjective factors are not wrong.

Elliot Silverstein, Director
Interview in *Directors at Work*, 1970

1273. There are no unimportant decisions in a movie.

Sidney Lumet, Director
Stated in his 1995 *Making Movies*

1274. If I can make five good scenes in (a) picture and don't annoy the audience, I think I'll be good.

Howard Hawks, Director
Stated in his 1972 *Hawks on Hawks*

1275. By judicious hinting it is possible to persuade an audience to put a shattering interpretation on the most innocuous things.... But you must be careful not to disappointment them.

Alfred Hitchcock, Director
Interview in *The Saturday Evening Post*, 1957,
on tricking the audience with a lesser surprise

1276. I'm never happy with (my) film ... if it were left to me, they'd have to pry the print out of my cold, bony fingers; I'd never let it go.

Kathryn Bigelow, Writer-Director
Interview in *Interview* magazine, 1990

1277. "I could do that better if I did it again."

Howard Hawks, Director
Stated in *Hawks on Hawks*, 1972, on what he
and all directors say about their finished films

1278. It does shatter your confidence to look at somebody else's wonderful work. Because their work is completed, edited, mixed, color corrected. And you're sitting there with a pile of unpromising dailies.

Woody Allen
Interview in *The New York Times Magazine*, 1997

1279. Do I watch rushes? No, that is a great preoccupation for the producers.

Federico Fellini
Cited in *Fellini — A Life*, 1986

1280. [B]est of all ... is to be alone with you, God, and the projectionist when you see the daily rushes.

Ingmar Bergman, Director
Interview in *Film Makers on Film Making*, 1983

1281. [W]hen you see our dailies; we must say, "God help me."

Ingmar Bergman
Interview in *Film Makers on Film Making*, 1983

1282. Don't commit suicide after the second day; just later on reshoot those first two days.

Ingmar Bergman
His advice to Pancho Kohner before his directorial debut, as cited in *The Hustons*, 1989

1283. Don't just expect things to go wrong, count on it!

Joe Cohn, MGM
Cited in *Mayer and Thalberg*, 1975

1284. I've only three things to tell you: don't screw your leading lady, don't screw your leading lady, and don't screw your leading lady.

Mel Frank
His advice to Pancho Kohner before his directorial debut, as cited in *The Hustons*, 1989

1285. [N]ot to do it.

John Huston
His advice to Pancho Kohner before his directorial debut, as cited in *The Hustons*, 1989

1286. There are extremists and prima donnas on every project.... You need to be skilled with people. There is a give and take. Getting the image is what is important.

Stephen Goldblatt, Cinematographer
Cited in *Contemporary
Cinematographers: On Their Art*, 1998

1287. (Directing is) a terrible drugged state. Total responsibility is a drug. Once you have it, you cannot kick it.

Richard Lester, Director
Interview in *Directors at Work*, 1970

1288. I found it laboriously irritating to direct. I have absolutely no powers of command. If I asked somebody to do something … they'd say, "What did you say?"

Walter Matthau, Actor
Cited in *Take 22: Moviemakers on Moviemaking*, 1984, on directing a movie his first and only time—1958

1289. I don't have the metabolic system to be a director. Directing is … a series of enormous jobs, behind which—unless you're willing to be a Philistine—is a visual, artistic viewpoint.

Richard Dreyfuss, Actor
Cited in *Take 22: Moviemakers on Moviemaking*, 1984

1290. I love the whole (directing) "process".… But it isn't easy, and it isn't fun. And anyone that says, "I'm having fun making a film" is a bloody liar, an insensate oaf.

Richard Lester, Director
Interview in *Directors at Work*, 1970

1291. Everyone says that directing is a great job because you have all this power. What power? I have the power not to sleep for months on end.

Penny Marshall, Director
Interview in *Harper's Bazaar*, 1996

1292. You may say you like a script, but then you have to ask yourself, "Do I really want to get up at 6 a.m. to make it?" That's the bottom line in moviemaking.

Amy Heckerling, Director
Interview in *People* magazine, 1991

1293. I came close to directing *City Slickers*, but it was too much to take on with the cows.

Billy Crystal, Actor
Cited in *Blockbuster Video* magazine, 1991

1294. The important thing … to understand is that you are running a nursery.

Jerry Lewis, Actor-Director
Interview in *Directors at Work*, 1970, on the directing of movie actors

1295. Shooting a film is organizing an entire universe…

Ingmar Bergman
Stated in his 1956 *Cahiers du Cinéma*

1296. It's hard enough to get a picture made and marketed. Woman directors are just one more problem we don't need.

Anonymous Studio Executive
Circa 1975, to director John Micklin Silver, as cited in *Women in Motion Pictures*, 1991

1297. I'm a director. I'm a woman. But don't classify man-directors, woman-directors—can't we just say director?

Penny Marshall, Director
Interview in *The New York Times Magazine*, 1992

1298. Actors and crews can tell in fifteen minutes if you're a good leader, and if you are, they'll be beside you whether you're a man or a woman or a buffalo.

Karen Arthur, Director
Cited in "Dialogue On Film—Karen Arthur," *American Film* magazine, 1987

1299. A female director is automatically thought of as being dominating.…

Anja Breien, Director
Cited in *Women Film Directors*, 1995

1300. I have more of a bubble-gum outlook on life than I think Welles did when he made *Citizen Kane*.

Steven Spielberg
On making his first feature film, as cited in *Steven Spielberg—The Unauthorized Biography*, 1996

1301. I'll spend the rest of my life disowning this movie.

Steven Spielberg
Cited in *Steven Spielberg —The Unauthorized Biography*, 1996, on *1941*

1302. Three hundred thousand bullet holes and not one tire went flat and nobody got nicked. The audience—we lost them right there.

Bob Daley, Malposo
Cited in *Clint Eastwood—A Biography*, 1996

1303. When you're directing children, you have to treat them as if they're forty.

Peter Bogdanovich, Writer-Director
Interview in *Take 22: Moviemakers on Moviemaking*, 1984

1304. I found out that there's no such thing as a trained bird, only a hungry bird. And we just had to wait, and wait and wait.

John Frankenheimer, Director
On *The Birdman of Alcatraz*, 1962, as stated in *John Frankenheimer—A Conversation with Charles Champlin*, 1995

1305. It's much easier to get comedy if you don't start out trying to be funny … get their attention with a good dramatic sequence.

Howard Hawks, Director
Stated in his 1972 *Hawks on Hawks*

1306. You have to commit yourself on a (comedy) motion picture stage to saying, "This will be funny a year from now when the film is released."

Elliot Silverstein, Director
Interview in *Directors at Work*, 1970

1307. There's no great mystery to film directing. In comedy all you have to do is subordinate everything to the joke.

Woody Allen, Writer-Director
Cited in *Woody Allen
— His Films and Career*, 1985

1308. You just get his heart as happy as yours and he'll be there.

Jerry Lewis, Actor-Director
Interview in *Directors at Work*, 1970, on
getting another actor to be a comic with you

1309. I think comedy and drama are completely related. I approach both with the same acting style.… But I think comedy is much more fragile to direct.

Norman Jewison, Director
Interview in *Directors at Work*, 1970

1310. Ve'll shoot dis mid out sound.

Eric von Stroheim, German film director
M.O.S. — "Without Sound" origin, as cited
in *Mayer and Thalberg*, 1975

1311. Anybody who has any talking to do, shut up!

Michael Curtiz
Director's common malapropism
on the set, as cited in *Bette and Joan
— The Divine Feud*, 1989

1312. Don't do it the way I showed you, do it the way I mean.

Michael Curtiz, Director
To Joan Crawford, as cited in *Bette and
Joan — The Divine Feud*, 1989

1313. No, no. Dog should bark from left to right.

Michael Curtiz, Director
Dissatisfied with the dog-actor's performance, as cited in *True* magazine, 1947

1314. OK, now ride off in all directions.

Michael Curtiz, Director
To actor Gary Cooper atop
his horse, as cited in *AMC:
American Movie Classics* magazine, 1996

1315. You are thrilled — excited! Let me see the tinkle in your eye.

Michael Curtiz, Director
Trying to motivate actor Errol Flynn for a
scene, as cited in *Liberty* magazine, 1948

1316. I'll lock myself in the sound booth. Then we'll have some quiet around here.

Michael Curtiz, Director
Asking for "quiet-on-the-set,"
as cited in *Liberty* magazine, 1948

Cinematography

9

1317. Careful analysis of the structure of film disproves the widespread assumption that film is an outgrowth of photography.

Peter Von Arx, Cinematographer
Stated in his 1983 *Film Design*

1318. Film was invented independently of photography. It had its origins in all the optical phenomena which alternated pictures in intervals making them thus appear to combine or move.

Peter Von Arx, Cinematographer
Stated in his 1983 *Film Design*

1319. The problem with movies is that there are too many people around to dilute the original concept. But with stills, it's just one person with a camera, and the image is sacred.

Roger Deakins, Cinematographer
Cited in *Movie Maker* magazine, 1998

1320. The photographer is like the cod, which produces a million eggs, in order that one may reach maturity.

George Bernard Shaw
Cited in *Bernard Shaw on Cinema*

1321. That man is not taking a movie picture with that coffee grinder!

Mrs. Plummer, Owner of the Plummer
Ranch, June 10, 1906
Site of the first motion picture made in
Southern California, today known as
Hollywood; as cited in *Cinematographers on
the Art and Craft of Cinematography*, 1987

1322. The camera — the object that may be the only true marriage of science and art — (is) in the business of recording and distorting reality....

Michael Aver
Stated in his 1975, *The
Illustrated History of the Camera*

1323. The criteria of any camera is the end result.

Michael Aver

Stated in his 1975
The Illustrated History of the Camera

1324. (Cinematography is) the utilization of the camera as a cinema eye — more perfect than a human eye for purposes of research into the chaos of visual phenomena filling the universe.

Dziga Vertov, Cinematographer
Interview in *Film Makers on Film Making*, 1983

1325. The lens of a movie camera can be likened to the eye of an attentive observer who sees only what he wants to see at any given moment.

V. I. Pudovkin, Russian Director
Cited in *The Complete Book of
Moviemaking*, 1972

1326. We have learned to love our camera; and every day we discover something new and fashion ever richer our scale of expression.

Günther Rittan, Director
Stated in *Cinematographers on the Art and
Craft of Cinematography*, 1987

1327. I think the camera is erotic. It is the most exciting little machine that exists.

Ingmar Bergman
Cited on the Internet Movie Database, 1998

1328. The most dangerous thing — the camera, because it has a personality all of its own.

Michael Caine, Actor
Interview in *Take 22: Moviemakers on
Moviemaking*, 1984, on the camera picking
up more than you want sometimes

1329. Ohhh, the camera is a wonderful friend. It is total. It's another actor and the director — it's everybody.

Olivia de Havilland, Actress
Cited in *Drama-Logue* magazine, 1986

1330. The camera eye is more perspicacious and

more accurate than the human eye. The camera eye has an infallible memory, and the filmmaker's eye is a multiple one divided.

Jean Rouch, Director, father of cinéma vérité
Stated in *Documentary Explorations*, 1971

1331. A mechanical eye — that's the movie camera. It refuses to use the human eye, as if the latter were a crib-sheet; it is attracted and repelled by motion, feeling through the chaos of observed events for a roadway for its own mobility and modulation....

Dziga Vertov, Cinematographer
Interview in *Film Makers on Film Making*, 1983

1332. Somehow (the) spirit of the person comes through. I guess that's what the camera is all about — picking up what's underneath.

Rhea Perlman, Actress
Interview in *US* magazine, 1996

1333. That camera is more dissecting than anything that's ever been invented. You stay in front of it long enough, and it tells ... what you had for breakfast. You can't fool it.

Lillian Gish, Actress-Director-Producer
Interview in *Reel Women: Pioneers of the Cinema*, 1991

1334. The camera is more than a recorder, it's a microscope. It penetrates, it goes into people and you see their most private and concealed thoughts.

Elia Kazan, Director
Cited in *Entertainment Weekly*, 1998

1335. The camera itself responds to the needs of the mind and acts as the imagination to realize the world of phenomena.

Hugo Münsterberg
Stated in his 1916 *The Film: A Psychological Study*

1336. We cannot make our eyes better than they have been made, but the movie camera we can perfect forever.

Dziga Vertov, Cinematographer
Interview in *Film Makers on Film Making*, 1983

1337. The camera is in one specific place because that is the story point and it always is the story point. All of the factors are determined by the story.

Richard Brooks, Writer-Director
Interview in *Directors at Work*, 1970

1338. I found that the placing of a camera was not only psychological but articulated a scene; in fact, it was the basis of cinematic style.

Charlie Chaplin
Stated in *My Biography — Charlie Chaplin*, 1964

1339. There has got to be a reason for moving (the camera). Use the camera like an information booth.

John Ford, Director
Cited in *Fred Zinnemann — An Autobiography*, 1992

1340. The camera can't talk back. It can't ask stupid questions. It can't ask penetrating questions that make you realize you've been wrong all along. Hey, it's a camera!

Sidney Lumet, Director
Stated in his 1995 *Making Movies*

1341. In the first place, the word "cameraman" is unfortunate ... it is too limited, too technical. "Chief artistic collaborator," were the phrase not so clumsy, would be less misleading.

Curt Courant, Cinematographer, 1935
Cited in the 1987 *Cinematographers on the Art and Craft of Cinematography*

1342. Consider. A camera is a machine, a vehicle for the film; the lens is a piece of dead glass; a lamp is a lamp; the film itself is a chemical product ... the man who can visualize a scene in terms of these dead things and from them create a work of living beauty, he is a creative artist. That is my cry.

Curt Courant, Cinematographer, 1935
Cited in *Cinematographers on the Art and Craft of Cinematography*, 1987

1343. All who are engaged in this task are apprentices of the new "camera-art" — for there is no master.

Günther Rittan, Director
Stated in *Cinematographers on the Art and Craft of Cinematography*, 1987

1344. The camera is objective, the subjectivity is my own.

Ermanno Olmi, Director
Stated in the *Film Forum*, 1985

1345. The cinematographer must be both an artist and an engineer, a technician and a painter of light.

Anna Kate Sterling, Author
Stated in her 1987 *Cinematographers on the Art and Craft of Cinematography*

1346. It's miraculous how these unsung heroes make us actresses look — like we don't.

Rosalind Russell, Actress
Cited in *Inside Oscar*, 1996, in presenting the Academy Cinematography Awards, 1940

1347. Four eyes are better than two.

D. W. Griffith, Producer-Director
Cited on the Internet Movie Database, 1998, referring to the cameraman

1348. One of the great, great unappreciated arts in cinematography today — what a first assistant (cameraman) does.
Allen Daviau, Cinematographer
Interview in *Moviemakers at Work*, 1987

1349. Do we steal? You bet, but we only steal from the very best!
Allen Daviau, Cinematographer
On people in his profession lifting ideas from one another, as stated in *Moviemakers at Work*, 1987

1350. Before I decide how to photograph something, I first of all think about how to improve whatever it is I'm photographing.
Akira Kurosawa, Director
Stated in *The Films of Akira Kurosawa*, 1965

1351. More important to me is to make each camera movement begin with a beautiful still picture and to end each scene with a beautiful still picture.
Gordon Parks, Director
Stated in his *Voices in the Mirror*

1352. It is important that the operative-technical moment be enveloped in the many emotions that are in the air in the moment one lives the scene … a collision with the moment.
Ermanno Olmi, Director
Stated in the *Film Forum*, 1985

1353. Every choice you make is going to have an effect, an outcome, on the shot or the scene.
Gordon Willis, Cinematographer
Cited in *Movie Maker* magazine, 1998

1354. A film is a sum of its parts and one shot is only as strong as what has come before it.
Caleb Deschanel, Cinematographer
Cited in *Movie Maker* magazine, 1998

1355. We appeal to the eye by a transient sequence of optical impressions, as the musician appeals to the ear by an acoustic sequence of sounds.
Günther Rittan, Director
Stated in *Cinematographers on the Art and Craft of Cinematography*, 1987

1356. You can't find in any other art, and … can't create a situation that is so close to dreaming as cinematography … at its best.
Ingmar Bergman, Director
Interview in *Film Makers on Film Making*, 1983

1357. The essence of the cinema lies in cinematic beauty.
Akira Kurosawa, Director
Cited in *The Films of Akira Kurosawa*, 1965

1358. Film for me is totally pictorial — the idea of the visual telling the story.
Steven Spielberg
Cited in *Steven Spielberg
— The Unauthorized Biography*, 1996

1359. Actors, directors, designers, write on your banner in bold letters the most important commandment of film art: the cinema's language is cinematographic!
Lev Kuteshov, 1918
Cited in *On the History of Film Style*, 1997

1360. Our art is reproved for being specifically cinematic. "You are not literary enough. You are not dramatic!" But a film ought to be filmic, or it is not worth making.
Lev Kuteshov, 1918
Cited in *On the History of Film Style*, 1997

1361. We rarely know why we make the choices we do at any given time. But the opportunities are always there and we follow them according to our instinct. Cinema is fantastic for us.
Vittorio Storaro, Cinematographer
Cited in *Movie Maker* magazine,
1998, on cinematography

1362. Privileged moments.
François Truffaut, Director
His description of filmed intervals of
beautiful imagery, as cited in
Great Film Directors, 1978

1363. For me, shooting is elucidation … each shot retains its life.
Alain Resnais, Director
Cited in *Films and Filming*, 1962

1364. I look upon (cinematography) as an added emotional quality to the script.…
Billy Williams, Cinematographer
Stated in the *Film Forum*, 1985

1365. The cinematographer's unique perversity is that in this absolutely chaotic, screwed up, very imperfect work, within the frame everything's perfect for an instant.
Allen Daviau, Cinematographer
Interview in *Moviemakers at Work*, 1987

1366. You do need the frame, otherwise, if there are no limits, there's no artistic transposition. I think the frame is a great discovery.
Nestor Almendros
Stated in the *Film Forum*, 1985

1367. It is very simple. I think the frame is like

life. Life, too, offers only certain possibilities. Film is like a square of life, it has the same boundaries....

R. W. Fassbinder, Director
Stated in the *Film Forum*, 1985

1368. The frame is the visual opportunity to express the written word.

Billy Williams, Cinematographer
Stated in the *Film Forum*, 1985

1369. [Y]ou can make the frame do anything you want it to do. It's a blank canvas. I find it limitless.

George Romero, Cinematographer
Stated in the *Film Forum*, 1985

1370. It's the very nature of film that implies that everything in the frame gives rise to the imagination of the spectator for that which is outside.

Benoit Jacquot, Director
Stated in the *Film Forum*, 1985

1371. Frequently in film, it is the things we hide, what we don't show, what is not in the frame, that is much more important than what's in the frame.

André Techine, Cinematographer
Stated in the *Film Forum*, 1985

1372. Sometimes the problem with the frame is like that with a second language: you have a dictionary but it isn't enough.

Claude Chabrol
Stated in the *Film Forum*, 1985

1373. (I shoot) to induce the viewer to see in a way that is best for me to show. The eye obeys the will of the camera....

Dziga Vertov, Cinematographer
Interview in *Film Makers on Film Making*, 1983

1374. Unlike painting, photography gives everything equal prominence.

David Lean
Cited in *David Lean—A Biography*, 1996

1375. Painting overwhelms and transforms nature by altering it. In contrast, film aims primarily at recording and revealing nature without changing it.

Siegfried Kracauer
Stated in his 1971 *Theory of Film*

1376. That's all frames in movies are: pictures, paintings.

Edward G. Robinson
Cited in *The Hustons*, 1989

1377. The great painters were so much a part of me ... Seurat ... Toulouse-Lautrec framed marvelously.

John Huston
Cited in *The Hustons*, 1989,
referring to framing a scene

1378. (The viewfinder) is an instrument of analysis: by blocking out everything else, you just focus on what counts.... It's like a microscope.

Nestor Almendros, Cinematographer
Stated in the *Film Forum*, 1985

1379. I ... never cropped my photographs, because you cannot crop movie film ... you have to learn to compose in a full frame.

Dennis Hopper, Actor-Director
Interview in *Reel Conversations*, 1991,
comparing photography to filming

1380. Images, not words, capture feelings in faces and atmospheres....

Sven Nykvist, Cinematographer
Cited in *Movie Maker* magazine, 1998

1381. (In silent film) the drama was inextricably entwined with the quality of photography, not just for the reason that you could see better, but from the point of view of mood.

Kevin Brownlow, Writer
Stated in his 1979, co-authored
Hollywood—The Pioneers

1382. Cinematic inflection ... a close-up is a question of feeling.

Charlie Chaplin
Cited in *Chaplin*, 1974

1383. [O]f close-ups ... a face is almost like a white paper on which you can inscribe letters ... to show faces you can read.

André Techine, Cinematographer
Stated in the *Film Forum*, 1985

1384. In each frame we direct the eye ... the impact is there without the audience having to search for it.

Allen Daviau, Cinematographer
Interview in *Moviemakers at Work*,
1987, on the cameraman's main function

1385. (Producers) have learned that pictures must be well composed, for a well composed picture is one at which the audience can look and see a lot with ease.

John C. Tibbetts, Lecturer
Stated during a 1929 National Film Society
lecture, "Introduction to the Photoplay"

1386. If (a camera) technique is to be perfect it must be imperceptible....

Jean Renoir, Director
Stated in his 1974, *Jean Renoir
— My Life and Times*

1387. Like some vital part in the mechanism of a watch ... the audience ... should never be aware of the camera.

Curt Courant, Cinematographer
Cited in *Cinematographers on the Art
and Craft of Cinematography*, 1987

1388. Camera setup is based on facilitating choreography for actor's movements. (To the contrary) it is the camera that is giving the performance and not the actor. The camera should not obtrude.

Charlie Chaplin
Stated in *My Autobiography
— Charlie Chaplin*, 1964

1389. If any of that behind the scenes work shows in the final product, then I think that work has been for nothing.

Roger Deakins, Cinematographer
Interview in *Contemporary
Cinematographers: On Their Art*, 1998

1390. I am constructing a relationship between the dynamic of the shot and the spirit of the scene.

Mike Leigh, Director
Cited in *Variety's On Production*, 1996

1391. Film thrives on presenting faces, streets, chance occurrences, casual glances. Its images corroborate our vision of reality.

Siegfried Kracauer
Stated in his 1971, *Theory of Film*

1392. My job is to create a visual environment that best supports the connection between the actor and audience, an environment which that magic can occur.

Jo Mayer, Cinematographer
Interview in *Contemporary
Cinematographers: On Their Art*, 1998

1393. (Too much camera movement) says "this is a motion picture." This isn't real.

John Ford, Director
Cited in *John Ford
— The Man and His Films*, 1986

1394. Cinematography should be unobtrusive. It should serve the story. It should be another dramatic tool ... style should be dictated by the material.

Carol Littleton, Film Editor
Interview in *First Cut*, 1992

1395. I wanted the camera to be an active participant.

Janusz Kaminski, Cinematographer
On his use of handheld cameras in the D-Day sequence in *Saving Private Ryan*, 1998, as cited in *The Hollywood Reporter*, 1999

1396. I don't believe in style ... you find what the picture looks like within the material.

John Seale, Cinematographer
Cited in *Movie Maker* magazine, 1998

1397. (Cinematography) is certainly not about imposing a style ... not about preconceived ideas. It's a question of remaining open ... to the needs of that day.

Chris Menges, Cinematographer
Interview in *Moviemakers at Work*, 1987

1398. The photography should enforce, not distract, from the thematic content. Selfish photography is like over-acting.

Curt Courant, Cinematographer
Cited in *Cinematographers on the Art
and Craft of Cinematography*, 1987

1399. Everybody sees the world from their own perspective and this uniqueness is what the DP brings to the film.

Roger Deakins, Cinematographer
Cited in *Movie Maker* magazine, 1998, in reference to the director of photography

1400. You will not find in my films any phony camera moves or fancy set-ups to prove that I am a moving picture director.

Billy Wilder, Director
Cited in *The Bright Side
of Billy Wilder, Primarily*, 1970

1401. Light is the most important tool we have to work with.... We need to think about light.

Laszlo Kovacs, Cinematographer
Cited in *Movie Maker* magazine, 1998

1402. A cinematographer is a master of light.

Laszlo Kovacs, Cinematographer
Cited in *Movie Maker* magazine, 1998

1403. My striving for simplicity derives from my striving for the logical light, the true light.

Sven Nykvist, Cinematographer
Cited in *Movie Maker* magzine, 1998

1404. I light the actors, and then I light the set. It's like a sheet of paper to write on; the figures are what is important, not the paper.

Lee Garmes, Cinematographer
Cited in *Film Makers on Film Making*, 1983

1405. I want light that works for the story. I like to start in the very background and work my way up to the foreground. It's like a puzzle.... I go for the contrast.

Donald M. Morgan, Cinematographer
Interview in *Contemporary
Cinematographers: On Their Art*, 1998

1406. If you want a real look, you need to add diffusion.

Rodger Pratt, Cinematographer
Cited in *American Cinematography*, 1997,
explaining his use of Christian Dior
stockings as a tool in back of the lens

1407. (Form and content) like light and darkness, what appears to be in conflict can sometimes lead to a seamless union and hold great power on the screen.

Gordon Willis, Cinematographer
Cited in *Movie Maker* magazine, 1998

1408. There's an element in film noir, the way light and shadow are used in such extreme contrast, that it is almost religious or spiritual or philosophic ... the age old notion ... of light against dark. Good against evil.

John Bailey
Cited in *American Cinema*, 1995

1409. In cinema it must be the camera which reveals the personality: plastically, one must sculpt the idea into a face by means of light and shade.

Robert Bresson, Director
Cited in *Great Film Directors*, 1978

1410. I've always loved what I call "God Lights," shafts coming out of the sky, or out of a spaceship, or coming through a doorway.

Steven Spielberg
Cited in *Steven Spielberg
— The Unauthorized Biography*, 1996

1411. Light in film noir is just barely there, and flares up when somebody lights a cigarette.... It's just eruptive and quick, and then it falls back into darkness.

John Bailey
Cited in *American Cinema*, 1995

1412. Nature's most beautiful light occurs at extreme moments, the very moments when filming seems impossible.

Nestor Almendros, Cinematography
Stated in his 1992 *A Man with a Camera*

1413. For comedy, I had a set formula: flood the scene with light. Comedy ... is no good unless it can be seen in minute detail.

Raoul Walsh, Director
Cited in *Directing
— Learn from the Masters*, 1996

1414. Think. Listen. Observe. Try to capture.

Allan King, Cinematographer
Interview in *Moviemakers at Work*, 1987

1415. When you are on the set, listen to the director ... actor ... words. Feel where you are and let the feeling of what is happening around you dictate how you should go about the job....

Chris Menges, Cinematographer
Interview in *Moviemakers at Work*, 1987

1416. Their eyes must tell them how the finished scene will look seen not through the viewfinder of the camera but projected on a screen.

Anna Kate Sterling, Author
Stated in her 1987 *Cinematographers on the
Art and Craft of Cinematography*

1417. The camera operator has to be aware of first where it's happening and everybody's moving toward the same goal and they are all breathing in the same breath. That's a moment of magic.

Allen Daviau, Cinematographer
Interview in *Moviemakers at Work*,
1987, on shooting scene after scene

1418. As in any other art form, you've got to take chances to get something exceptional.

Allen Daviau, Cinematographer
Stated in *Moviemakers at Work*, 1987

1419. Give to the director and the actors and the writer the freedom to experiment ... give something original, so that the work doesn't become stylistically dogmatic, so that the work is fresh.

Chris Menges, Cinematographer
Interview in *Moviemakers at Work*, 1987

1420. I like going for the shot that gives the actors the most freedom ... gives a sense of pace, and a sense of time and a sense of place ... shots that develop.

Chris Menges, Cinematographer
Interview in *Moviemakers at Work*, 1987

1421. Time and Space. Film art is the only art form that allows us to dominate both.

Jean Cocteau
Stated in his 1954 *Cocteau on the Film*

1422. If you pan across a face and you miss the words, don't always worry about the words, because sometimes what people are doing is more important than what they are saying.

Chris Menges, Cinematographer
Interview in *Moviemakers at Work*, 1987

1423. The camera should follow the actor as he moves; it should stop when he stops.

Akira Kurosawa, Director
Cited in *The Films of Akira Kurosawa*, 1965

1424. I never used changes of focus. Those variations of the distance between foreground and background seem to me artificial.

Jean Renoir, Director
Stated in his 1974 *Jean Renoir
— My Life and Times*

1425. Why you use the big head, it's to show something important.

John Huston, Director
Cited in *The Hustons*, 1989,
on using a "long shot" close-up

1426. The success of the film is dependent on the lab's excellent processing of the negative.... It's no good dreaming and having visions if the work is not printable....

Chris Menges, Cinematographer
Interview in *Moviemakers at Work*, 1987

1427. Somebody had the nerve to look at reality and say: I like that. I'm going to put that on film exactly the way it is and not overwhelm the image with my technology or my craft or my personality.

Philippe Rousselot, Cinematographer
Cited in *Movie Maker* magazine, 1998, on
David Lean's *Lawrence of Arabia*

1428. Since I lack imagination, I seek inspiration in nature, which offers me an infinite variety of forms.

Nestor Almendros, Cinematographer

Stated in his 1992 *A Man with a Camera*, on
the most beautiful light being natural light

1429. (In nature films) anticipation is the single most important tool a DP needs to have ... control the moment, rather than being controlled.

John Seale, Cinematographer
Cited in *Movie Maker* magazine, 1998

1430. I'm in motion pictures because I love making art with technology.

Allen Daviau, Cinematographer
Interview in *Movie Makers at Work*, 1987

1431. We know there is no magical, electronic wizard-device which will change premeditated mediocrity to something better.

Haskell Wexler, Cinematographer
Interview in *Action!* magazine, 1967

1432. Nothing is worse than the abuse of technical devices.

Nestor Almendros, Cinematographer
Stated in his 1992 *A Man with a Camera*

1433. Don't let the equipment or the technique divorce you from the people whose story you're trying to tell when you are shooting....

Chris Menges, Cinematographer
Interview in *Moviemakers at Work*, 1987

1434. Despite the advances in CGI (computer generated imagery) and so forth, it's the close-up that remains the great invention of cinema.

Peter Weir, Director
Interview in *Premiere* magazine, 1998

1435. Commercials can be to cinematography what NASA has been to so many sciences. You have somebody who is financing research on the edge.

Allen Daviau, Cinematographer
Interview in *Moviemakers at Work*,
1987, on not shooting only features

10

Production Design

1436. The stage setting surrounds the actors. In the movies, once the scene is filmed ... the actors surround the set ... sets are but backgrounds of which they play....

Robert Henderson, Author
From his book, *D.W. Griffith:*
His Life and Work, 1972

1437. Every emotion can be expressed in terms of form and color. Through physical marshaling of objects, through contours and balance, through light and shade and their gradation, the world's grief and ... laughter may be deftly and exactly expressed.

Hugo Ballin, Production Designer
Cited in the March issue of
Motion Picture Classic, 1919

1438. There is no location that is completely acceptable to the story.... One has to reinterpret the script and, of course, this is what (production) design is all about.

John Stoll, Set Designer
Cited in *Film Design,* 1974

1439. The great attraction for me has always been ... to be in another world, in another time.

Patrizia von Brandenstein,
Production Designer
Interview in *Moviemakers at Work,* 1987

1440. In the film world the producer and director and cameraman are so full of themselves that it is not sufficiently acknowledged that the art director is the creator of those miraculous images up there on the big screen.

Michael Powell, Director
Cited in *A Life in the Movies,* 1986

1441. Most men "above the line," those who set studio policy, just do not know the scope of the art director's knowledge of motion picture production.

Statement in the monthly bulletin of the
Society of Motion Picture Art Directors,
March 1951

1442. The art director is responsible for everything you see on the screen ... that doesn't move ... and is usually out of focus.

Stanley Fleisher, Supervising Art Director
Cited in *What an Art Director Does: An*
Introduction to Motion Picture Design, 1994

1443. The artistic value of innumerable productions would be greatly enhanced if only producers would take the art director into their confidence in the planning of a film.

Cited in *Sight and Sound,* September, 1934,
"The Artist and the Film"

1444. It is not generally recognized by the public that the most genuinely creative member of a film unit, if the author of the original story and screenplay is excluded, is the art director....

Michael Powell, Director
Cited in *A Life in the Movies,* 1986

1445. The art director ... is responsible for the emotional content of his background and sometimes this is produced by a single windswept tree or a lonely figure on a misty heath ... so we will start with the element!

Edward Carrick, Author
Stated in his *Designing for Films,* 1949

1446. (The art director must have) new ideas and rapid visualization ... a knowledge of how to fake so as to cheat the camera....

Frank H. Webster, Author
Stated in his book *The Art*
of the Art Director, 1923

1447. (The production designer must) enhance communication by visual means, and produce settings that advance the story.

Ward Preston, Author–Production Designer
Cited in *What an Art Director Does: An*
Introduction to Motion Picture Design, 1994

1448. Color is an optical experience, and the capacity to see, think and feel in colors, is a natural gift. We may presume that painters, in general, have that gift.

Carl Th. Dreyer
Cited in *Filmmakers on Filmmaking*, 1983

1449. Probably the most underrated of cinema artists, the art director may dominate the visual quality of a film....

Ephraim Katz, Writer
Cited in *The Film Encyclopedia*, 1979

1450. Do you realize that there is not a single shot made in a picture that is not laid out by this biped, the art director?

W. R. Wilkerson
Interview in *The Hollywood Reporter*, 1939

1451. It's astonishing how little credit in this land of all credits, goes to the creation of sets for motion pictures....

W. R. Wilkerson
Interview in *The Hollywood Reporter*, 1939

1452. In Hollywood and elsewhere, scenery is not "box office." Though essential to the narrative film, art direction does not sell many tickets.

Charles Affron, Author
Stated in his co-authored
Sets in Motion, 1995

1453. The set designer has to have an important statement to make, like a film director, like an actor, like a screenwriter.

Eiko Ishioka, Production Designer
Interview in *Moviemakers at Work*

1454. The process of (a production designer) is primarily emotional and not visual.

Harry Horner, Production Designer
Interview in *Photoplay*, 1917

1455. Your (design) work should be invisible.

Polly Platt, Production Designer
Interview in *Filmmakers on Filmmaking*,
1983, on being aware of the sets

1456. Technology is like my paint, my brush; it cannot be my concept.

Eiko Ishioka, Production Designer
Interview in *Moviemakers at Work*, 1987

1457. I, for one, do not like extremely realistic sets. I am for simplicity and beauty and you can achieve that only by creating an impression.

Anton Grot, Art Director
Cited in *An Introduction to Film Studies*, 1996

1458. (Movie) decor exploits "the reality effect" both when it represents the everyday and when it represents the "real" of its genre.

Mirella Jona Affron, Professor-Author
Stated in her co-authored *Sets in Motion*, 1995

1459. In most films, decor carries a low level of narrative weight. It sets time, place, and mood and subscribes to the generally accepted depiction of the real.

Mirella Jona Affron, Professor-Author
Stated in her co-authored *Sets in Motion*, 1995

1460. Things seen from one angle look entirely different when seen from another, but things don't change. It's all in how we look at them! It's all a matter of perspective, dammit!

Karl Brown, Cameraman
Commenting on the art design philosophy
of scenic designer Walter L. Hall, in the
September 1985 *American Film* issue

1461. It is up to the camera to present the décor in the right way, it's not for the setting to conform to the camera.

Alain Resnais, Director
Interview in *Films and Filming*, 1962

1462. Success is when everyone believes — if you believe my world that I've put up there (on the screen).

Patrizia von Brandenstein,
Production Designer
Interview in *Moviemakers at Work*, 1987

1463. The style becomes illusionistic; the style is saying, "Come into this world."

David Bordwell
Cited in *American Cinema: One Hundred
Years of Filmmaking*, 1995

1464. It's just like being there but with better weather.

Billy Wilder, Director
Upon looking through the lens at a Paris
studio set design, as cited in his
bibliography, *The Bright Side of
Billy Wilder, Primarily*, 1970

1465. The atmosphere that's created by some of these "unregistering" bits of detail is very pervasive and gets to the actors; it influences them, therefore, it influences the whole scene.

Robert Wise, Director
Interview in *Directors at Work*, 1970

1466. In order to forcefully emphasize the locale I frequently exaggerate — I made my English subject more English ... and I over-Russianize Russia.

William Cameron Menzies, Art Director
Cited in *The Art Director*
— Behind the Screen, 1938

1467. The "look" the production designer establishes can involve the audiences emotionally as much as story lines and dialogue.

Robert Olson, Author
Stated in his book *Art Direction*
for Film and Video, 1993

1468. The quality of the set influences the quality of the actors' performances ... the actors can move about them naturally.

Akira Kurosawa, Director
Stated in his autobiography,
Akira Kurosawa, 1982

1469. The decor expresses the psychology of the character, acting as a mirror of their personalities, or of subordination, where decor is subject to the actions of the characters.

Mirella Jona Affron, Professor-Author
Stated in her co-authored *Sets in Motion*, 1995

1470. Actors have a narrative analog in character just as decor has in fictional space. And ... subject to photography, actor and decor, it is the human figure that is privileged in film....

Charles Affron, Professor-Author
Stated in his co-authored *Sets in Motion*, 1995

1471. My sets have a spirit like a human being. Sets have a spirit and a voice.

Eiko Ishioka, Production Designer
Interview in *Moviemakers at Work*, 1987

1472. You're directing the actors. Which is, in essence, what an art director does ... Directors are essentially people directors ... and we're there to help them.

Rich Cheatham
Interview at the Doheny Library, St. John's
Seminary, Camarillo, California, 1980

1473. I most vehemently and definitely agree ... that a set cannot be shown to a director too soon.

Mordecai Gorelik
Interview in *Sight and Sound*, Autumn, 1946

1474. You build a wonderful set, and then you put these (actors) in it and they ruin it. As soon as they enter there is no more decor.

William Cameron Menzies, Director
Interview in *Cinematographe*, 1982

1475. (Set designers) were creators of places where action happened, never of action itself.

George Gibbons, Art Director
Cited in *Sets in Motion*, 1995

1476. It all starts with the story. Design decisions follow, their purpose, in general, to support the narrative ... to serve the story.

Charles Affron, Author
Stated in his co-authored *Sets in Motion*, 1995

1477. Good sets must be planned so that no unnecessary movements slowing up the action need ever be included.

Morton Eustis
Interview in *Theatre Arts Monthly*, 1937

1478. The design of a set reflects industrial as well as narrative pressures.

Charles Affron, Author
Stated in his co-authored *Sets in Motion*, 1995

1479. Directors want to know how do you get into a scene and how do you get out of it.

Harry Horner, Art Designer
Interview in *Photoplay*, 1917

1480. A photograph can ... show what exists; only the film reel can show what happens. Structural design in a film must adjust itself accordingly.

Hugo Häring, Film Architect
Stated in *Film Architecture — Set Designs*, 1996

1481. Like the notes of the basic scale when expanded into a symphony, color has seemingly unlimited variation and enormous capacity to manipulate our emotions. It is, therefore, one of the most powerful tools of the designer.

Marjorie Elliott Bevlin, Costume Designer
Cited in *The Costume Designer's Handbook*, 1992

1482. The camera sees the last coat of paint.

Ward Preston
One of the Commandments of Art Direction as cited in
What an Art Director Does: An Introduction
to Motion Picture Design, 1994

11

Locations

1483. The decors of cinema are everywhere, not on sound stages alone but in city streets and natural landscapes as well, and the "real" locations (have) the same fictional status we ascribe to constructed decor.

> Charles Affron, Author
> Stated in his 1995 *Sets in Motion*

1484. Some filmmakers decide to tell a story and then choose a décor which suits it best. With me it works the other way around ... out of that (place) develops the theme of my films.

> Michelangelo Antonioni, Director
> Interview in *50 Major Film Makers*, 1975

1485. Some of our most exquisite murders have been domestic; performed with tenderness in simple, homey places like the kitchen table.

> Alfred Hitchcock
> Cited in *The Art of Alfred Hitchcock*, 1975

1486. A tree is a tree, a rock is a rock; shoot it in Griffith Park.

> Film Industry Saying
> Cited in *Film Makers on Film Making*,
> 1983, as a traditional Los Angeles film
> location for the "real" thing

1487. Hollywood doesn't know anything about the United States ... you could route a factual crew ... for years recording the looks and customs indigenous to this country and not be tiresome or repetitious.

> Pare Lorentz
> Interview in *McCalls* magazine, 1939

1488. I wasn't going to let some fool from Idaho or Encino direct a movie about living in my neighborhood.

> John Singleton, Screenwriter-Director
> Cited in *Inside Oscar*,
> 1996, of *Boyz 'n' the Hood*

1489. The film commission, wherever it is located, is the point where the art, the industry and the politics of filmmaking converge.

> Nancy Littlefield, Former President,
> Association of Film Commissions
> Cited in *American Premiere* magazine
> 1982, on the promotion of locations

1490. Hollywood, Ohio can be any Ohio town when the Ohio Film Bureau is successful in convincing filmmakers to shoot on location in Ohio.

> Eva Lapolla, Assistant Manager,
> Ohio Film Bureau
> Interview in the 1983 booklet,
> "Feature Film Making in Ohio"

1491. The big difference is what we get for nothing from a community that really wants you.

> Martin Jorow, Independent Producer
> On the location selection process, as cited
> in *Current Research in Film*, 1991, vol. 5

1492. The first thing producers consider when they go on location is labor, labor, labor.

> Thomas Nolan, Economics Research Associate
> Cited in *Variety*, 1997

1493. For a psychological story, where the characters and their inner emotions and feelings are the key thing ... the studio is the best place.

> Stanley Kubrick, Director
> Cited in *Kubrick — Inside a
> Film Artist's Maze*, 1982

1494. The secret lay in picking the right place to begin with and then doing as little as possible with it.

> Carlo de Palma, Cameraman
> Cited in *Making Movies* by Sidney Lumet,
> 1995, on good location scouting

1495. My pictures are set on the bed, under the bed or in the bathroom. They need a minimum of cinerama.

> Billy Wilder, Director

Cited in The Bright Side of Billy Wilder,
Primarily, 1970, on his opposition
to filming on exterior locations

1496. Mountains are much more difficult to photograph than women; moody and elusive, they don't reveal themselves easily. It takes a very good eye to find their best side.

Fred Zinnemann, Director
Stated in *Fred Zinnemann*
— An Autobiography, 1992

1497. King Vidor grew up in Texas. So, if you look at a Vidor film you understand space, the way he sees it. You look at a picture of mine, I'm in a building.

Martin Scorsese, Director
Interview in *Fade In* magazine, winter,
1997/98, alluding to his city roots

1498. Don't make pictures with a lot of ice and snow. People don't want to see ice and snow, they want beaches and palm trees.

Fred Zinnemann
Recited in his 1992 *Fred Zinnemann*
— An Autobiography, 1992 as
a film industry axiom

1499. In movies you go to places no tourist would ever go.

David Lean
Stated in *David Lean — A Biography*, 1996

1500. There is Paramount Paris and Metro Paris, and of course the real Paris. Paramount's is the most Parisian of all.

Ernst Lubitsch, Director
Cited in *Ernst Lubitsch: A Critical Study*

1501. European countries all have strong national identities. We don't have to dream anything up.

Catherine Deneuve, Actress
Cited in the *Santa Barbara News-Press*,
1998, on European filmmaking

1502. New York (City) is intrinsically more theatrical than any other city in the world.

Patricia Reed Scott,
N.Y. City Film Commissioner
Cited in *Variety's — On Production*, 1996,
referring to N.Y.C. as ideal for film shoots

1503. I'd rather make a film in the Bronx than on Park Avenue.

Paul Newman
Stated in the 1989 biography *Paul Newman*

1504. [I]t almost makes you forget all the dog poop on the streets.

Maureen Stapleton, Actress
Cited in *Woody Allen — His Films and*

Career, 1985, after viewing the Woody
Allen movie *Manhattan*, 1979

1505. (Federico) Fellini loves squalor. It never ages.

Bernardino Zapponi,
Italian Novelist-Screenwriter
Cited in *Fellini — A Life*, 1986, referring to
the director's most common film settings

1506. (The typical film noir settings) — broken-down beaneries, low-rent apartments, rain-slick urban streets, posh nightclubs, boxing arenas, sleazy massage parlors.

Jeanine Basinger, Writer
Stated in her 1995 *American Cinema:*
One Hundred Years of Film Making

1507. Is there any such place as Key Largo?

John Huston
Cited in *The Hustons*, 1987,
upon arriving in Key West, Florida,
to shoot *Key Largo*, 1947

1508. My God, there's no scene in Chinatown and it's called "Chinatown."

Anonymous Studio Executive
Cited in *Film Makers on Film Making —*
Vol. II, 1983, commented
before filming the movie, 1973

1509. I just want writers to go someplace one time and see the damn place they are writing about.

Phil Oakley, Louisiana Film Industry Office
Cited in *Variety*, 1982

1510. John Ford('s) different Westerns often used the one landscape. You would always see the same cactus sticking up.

Freddie Young, Cinematographer
Cited in *David Lean — A Biography*, 1996

1511. When I needed a canyon or a desert, whatever the scene called for, I would find one in *Arizona Highways* (magazine) and describe it from the caption.

Elmore Leonard, Screenwriter
Interview in *Film Comment* magazine, 1998

1512. We went on location in Arizona and it snowed. We should have called it *Duel Without Sun*.

Joseph Cotton, Actor
Cited on the Internet Movie Database, 1998

1513. You never realize how many palm trees there are in L.A. until you try to make shots look like the South.

Ice Cube, Actor-Director
Interview in *Entertainment Weekly*, 1998

1514. Rome was really the star of the film. The "Babylon" of my dreams. I chose it for its permanence.

Federico Fellini
Stated in his 1986, *Fellini — A Life*

1515. In the middle of Rome … there was a zoological garden. It was … everything we needed.

John Huston
Cited in *The Hustons*, 1989, for the
Garden of Eden in his film, *The Bible*

1516. There's only one asset to a foreign location, and that is its authenticity. There is no other asset. None whatsoever … the Italian town is an Italian town.

Stanley Kramer, Producer-Director
Interview in *Directors at Work*, 1970

1517. Americans are not as moved by stained glass windows as the British are.

Marilyn Monroe, Actress
Cited in the 1990 *Clown Prince of
Hollywood*, filming in London, complaining
to Jack Warner of the time spent
shooting church and palace scenes

1518. If I were to make another picture in Australia today, I'd have a policeman hop into the pocket of a kangaroo and yell, "Follow that car!"

Alfred Hitchcock
Cited in *The Art of Alfred Hitchcock*, 1975

1519. If you've got to make a picture about the end of the world, Melbourne is the right place to do it.

Ava Gardner, Actress
Cited in *Variety*, 1997, referring to the Australian location for *On the Beach* years later

1520. I found out for the first time that there was a world where nobody heard of Frank Sinatra.

Red Buttons, Actor
Cited in *Hawks on Hawks*, 1971
shooting *Hatari* in the bush
country of Tanqayika, Africa, 1962

1521. We chose to go to Italy, because being in that culture and around that language would influence the movie, enrich it.

Francis Ford Coppola, Screenwriter-Director
Interview in *Reel Conversations*, 1991, with
the three *Godfather* films

1522. You have to fight the jungle all the time, and that gets into your performance.

John Huston
Cited in *The Hustons*, 1989,
defending his decision to film on
location for *The African Queen*, 1951

1523. On long jobs out of the country, you pick people as much for their expertise as you do for their ability to survive psychologically.

Chris Newman, Sound Recordist
Interview in *Moviemakers at Work*, 1987

1524. I hate the idea of two years working in ten different countries and getting dysentery in each one of them.

Steven Spielberg
Cited in *Steven Spielberg
— The Unauthorized Biography*, 1996

1525. I'd rather die than live in the country. I've always been at two with nature.

Woody Allen, Writer-Director
Cited in *Woody Allen — His Films
and Career*, 1985, as to why most
of his films are urban settings

1526. The only two Spanish words (Humphrey Bogart) thought worth learning (were) "Dos Equis."

Evelyn Keyes
Cited in *The Hustons*, 1989, on location in
Mexico for *Treasure of the Sierra Madre*, 1948

1527. Everybody else gets these great epic locations like Europe and China and I get Cincinnati or some tavern in Virginia.

Jodie Foster, Actress
Interview in the *Santa Barbara
News-Press*, 1998

1528. When I'm making a movie I become celibate. Location shooting is the "Rites of Spring" to most film crews.

Steven Spielberg
Cited in *Steven Spielberg
— The Unauthorized Biography*, 1996

1529. Hollywood itself is not an exact geographical area, although there is such a postal district. It has commonly been described as a state of mind, and it exists wherever people connected with the movies live and work.

Hortense Powdermaker
Stated in *Hortense Powdermaker*, 1950

1530. Hollywood. We live here … so you don't have to.

Local industry saying

1531. It's a little insane asylum and they are all inmates.

Billy Wilder, Screenwriter-Director
On Hollywood, as cited on
the Internet Movie Database, 1998

1532. Hollywood — the American City of Oz, which looks that way because you're wearing colored glasses.

Gary Cooper, Actor
Interview in the *Rochester Democrat Chronicle*, 1936

1533. If you are going to start in the wristwatch business ... you go to Switzerland. If you want to make movies, you go to Hollywood.

Billy Wilder, Director
Cited in *The Bright Side of
Billy Wilder, Primarily*, 1970

1534. Hollywood is no more than the product of Broadway's success.

Jean Renoír, Director
Stated in his 1974 *Jean Renoír
— My Life and Times*

1535. If New York is the Big Apple, to me, Hollywood ... is the Big Nipple.

Bernardo Bertolucci, Italian Director
Cited in *Inside Oscar*, 1996

1536. Dahling, how does one get laid in this dreadful place?

Tallulah Bankhead
Cited in *Mayer and Thalberg — The Make
Believe Saints*, 1975, to Irving
Thalberg upon arriving in Hollywood

12

Roles

1537. There are no small parts, only small actors.
Konstantin Stanislavski, Acting Teacher
Cited in *Film Comment* magazine, 1997

1538. Roles can be short, but they're all as important for that length of time.
William Wyler, Director
Interview in *Directors at Work*, 1970

1539. It's better to play small roles when you're doing well because then you don't notice them getting smaller later on.
Tony Curtis
Cited in *The Hustons*, 1989

1540. Small roles, senseless roles. If a role is beautifully written, that's fine with me — it then becomes a great role.
Barbara Hershey, Actress
Interview in *Detour* magazine, 1997

1541. To be an actor is to play any role, big or small, that has something of importance to say.
Montgomery Clift, Actor
Cited in the *Citizen News*, 1962

1542. I don't need a big part. Bigness isn't bestness; sometimes lessness is bestness.
Clint Eastwood
Cited in *Clint Eastwood — A Biography*, 1996

1543. I can't tell you how many times I have looked at a script and requested a role other than what was suggested.
Peter O'Toole, Actor
Interview in *GQ* magazine, 1985

1544. If you're going to do junk, don't fool yourself that it isn't.
George Cukor
Cited in *George Cukor — A Double Life*, 1991

1545. Hollywood used to build stories to fit the stars.... Today they write roles and try to fit actors into them.
Rita Hayworth, Actress
UPI wire service story, c. 1950

1546. [T]here are these roles that every once in a while you get that are cathartic because they give you back your sense of being a good actor.
John Travolta, Actor
Interview in *The Hollywood Reporter*, 1996

1547. I didn't set out to play heroes. I set out to be the best actor I could be.
Gregory Peck, Actor
Cited in *The Boston Sunday Globe*, 1997

1548. [P]erhaps there's a greater advantage — a greater commercial advantage — in accepting your age and playing roles depicting the problems of your age.... But the ego dies hard.
Gena Rowlands, Actress
Interview in *Take 22: Moviemakers on Moviemaking*, 1984

1549. The day of the strongman is over. It's like to be a man today is to be nonconfrontational. That's why the hero's a victim.
Sylvester Stallone, Actor
Interview in *Esquire*, 1996

1550. I think that not smoking cigars made me feel a little more like a leading man ... that's my theory — that a man who doesn't smoke is more of a leading man.
Walter Matthau, Actor
Interview in *Take 22: Moviemakers on Moviemaking*, 1984, on defining a role

1551. Movie characters stand for something rather than being something. They're symbols.
John Huston
Cited in *The Hustons*, 1989

1552. The loudest statement you can make is be black and make movies for everybody.
Eddie Murphy, Actor
Interview in *The Los Angeles Times*, 1989

1553. He transformed a suicidal gamble into a modern profession.
Charlton Heston, Actor
Cited on the Internet Movie Database,
1998, on Hollywood's pioneer
stuntman, "Yakima" Canutt

1554. [S]uccess narrows the roles you get to play; race narrows the roles you get to play.
Denzel Washington, Actor
Cited in *USA Weekend*, 1998

1555. The interesting characters are the ones who are not holding on quite as tight to life.
Jessica Lange, Actress
Cited in *The Los Angeles Times*, 1998

1556. I'll do a Batman when it's called "Death Comes to Batman."
Spencer Tracy, Actor
Cited in a 1965 AP Newsfeature Wire, on
being offered a cameo role in a Batman movie

1557. One of the greatest novels in Western literature, and all everybody is asking is, "Do you sing in it?"
Liam Neeson, Actor
In the movie version of *Les Misérables*, 1998,
as cited in the *Santa Barbara News-Press*

1558. I even treated *Twister* like Shakespeare.
Helen Hunt, Actress
Cited in *Time* magazine, 1997,
on preparing for movie roles

1559. I don't look Shakespeare, I don't talk Shakespeare, I don't like Shakespeare, and I won't do Shakespeare.
Clark Gable
Cited in *Mayer and Thalberg
— The Make Believe Saints*, 1975

1560. I didn't want to die and go to actor heaven or actor hell and have some guy say, "You were a star and you didn't do Shakespeare?"
Dustin Hoffman, Actor
Interview in *People* magazine, 1989, performing
in *The Merchant of Venice* at age 51

1561. I won't play a man who sleeps with a woman whose serviceman husband is overseas.
Clark Gable, Actor
Cited on the Internet Movie Database, 1998

1562. "I'm doing a Johnny Depp."
Common quote among young actors
taking big risks in choosing roles,
as cited in *Biography* magazine, 1998

1563. [A] lot of movie stars play themselves because that's what they're expected to do, and on some level that's what they can do....
Kevin Spacey, Actor
Cited in *Entertainment Weekly*, 1998

1564. [N]othing transcended personality.
Charlie Chaplin
On creating the role of his character, the
little "Tramp," as cited in *Chaplin*, 1974

1565. The average man is the man I know, like and understand the best, because I am one of him.
Gary Cooper, Actor
Interview in *Silver Screen* magazine, 1941,
on the roles he's comfortable playing

1566. I've always played characters who were looking for home.
Richard Gere, Actor
Interview in *Vanity Fair*, 1994

1567. Different roles require different energies. Some are closer to you than others, and some require you to step miles away from who you are. And you can't make the trip every night back to yourself. It's just too far to walk.
Sean Patrick Flanery, Actor
Interview in *Interview* magazine, 1998

1568. Your personal life evaporates when you throw yourself into a film ... what you're thinking about is, I'm this character and I live in this world.
Sean Patrick Flanery, Actor
Interview in *Interview* magazine, 1998

1569. I look for a moment in the script to define myself as the character ... as I'm defining myself as that character, I'm also defining an aspect of myself.
Danny Glover, Actor
Interview in the *Village View*, 1991

1570. If a person thinks that I am the person I played, that's terrific. That's every actor's dream!
Clint Eastwood
Cited in *Clint Eastwood — A Biography*, 1996

1571. I'm really not the characters I play. I don't know what Cruella's going to do.
Glenn Close, Actress
Interview in *W* magazine, 1996,
on her role in *101 Dalmations*

1572. I like doing common men because it's a way of celebrating the garbage man....

James Earl Jones, Actor
Cited in *Venice* magazine, 1996

1573. Remember, he's just a mouse.

Walt Disney, Creator-Producer
Cited in *Disney's Art of Animation*, 1991,
on cautioning animators not to
outreach Mickey's capabilities

1574. Although we didn't think the first film was that violent ... we thought we should address that problem.... On the other hand, they are what they are: "Teenage Mutant Ninja Turtles."

David Chan, Producer
Interview in *Drama-Logue* magazine, 1991

1575. And there is no question: they'll think that I am the character. But they think that in everything I do. I don't care. That is one of the curses or the blessing of what I do. That is why they come or why they stay away.

Woody Allen
Interview in *The New York Times Magazine*, 1997

1576. I don't think I could play someone ... "stupid." I'm just too fucking bright.

Richard Dreyfuss, Actor
Cited in *Time-Out*, 1996

1577. In your early 20s you get asked to play a lot of guys who like doing panty raids.

Ethan Hawke, Actor
Cited in *Premiere* magazine, 1998

1578. In Westerns ordinarily they just stand me there and run everybody up against me.

John Wayne
Interview with Roger Ebert, cited in *John Wayne's America*, 1997

1579. I've gone from saint to whore and back to saint again, all in one lifetime.

Ingrid Bergman
Cited in *Entertainment Weekly 100*, "The 100 Greatest Movie Stars of All Time," 1997

1580. Walter Huston, the hard and heartless man of iron.

Walter Huston
Complaining on the "rut" of his film roles, as cited in *The Hustons*, 1989

1581. I'm sick of carrying guns and beating up women.

James Cagney, Actor
Stated in 1930, as cited in *Inside Oscar*, 1996

1582. There's nothing less interesting than a goody-goody, and I played lots of them. The best thing to play is a bitch with a heart of gold.

Claudette Colbert, Actress
Cited in *Architectural Digest*, 1998

1583. They treat me like a bitch in heat.

Jean Harlow, Actress
Cited in *Architectural Digest*, 1994,
on being type cast as the harlot

1584. Meryl Streep never did nudity. I'm not her, but I'm me and I'm not gonna do it.

Renee Zellweger
Cited in the *Santa Barbara News-Press*,
1998, when asked to do a nude
scene in *Jerry Maguire*, 1997

1585. Just because Charlie Chaplin played a tramp doesn't make tramps out of all Englishmen....

Stepin Fetchit, Actor
Interview in *The Los Angeles Times*,
1968, defending his roles as
a black, bumbling, lazy character

1586. I don't "Tom" in movies. Why, I've never even said, "Yassuh boss." I'm a comedian, not a clown.

Stepin Fetchit, Actor
c. 1955

1587. What would you expect me to play? Clark Gable's leading lady?

Hattie McDaniel, Actress
Cited in *Artrage Autumn*, 1989,
answering criticism for perpetuating
offensive racial stereotypes, c. 1940

1588. Why should I complain about making seven thousand dollars a week playing a maid? If I didn't I'd be making seven dollars a week actually being one.

Hattie McDaniel, Actress
Cited in *Artrate Autumn*, 1989, on her part
in *Gone with the Wind*, c. 1940

1589. I'm frightened to death of the water and yet it seems that I'm always required to go into it on every one of my pictures.

Natalie Wood, Actress
Interview in *The Tribune Chronicle*, 1981

1590. Joan Crawford never dies in her movies, and she never loses her man to anyone.

Joan Crawford
To producer Jack Warner, as cited in
Bette and Joan—The Divine Feud, 1989

1591. What was good for me was good for the picture.

Mae West
Cited in *The Great Movie Comedians*,
1990, on the scripting of her roles

1592. I don't mind being labeled a character actor. There's something great about having expectations of certain actors, and having to live up to them.

Samuel L. Jackson, Actor
Interview in *Detour* magazine, 1995

1593. As soon as people see my face on the movie screen, they know ... first, I'm not going to get the girl, and, second, I'll get a cheap funeral before the picture is over.

Lee Marvin, Actor
Cited in *Inside Oscar*, 1996

1594. I want to be the first actor who goes from a black mask of *Zorro* to a white one in the *Phantom of the Opera*.

Antonio Banderas, Actor
Interview in *Movieline* magazine, 1998

1595. Every man I knew had fallen in love with *Gilda* and wakened with me.

Rita Hayworth, Actress
Cited in *Chronicle of the Cinema*,
on her star role in *Gilda*, 1946

1596. I didn't come to make Casanova, I came to make Federico Fellini's Casanova.

Donald Sutherland
1977, as cited in *Fellni — A Life*, 1986

1597. Most actors want to play Othello, but all I've really wanted to play is "Chance the Gardner."

Peter Sellers, Actor
Cited in *Inside Oscar*, 1996, on *Being There*, 1979

1598. It was Sergeant Alvin York who won this award. Because to the best of my ability, I tried to be Sergeant York.

Gary Cooper, Actor
Cited in *Hawks on Hawks*, 1972, upon receiving the Best Actor Oscar for that role, 1942

1599. Since I'm representing a man's life, I owe it to him and his name to give it my blood, sweat and tears — everything that he gave.

Ving Rhames, Actor
Interview in *Esquire*, 1998, on his biopic role, Sonny Liston, 1998

1600. It's a different notion to play someone who walked on the earth. There's another kind of

responsibility to do justice to someone who actually lived....

Avery Brooks, Actor
Interview in *The Los Angeles Times*,
1992, on Biopics

1601. I don't have any sex with Jack, no sex at all.

Walter Matthau, Actor
Cited in *Entertainment Weekly*, 1998, about *The Odd Couple II* co-star Jack Lemmon

1602. [N]ever ... should I take a part unless on the first reading I could shout inside, "Yeah, I know her!"

Anne Bancroft, Actress
Interview in *Films in Review* magazine, 1980

1603. All I do is run around barns and lose my pants.

Will Rogers, Actor
On his unhappiness with his film roles, as cited in *The Great Movie Comedians*, 1978

1604. I wasn't "born to play this part," I was born to have a nice life and not strain myself too much.

Robert Mitchum, Actor
Cited in *Details* magazine, 1993

1605. But this movie isn't falling on me. The only thing I can do wrong is not be funny.

Chris Rock, Actor-Comedian
Interview in *Entertainment Yearbook*, 1998, on his role in *Lethal Weapon 4*, 1998

1606. [I]t's always appealing to play a character who has to overcome himself as well as an obstacle.

Clint Eastwood
Cited in *Clint Eastwood — A Biography*, 1996

1607. The little fellow in trouble always gets the sympathy of the mob. Knowing that ... I always accentuate my helplessness.

Charlie Chaplin
Cited in *Chaplin*, 1974, on the character role of "The Tramp"

1608. When you have a character that's really conflicted, that's really good food for an actor.

Delroy Lindo, Actor
Interview in *Venice* magazine, 1997

1609. You know, this is Oscar material ... because the role has you severely crippled and then you get to die.

Kevin Kline, Actor
Interview in *Playboy*, March, 1998, reciting what agents often say to sell a role to an actor

1610. Who wants to see some dame go blind and die?

Jack Warner, Studio Producer
To Bette Davis about the lead role in
Dark Victory, for which she was later
awarded the 1939 Oscar for Best Actress

1611. [I]s it worth playing all those demented old ladies to maintain star status?

Myrna Loy, Actress
Cited in *Bette and Joan—A Divine Feud*,
1989, on Bette Davis

1612. Katie will eventually get dysentery, then she will understand what the part is about.

John Huston
On Katharine Hepburn's role in
The African Queen, 1951, as cited in
The Hustons, 1989

1613. I didn't shoot that dog. He was a dog actor. He went home and had a good dinner that night.

Gregory Peck, Actor
On a scene from *To Kill a
Mockingbird*, 1962, as cited in
the *Santa Barbara News-Press*, 1998

1614. At least it creates more character roles for those who still have their own faces.

Pauline Kael, Critic
Interview in *Modern Maturity* magazine,
1998, on actors having plastic surgery

1615. John Huston was used for his rotting charm…. He drags his legend right into a role….

Pauline Kael
Cited in *The Hustons*, 1989, on *Chinatown*, 1974

1616. If you [Peter O'Toole] had been any prettier, it would have been *Florence of Arabia*.

Noel Coward
On O'Toole's role of *Lawrence of
Arabia*, 1962, as cited in *Entertainment
Weekly 100*, "The 100 Greatest
Movie Stars of All Times," 1997

1617. I like Donald Sutherland because he has a wonderfully stupid look. He looks unborn. I want a character who is unborn, still in the placenta.

Federico Fellini
Stated in *Fellini—A Life*, 1976, for *Casanova*, 1977

1618. They didn't like me until I got into a leg show.

Katharine Hepburn
Cited in *Entertainment Weekly 100*, "The 100
Greatest Movie Stars of All Time," 1997

1619. The average person doesn't realize that even big stars have to fight for roles.

Rick Yorn, Manager
Cited in *Los Angeles* magazine, 1997

1620. It's never about money. It's always about what the story is.

Tom Hanks
Cited in *The New York Times Magazine*, 1997

1621. I don't want the part for money, chalk or marbles.

Clark Gable, Actor
Cited on the televised A&E *Biography*,
"Clark Gable," 1998, on the role of Rhett
Butler in *Gone with the Wind*, c. 1939

1622. Days off!

Spencer Tracy, Actor
Interview in *Screen Actor* magazine, 1968,
when asked what he looks for in a script

1623. If an actor gets a good role, play it for what the producer can afford. You can't keep the money but you can keep your performance.

Montgomery Clift, Actor
Cited in the *Citizen News*, 1962

1624. I'll accept the role if I don't have to act.

Martin Scorsese
Cited in *Fade In* magazine, 1997

1625. You can make me the best man in the world or the worst, but never make me cheap.

John Wayne
Cited in *Steven Spielberg
—The Unauthorized Biography*, 1996

1626. I was willing to have my head cut off for the part of Maria.

Ingrid Bergman, Actress
Stated in *Ingrid Bergman—My Story*, 1980,
when asked if she would have her hair cut
off shorter in *For Whom the Bell Tolls*, 1943

1627. In the last analysis, you have to develop your own projects.

Paul Newman
Referring to getting choice roles,
as cited in *Paul Newman*, 1989

1628. Actually, I had planned to commit suicide.

Robert Mitchum
Cited in *David Lean—A Biography*, 1996,
giving his reason for declining a movie role

1629. I'm not having sex for money — that's why

I'm not a call girl. I'm acting, and everything I do is for the film.

Tia Bella, Porn star
Interview in George magazine, 1998

1630. I've played a white knight a few times. And you know what … I noticed? Bad guys get to smile a lot more.

Matthew McConaughey, Actor
Interview in Interview magazine, 1998

1631. Nobody wants to see a part that's been grafted from other modern action archetypes.

Max Wong, Production Executive
Cited in Moviemaker magazine, 1998

1632. [A] hero is only weighed against the power and charisma of the villain. So the villain is more important than the hero.

Sylvester Stallone, Actor
Interview in Esquire magazine, 1996

1633. Playing an actress is unlike playing an ordinary woman … her all-encompassing ego makes her seem completely pagan, but an articulate pagan.

Bette Davis
Cited in Bette and Joan — The Divine Feud, 1989

1634. Actresses are like a prism. There's a reality about them that's incredibly touching and yet at the same time you wonder if that's real.

Gabriel Byrne, Actor
Interview in Movieline magazine, 1998

1635. Movie goers tend to want their actresses to remain romantic heroines — forever.

Anne Thompson, Writer
Cited in Premiere magazine, 1998

1636. It's a mistake to think that if you put a villain on the screen, he must sneer nastily, stroke his black moustache or kick a dog in the stomach…. The really frightening thing about villains is their surface likeableness.

Alfred Hitchcock
Interview in The Saturday Evening Post, 1957

1637. I didn't want what happened to Charlie Chaplin to happen to me. When he discarded the little tramp, the little tramp turned around and killed him. The little girl made me.

Mary Pickford, Actress-Producer
Referring to her most common career roles,
cited in The Parade's Gone By, 1969

1638. A gangster doesn't think of himself as a hus-

tler. I assume he thinks of himself as a businessman.

Delroy Lindo, Actor
Cited in Warner Brothers,
1975, on defining the role

1639. I'm a morale-builder. If you have the lead in a movie, it's your duty.

Louis Gossett, Jr., Actor
Interview in Moviegoer magazine, 1986

1640. The analysis of the text is the education of the actor.

Stella Alder, Acting Teacher
A stage and screen actors' axiom

1641. I search for it intellectually and then recreate it through the character armor … by osmosis, … by induction, the character starts to come to life.

James Woods, Actor
Interview in Film Comment magazine, 1997

1642. In order to be a good straight man, you must be a good actor.

Jim Mulholland
Cited in The Great Movie
Comedians, 1978, on Bud Abbot

1643. My characters are truth-seekers. And they are willing to experience hell if that's what it takes to discover who they are.

Oliver Stone, Screenwriter-Director
Interview in Reel Conversations, 1991

1644. [A] film called into being by a cooperative effort in which all contributions have the same degree of permanence, is the nearest modern equivalent of a medieval cathedral….

Irwin Panofsky, Art Historian
Referring to all film roles having equal impor-
tance, as cited in Film: An Anthology, 1975

1645. I just opened my mouth. The thing about it is, it's English.

Laurence Fishburne, Actor
Interview in Boxoffice, 1995, on
Shakespeare's language for
Othello not being intimidating

1646. In "Die Hard" … I spend a lot of time going, "Oh, shit! Oh, shit!" That kind of thing. And occasionally we'd stop to act.

Samuel L. Jackson, Actor
Interview in Detour magazine,
1995, on action movie roles

1647. As far as film projects go, I'm drawn to what I'm afraid of.

Jeff Bridges, Actor
Interview in US magazine, 1991

1648. I ain't putting no chains around my neck. I'm not in the mood.

> Denzel Washington, Actor
> On turning down a part in
> *Amistad*, 1997, as cited in
> *The Los Angeles Times Magazine*, 1998

1649. It is pretty easy to fool an audience with a little crêpe hair and a dialect.

> W. C. Fields, Actor
> On his on-camera persona roles,
> as cited in *Inside Oscar*, 1996

1650. I was going to Hollywood and become a cowboy.

> Sidney Poitier
> Interview in *Film Makers on Film Making*,
> 1983, on his acting dreams at age 13

1651. I've been asked to run for the Senate ... I've already been President three times....

> Charlton Heston, Actor
> Cited in *Modern Maturity* magazine, 1998

1652. By God, if I ever did play a president, he is the only one I could get away with.

> John Travolta, Actor
> Interview in *George* magazine, 1998, on
> President Clinton, in *Primary Colors*, 1998

1653. It's a great role, and somebody's gonna do it, so it might as well be Billy Bob Thornton.

> President Bill Clinton
> Cited in *George* magazine, 1998,
> on the role of Richard Jemmons, a.k.a.
> James Carville, in *Primary Colors*

13

Casting

1654. I believe that in every form of artistic endeavor, there is first of all a process of selection.
Míchelangelo Antonioni
Cited in *Film Culture* magazine, 1962

1655. For me, casting is not everything; but it comes close.
Warren Beatty
Cited in *American Premiere*, 1992

1656. Usually people don't trust actors enough to hire them for their acting, unless they already have a reputation.... They trust hiring someone who is the character, much more than they trust someone to act it.
Sally Field, Actress
Interview in *Screen Actor*, 1986

1657. A great number of competent actors ... could have acted the part but couldn't have looked it.
Raphael D. Silver
Interview in *Film Forum*, 1985

1658. It's not just a matter of having a good actor; you have to have exactly the right actor.
Tony Richardson, Director
Interview in *Films and Filming*, 1961

1659. I am well aware of the fact that the present cumbersome and haphazard method by which screen talent is selected will not endure long. Time will find this matter adjusted upon a basis of merit....
D. W. Griffith
Interview in *Collier's* magazine, 1924

1660. If you cast well then half the battle is already won.... You reached into a crowded world and pulled a man, a woman or a child from thin air and plugged them into your vision.
Steven Spielberg, Director
Cited in *Take 22: Moviemakers on Moviemaking*, 1984

1661. Steven (Spielberg) is one of those people who do their direction of actors in the casting.
Paul Freeman
Cited in *Steven Spielberg — The Unauthorized Biography*, 1996

1662. Someone comes in, and they can either do it or not. And you pick that person who can do it the best. I mean, it's really no more mysterious than that.
Woody Allen
Interview in *The New York Times Magazine,* 1997

1663. There (are) no big or small parts. All parts (are) star parts, even if they lasted five seconds.
Frank Capra, Producer-Director
Stated in his 1971 *Frank Capra — The Name Above the Title*

1664. One person can paint a picture; one person can sing a song; one person can write a poem, but it takes a whole lot of people to make a movie.
Hollywood saying

1665. There is too much talent and not enough work in the movies.
Lillian Gish, Actress
Cited on the Internet Movie Database, 1998, referenced circa 1930

1666. When I was in casting, I thought the only thing agents did was give out incorrect availabilities and misquote actors' prices.
Toni Howard, Co-chair of Motion Picture Talent at ICM
Cited in *Movieline* magazine, 1998

1667. As far as actors are concerned, casting directors are the keys to the kingdom.
Noel Black, Director
Cited in *Your Film Acting Career*, 1989

1668. Nobody pays me to keep people out of work.
Jim Gibson, Theatrical Agent
Cited in *Your Film Acting Career*, 1989, referring to actors not being selected

1669. The most distressing thing is when an actor feels the people he's going to read for are enemies…. We all want you to be terrific.
Ron Stephenson, Casting Director
Cited in *Your Film Acting Career*, 1989

1670. You can't ask anything of the people who you audition for. That's one of the key things. You come in telling, you don't come in asking.
Sally Field, Actress
Interview in *Screen Actor*, 1986

1671. Disney, of course, has the best casting. If he doesn't like an actor, he just tears him up.
Alfred Hitchcock, Director
Cited on the Internet Movie Database,
1998, on Walt Disney animated pictures

1672. The studios recognize the marketing potential of discovering someone.
Bryan Lourd, Agent
Cited in *Premiere* magazine, 1998

1673. There's something marvelously efficient about working with actors that you know. There's less time wasted with diplomacy and more time used in getting the performance.
Sydney Pollack, Director
Interview in *Take 22: Moviemakers
on Moviemaking*, 1984

1674. (Actors who have) been used thousands of times … are like old worn coins that the public doesn't respond to freshly and so doesn't believe in the character they are playing.
Tony Richardson, Director
Interview in *Films and Filming* magazine, 1961

1675. (Being) committed to a star (as a producer) … [i]n a way, that would be like a painter saying, "Gosh, I've got all this red. Now, what can I do with red? I've got to do a lot of red pictures.
Richard Lester, Director
Interview in *Directors at Work*, 1970

1676. Talent is like a precious stone … you take care of it … you put it in a safe … you clean it, polish it, look after it.
Louis B. Mayer, Studio Head–Producer
Cited in *Mayer and Thalberg—The Make
Believe Saints*, 1975, referring to contract actors

1677. I like actors less than I do personalities.
Howard Hawks, Director
Stated in *Hawks on Hawks*, 1972

1678. We can't afford to ignore talent because we don't like the personality that goes with it.
Irving Thalberg
Cited in *Mayer and Thalberg*, 1975

1679. I believe in choosing distinct types and then seeing that the actor puts his own personality into his parts, instead of making every part in a picture reflect my personality.
Ida May Park, Director
Interview in *Photoplay*, 1918

1680. The camera likes some people and the camera dislikes other people.
Howard Hawks, Director
Stated in *Hawks on Hawks*, 1972

1681. I don't think that any of the greats can ever be really bad (actors) because they have something special, and the camera brings it out.
Mervyn LeRoy, Director
Interview in *Films of the
Golden Age* magazine, 1998

1682. I want to make it as easy as possible. I don't like people to act. I want their character on the screen to be it. For me, that's what casting is about.
Andre de Toth, Director
Interview in *Movie Maker* magazine, 1998

1683. You shouldn't have bought the pig in the sack.
Ingrid Bergman
Cited in *Ingrid Bergman—My Story*, 1980,
to producer David O. Selznick for
wanting to transform her personal image

1684. The truly popular movie comedians had one quality that set them apart … humanity.
Leonard Maltin, Film Critic—Author
Stated in his 1978 *The Great Movie Comedians*

1685. All great comic films laugh at the absurdity of the world, but laugh most of all at the comic's persona: Chaplin, Keaton, Lloyd, and early Woody Allen all have this in common.
Douglas Brode, Author
Cited in *Woody Allen
—His Films and Career*, 1985

1686. I'm looking for work, as an actor or actress.
Walter Matthau, Actor
Cited in *Inside Oscar*, 1996

1687. I'll read without clothes if he wants.
Gloria Stuart, Actress
Cited in *Entertainment Weekly*, 1998, at age
87, when asked if she would read without
makeup for a possible part in *Titanic*, 1997

1688. I will play anything, but Henry V and that sort of stuff.
Clint Eastwood
Cited in *Clint Eastwood—A Biography*, 1996

1689. What a challenge! I can't imagine how you will ever get Jean Harlow to play a tart.

Herman J. Mankiewicz, Screenwriter
Cited in *George Cukor—A Double Life*, 1991

1690. Any part, any time, any price, anywhere.

James Woods, Actor
Cited in *Film Comment* magazine, 1997, referring to a message left by him on Martin Scorsese's answering machine

1691. [A]s genuine as a fingerprint.

John Huston
Selecting for the role of Eve, Ulla Bergryd for the film *The Bible*, as cited in *The Hustons*, 1989

1692. The sonuvabitch looked like a man.

Raoul Walsh, Director
Cited in *John Wayne's America*, 1997

1693. No one is as good as Bette (Davis) when she's bad.

Movie Poster
For *In This Our Life—1942*, as cited in *Entertainment Weekly 100*, "The 100 Greatest Movie Stars of All Time," 1997

1694. If John Huston calls, tell him I died.

Robert Mitchum
Cited in *The Hustons*, 1989, on not wanting the lead role in *The Misfits*, c. 1959

1695. I can't imagine Clark Gable chasing you for ten years.

David O. Selznick, Producer
Cited in *Bette and Joan—The Divine Feud*, 1989, rejecting Katharine Hepburn as Scarlett for *Gone with the Wind*, c. 1939

1696. A lot of the parts I want they give to Robert Redford.

Walter Matthau, Actor
Interview in *Take 22: Moviemakers on Moviemaking*, 1984

1697. If you were casting *High Noon* today, who could leave Grace Kelly behind and walk down the street like Gary Cooper did? I think only Sean Connery could.

Larry Gordon, Producer
Interview in *GQ*, 1989

1698. There are two kinds of romantic leading men in American movies. There's the godlike person you've never met, like Cary Grant, and there's the boy next door you've known all your life, like Jimmy Stewart.

Nora Ephron, Director
Interview in *The Los Angeles Times Calendar*, 1993

1699. Until I came along, all the leading men were handsome, but luckily they wrote a lot of stories about the fellow next door.

Gary Cooper, Actor
Cited in *Chronicle of the Cinema*, 1995

1700. If you've got an obnoxious character you want the audience to like, he's your man.

Sean Mitchell, Writer
On Richard Dreyfuss, as cited in *The Los Angeles Times Calendar*, 1991

1701. If Dustin Hoffman wants to act in your movie, you know two things — that you're about to spend a season in hell, and that when it's finished what you've made will have greatness in it.

Stephen Schiff, Critic
Interview in *The Sunday Times*, London, 1993

1702. I was in a movie Marlon Brando was in, I figured I must have been pretty good.

Laurence Fishburne
Interview in *Boxoffice*, 1995, referring to *Apocalypse Now*, 1979, at age 14

1703. If blue eyes are what it's all about, and not the accumulation of my work as a professional actor, I may as well turn in my union card right now and go into gardening.

Paul Newman
Cited in *Paul Newman*, 1989

1704. Can't act. Can't sing. Slightly bald. Can dance a little.

Talent Scout, 1933
Cited in *Chronicle of the Cinema*, 1994, on Fred Astaire

1705. You've just thrown away 500 bucks on a (screen) test. Didn't you see the size of that guy's ears?

Darryl F. Zanuck
On rookie actor Clark Cable, as cited in *Films of the Golden Age* magazine, 1998

1706. I just lacked the look that decade called for.

Clint Eastwood
Cited in *Clint Eastwood—A Biography*, 1996, referring to the 1950s

1707. "C" comes before "D" and "S"; so count me in.

Joan Crawford, Actress
Cited in *Bette and Joan—The Divine Feud*, 1989, learning that the new film's credits would be alphabetical with co-stars Bette Davis and Barbara Stanwyck

1708. For audiences to hate me, they would first have to notice me.

Bette Davis, Actress
Cited in *Bette and Joan—The Divine Feud*,
1989, fighting with Jack Warner for better roles

1709. Forget it. Mayer never chased me around his desk. Of course, he never gave me good parts either.

Angela Lansbury, Actress
Cited on the Internet Movie Database,
1998, on producer Louis B. Mayer

1710. Don't use me in your movie. Get a giant, or a dwarf, or even better, use a puppet that looks like Fellini.

Federico Fellini
Cited in *Fellini—A Life*, 1986, on
being cast for *Alex in Wonderland*

1711. No, thank you. I'm tired. Please, oh please, just let me stay home.

Peggy Ashcroft
On initially declining a part in
A Passage to India at age 75,
in 1983, later winning the Oscar for
her Best Supporting Actress role, 1985

1712. I asked for a first violinist and instead got a soloist.

David O. Selznick, Producer, *A Farewell to Arms*
Cited in *The Hustons*, 1989,
on firing director John Huston, 1956

1713. I'm not going to test you. You have the role. And I have a .22. If you don't come through for me, I'll shoot out every arc light on the set and maybe you too.

Bill Wellman, Producer
To actress Ida Lupino, 1965,
as cited in *The Los Angeles Times*

1714. I see it up there—Barrymore and Huston—and let's have our grandfathers and our fathers looking down and smiling.

Drew Barrymore, Actress
Cited in *Movieline* magazine, 1998, to
Cinderella co-star Anjelica Huston on
being the legacies of famous film stars

1715. I'm even jealous of Julia Roberts as Tinkerbell.

Richard Dreyfuss
Cited in *Steven Spielberg—The Unauthorized Biography*, 1996, referring to
casting opportunities other actors get

1716. It's only about how you look. In Holly-wood, age is always an issue because it's made an issue.

Mimi Rogers, Actress
Cited in *Movieline* magazine,
1998, on getting youthful roles

1717. What has age to do with talent?

Spencer Tracy, Actor
Cited in *Film Comment* magazine, 1968

1718. For 50 pesos, señor, you can shoot them in the arms and legs. But mind you, no killing.

Mexican casting agent
To director John Huston on the hiring of
local extras in Tampico, Mexico, for
The Treasure of the Sierra Madre,
1947, as cited in *The Hustons*, 1989

1719. When (producers) want someone to be rotten and dastardly, the first thing they say is, "We've got to get someone who's a foreigner."

Michael Caine, Actor
Interview in *Take 22: Moviemakers
on Moviemaking*, 1984

1720. We haven't seen one movie where the hero is black.... I just want one to cheer for. Like I cheer for Terminator ... for Rambo ... for James Bond. I just want one....

Robert Townsend, Actor-Director
Interview in *Interview* magazine, 1991

1721. Black actors will look at the trade papers and if the casting list doesn't say "black sergeant," they won't go out for the part. And if the script doesn't say "black sergeant," the producers and directors won't look for one.

Louis Gossett, Jr., Actor
Interview in *People* magazine, 1982

1722. I think it is very uninspired of casting directors to wait for the role to say "black woman".... They are simply denying their imaginations.

Alfre Woodard, Actress
Interview in *The Christian Science Monitor*, 1987

1723. It would not be accurate to say that serious black actors don't get a chance at dramatic roles. For any actor to get cast in any part is a very long shot.

Charlton Heston, Actor
Referenced at an AMPAS meeting in 1989
regarding the previous 25 years

1724. To me, the "talking head" is the essence of cinema.... If you've got the right face saying the right things at the right moment, you've got everything cinema can offer.

David Cronenberg, Director
Interview in *Inner Views: Filmmakers
in Conversation*, 1992

1725. Typecasting is slow death for actors.
Irving Thalberg, MGM
Cited in *Mayer and Thalberg*, 1975

1726. The minute they can pin you down, you are stuck like a butterfly on a piece of paper.
Minnie Driver, Actress
Interview in *Biography*, 1998, on typecasting

1727. Most actors hate the term of typecasting. But it is more important in them as creative people, as artists that they have an ability, an aura, a mood or a look, a feel that has a great deal to do with the role.
Norman Jewison, Director
Interview in *Directors at Work*, 1970

1728. Show me a blond leading man.
Louis B. Mayer
Cited in *Mayer and Thalberg*, 1975, protesting
the use of Nelson Eddy in a lead role, 1933

1729. Being blond, blue-eyed and having a lot of energy is an image that people connect with the girl next door.
Doris Day, Actress
Interview in *Ms.* magazine,
1976, on being typecast

1730. I like to take actors who've always played heavies and make them nice people — or the other way around.
Guy Hamilton, Director
Interview in *Take 22: Moviemakers
on Moviemaking*, 1984

1731. Whenever they need somebody to deliver a baby, they say, "See if you can get Matthau."
Walter Matthau, Actor
Interview in *Take 22: Moviemakers
on Moviemaking*, 1984

1732. Gino Corrado for "waiter"? He's the waiter in every movie ever made.
Orson Welles
Cited in *Orson Welles:
The Road to Xanadu*, 1996

1733. You know, I'm a kosher colored kid from Brooklyn — I'm not supposed to be able to do ("Othello").
Laurence Fishburne, Actor
Interview in *Boxoffice*, 1995, to his director

1734. But I (come) from Sweden where acting meant certainty of change. You got inside somebody else's skin.
Ingrid Bergman, Actress
Stated in *Ingrid Bergman — My Story*, 1980,
not wanting the Hollywood typecasting

1735. I believe I was lacking the things they wanted an actress to lack.
Elizabeth Hartman, Actress
Cited in *Inside Oscar*, 1996, being
cast for a role of a "luckless" girl

1736. I like to use real people ... to fill in the landscape around the actors; it helps their reality.
Henry Jaglon, Director
Interview in *Film Forum*, 1985

1737. Films (are) novels filled with living people. I cast actors that I (believe) could be those living people.
Frank Capra, Producer-Director
Stated in *Frank Capra
— The Name Above the Title*, 1971

1738. Now, you see why I use amateurs (locals). If I'd used actors they wouldn't carry all that (equipment).
Roberto Rossellini, Producer-Director
Cited in *Ingrid Bergman — My Story*,
1980, on not casting professional actors

1739. People accused me of filling my films with freaks. Then I looked around me and felt my characters were normal by comparison.
Federico Fellini
Cited in *Fellini — A Life*, 1986

1740. I picked ugly people. I tried to make it as real as possible....
Irving Rapper, Director
Cited in *George Cukor — A Double Life*, 1991

1741. The face means everything. I'd rather have a great face than a great actor in a lot of cases.
Federico Fellini
Cited in *Clint Eastwood — A Biography*, 1996

1742. Our "nuns" carried makeup cases and smoked cigarettes between set-ups....
Fred Zinnemann, Director
Stated in *Fred Zinnemann — An
Autobiography*, 1992, on the actresses
cast for *The Nun's Story*, 1959

1743. I'm not looking for an actress who can play a lady, I want an actress who is a lady.
Orson Welles
Cited in *Orson Wells: The Road to Xanadu*,
1996, to actress Ruth Warrick,
"Emily" in *Citizen Kane*, c. 1940

1744. It's very hard when you have an icon playing an ordinary person.
Steven Spielberg
Cited in *Steven Spielberg
— The Unauthorized Biography*, 1996

1745. Sex appeal is difficult to define. And when you try, it becomes even less clear.

Sean Connery, Actor
Interview in *People* magazine, 1989

1746. To me, sex is class, something more than a wiggly behind. If it weren't, I know two hundred whores who would be stars.

Frank Capra, Producer-Director
Stated in his 1971 *Frank Capra*

1747. Casting was a great way to be paid for being opinionated.

Toni Howard, Co-chair of
Motion Picture Talent at ICM
Cited in *Movieline* magazine, 1998

1748. The popular American sport of castigating actors for taking parts in bad movies is based on the erroneous assumption that movie stars are captains of their fate.

Richard Dreyfuss
Cited in *The Los Angeles Times Calendar*, 1991

1749. (Casting) finally comes down to a guess.

Tim Burton, Director
Interview in *Inner Views:*
Filmmakers in Conversation, 1992

1750. If the movie gods are going to shine on you, they will.

Ray Liotta
Cited in *Movieline* magazine, 1998, Actor

14

Acting

1751. (Movies:) It's the grandest show business I know anything about and the only place where an actor can act and at the same time sit down in front and clap for himself.

Will Rogers
Cited in *His Wife's Story* biography, 1941

1752. Great actors are produced by great films.

Roger Ebert
Cited in *Questions for the Movie Answer Man*, 1997

1753. It takes a long time for an actor to get over the thought that whatever he's doing at the moment may be his last job.

Clint Eastwood
Cited in *Clint Eastwood — A Biography*, 1996

1754. What interested me about acting was character work. Craft was important.

Robert Redford
Cited in *The New York Times Magazine,* 1997

1755. I resent people who have big talents and don't work at it, because I have a tiny talent and I squeeze the tube about as dry as it is going to get.

Paul Newman
Stated on *The Today Show* — NBC

1756. To be an actor it is essential to be an ego-maniac; otherwise, it doesn't work.

David Niven
Cited in *Bette and Joan — The Divine Feud,* 1986

1757. You have to have a certain amount of ego in filmmaking … you have to get in front of the camera and think that it is all about you.

Gene Hackman, Actor
Interview in *The Los Angeles Times Magazine,* 1994

1758. Good actors make you feel good.

Anjelica Huston
On playing scenes, as cited in *The Hustons,* 1989

1759. You learn acting from life, and that goes on around you all the time.

Ingrid Bergman

1760. The development of the person precedes the craft.

Gilbert Cates, Director
Interview in *Film Makers on Film Making,* 1983, on becoming an actor

1761. (The best actors are) very humble people, almost embarrassed about their own personality. They're not quite sure how to manifest in real life. As soon as they find a character, they just come alive.

Sam Shepard, Actor-Director-Playwright
Interview in *Premiere* magazine, 1998

1762. The scenes and characters I play don't affect me or my personal life, but my personal life, I think, affects the characters and scenes I play.

Gary Cooper, Actor
Interview in *Silver Screen* magazine, 1941

1763. If you want to be an actress, throw your contract in the ash can and wait for good parts.

Hedda Hopper, Hollywood columnist
Cited in *The Chicago Sunday Tribune,* 1949

1764. Acting is fine, just don't get caught at it.

Spencer Tracy
Cited in *The Camera Smart Actor,* 1994

1765. I had to resort to acting.

Gregory Peck, Actor
On how could he play a despicable character like Josef Mengele in *The Boys from Brazil*

1766. Saying a gay man can't convincingly make love to a woman on the screen — of course he can. It's called acting.

Sir Ian McKellen, Actor
Cited in *Vanity Fair,* 1999

1767. I'd like to learn a little more about acting before it's too late.

Ralph Richardson, Actor
Commenting late in his life — age 80,
c. 1982 as cited in *Variety*, 1997

1768. The more I see good actors, the more I understand. What I've been doing is mugging … but there's another way to go. I could, for instance, learn how to act. That would be nice.

Chevy Chase, Actor, 1988
Interview in *Playboy*, June, 1988

1769. An actor is fooling with reality … doing strange, bizarre, magical things.

Jon Voight, Actor
Interview in *CUE*, New York, 1979

1770. An actor is akin to the magician — an illusionist in the profession of making things look real.

Brian Adams, Author
Written in his *Screen Acting*, 1986

1771. A magician is an actor impersonating a magician.

Jean Eugene Robert-Houdin
Cited in *True and False: Heresy and Common Sense for the Actor*, 1997

1772. Acting is only the second oldest profession, but society has always looked on both trades with equal suspicion.

Charlton Heston
Cited in *Movie Business: American Film Industry Practice*, 1972

1773. Acting is like begging in India … an honorable and humble experience.

Nathan Lane, Actor
Upon receiving a People's
Choice Award, 1999, on CBS

1774. You spend all your life trying to do something they put people in asylums for.

Jane Fonda
Cited on the Internet Movie Database, 1998

1775. It became a little bit real…. Acting always brings out demons.

Mira Sorvino
On the actor's playing a scene too
realistically in *Replacement Killers*, 1998

1776. The only difference between an actor professionally and an actor in life is the professional knows a little bit more about it … and they get paid for it.

Marlon Brando
Interview in *Conversations with Brando*, 1991

1777. I shall prepare a face to meet the faces that I meet.

T. S. Eliot, Poet
Recited by Marlon Brando, interviewed
in *Conversations with Brando*,
1991, on everyone being an actor

1778. If you think you're a great actor 'cause you won an Oscar, you're crazy.

Joe Pesci
Commenting upon winning his Oscar
at the 1991 Academy Awards party

1779. It's not all that fancy. Life's what's important — acting is just waiting for a custard pie. That's all.

Katharine Hepburn
Interview in *Biography* magazine, 1998

1780. Acting is a heartbreaking business. You're using your emotions.

Kirk Douglas
Cited in *Screen Acting*, 1986

1781. Who acts undertakes to suffer.

Aeschylus
Cited in *Funny Business:
The Craft of Comedy Writing*, 1985

1782. (Acting) — for me it's like tearing your soul apart for money.

Sean Penn, Actor
Interview in *The Los Angeles
Times Calendar*, 1991

1783. Being the wood that the nail banged into doesn't feel good — that's what acting (is).

Sean Penn, Actor
Interview in *Los Angeles Style* magazine, 1991

1784. Acting is not an important job in the scheme of things. Plumbing is.

Spencer Tracy
Cited on the Internet Movie Database, 1998

1785. I don't think acting is all that wonderful; I am not so proud to be an actress.

Greta Garbo
Commenting to director George Cukor,
as cited in his biography, *George Cukor
— A Double Life*, 1989

1786. Sometimes you want to tell the (audience), "If you only knew what we've been going through!"

Burt Lancaster, Actor
Interview in *Take 22: Moviemakers
on Moviemaking*, 1984

1787. Well, the truth is, no actor has any real power. Every single one of us is in service to somebody.

Sharon Stone
Cited in *The New York Times Magazine,* 1997

1788. An actor tells a story the way his conscience dictates is best to tell it … it's up to their conscience and artistic sense.

Harvey Keitel, Actor
Interview in *Playboy,* November, 1995

1789. You can't get it out of them unless it's in them (actors).

Elia Kazan, Director
Cited in *Entertainment Weekly,*
1998, as his acting axiom

1790. Every great movie actor is adroit at being themselves.

Robert Towne, Writer-Director
Cited on a 1999 televised cable interview

1791. There are some scenes, some parts, that are actor proof. If you don't get in the way of a part it plays by itself.

Marlon Brando
Interview in *Conversations with Brando,* 1991

1792. If St. Peter asks my opinion of Thespians, I will say, "God bless them all! From stars to extras, from hams to shams, bless them all!"

Frank Capra, Producer-Director
Stated in his *Frank Capra
— The Name Above the Title,* 1971

1793. Acting is damned hard work. It's not something to fool around with.

John Wayne
Cited in *Screen Acting,* 1986

1794. Quite simply, it's very hard to do good work. It always was and it always will be.

Dustin Hoffman
Interview in *The Sunday Times London,* 1993

1795. The first thing you learn as an actor is that it's a cold bucket of water everyday.

Peter O'Toole, Actor
Interview in *European Travel & Life,* 1990

1796. Acting great parts devours you.

Sir Laurence Olivier
Cited in *Screen Acting,* 1986

1797. If it's a terribly difficult part, I don't see him

at all. Oh, he's there, all right, but he isn't. He's off inside his head somewhere.

Joanne Woodward
Cited in *Entertainment Weekly 100,* 1998, referring to her actor husband Paul Newman

1798. Acting is not an all-consuming thing, except for the moment when I am actually doing it.

William Holden
Cited in *Entertainment Weekly 100,* 1998

1799. The actor works with himself as surely as a philosopher does with his brain, or a prostitute with her body.

Micheál Mac Liammoir
Cited in *Orson Welles: The Road to Xanadu,* 1996

1800. For an actor, the only way you can work is from your senses.

Jessica Lange, Actress
Interview in *American Film* magazine, 1990

1801. An actor's discomfort sometimes works well for him. It is not out of the realm of possibility to have the audience mistake discomfort for rage. At which time the actor is way ahead of the game.

Paul Newman
Stated in *Paul Newman,* 1989

1802. I … dared to play certain key moments out of control, as a skier will throw all restraint to the winds in order to achieve a new mark.

Sophia Loren
Cited in *Sophia Loren — A Biography,* 1998, on her performance in *Two Women*

1803. Only the great, great actors have an inexhaustible source of variety. Brando, when he is really on, when he is interested, when he is involved, can do it.

Paul Newman
Stated in *Paul Newman,* 1989

1804. Actors are like sponges, everything they see is absorbed in the body and you squeeze little parts of it whenever you need it.

Alfre Woodard, Actress
Interview in *Drama-Logue* magazine, 1983

1805. Bad acting is the same the world over and that when an actor has talent, this too is universal.

Jean Renoír, French director
Stated in his autobiography, *Jean Renoir —
My Life and Times,* 1974

1806. Italy is full of actors, fifty million of them

... and they are almost all good; there are only a few bad ones, and they are on the stage and screen.
Orson Welles
Cited in *Sophia Loren—A Biography*, 1998

1807. To be a good actor you have to be a child.
Paul Newman
Stated in *Paul Newman*, 1989

1808. If you think about it, it's a bit silly being an actor because we're a bit like children playing at being someone else. You play with a character that has nothing to do with your real life.
Michael Douglas, Actor
Interview in *Hello* magazine (UK), c. 1989

1809. The ideal thing would be to act just by yourself, in a room somewhere. The next best thing is doing it in front of a minimal crew and, after that, appearing before small audiences of people.
Clint Eastwood
Cited in *Clint Eastwood—A Biography*, 1996

1810. I think that's what's addictive about acting. That for a few seconds you get a hit of being in some other world.
Gabriel Byrne
Interview in *Movieline*, 1998

1811. I had no desire to be an actor. If I had, I would have said, "Could I have a spear to hold."
Orson Welles
Stated in *Orson Welles: The Road to Xanadu*, 1996

1812. The poor Burtons had to spit at each other and hit each other for days.
Mike Nichols, Director
On Elizabeth Taylor and Richard Burton in *Who's Afraid of Virginia Woolf?* 1966, as cited in *Chronicle of the Cinema*, 1995

1813. Most of us would put the imagination first in the actor's equipment.
Minnie Maddern Fiske
Stated in *Mrs. Fiske: Her Views on Actors, Acting and the Problems of Production*, 1917

1814. It isn't beauty or personality or magnetism that makes a really great actress. It is imagination....
Laurette Taylor
Interview in *The Green Book* magazine, 1914

1815. Drama is imagination. Dramatically ... you vitiate the power of a good obscene word if you use it too much ... there may be more drama in not saying the obscenity.
Walter Matthau
Interview in *Take 22: Moviemakers on Moviemaking*, 1984

1816. Acting is a way of dreaming. My acting is an extension of my dreaming.... I cast myself into the role of my fantasies.
Mel Gibson
Cited in *Screen Acting*, 1986

1817. "Technique" is the occupation of a second-rate mind. Act as you would in your fantasy.
David Mamet, Writer-Director
Written in his *True and False*, 1997

1818. My pictures are make-believe. Actors should do the same.
Alfred Hitchcock, Director
Cited in *Screen Acting*, 1986

1819. Acting is an illusion, as much an illusion as magic. It's the ability to dream on cue. Actors have to dream to order.
Ralph Richardson
Cited in *Screen Acting*, 1986

1820. (Acting is) a game of pretends. For what is acting but lying, and what is good acting but convincing lying?
Sir Laurence Olivier
Cited in *Screen Acting*, 1986

1821. Acting is just one big bag of tricks.
Sir Laurence Olivier
Cited in *Screen Acting*, 1986

1822. I like leaving surprises for the director.
John Travolta, Actor
Interview in *Los Angeles* magazine, 1998

1823. Acting is the expression of a neurotic impulse.
Marlon Brando
Cited in *The Stanislavsky Heritage*, 1965

1824. Some performers can communicate their neuroses, their joys and their sorrows.... Others of us remain in an unfathomable, amorphous state — undefined inside.
Sylvester Stallone, Actor
Interview in *The Los Angeles Times Calendar*, 1998

1825. I think people become artists in order to express or ease the contradiction between their conscious mind and their unconscious.
Steve Martin, Actor
Interview in *Parade* magazine, 1998

1826. Acting is an opportunity to dip into emotions you might not have the time or inclination to explore.

Jessica Lange, Actress
Interview in *Vogue*, 1990

1827. To me, acting is the most logical way for a person with problems to express himself.

James Dean, Actor
Cited in *Hollywood Studio* magazine, 1985

1828. The mind is always the great factor, not the emotions, in acting.... It is the brain every time which wins out in the long run.

Lon Chaney, Actor
Interview in *The Morning Telegraph*, 1924

1829. The actor's art is to express in well-known symbols what an individual man may be supposed to feel; and we, as spectators, recognizing these expressions, are drawn into sympathy.

Genevieve Stebbins
Cited in *Delsorte System of Expression*, 1902

1830. Acting, when it is done at its best, is behaving as if you were alive in a set of given circumstances that are different from your own given circumstances.

Joan Darling, Director
Cited in *Acting Is Everything*, 1981

1831. Acting is as distinguished as a piece of music.

Kirk Douglas
Cited in *Screen Acting*, 1986

1832. "Action" is not physical movement. "Action" is an internal occurrence.

Unknown
On acting, as cited in
The Language of Show Biz

1833. Acting is a verb.

Sidney Lumet, Director
Stated in his *Making Movies*, 1995

1834. The Stanislavsky "Method," and the technique of the schools derived from it, is nonsense. It is not a technique out of the practice of which one develops a skill — it is a cult.

David Mamet, Writer-Director
Written in his *True and False*, 1997

1835. I've read ... from Strasberg to Stanislavsky and, in my opinion, you just take what you need and discard the rest.

Johnny Depp
Interview in *Biography* magazine, 1998

1836. There's no method to acting. There might

be a method to getting there, learning ... preparing to act, but not to doing it. You could compare it to a method boxer.

Morgan Freeman, Actor
Interview in *Los Angeles View*, 1995

1837. It's as if they're trying to impose their psychiatric difficulties on the audience.

Joan Crawford
Cited in *Inside Oscar*, 1996,
commenting on "method" actors

1838. What measure of serenity I have in my life today is the direct result of analysis. It brought me every possible benefit.

Paul Newman
Stated in *Paul Newman*, 1984

1839. I do not assume that the doctor, or the musician or the dancer or painter, strives first to bring himself to a "state," and only then directs his efforts outward.

David Mamet, Writer-Director
Criticizing "method" acting in
his *True and False*, 1997

1840. There are those actors who explain to you that they know exactly how they're going to do the part ... then there is the other method, which is to have no method at all. This is mine. I didn't choose it, nor did I decide that it was a method.

Simone Signoret, Actress
Stated in her biography, *Nostalgia
Isn't What It Used to Be*, 1978

1841. Intellectualizing ... has little to do with acting, and is liable to fall into arid dogma. Simplicity of approach is always best.

Charlie Chaplin
Stated in *My Autobiography
— Charlie Chaplin*, 1964

1842. I'm not really sure how (acting) works.... I don't want to break down the process of acting. I think there could be a danger of constipating it.

Nicolas Cage, Actor
Interview in *The Los Angeles
Times Magazine*, 1996

1843. I feel a real need not to think, not to analyze. When I'm filming I need someone who's going to think and analyze for me — the director.

Simone Signoret, Actress
Stated in her biography, *Nostalgia Isn't
What It Used to Be*, 1978

1844. The actor who thinks too much is driven by the ambition to be great. It is a terrible obstacle which runs to the risk of eliminating much truth from his performance.

> Míchelangelo Antonioni
> Interview in *Film Culture* magazine, 1961

1845. I'm not a method actress. I don't dig directors who want me to analyze my role. The only method I have goes, "Dear God, I hope I make it today."

> Ida Lupino, Actress/Director
> Interview in the *Los Angeles Express*, 1972

1846. When I first read a script, my response is not intellectual, it's emotional.

> Annette Bening, Actress
> Interview in *The Los Angeles Times Calendar*, 1991

1847. I'm not a method star. What I try to do is play a part honestly, how it reacts to me.

> Spencer Tracy, Actor
> Interview in *The San Francisco Examiner & Chronicle*, 1967

1848. I have a "method." I'm a fully trained actor.

> Sean Connery, Actor
> Interview in *Vanity* magazine, 1993

1849. Every good actor has a method, whether it is something he realizes or not.

> Montgomery Clift, Actor
> Cited in *The Citizen News*, 1960

1850. Your salary.

> Alfred Hitchcock
> Responding to an actor's request for a scene's motivation, as cited in *David Lean — A Biography*, 1995

1851. There's nothing depending upon your performance except your whole career.

> Alfred Hitchcock, Director
> Commenting to an actor waiting before the camera, 1957, cited in *The Saturday Evening Post*

1852. Honey, just think of Coca-Cola and Frank Sinatra.

> Paula Strasberg
> The acting coach's advice cited in *Clown Prince of Hollywood*, 1990

1853. I do not need to think I have two legs. I have them.

> Míchelangelo Antonioni
> Interview in *Film Culture* magazine, 1961

1854. (The audience) will invest you with the feelings they expect you to have! So you can trust being simple. You must be simple!

> Eric Stephan Kline, Author
> Cited in *Acting for the Camera*, 1997

1855. Make film acting simple. Don't clutter it up with a lot of overly-physical gymnastics.

> George Cukor, Director
> Cited in *Screen Acting*, 1986

1856. The secret of movie acting is — seeming to do nothing before the camera.

> Alec Guinness, Actor
> Interview in *The Dial* magazine, 1981

1857. A lot of actors do what I call the constipate school of acting. It becomes "uuhhh" … I like acting you can't catch. When you make it look easy, you're doing it right.

> Burt Reynolds, Actor-Director
> Interview in *Take 22: Moviemakers on Moviemaking*, 1984

1858. The skill of acting is like the skill of sport, which is a physical event. And like that endeavor, it's difficulty consists to a large extent in being much simpler than it seems.

> David Mamet, Writer-Director
> Written in his *True and False*, 1997

1859. I've tried to make movie acting not acting — but just being a person, even though it isn't me.

> Michael Caine
> Interview in *Take 22: Moviemakers on Moviemaking*, 1984

1860. [T]he film actor should content himself with saying his lines. He should not allow himself to show that he already understands them. Play nothing, explain nothing.

> Robert Bresson, Director
> Cited in *Great Film Directors: A Critical Anthology*, 1978

1861. When you make it look easy, that's when you're doing it the best.

> Morgan Freeman
> Cited in *Paul Newman*, 1989

1862. Good acting, like good anything, doesn't look like there's a lot of effort with it.

> Clint Eastwood
> Cited in *Clint Eastwood — A Biography*, 1996

1863. Increasingly my approach to performing is to be totally abandoned, as unprepared and unintellectualized as possible.

> Sigourney Weaver
> Interview in *Entertainment Yearbook*, 1998

1864. I find more juices to spend on my work if my work makes a comment.
Sidney Poitier, Actor
Interview in *The New York Times*, 1967

1865. The tendency with actors is to think that if you're doing more, you're doing more.
Sydney Pollack, Director
On keeping the performance simple, as
cited in *Acting for the Camera*, 1997

1866. I was used to working on a tightrope onstage. A movie is just a line painted on the floor.
Al Pacino, Actor
Interview in *Esquire* magazine, 1996

1867. Making it simple.
Sir John Gielgud
On what is the most difficult thing for him in
acting, as cited in *Acting for the Camera*, 1997

1868. An actor's concern with talent is like a gambler's concern with luck. Luck … is either going to favor everyone equally or going to exhibit a preference for the prepared.
David Mamet, Writer-Producer
Written in his *True and False*, 1997

1869. A concern with one's talent is like a concern with one's height — it is an attempt to appropriate prerogative which the gods have already exercised.
David Mamet, Writer-Producer
Written in his *True and False*, 1997

1870. There is no such thing as an important actor or an unimportant one. There is only the actor who gives full expression to the purpose to which he owes his presence.
Josef von Sternberg
Interview in *Film Culture* magazine, 1955

1871. Most of acting is reacting, and you only react if you're listening. I think if you have a talent for acting, it is the talent for listening.
Morgan Freeman
Interview in *Los Angeles View*, 1995

1872. If actors have talent, they're easy to shoot. If they don't, nothing helps.
Mervyn LeRoy, Director
Cited in *Screen Acting*, 1986

1873. I learned (acting) in the most terrifying way — in front of the public.
Michael Caine
Interview in *Take 22: Moviemakers
on Moviemaking*, 1984

1874. Every actor that I know is, without exception, terrified.
Richard Attenborough, Actor-Director
Interview in *Film Makers on
Film Making*, Vol. II, 1983

1875. Mary dear, hold my hand, tell me I won't make an ass of myself.
Sidney Greenstreet
To Mary Astor prior to his first movie
scene, as cited in *The Hustons*, 1989

1876. Courage is being scared to death and saddling up anyway.
John Wayne
Cited in *Acting Is Everything*, 1981

1877. In our film profession you may have Gable's looks, Tracy's art, Marlene's legs or Liz's violet eyes … (but they) don't mean a thing without that swinging thing called courage.
Frank Capra, Producer-Director
Stated in his *Frank Capra
— The Name Above the Title*, 1971

1878. It doesn't get any better not doing it.
Michael Rhodes, Producer
Cited in *Your Film Acting Career*,
1989, on taking acting classes

1879. There is no teacher like performing.
Ed Asner, Actor
Cited in *Acting for the Camera*, 1997

1880. Show up on time and know your lines.
Humphrey Bogart
Cited in *Screen Acting*, 1986,
on being a professional

1881. Be the first on the set, word perfect.
Richard Burton
Cited in *Screen Acting*, 1986,
on being a professional

1882. Plant your feet and tell the truth.
James Cagney
Cited in *Clint Eastwood — A Biography*, 1996

1883. [J]ust know your lines and don't bump into the furniture.
Spencer Tracy
Cited in *Entertainment Weekly 100*, 1998

1884. Most actors are expected to come with their parts in their pockets and their emotions spring-loaded.
Marlon Brando
Interview in *Conversations with Brando*, 1991,
on some directors not liking improvisation

1885. I just learn the lines and pray to God.
Claude Rains
Interview in *Film Makers on
Film Making*, Vol. II, 1983,
when asked how he approaches a role

1886. Oh, it's really not so much, just get up and do it.
Dan O'Herlihy
Cited in *Clint Eastwood—A Biography*, 1996

1887. Suddenly somebody shouts "Quiet!" and you've got to present your wares.
Richard Attenborough
Interview in *Film Makers on
Film Making*, Vol. II. 1983

1888. The word "Action!" frees me ... the transformation is something I cannot explain ... too much analysis might destroy it.
Sophia Loren
Cited in *Sophia Loren—A Biography*, 1998

1889. You try to stay enigmatic. That's my job: to be other people.
Jack Nicholson
Cited in *Sports Illustrated*, 1986

1890. So this is acting. I don't have to act, I just have to be.
Robin Williams
On building a character, as cited in
Entertainment Weekly, 1998

1891. I'm more effective playing parts which are farthest from my own self.
Paul Newman
Stated in *Paul Newman*, 1989

1892. I think that once you get the physical quality of a character, the inner person comes by itself.
Paul Newman
Stated in *Paul Newman*, 1989

1893. I played at being someone I wanted to be, until I became that person. Or he became me.
Cary Grant
Cited in *Entertainment Weekly 100*, 1998

1894. I'm just trying to play the human being.
Anthony Hopkins
Cited in *Entertainment Weekly 100*, 1998

1895. I wear the character's attitudes, try them on for size in order to take on the mood, the feeling....
Kirk Douglas
Cited in *Screen Acting*, 1986

1896. Don't force the character on yourself; find the character in yourself.
Eric Stephan Kline, Author
Cited in *Acting for the Camera*, 1997

1897. Never play the character—let the character play you.... I can take his mannerisms or thoughts and let them play through me.
James Woods
Interview in *Film Comment* magazine, 1997

1898. I cannot feel I've got a character set until I'm in his skin. I possess the character. It's like entering his soul.
Jack Lemmon
Cited in *Screen Acting*, 1986

1899. We must see people, not actors in the roles they play.
Alfred Hitchcock, Director
Cited in *Screen Acting*, 1986

1900. I'm a medium, not an orator ... my work enables me to come out of myself. I like what I do, not what I am.
Orson Welles
Stated in *Orson Welles: The Road to Xanadu*, 1996

1901. If you expect the audience to suspend disbelief, then you must do it first; you must believe in who you are.
Eric Stephan Kline, Author
Cited in *Acting for the Camera*, 1997

1902. I'm envious of guys like Olivier and Guinness who seem to have an almost inexhaustible supply of characters in them—all different.
Paul Newman
Stated in *Paul Newman*, 1989

1903. The three totally original characteristics of (Ingrid Bergman) work: truth, naturalness and fantasy.
Gustav Molander, Swedish actor
Cited in *Ingrid Bergman—My Story*, 1980

1904. (Jackie Coogan could) apply emotion to the action and action to the emotion.
Charlie Chaplin
Cited in *Chaplin*, 1974, on his
discovery of the 4-year-old actor

1905. She knew everyone's dialogue, and if you forgot a line, she gave it to you.
Alice Faye
Cited in *Entertainment Weekly 100*,
1998, commenting on Shirley Temple

1906. Bette (Davis) does not play a part, she attacks it. She comes on hungry.

Joseph Cotton
Cited in *Bette and Joan—The Divine Feud*, 1989

1907. When you step outside of yourself it's nothing to admit consciously but you know, like when you're riding a horse ... when you know you're in a good stride....

Alfre Woodard, Actress
Interview in *Drama-Logue* magazine, 1983

1908. What I bring to acting is all that I was, I am and hope to be.

Clark Gable
Cited on "Clark Gable," an A&E *Biography*, 1998

1909. I have been an actress. I want to be a good actress now.

Mary Pickford
Speaking to a producer at age 15, 1908

1910. Generally speaking, when a character cries in a movie, the audience doesn't. To hold back tears is more affecting than to let it all out.

Peter Bogdanovich, Writer-Director
Interview in *Take 22: Moviemakers on Moviemaking*, 1984

1911. Actor's who are acting generously are very much like jazz musicians: they are within the scene, but they are doing things that aren't exactly written. The unspoken word, the notes they are throwing in.

Clint Eastwood, Director
Interview in *Inner Views: Filmmakers in Conversation*, 1992

1912. Words are not important; it's what's under the words, what's making them happen, that's important!

Eric Stephan Kline, Author
Cited in *Acting for the Camera*, 1997

1913. The easiest thing about being an actor is memorizing lines! The stuff you don't see is the exploration of the character.... What's being said isn't all that important.

Tom Cruise, Actor
Interview in *W* magazine, 1997

1914. Emotions are often difficult for the actor to achieve because in real life he is ashamed to reveal that he is capable of experiencing them.

Eric Stephan Kline, Author
Cited in *Acting for the Camera*, 1997

1915. Don't judge too quickly. Don't patronize.

Don't make statements. Don't set people aside. Give them their due.

Robert Duvall
Stating his credo on acting and character development in a 1998 *Time* magazine interview

1916. Drama is when you fight hard not to do something.

Kevin Costner
Interview in *Premiere* magazine, 1998

1917. It's easy for an actor to explode. What's hard is to keep from exploding.

Raul Julia, Actor
Cited in *The Village Voice*, 1976

1918. The only reason to rehearse is to learn to perform the (screenplay).

David Mamet, Writer-Director
Written in his *True and False*, 1997

1919. Preparation is what acting is all about.

Peter O'Toole, Actor
Interview in *US* magazine, 1989

1920. Acting in a way is like investigative reporting. You search out your character.

Denzel Washington, Actor
Interview in *Vanity Fair*, 1995

1921. There's always something to research, even if you're playing a short-order cook.

Al Pacino, Actor
Interview in *Time Out London*, 1993

1922. I don't do much in the way of research ... if it's not on the page, where are you going to find it?

Morgan Freeman, Actor
Interview in *Los Angeles View*, 1995,
on having confidence in the script

1923. Overanalyzing (your acting) can contaminate the process. I don't mean to sound overly delusional about what I do as a performer, but I like to leave it to its own kind of magic.

Dwight Yoakam, Actor-Singer
Interview in *Interview* magazine, 1998

1924. The best thing is, just do it and not explain it. It doesn't need any explaining.

Robert De Niro
Cited on the Internet Movie Database, 1998

1925. If I sat down and really looked at people's expectations, I would get paranoid and not be able to create anything.

Jim Carrey
Interview in *Movieline*, 1998

1926. Never do one foot of film without reviewing what is coming before and ... after.
George Arliss, Director
On screen acting, interviewed in *Film Makers on Film Making*, Vol. II, 1983

1927. The actor needs to know what each shot is "telling," and how it helps to illuminate his character's story.
Richard Brestoff, Actor-Author
Stated in his *The Camera Smart Actor*, 1994

1928. (The task of the film actor) is creating the illusion of a continuous performance.
Vladmir Pudovkin, Director
Cited in *The Camera Smart Actor*, 1994

1929. You can always do it better.
Charlton Heston
Interview in *Film Makers on Film Making*, Vol. II, 1983

1930. We did the scene over and over again. They were ... happy days.
Jimmy Stewart
Cited in *Entertainment Weekly 100*, 1998, commenting on a kissing scene with Jean Harlow

1931. I improvise in front of the camera because I think the actor influences the camera ... and that the camera influences the actor.... I think the thing must be born on the set.
Elio Petri, Director
Speaking at the New York Film Forum, 1985

1932. Improvisation has to be worked out as carefully as a three-act play.
Nicolas Ray, Director
Interview in *Film Makers on Film Making*, Vol. II, 1983

1933. To improvise on an improvisation is always shit.
Ingmar Bergman, Director
Interview in *Film Makers on Film Making*, 1983

1934. The dramatic art is a collective art and, therefore, however talented the actor may be, he will not be able to make full use of his ability to improvise if he isolates himself from the ensemble of his partners.
Michael Chekhov
Cited in *Clint Eastwood—A Biography*, 1996

1935. Improvisation is an extraordinary egotism.
Michael Caine
Cited in *Film Makers on Film Making*, 1983

1936. Listen. I'll say my lines and kiss any actress my paycheck says to kiss; whether I like 'em or not.
Sterling Hayden
Cited in *Bette and Joan—The Divine Feud*, 1989

1937. I will kiss anybody, including pariah dogs, and I don't care who is looking.
Richard Burton
Cited in *Sophia Loren—A Biography*, 1998, on doing love scenes on camera

1938. There is no such thing as over-acting: an actor plays "false" or he plays "true." If he plays true he may allow himself all manner of exaggeration.
Jean Renoir, Director
Written in his *Jean Renoir—My Life and Times*, 1974

1939. (I urge my actors) not to act (but) to aim at sincerity.
Charlie Chaplin
Cited in *Chaplin*, 1974

1940. Don't act. Just don't act.
Laurence Fishburne, Actor
Quoting the advice director Francis Ford Coppola gave him

1941. The effort is to let yourself go and do it. The job of the actor is to get out of the way of the material.
Morgan Freeman, Actor
Interview in *Venice* magazine, 1995

1942. Searching for the truth should be every actor's occupation.
Louis Jourdan
Cited in *Screen Acting*, 1986

1943. Acting is: whenever or whatever you say—mean it.
James Cagney, Actor
Cited in *Drama-Logue* magazine, 1986

1944. What really counts in film acting ... is not technique or professionalism—just truth.
John Huston
Cited in *The Hustons*, 1989

1945. Strip your work of its affections. It is now a more realistic world. Play for realism. Play without fear, without caution.
Sir John Gielgud
Cited in *Screen Acting*, 1986

1946. It's a mysterious thing ... if the actor "has it," it means that he can be taking stuff out of a supermarket freezer and there's something special about it.

Philip Kaufman, Director
Interview in *Vanity Fair*, 1993

1947. Find your mark, look the other fellow in the eye, and tell the truth.

James Cagney
Cited in *True and False: Heresy and Common Sense for the Actor*, 1997

1948. (Acting) is not so much about finding the truth as revealing it ... things are only revealed to you when you are ready to deal with them.

Laurence Fishburne, Actor
Interview in *Buzz* magazine, 1994

1949. If the line is phony, I'll forget it — if it's true, I won't.

Michael Caine
Interview in *Take 22: Moviemakers on Moviemaking*, 1984

1950. The truth is the truth, it doesn't matter how you get there.

Forest Whitaker, Actor
Interview in *Playboy*, March, 1992, on the British way of acting versus the American way

1951. As soon as one tries to express oneself through mimicry, through gestures, through vocal effects, what one gets ceases to be cinema and becomes photographed theater.

Robert Bresson, Director
Cited in *Great Film Directors: A Critical Anthology*, 1078

1952. If (the performers) tell me it didn't feel good to them, then I know it will never feel good to an audience. Then we (shoot) it over until they feel it.

Mervyn LeRoy, Director
Interview in *Films of the Golden Age*, 1998

1953. Performing is elusive. Sometimes an idiot can do it, and sometimes a genius can't.

Steve Martin, Actor
Cited in *Life* magazine, 1992

1954. Whatever dramatics, or dynamics, I can offer a movie ... at my best, I can be real. If real is the nitro and the script is glycerine ... then we can make some bombs go off.

Sean Penn, Actor
Interview in *Time Out* magazine, 1996

1955. I can't cheat when I act. I know that the cinema is an illusion, but not for me.

Robert De Niro
Cited on the Internet Movie Database, 1998

1956. Acting is honesty. If you can fake that, you've got it made.

George Burns
Cited in *Screen Acting*, 1986

1957. The actor is not only an interpreter ... a carrier of ideas ... but himself can be a good creative artist.

Josef von Sternberg
Interview in *Film Culture* magazine, 1955

1958. The film actor should work not on the psychological level but on the imaginative one. And the imagination reveals itself spontaneously — it has no intermediaries upon which one can lean for support.

Míchelangelo Antonioni
Interview in *Film Culture* magazine, 1961

1959. The film actor should arrive for shooting in a state of virginity. The more intuitive his work, the more spontaneous it will be.

Míchelangelo Antonioni
Interview in *Film Culture* magazine, 1961

1960. Whether I'm doing an action movie or a love story, my approach to the work remains the same. It's all about trying to do something original....

Nicolas Cage, Actor
Interview in *The Los Angeles Times*, 1997

1961. Walk into each role like you don't even know how to act and therefore you were bound to find something unique.

James Earl Jones, Actor
Interview in *Venice* magazine, 1996

1962. There are more than a thousand ways an actor can enter a room and slap someone across the face. But there is only one right way.

Míchelangelo Antonioni
Interview in *Film Culture*, Spring 1962

1963. Actors must take risks. Otherwise nothing is gained.... Taking risks is what always keeps acting new.

Faye Dunaway, Actress
Interview in *GQ* magazine, 1983

1964. What I'm really trying to do with the actors is to get them to be less creative and just use their own natural selves more ... behavioral (not actorial). Behavior is what it is.

Robert Altman, Director
Interview in *Inner Views: Filmmakers in Conversation*, 1992

1965. I followed my nose — which is a pretty long trip.

Dustin Hoffman, Actor
On preparing to play his first Shakespeare-an role, as cited in *People* magazine, 1989

1966. I create behavior that tells a story.

Harrison Ford
Cited in *Screen Acting*, 1986

1967. As important as anything you say is what you do because the doing tells the audience far more than any words can tell.

Eric Stephan Kline, Author
Cited in *Acting for the Camera*, 1997

1968. Acting is not the memorizing of lines while wearing a disguise, but the clear reconstruction of the thoughts that cause the actions and the lines.

Josef von Sternberg
Interview in *Film Culture* magazine, 1955

1969. An ability to lean in any direction, look like many people but still project a personal charisma through each characteristic.

Jack L. Warner, Studio Head–Producer
Cited in *Screen Acting*, 1986, on
what makes a great screen actor

1970. What's left unsaid ... the internal life of a character that comes out in little things like a gesture ... (are) the subtleties of acting, rather than the broad strokes.

Jessica Lange, Actress
Interview in *American Film* magazine, 1990

1971. Sometimes one must exaggerate just a bit before the camera.

Lon Chaney, Actor
Interview in *The Morning Telegraph*, 1924

1972. The last thing you want to be in acting is an introvert....

Audrey Hepburn, Actress
Interview in *People* magazine, 1989

1973. As an actor, I want to startle the people in a subtle kind of way — the way people are startled when they catch sight of themselves in a mirror.

Laurence Fishburne, Actor
Interview in *Buzz* magazine, 1994

1974. Acting is about scaring myself a little bit.... The skill is doing it again and again and again.

Annette Bening, Actress
Interview in *The Los Angeles
Times Calendar*, 1991

1975. You really have to trust the director; you have to surrender your vanity to the director.

Anne Jackson
Interview in *Take 22: Moviemakers
on Moviemaking*, 1984

1976. The thing that I've been able to learn ... is to allow the director to boss me around.

Tom Hanks
Interview in *The Hollywood Reporter*, 1995

1977. You're trying to reach the director. It's a very egotistic pleasure; it's really like lovemaking.

Jeanne Moreau
Interview in *Film Makers on Film Making*, 1983

1978. There is nothing more adrenaline giving to an actor than seeing his director stuff his mouth with his handkerchief.

Malcom McDowell
Cited in *Stanley Kubrick — A Biography*,
1997, commenting on Stanley Kubrick

1979. The only way I prepare myself for a film and a director is to be empty. I am ready to be filled up.

Jeanne Moreau
Interview in *Film Makers on Film Making*, 1983

1980. It's wise to dump your bag of tricks after every movie and not carry them to the next role.

Gene Hackman, Actor
Cited in a *Venice* magazine
interview by James Earl Jones, 1996

1981. We must not lie to the actors ... better actors like the truth more.

Ingmar Bergman, Director
Interview in *Film Makers on Film Making*, 1983

1982. I don't want life reproduced up there on the screen. I want life created.

Sidney Lumet, Director
Stated in his *Making Movies*, 1995

1983. If actors do as they're told, the result will be a film in which all of the parts seem to have been rendered by the same interpreter. What could be more tedious?

Jean Renoír, Director
Stated in his *Jean Renoír
— My Life and Times*, 1974

1984. If an actor doesn't have experience, I don't have time on the set to teach him how to respond. My job is to direct a film, not coach an actor.

Daniel Mann, Director
Cited in *Screen Acting*, 1986

1985. The actor is kind of a Trojan horse in the citadel of the director.

> Míchelangelo Antonioni
> Interview in *Film Culture* magazine, 1961

1986. The actor is the weakest scaffolding on which to build a foundation. What really counts is the director and the script ... we're the tools.

> Tom Hanks, Actor
> Interview in *Vim and Vigor* magazine, 1996

1987. Whenever (George Cukor) tries (to tell me) how to say my lines, I just tell him to play the part and I'll direct the film.

> Spencer Tracy
> Cited in *George Cukor—A Double Life*, 1989

1988. Motivations, meanings, scene impact and quality of writing fascinate me. It sometimes results in disagreements with directors.

> Paul Newman
> Stated in *Paul Newman*, 1989

1989. I've always considered myself to be the author's advocate.

> Peter O'Toole, Actor
> Interview in *Playboy*, September, 1965

1990. Actors want to direct because they get fed up with the restriction of acting inside their own selves.

> Paul Newman
> Stated in *Paul Newman*, 1989

1991. An actor only needs a sympathetic director who's got the camera at the right distance.

> Michael Powell
> Speaking at the New York Film Forum, 1985

1992. If I was hanging from an elk's head and they said, "Hold it," I held it—even if they went to lunch.

> Virginia Fox
> Cited in *The Zanucks of Hollywood*, 1989,
> commenting on taking direction—1923

1993. Some of the greatest direction I've ever received is "That was terrible. I didn't believe a moment of that...."

> Tom Hanks, Actor
> Interview in *The Hollywood Reporter*, 1995

1994. Knowledge of the logical and psychological reasons for camera positions transforms the actor from a photographed object, to a creative collaborator.

> Richard Brestoff, Actor-Author
> Stated in his *The Camera Smart Actor*, 1994

1995. The chemistry between certain people and the camera ... it's something you can't go to acting school for.

> Robert Wise, Director
> Stated in his 1995 *Robert Wise: On His Films*

1996. Film acting is about nuance. The things you do for the camera are infinitesimal and wouldn't be perceived in a theater.

> Kevin Kline
> Interview in *Playboy*, March, 1998

1997. You don't have to kick it out to an audience ... Let the camera do the work.

> George Cukor
> Cited in *George Cukor
> —A Double Life*, 1989, on screen acting

1998. In front of the camera I have to be careful what I think—it all shows.

> Shirley MacLaine
> Cited in *Look* magazine

1999. When the camera comes close up, do something so you won't be frightened by it.

> Vittorio De Sica
> Cited in *Sophia Loren—A Biography*, giving
> advice to young film actress Sophia Loren

2000. The camera is a Cyclops living in a flat world ... the actor ... must use a kind of psychological lighting and shading to give depth to his creations.

> Richard Brestoff, Actor-Author
> Stated in his *The Camera Smart Actor*, 1994

2001. The actor is the servant of the camera. The camera is what tells the story.

> Charlton Heston
> Interview in *Film Makers
> on Film Making*, Vol. II, 1983

2002. The camera has to be the best friend of the actor....

> Ingmar Bergman, Director
> Interview in *Film Makers on Film Making*, 1983

2003. If you don't deliver, they can't morph good acting.

> Sylvester Stallone, Actor
> Interview in *Time* magazine, 1997

2004. It's very important to get to people's emotions, to remind them that they've got emotions lying around.

> Paul Newman
> Stated in *Paul Newman*, 1989

2005. Emotion is a vital part of a performance; over-emotionalizing is not.
> Eric Stephan Kline, Author
> Cited in *Acting for the Camera*, 1997

2006. You have to learn to take off your clothes emotionally on-stage.
> Paul Newman
> Stated in *Paul Newman*, 1989

2007. To do the job really well you have to allow yourself to be vulnerable.
> Gene Hackman
> Cited in *Paul Newman*, 1989

2008. Actors are very delicate instruments … they have to, to some degree, expose areas of themselves that are terribly personal … their ego is forever exposed.
> Sidney Poitier, Actor
> Interview in *American Film*, 1991

2009. I've always felt that an actor has to be in touch with his own anger about something.
> Clint Eastwood
> Cited in *Clint Eastwood—A Biography*, 1996

2010. (Student actors) learned about the mechanism of feeling.
> Marlon Brando
> Referring to his acting teacher, Stella Adler,
> as cited in *Conversations with Brando*, 1991

2011. For an actor to give the appearance of reality, he cannot pretend or make believe he is thinking…. His thoughts must be real thoughts in order to produce real and believable actions.
> Edward Dwight Easty
> Stated in *On Method Acting Manual*, 1966

2012. The audience never knows the thoughts which go on in the actor's mind and any which produce real behavior can and should be utilized.
> Edward Dwight Easty
> Stated in *On Method Acting Manual*, 1966

2013. Spontaneity is the element that gives the audience a strong sense of reality — the feeling that … it's actually happening for the first time.
> Raoul Walsh, Director
> On being opposed to too many rehearsals, as cited
> in *Directing—Learn from the Masters*, 1996

2014. The dance, to me, is all-important. The place where you stand, how you use your space … in relation to other people in the scenes, how you dance with them — that's what it's all about.
> Tony Richardson, Director
> Interview in *Films and Filming*, 1962

2015. Think the scene! I don't care what you do with your hands or your feet.
> Charlie Chaplin, Director
> Cited in *The Great Movie
> Comedians*, 1978, commenting
> on actors playing it with their brains

2016. Inspirational acting breeds communion and oneness with the artist and his audience.
> Charlie Chaplin, Actor-Director
> Cited in *Screen Acting*, 1986

2017. The audience is on your side, and does half your work. That's their "job"; they pay money to empathize with you.
> Eric Stephan Kline, Author
> Cited in *Acting for the Camera*, 1997

2018. An actor has to be able to make an audience forget where it is and take them along with him as the story unfolds. If he can't do that, he'd better go back to pumping gas.
> Jack L. Warner, Studio Head–Producer
> Cited in *Screen Acting*, 1986

2019. If I'm really doing my (acting) job correctly, you should sit there and say, "I'm involved with this person" and have no idea there's an actor there.
> Michael Caine
> Interview in Take *22: Moviemakers
> on Moviemaking*, 1984

2020. If you want something from an audience, you give blood to their fantasies. It is the ultimate hustle.
> Marlon Brando
> Interview in *Conversations with Brando*, 1991

2021. (The actor) is as free of the necessity of "feeling" as the magician is free of the necessity of actually summoning supernormal powers. The magician creates an illusion in the mind of the audience. So does the actor.
> David Mamet, Writer-Director
> Written in his *True and False*, 1997

2022. An actor's job is not to feel things, it is to make the audience feel them.
> Richard Dreyfuss
> Cited in *Acting Is Everything*, 1981

2023. Don't sell it! Remember, they're peeking at you….
> Charlie Chaplin, Director
> Cited in *The Great Movie Comedians*, 1978,
> with advice to his actors not to overact

2024. This anesthetized society … I want to really get to an audience and wake them up.
> Paul Newman
> Stated in *Paul Newman*, 1989

2025. The actor is the opposite of a scarecrow — it is his function to attract.

Josef von Sternberg
Interview in *Film Culture* magazine, 1955

2026. The audience is always a little ahead of you.

Humphrey Bogart
Cited in *The Hustons*, 1989

2027. Above all, it is the actor ... which link[s] the viewer to the events pictured on the screen.

Elena Oumano, Author
Speaking at the New York Film Forum, 1985

2028. There's nothing more pathetic than to be complacent in the arts.

Sylvester Stallone, Actor
Interview in *Time* magazine, 1997

2029. Always leave them wanting more.

Old acting adage

2030. Doing comedy is like emotional hang gliding, and acting is like oil drilling.

Robin Williams
Interview in *Movieline*, 1998

2031. Dying is easy, comedy is hard.

Edmund Kean
The actor on his death bed, as cited in *Funny Business: the Craft of Comedy Writing*, 1985

2032. Any actor knows that comedy is more difficult, requires more artistry.

W. C. Fields
Cited in *Inside Oscar*, 1996

2033. Always I try to contrast my seriousness of manner with the ridiculousness of the incident.

Charlie Chaplin
Cited in *Chaplin*, 1974

2034. Why should the comic be the only guy who's not allowed to laugh?

Red Skelton
Cited in *The Great Movie Comedians*, 1978, on laughing with his audience

2035. Films are frustrating for an actor, they're more "show me, show me," whereas theater is more "tell me, tell me."

Samuel L. Jackson, Actor
Interview in *Venice* magazine, 1993

2036. (John Wayne had) an "I-own-the-world" way of walking.

Howard Hawks, Director
Cited in *John Wayne's America*, 1997

2037. For Hawks, to walk is to be.

Gerald Mast
Commenting that director Howard Hawks considered an actor's physical attitude his most important asset, as cited in *John Wayne's America*, 1997

2038. He kept calling me a clumsy bastard and a big oaf and kept telling me I moved like an ox.

John Wayne
Cited on the Internet Movie Database, 1998, recalling director John Ford

2039. Goddamit, be graceful — like me!

John Wayne
Admonishing his cast while directing *The Alamo*, as cited in *John Wayne's America*, 1997

2040. There are a hundred rules for being a hero. Never blink your eyes when you shoot ... never move your head when you say your lines.... Show no emotions. Never skip or hop.... When reloading a gun, do not look at the gun.... Every gesture has to separate you from the rest of the bunch if you want to play a stud.

Arnold Schwarzenegger, Actor
Interview in *The Los Angeles Times Magazine*, 1996

2041. Always look the victim straight in the eye when you are telling a lie.

Arnold Schwarzenegger, Actor
Interview in *The Los Angeles Times Magazine*, 1996

2042. Talk low, talk slow, and don't say too much.

John Wayne
Cited on the Internet Movie Database, 1998

2043. I can tell if they can ride at all by the time they put a toe in the stirrup.

Yakima "Yak" Canutt, Stuntman
Cited in *John Wayne's America*, 1997

2044. Cajun is actually a bad actor's way of doing a Brooklyn accent.

Walter Matthau
Interview in *Take 22: Moviemakers on Moviemaking*, 1984

2045. Dancing is acting. It's attitude.

John Travolta, Actor
Interview in *GQ* magazine, 1995

2046. Dancing badly is a real art.

John Travolta, Actor
Interview in *The Hollywood Reporter*, 1996

2047. Like an old Model T Ford, I had to be cranked up.

Marie Dressler
Commenting at the Academy Awards on
working in her advanced years — 1931

2048. If forty years ago there was a great one-legged actor, should we all amputate ourselves and say, "Let's go back to the true spirit of acting?"

Richard Lester, Director
Interview in *Directors at Work*, 1970, on
actors being creative and original

2049. In most films, if you talk for 15 minutes, you've talked a whole lot.

Samuel L. Jackson, Actor
Interview in *Playboy*, April 1995

2050. It's a very privileged existence to shoot for a few minutes and then go back to your trailer and make phone calls.

Johnny Depp
Interview in *Biography* magazine, 1998

2051. "You just want to show off and get paid for it."

Katharine Hepburn
Quoting her father at home upon her
announcement she wanted to be an actress

2052. (A stunt guy) would give me a scale of how painful (each stunt was) going to be. Then I'd jump in and get the final pounding, as it were.

Tom Cruise, Actor
Interview in *Boxoffice* magazine, 1998, referring
to his role in *Mission Impossible,* 1997

2053. You do not take money for nothing. You are being paid to cry. So cry!

Sophia Loren
Cited in *Sophia Loren — A Biography*, 1998,
upon slapping an actor to cry for a film scene

2054. Please, please don't start the film (shooting) with a love scene.

Ingrid Bergman
Her plea with the director so she could know
the leading man better, as stated in her autobiography, *Ingrid Bergman — My Story*, 1980

2055. I like working with animals. They're unpredictable. My theory was always, I follow the dog.

Jack Nicholson
Interview in *Entertainment Weekly*, 1998

2056. Children are marvelous little actors. They don't know enough to be bad.

William Wyler, Director
Interview in *Directors at Work*, 1970

2057. The good ones don't remind you of anybody else.

John Huston
Referring to actors, as cited in *The Hustons*, 1989

2058. It's the sex personality, it's not the words. The censors could never beat that.

Mae West
Cited in *The Great Movie Comedians*, 1978

2059. I've always kept my clothes on for the camera ... There isn't all that much for audiences to look forward to after all that (nudity).

Rita Hayworth, Actress
c. 1971

2060. I'm not going to do a nude scene because when you take off your blouse you're not the character anymore, you're Bernadette Peters with her blouse off.

Bernadette Peters, Actress
Interview in *Playboy*, January 1993

2061. Pantomime ... is the prime qualification of a successful screen player....

Charlie Chaplin
Cited in *Chaplin*, 1974

2062. This is a delicate and serious art, and not one in which amateurs or inexperienced flingers should try to win reknown.

Del Lord, Actor
Commenting on the dramatic art of pie-throwing,
as cited in *Film Makers on Film Making*, 1983

2063. If you have a cigarette to light and it doesn't light, you take it out on the match and the cigarette — so you're a great artist too.

Jack Warner
Cited in *George Cukor — A Double Life*, 1991

2064. (Actors) want (an agent) with an eyeshade who they think sits and reads scripts all night.

Sue Mengers, Agent
Interview in *Film Makers on Film Making*, 1983

2065. I'm, as an actor, not out to play my political feelings.

Clint Eastwood
Cited in *Clint Eastwood — A Biography*, 1996

2066. Very few leading men understand the importance of the tenor range.

Orson Welles
Interview in *Film Makers on*
Film Making, Vol. II, 1983

2067. My best performance is on the cutting room floor.

> Old complaint among film actors
> Cited in *Take 22: Moviemakers on Moviemaking*, 1984

2068. You learn acting from life, and that goes on around you all the time.

> Ingrid Bergman, Actress
> Stated in *Ingrid Bergman — My Story*, 1980

15

Costume Design

2069. Each element (in movie making) has its own particular relation to the drama ... and each element — the word, the actor, the costume — has the exact significance of a note in a symphony.

Robert Edmond Jones, Costume Designer
Cited in *The Costume Designer's Handbook*, 1992

2070. What we do is create an illusion ... It is a cross between magic and camouflage.

Edith Head, Costume Designer
Interview in *Film Makers on Film Making*, Vol. II, 1983

2071. We, the couturiers, can no longer live without the cinema any more than the cinema can live without us. We corroborate each other's instinct.

Lucien Lelong, Designer
Cited in *Movie Classic 8*, "Do Movies Influence the Paris Designers," 1935

2072. (The film's producers) have three magicians — hairstylist, makeup artist, and clothes designer....

Edith Head, Clothes Designer
Interview in *Film Makers on Film Making*, Vol. II, 1983

2073. (The Oscar) is one of the highest (honors) in the world of fashion since much of the most exciting thinking in design is done by film people.

Julie Harris, Costume Designer
Cited in *Inside Oscar*, 1996, commenting on her winning the Oscar for best costume design (black & white) for *Darling*, 1965

2074. I have no patience with costume designers who view actors as pliable dolls on which to drape fabric.

Arvin Brown, Artistic Director
Cited in *The Costume Designer's Handbook*, 1992

2075. You don't just design something and say goodbye.

Anthea Sylbert, Costume Designer
Interview in *Film Makers on Film Making*, 1983

2076. Everybody is an expert because everybody wears clothes....

Anthea Sylbert, Costume Designer
Interview in *Film Makers on Film Making*, 1983

2077. I do not design for people, but with people.

Edith Head, Costume Designer
Cited in *Fashion in Film*, 1990

2078. (Doris Langley Moore) could look at a seam and say it was made in 1862 and not 1863....

Angela Allen
Cited in *The Costume Designer's Handbook*, 1992

2079. An admirable (costume) design is meaningless if the actor cannot wear it with conviction ... and find some grains of the character's identity in the clothes.

Arvin Brown, Artistic Director
Cited in *The Costume Designer's Handbook*, 1992

2080. Neither a setting nor a costume is good if the actor is uncomfortable. Part of the designer's job is to give the performer every physical and psychological, as well as visual, assistance.

Jo Mielziner, Costume Designer
Cited in *The Costume Designer's Handbook*, 1992

2081. Each separate costume we create for a screenplay must be exactly suited both to the character it helps to express and to the occasion it graces.

Robert Edmond Jones, Costume Designer
Cited in *The Costume Designer's Handbook*, 1992

2082. A sensitive (costume) designer can guide the actors toward that very discovery of a character's inner nature....

Arvin Brown, Artistic Director
Cited in *The Costume Designer's Handbook*, 1992

2083. If asked to wear clothes that violate his ...

own deep sense of reality ... a bit of breath will have been knocked out of the character, and breathing — life — is what (acting) is all about.
Arvin Brown, Artistic Director
Interview in *Moviemakers at Work*, 1987

2084. Sometimes a garment will trigger a whole new concept of who the character is.
Kristi Zea, Costume Designer
Interview in *Film Makers on Film Making*, 1983

2085. (The movie) must never be about the costumes; it must always be about the characters. You must not leave a movie whistling the clothes.
Anthea Sylbert, Costume Designer
Cited in *Film Makers on Film Making*, 1983

2086. Character comes out of design and vice versa.
Polly Platt, Costume Designer
Stated in her 1995 *Making Movies*

2087. Nothing helps actors more than the clothes they wear.
Sidney Lumet, Director

2088. She's given me the whole bloody character now.
Sean Connery
Cited in *Making Movies*, 1995, on being outfitted by costume designer Ann Roth

2089. I didn't know what in the world to do with (the role) of (Baby) Jane until I got into the clothes.
Bette Davis
On *Whatever Happened to Baby Jane?* 1962, as cited in *Film Makers on Film Making*, Vol. II, 1983

2090. I owe a lot of my performance to the corset I had to wear ... the blood rushes to your face. So that explains "radiant."
Emma Thompson, Actress
Cited in *Inside Oscar*, 1996, referring to *Howards End*, 1993

2091. I prefer to play parts where I can wear old clothes ... so when I am comfortable I act more natural. It's the same when I'm "wearing" a part that fits me, comfortable.
Gary Cooper, Actor
Interview in *Silver Screen* magazine, 1941

2092. (With animation) we can invest the clothing of a character with the capacity to reflect the character's mood. Always remember that clothing can "act," too.
Shamus Culhane, Animator
Stated in his 1988 *Animation*

2093. Clint Eastwood at the time had only two expressions — with a hat and without a hat.
Sergio Leone, Director
Cited on the Internet Movie Database, 1998, referring to his "spaghetti westerns," in the sixties

2094. The dripping yellow dress made Sophia (Loren) a poster girl all over the world.
Jean Negulesco, Director
Cited in *Sophia Loren — A Biography*, 1998, referring to *Boy on a Dolphin*, 1961

2095. The closer (Sophia Loren) resembles a statue, the better she looks and the better proportioned her clothes appear.
Edith Head, Designer
Cited in *Sophia Loren — A Biography*, 1998

2096. Lana Turner is to an evening gown what Frank Lloyd Wright is to a pile of lumber.
Rex Harrison

2097. (George) Cukor wanted Greta Garbo to look as she does in reality ... in bulky, ugly clothes.
Joseph Ruttenberg
Cited in *George Cukor — A Double Life*, 1991, on his proposed wardrobe for the film *Two-Faced Woman*, 1941

2098. He was a very heavy character to wear ... looking like you've been up all night doing drugs, can be weighty.
Laurence Fishburne, Actor
On the costume to play Ike Turner in *What's Love Got to Do with It?*, 1993, as cited in *US* magazine

2099. I am sick of Cinderella parts, of wearing rags and tatters. I want to wear smart clothes and play the lover.
Mary Pickford, Actress
Cited in *Inside Oscar*, 1996

2100. I always hated to take off the colorful costumes (from *Pride and Prejudice*) and put on slacks, feeling something like Cinderella after the ball.
Greer Garson, Actress
On the nineteenth century English period film, quoted in a 1940 MGM press release

2101. I went to Sears and bought my dresses off the rack.
Joan Crawford, Actress
Cited in *Bette and Joan — The Divine Feud*, 1983, referring to her role in *Mildred Pierce*, 1945

2102. RKO made the same films with me in it for

10 years. They were so alike I wore the same suit in six of them and the same Burberry trench coat.
> Robert Mitchum, Actor
> Interview in *Big Reel* magagzine, 1997

2103. I would not walk out of a picture for anything as trivial as a costume.
> Lana Turner, Actress
> Cited in *Inside Oscar*, 1996, accused of
> walking out of an Otto Preminger
> production over a costume dispute

2104. Every year [Warner Bros.] studio gave a banquet for all the employees. Even the back lot fellows go into the wardrobe department and come out with tuxedos to wear to dinner.
> Ronald Reagan, Actor
> Cited in *Clown Prince of Hollywood*, 1990

2105. The costume designer is irrevocably linked to the past as well as the present, and influenced as much by history as by the events of the contemporary scene.
> Motley
> Cited in *The Costume Designer's Handbook*, 1992

2106. Ordinary clothes automatically become extraordinary on the ... screen. The frame around the events invites intensified attention to what is being worn....
> Anne Hollander
> Cited in *The Costume Designer's Handbook*, 1992

2107. Once, in the darkness of a movie theater, someone is fascinated by the dress, the presence of a figure on the screen. From that moment, they are driven to make that image their own.
> Regine Engelmeier
> Cited in *Fashion in Film*, 1990

2108. The dress in modern films may be of little importance, but costume pictures add notes, bars, and passages to the symphony of dress.
> Lillian Churchill, Fashion Reporter,
> *New York Times Magazine*
> Cited in *Hollywood and History*
> *— Costume Design in Film*, 1987

2109. Costume pictures ... generally become as unconvincing and artificial as fancy-dress balls in a small college gym unless (the costumes) ... are built and tailored exactly as ... in the days of the story.
> Mitchell Leisen, Designer-Director
> Cited in the 1973 *The Career of Mitchell Leisen*

2110. On (some) pictures, I've wanted a hodge-podge ... everything had to feel accidental.
> Sidney Lumet, Director
> Stated in his 1995 *Making Movies*

2111. All my movie going life I've wanted somebody to knock somebody out and take his clothes — and not have the clothes fit.
> Judith Crist, Film Critic
> Interview in *Take 22: Moviemakers on
> Moviemaking*, 1984, commenting
> that director Steven Spielberg made it
> happen in *Raiders of the Lost Ark*, 1981

2112. Can it be done in modern dress?
> Harry Rapf
> Cited in *Mayer and Thalberg— The Make
> Believe Saints*, 1975, on proposed MGM
> movie on the life of the Virgin Mary

2113. I speak to the art director, to make sure I do not design a lilac dressing gown for a lilac bedroom.
> Edith Head, Costume Designer
> Cited in *Fashion in Film*, 1990

2114. The suit or armor in *Excalibur* ... was torture because they didn't design any trap doors for ... obvious functions. ... and you would just see clouds of steam coming out of the armor.
> Gabriel Byrne, Actor
> Interview in *Movieline* magazine, 1998

2115. Clothes don't fit correctly.
> Polly Platt, Costume Designer
> Cited in *Film Makers on Film Making*,
> 1983, on realism in film wardrobe

2116. If you have a large bust, don't put on clothes so tight you suggest a sausage.
> Edith Head, Costume Designer
> Cited on the Internet Movie Database, 1998

2117. (Then) let's make a movie about poor people.
> Anthea Sylbert, Costume Designer
> Responding to the news that that
> a planned film had no budget for
> "wardrobe," as quoted in her interview in
> *Film Makers on Film Making*, 1983

2118. One day I saw women walking alone dressed in a fantastic and extraordinary way, so fascinating that it set light to my imagination.
> Federico Fellini
> Cited in *Fellini— A Life*, 1986,
> prior to filming *La Dolce Vita*, 1958

2119. It cannot be denied that clothes in period pictures do affect the modes of the moment.
> Lillian Churchill, Fashion Reporter,
> *New York Times Magazine*
> Cited in *Hollywood and History*
> *— Costume Design in Film*, 1987

2120. I'm more interested in fashion as an art form....

Sandy Powell
Cited in *Premiere* magazine, 1998

2121. The ... difficult thing about doing a movie (wardrobe) that takes place "today" is that it's really going to take place next year.

Anthea Sylbert, Costume Designer
Interview in *Film Makers on
Film Making*, 1983, on style changes

2122. We have a thousand delicious memories of the movie (*Tom Jones*), but what we came away with was a really insatiable craving for: the Tom Jones shirt.

Vogue magazine, 1964

2123. Paris is all agog about "Zaza" clothes....

Edith Head
Cited in *Hollywood and History — Costume
Design in Film*, 1987, on a cable
from the costume designer in Paris
to Paramount Pictures, referring to
the 1939 movie with Claudette Colbert

2124. Accessories make the costume.

Bette Davis
Cited in *Bette and Joan — The Divine Feud*, 1989

16

Make-Up

2125. To be able to change identity as well as our appearance is a basic human wish.

> Way Bandy
> Cited in *The Face of the Century*, 1995,
> from the author, *The Way of Beauty*

2126. The word "glamour" is from the Scotch word for magic.

> Mary Tanner
> Cited in *The New York Times*, 1997

2127. The first thing was always how the star looked.

> Lawrence Kasdan
> Cited in *American Cinema*, 1995

2128. (The make-up) artists have the power to transform us from the cocoon of the dressing room to the butterfly of the film.

> Carrie Fisher
> Written for the Academy Awards presentation
> for Best Make-Up in a Film, 1998

2129. Make-up is (the actor's) armor, their Excalibur, their Red Badge of Courage, ... they are a race of nobles; they drink out of the Big Dipper.

> Frank Capra, Producer-Director
> Stated in his 1971 *Frank Capra
> — The Name Above the Title*

2130. (The Americans) have developed the art of make-up to the utmost of unreality.

> Jean Renoir, French Director
> Stated in his 1974 *Jean Renoir
> — My Life and Times*

2131. There is a corrective formula for everything that is wrong with the feminine face ... the (make-up) miracle men know what it is.

> Adele Whitely Fletcher
> 1939 interview in *Photoplay* article, "Miracle
> Men at Work to Make You Lovelier"

2132. So important is the movie studio glamour business that make-up men rank just above directors ... every lot ... possesses a small herd of these make-up maestri.

> *Stage* magazine, 1936

2133. One of the great things about (the makeup) artist is that you don't first execute an idea or vision. You expound and improve upon it or you create a better one. You always make the film better.

> Michael Key, Writer
> Interview in *Make-up Artist* magazine, 1997

2134. The artistry of the makeup artist, and the ramifications of his painstaking skills ... is hardly apparent upon the surface of a thin layer of grease paint.

> Mel Archer, Make-up Designer
> Interview in *Production Design* magazine, 1951

2135. Make-up only touches perfection when it passes unnoticed.

> Kate de Castelbajac
> Stated in her 1995 *The Face of the
> Century—100 Years of Make-up and Style*

2136. Don't try to improve or change Nature's selection or you will appear artificial.

> Jeff Dawn, Make-up Artist
> Interview in *Make-up Artist* magazine,
> 1998, on natural color shades

2137. A few years ago, any woman using those devil's tricks would have been called "fast" and cut dead by the minister's wife.

> Hollywood columnist
> After viewing the beautifully made-up actress
> Greta Garbo, in her screen debut, 1925

2138. Grease paint is Max Factor's LSD. It comes in tubes.

> Frank Capra
> Stated in his 1971 *Frank Capra
> — The Name Above The Title*

2139. In black-and-white we worked with contrasts of light and shade. In color, this is not the case. We are now ... seeking to imitate and enhance the subject's natural coloring.

Max Factor, Make-up Artist
Cited in *Max Factor's Hollywood*, 1995,
upon the advent of color movies, circa 1927

2140. No make-up is good make-up, unless the other fellow doesn't know you have it on.

Max Factor
Cited in *Max Factor's Hollywood*,
1995, on movie actors' "greasepaint"

2141. (With makeup) it is this sense of "believability" versus "reality" that separates theatre from film and photography.

Gary Christiansen, Make-up Artist
Interview in *Make-up Artist* magazine, 1998

2142. [E]ffect an alteration in her appearance, one that would make her nationally known and talked about almost overnight.

Howard Hughes, Producer
Commenting to Max Factor about a new
actress named Jean Harlow, circa 1928, as
cited in *Max Factor's Hollywood*, 1995

2143. [E]ven Max Factor cannot make a Chiquita banana out of a dwarf pickle.

Raoul Walsh, Director
Cited in *Directing — Learn from the Masters*, 1996

2144. Ten different make-up artists showed me how to do a black eye.

Michael Westmore, Make-up Artist
Interview in *Moviemakers at Work*, 1987

2145. The only thing the leading man in a film has to be sure of is that his haircut in the back is in perfect shape.

Anonymous Actor
Cited in *Film Makers on Film Making*, 1983

2146. There might be a new Hollywood glamour, but it's not painted on. It comes from inner strength.

Jeanine Lobell
Cited in *The New York Times Magazine*, 1997

2147. (Greta Garbo) was the first (actress) to be glamorized in the modern Hollywood sense, and she remains to this day the outstanding product of the art.

Frederick Hall
Cited in *The Face of the Century*, 1995,
from the columnist of *Stage* magazine, 1934

2148. I'm a good artist, but every day I paint the same picture — my face.

Claudette Colbert
Cited in *Vanity Fair*, 1998

2149. Well, I do know how to apply makeup.

Sigourney Weaver, Actress
Cited in *Entertainment Yearbook*, 1998, stating
her qualifications to someday teach acting

2150. My rule of thumb is, unless there's a point to it, why make me look uglier than I actually look?

Sigourney Weaver
Interview in *Premiere*, 1998

2151. Always shoot your close-ups first thing in the morning, honey, 'cause your looks ain't gonna hold out all day.

Ava Gardner
Cited in *Sophia Loren — A Biography*, 1998,
on her advice to young Sophia Loren

2152. Understand this, you are not going to take one eyebrow or one hair away.... If you alter anything, I'll kill you.

David O. Selznick, Producer
Cited in *Ingrid Bergman — My Story*,
1980, to his studio make-up srtists
on new actress Ingrid Bergman

2153. Touch this and Ann Miller will tap dance all over your face.

Sign on make-up room shelf
protecting actress Ann Miller's private
supply of eye shadow, as cited in
Max Factor's Hollywood, 1995

2154. Christ! This will play hell with my love life.

Bette Davis
Upon having her head and eyebrows
shaved for a role, as cited in *Bette and
Joan — The Divine Feud*, 1989

2155. When Sophia (Loren) first saw herself made up to be eighty, she burst into tears.

Peter Ustinov
Cited in *Sophia Loren — A Biography*,
1998, referring to her role in *Lady L*

2156. (It) looked like somebody dipped me into an old guy....

Billy Crystal, Actor
Interviewed in *The Los Angeles Times
Calendar*, 1992, on his make-up
for *Mr. Saturday Night*

2157. A line here, a shadow there will produce

entirely different effects when employed in different lights ... one must experiment endlessly....

Lon Chaney, Actor
Interview in *The Morning Telegraph*,
New York City, 1924

2158. (Lon Chaney) in effect assumed his roles from the outside in.

Beth Werling
Interview in *Terra* magazine, 1996,
on *The Man of a Thousand Faces*

2159. (Johnson's face) is touched by life rather than retouched by an ever-hovering make-up man.

The Saturday Review, 1946
Praising the unglamorous average
look given to actress Celia Johnson
in *In Which We Serve*

2160. Sure, it's just not my real hair.

John Wayne, Actor
When asked if his hair was real, as
cited in *Max Factor's Hollywood*, 1995

2161. If I lost my squint, I think my whole career would go down the tubes.

Clint Eastwood
Cited in *Clint Eastwood—A Biography*, 1996

2162. (My horse and I) were in makeup together every morning fighting over the Trades and bran muffins. I just wanted him to look different.

Billy Crystal

Interview in *The Valley Vantage*,
1994, referring to *City Slickers II*

2163. No actor ever morphed himself with such cruel imagination (as Lon Chaney).

Ty Burr, Senior Writer, *Entertainment Weekly*
Stated in *Entertainment Weekly 100*, 1997

2164. (With horror films) there is dirt, blood, wounds, appliances and characters – everything a makeup artist loves.

Jeff Dawn, Make-up Artist
Interview in *Make-Up Artist*, 1998

2165. If you want to become a real actress, the first thing you do is let your eyebrows grow, get your hair back to its natural shade and scrub all that goo off your face.

Hedda Hopper, Hollywood Columnist
Advice to unknown actress

2166. The computer allows the makeup artist to create a visual agreement between him/herself and the decision-makers ... of the production.

Michael Key, Writer
Interview in *Make-Up Artist* mgagzine,
1998, on digital design by makeup artists

2167. When the actor walks onto the set looking exactly like the (makeup) design, you are the hero.

Michael Key, Writer
Interview in *Make-Up Artist* magazine, 1998

17

Color

2168. Up to now the moving picture industry has been like an artist who was allowed only to use pencil or charcoal. Now Technicolor has given us paints.

> Rouben Mamoulian, Director
> Cited in *The Technicolor Years*,
> 1980, commenting in 1935

2169. Science and art, the handmaidens of the cinema, have joined hands to endow the screen with a miraculous new element — color.

> *New York Times*
> Review of the movie *Becky Sharp*, 1935, as
> cited in *The Technicolor Years*, 1980

2170. They alone speak with more eloquence than can be described by words....

> Dr. Herbert T. Kalmus, Inventor of Technicolor
> Cited in *The Technicolor Years*, 1980

2171. To the many other rhythms in films, it is necessary ... to add the color rhythm.

> Carl Th. Dreyer
> Interview in *Film Makers on Film Making*, 1983

2172. The colors for the scenes must be in (the director's) mind's eye from the beginning. The director must create in color.

> Carl Th. Dreyer
> Interview in *Film Makers on Film Making*, 1983

2173. Color is a factor in art, and must be used where it has a function to fulfill.

> Andrzej Wajda, Director
> Interview in *Films and Filming*, 1961

2174. If rainbows were in black and white....

> Technicolor Company
> The headline of their first advertisement,
> 1930, cited in *The Technicolor Years*, 1980

2175. My role was playing ringmaster to the rainbow.

> Natalie Kalmus

Promoter of her husband's (Herbert) Technicolor process in the movies, as cited on the Internet Movie Database, 1998

2176. Natalie Kalmus was Technicolor.

> Jack Cardiff
> Cited in *Premiere* magazine, 1998, on the wife
> of Herbert Kalmus, founder of Technicolor

2177. Color ... was invented and set up lab-wise to be candy. The color itself was a form of entertainment, a novelty. "Look how colorful this is!"

> Elia Kazan, Director
> Interview in *Directors at Work*

2178. They gave the color to the terrible scripts as an added inducement to get the public in.

> Bette Davis, Actress
> On the transition from black
> and white films to color, as cited
> in *Chronicle of the Cinema*, 1995

2179. One of the things I look for in a colored film is the palette. What palette do I use? Just as a painter....

> John Huston
> Cited in *The Hustons*, 1989

2180. I want to paint the film as one paints a canvas; I want to invent the color relationships....

> Michelangelo Antonioni
> Interview in *Film Culture* magazine, 1962

2181. The unrivaled beauty of the different episodes is mindful of the paintings of the old masters.

> *New York Times*
> Reviewing the first color feature film,
> *The Black Pirate*, 1926, as cited
> in *The Technicolor Years*, 1980

2182. You can use (color) as a painter does: you want to shock people, you throw color at them.

> John A. Alonzo, Cinematographer
> Interview in *Film Makers on Film Making*,
> Vol. II, 1983

2183. To demand that color in color films should be "natural" is to misunderstand all that is involved.

Carl Th. Dreyer
Interview in *Film Makers on Film Making*, 1983

2184. (Directors want) color that is an emphasis factor, the way color is in life, and to catch the poetry of the essential gray in life.

Elia Kazan, Director
Interview in *Directors at Work*, 1970

2185. (Alfred) Hitchcock has, thanks to color, been able to make the cruelty of his scenes almost beautiful.

Peter Cowie
Stated in his *50 Major Film Makers*, 1975

2186. (Walt Disney cartoon) color ... is wild, fantastic, subtle, or merely literal, for it depends not upon the real colors of objects but upon the pigmentation dictated by his imagination.

Lewis Jacobs, Writer
Stated in his *The Rise of American Film*, 1939

2187. Color is basically immobile, and yet it must move. Color is wrong for a film that tries to be as subjective as mine ... the only way to use (color) is subjectively.

Federico Fellini
Cited in Cited in *Fellini—A Life*, 1986

2188. Where yellow is emphasized and compensatory, there is likely to be superficiality.

The Luscher Color Test
As recited by Alfred Hitchcock
in his 1983 biography, *Hitchcock*

2189. Lighting should be treated as it is for black and white film....

Akira Kurosawa, Director
On lighting color scenes, stated in his
1982 biography, *Akira Kurosawa*

2190. Color is a double-edged sword ... if you need a sunrise in black and white, you can shoot a sunset and get away with it. But a sunrise is entirely different in color from a sunset.

Franz Planer, Director of Photography
Cited in *The Technicolor Years*, 1980

2191. Black and white are too little used in color films. They have been forgotten in the childish rapture over the many bright colors in the paint-box.

Carl Th. Dreyer
Commented in 1955, as cited in
Film Makers on Film Making, 1983

2192. I have rarely experienced a "bouquet" in a film theater....

Ray Bradbury
Cited in *The Hustons*, 1989, on the innovative
use of color effects in *Moulin Rouge*

2193. It was a psychological story, and I didn't want to have the distraction of too many colors.

John Huston
On *Reflections in a Golden Eye*,
1967, cited in *The Hustons*, 1989

2194. I think that color on the screen must be applied in physiological doses, not mechanically.

Andrzej Wajda, Director
Interview in *Films and Filming*, 1961

2195. The ... picture was ... about waste, and you get more waste in black and white.

Arthur Miller
Cited in *The Hustons*, 1989, on
The Misfits in black and white

2196. There are only two colors you can use in cinema—black and white.

Federico Fellini
Cited in *Fellini—A Life*, 1986

2197. Black and white (film) has its own potency, in that it gives a film an abstract quality. It has the advantage that it can never be realistic.

Jean Renoír, Director
Stated in his 1974 *Jean Renoír
—My Life and Times*

2198. Black and white (film) is already stylized; it's a transposition of reality.

Louis Malle, Director
Interview in *Film Buff*, 1976

2199. When have you ever seen a black and white stage play?

Norman Jewison, Director
Interview in *Directors at Work*, 1970

2200. If the colors (of the scene) were reproduced they would blaze horribly. They would consume the dramatic action that must all be left to the actors.

Douglas Fairbanks, Sr., Actor
Interview in *The Morning Telegraph*, New York
City, 1923, on his opposition to color movies

2201. Color photography, when it is well done, is suitable for travelogues and the like, but surely not for pictures in which human emotion is the strongly dominating ingredient.

Douglas Fairbanks, Sr., Actor
Interview in *The Morning
Telegraph*, New York City, 1923

2202. One hour of color is too much color at one sitting.
Unknown Film Critic
1935, as cited in *The Technicolor Years*, 1980

2203. Inclusion of color stifles the greatest of audience reactions; it does not stimulate the imagination. Color, of itself, will not impart dramatic punch.
Unknown Critic
1935, as cited in *The Technicolor Years*, 1980

2204. You know, color goes a little screwy at times and I'm not just sure I want to make a Technicolor picture.
Carole Lombard, Actress, 1938
Cited in *The Technicolor Years*, 1980

2205. Technicolor makes me look like death warmed over.
Bette Davis, Actress
Cited in *Bette and Joan — The Divine Feud*, 1989

2206. Faces in color tend to look like meat, veal, beef, bologna.
Orson Welles, Director
Cited in the Internet Movie Database, 1998

2207. Pirates need color.
Douglas Fairbanks, Sr., Actor
On his future film *The Black Pirate*, 1923, cited in *Pulse* magazine, 1996

2208. Even the dialogue sounds phony when the picture is in color. Everybody looks blue or red. It's like shooting in a jukebox.
Billy Wilder, Director
Cited in *The Bright Side of Billy Wilder, Primarily,* 1970, on his dislike of filming in color

2209. I'm going to colorize *Casablanca* just to piss everybody off.
Ted Turner, Media Mogul
Cited in the Internet Movie Database, 1998

2210. Keep Ted Turner and his goddamned Crayolas away from my movies.
Orson Welles, Director
Cited in the Internet Movie Database, 1998

2211. Just think, for the first time, you can actually see the losers turn green.
Bob Hope
Speaking as the emcee, 1965 Academy Awards ceremony, for the first time televised in color, April 18, 1966

2212. The color was a character of its own.
William Goldberg, Editor
On color being the principal feature of the story in *Pleasantville*, 1998, as cited in *The Hollywood Reporter*, 1999

18

Sound and Music

2213. It was my aim to tell the story through pictorial nuances ... the audience could listen with their eyes.

Ernst Lubitsch, Director
Stated in a letter to Herman G. Weinberg,
printed in 1962, on his silent film days

2214. It all started with the pianist in the early movie theaters ... the fact remains that the silent movie needed music as a dry cereal needs cream.

Kurt Weill
Interview in *Harper's Bazaar*, 1947

2215. The early filmmakers had no desire to allow external annoyances to compete for attention with their visual product: music was their panacea for encouraging audience empathy.

Hans-Christian Schmidt
Translated from the Swiss book *Filmmusik*,
1982, on the use of live theater organ music

2216. We communicated by means of music: it was the sound of their inner life.

Jean Paul Sarte
Commenting on the background
musical score for silent films, 1915

2217. Score-makers, conductors, and organists should throw themselves into the work as the great actors do, and make themselves the creators of the characters and story, 'til it becomes a living flesh and blood organism.

Frank Stewart Adams, Writer
Interview in *The American Organist*, 1921

2218. The theater organ shouts vengeance, frantically claws the enemy, wails with impassioned grief, screams with victory, sobs thickly with love, moans with remorse, cries like a baby, giggles like a young girl, does a Charleston, barks like a dog, and finally shoots itself with a bass drum.

Harry J. Colwell, Writer
As written in *The American Organist*, 1927

2219. Adding sound to movies would be like putting lipstick on the Venus de Milo.

Mary Pickford, Actress
Cited on the Internet Movie Database, 1998

2220. If audiences wanted to read, they would stay at home with a book.

D. W. Griffith, Producer-Director
Referring to subtitles in movies versus talkies.
Cited on the Internet Movie Database, 1998

2221. Novelty is always welcome, but talking pictures are just a passing fad.

Irving Thalberg
Comment to the press when asked
about the future of "talkies," 1927

2222. Talkies are spoiling the oldest art in the world — the art of pantomime.

Charlie Chaplin, Actor-Director
Lamenting the new popularity of
"talkies" and the declining popularity
of silent movies, 1928

2223. Let them develop (sound) if they can. Then we'll see about it.

Louis B. Mayer
Comment to the press when asked about the future
of "talkies" at MGM, 1927, following Warner
Bros.' "talkie" debut of *The Jazz Singer*

2224. The silent screen had grown a larynx!

Frank Capra, Director
After hearing the first film "talkie,"
1927, as recalled in his autobiography,
The Name Above the Title

2225. "At last, pictures that talk like living people!"

Early advertisement for
Vitaphone Talking Pictures, 1927

2226. [T]he purpose of all artistic creation is the knowledge of man, and is not the human voice the best means of conveying the personality of a human being?

> Jean Renoir, Director
> On welcoming the advent of "talkies" to the
> world of cinema, 1927, as stated in his
> autobiography, *My Life and Times*, 1974

2227. Sound film was a regression…. With sound came the words; that was the trouble, theater came in.

> Louis Malle, Director
> Interview in *Film Buff*, 1976

2228. (The silent film) international language was over … the human species had lived on the face of the globe for thousands of years and there had never before been a language in which they could all speak to each other.

> Cedric Belfrage
> Lamenting the lost universal language
> of silent film with the advent of
> English speaking "talkies," 1929

2229. The sound film will teach us to analyze even chaotic noise with our ear and read the score of life's symphony.

> Béla Balázs
> Cited in *Theory of Film*, 1970

2230. [S]ound works enormously, deeply, and it doesn't always travel through the intellect. It's a poetic way to speak to someone.

> Yves Yersin, Director of silent films
> Cited in *Film Forum*, 1985

2231. Sound is only an element of the spectator's regard. But the sound, paradoxically, has a rapport with the regard.

> Benoit Jacquot
> Cited in *Film Forum*, 1985

2232. Who the hell wants to hear actors talk? The music. That's the big plus with this.

> Harry Warner, Warner Bros. Producer
> Upon hearing a motion picture sound
> experiment for the first time, 1925, as
> cited in the 1990 biography of Jack L.
> Warner, *The Clown Prince of Hollywood*

2233. There is no voice in the world like the voice of music.

> D. W. Griffith
> 1924, on his opposition to
> human voices in motion pictures

2234. The screen, in acquiring the gift of speech, had taken on new possibilities. It was my ambition to make screen stories live.

> Darryl F. Zanuck, Producer
> Cited in *Twentieth Century's Fox*, 1997

2235. With the advent of (movie) sound, photography was forced to give way to its (new) brother … and the poor cameraman played second fiddle to a new instrument — the microphone.

> Virgil E. Miller, Cinematographer
> Cited in *Cinematographers on the Art
> and Craft of Cinematography*, 1987

2236. In the silent film, earth and sky could dwarf most scenery, and music was used to frame and enhance the story being told.

> Lillian Gish, Actress
> Cited in *Sounds for Silents*, 1969

2237. Put three speakers behind the screen and spread the music around.

> Sam Warner, Head of Warner Bros. Studios
> As the first to produce "talkies," 1927, quot-
> ed on the Internet Movie Database, 1998

2238. On location doing exteriors … the sound-man was God. Whatever he said went.

> Hal Mohr, Director of Photography
> Cited in *The Reel Tinsel*, 1970

2239. Film fascinated composers right from the start. The new medium looked like a new kind of opera, without tenors.

> Alex Ross, Writer
> As written in *Scoring for Oscar*, 1998

2240. With new concert music basically dead, film is the last bastion of music as composition.

> Lukas Kendall, Editor-Publisher
> Written in his editorial of
> *Film Score Monthly*, June 1998

2241. The philosophy (of film music) is to come into the assignment as if it's the first thing you've ever done….

> John Barry, Film Composer
> Cited in *Overtones and Undertones:
> Reading Film Music*, 1994

2242. I've had lots of (film score) theories as the years have gone by, and I keep changing my theories so they're all useless, really.

> Anne Dudley, Film Composer
> Interview in *Film Score Monthly*, 1998

2243. The final function of film music … is to complete the psychological meaning of the scene.

> Miklós Rozsc, Film Composer
> Cited in *Overtones and Undertones:
> Reading Film Music*, 1994

2244. When we're inspired by things through our work, the work becomes inspired….

> Philip Glass, Film Composer
> On film scoring as cited in
> *Film Score Monthly*, 1998

2245. Film music is utilitarian ... some quite beautiful in their own right. A teapot is made for a purpose, but it can also be a work of art.
David Raskin, Film Composer
Cited in *Music for the Movies*, 1997

2246. Film is the closest art form to music there is. That which is as liquid ... that an image brings to mind.... That's how liquid thoughts are — images. The closest thing to that is music.
Richard Brooks, Writer-Director
Interview in *Directors at Work*, 1970

2247. It's the art of seduction. You're always seducing the audiences.
Sidney Levin, Film Editor
Interview in *First Cut*, 1992,
commenting on music editing

2248. Love in the sixteenth century is still love in the 21st century.
Jerry Goldsmith, Film Composer
On creating mood music
for a futuristic film, as stated in
Film Makers on Film Making, 1983

2249. Once you find the emotional line, which is, "Where can I take you on this journey?"— if you can feel that, it sure is going to be easy.
Ted Winterburn, Film Editor
Interview in *First Cut*, 1992,
commenting on sound editing

2250. The producer is its lungs, the director is its brains, the cameraman is its eyes, and the composer is its ears....
Lalo Schifrin, Film Composer
Cited in *Music for the Movies*,
1997, on the anatomy of a film

2251. The omniscience of producers isn't taxed as much in the fields of writing, photography and acting as it is in music, which seems to be a closed shop to them.
Hugo Friedhofer, Film Composer
Cited in *Music for the Movies*, 1997

2252. Ideally speaking, the composer should make you see something in that film that you couldn't have seen without the music.
Leonard Rosenman, Composer
Interview in *Film Makers on Film Making*, 1983

2253. Music is as important as some of the actors ... if not more important. The film composer is an actor in the films.
Tim Burton, Director
Interview in *Inner Views:
Filmmakers in Conversation*, 1992

2254. The composer for films is a dramatist ... it is how he sees the "mise-en-scène" musically....
Leonard Rosenman, Composer
Referring to the "placement in the scene" in an
interview for *Film Makers on Film Making*, 1983

2255. An artist expresses himself strongest in his own personality. If you feel the movie is close to that kind of personality, you have to go to that composer.
Paul Verhoeven, Director
Interview in *Film Score Monthly*, 1997

2256. America is the only country in the world with so-called "film-composers"— every other country has composers who sometimes do films.
Bernard Herrmann, Film Composer
Commenting on his dislike of the title —
1944, as quoted in *Music for the Movies*

2257. Commercial art is definitely more demanding than art with a capital "A."
Stewart Copeland, Film Composer
Interview in *Film Score Monthly*, 1997

2258. A lot of composers make the mistake of thinking of a film as a concert platform on which they can show off. This is not the place.
Max Steiner, Film Composer
Cited in *The Reel Tinsel*, 1970

2259. Any composer today is sitting there with this film ... and they have no idea what they're going to do. The only thing you can do is sit there and open up the veins and bleed all over the page.
Hans Zimmer, Film Composer
Interview in *Film Score Monthly*, 1997

2260. That everyone knows his own job and music too.
Jerry Goldsmith, Composer
On an old Hollywood saying, as cited in
Film Makers on Film Making, Vol. II, 1984

2261. So much of filmmaking today ... is done by committee decision — and nothing is worse for music than a committee decision.
John Scott, Film Composer
Cited in *Music for the Movies*, 1997

2262. Never forget that music is much too important to be left entirely in the hands of professionals.
Robert Fulghum, Writer
As written in his book, *Maybe Maybe Not*

2263. If (Richard) Wagner had lived in this century, he would have been the Number One film composer.

> Max Steiner, Film Composer
> Cited in *The Reel Tinsel*, 1970, on Wagner's
> incidental scoring behind his operas

2264. I'm trying to interpret the film through the director's head ... a composer is kind of like a psychic medium. They're holding their séance and trying to tap into the director's spirit.

> Danny Elfman, Film Composer
> Interview in *Film Score Monthly*, 1997

2265. Most directors are antimusical. They don't understand, they're fearful of what music might do to their carefully contrived balances.

> David Raksin, Film Composer
> Cited in *Overtones and Undertones:*
> *Reading Film Music*, 1994

2266. The director who makes your life difficult is probably the director who makes a better movie.

> Stewart Copeland, Film Composer
> In a *Film Score Monthly* interview,
> discussing music collaboration
> between the composer and director, 1998

2267. You have to do good films; then the music will appear better too.

> Leonard Rosenman, Composer
> Interview in *Film Makers on Film Making*, 1983

2268. The problems confronting the film composer are never the same twice and require in every instance another solution.

> Hugo Friedhofer, Film Composer
> Cited in *Music for the Movies*, 1997

2269. There are no new sounds, only new ideas, and they don't come along very often.

> Bernard Herrmann, Film Composer
> Cited in *Music for the Movies*, 1997

2270. The film composer has to bear in mind that we are a visually oriented society ... more of our brain is given over to view than to hearing.

> Leonard Rosenman, Film Composer
> Interview in *Film Makers on Film Making*, 1983

2271. We are craftsmen, and we become artists if what we do is good enough. But I confess I feel that art has been attained rarely on the screen.

> Henry Mancini, Film Composer
> Cited in *Music for the Movies*, 1997

2272. Film is the youngest of the arts and ... scoring is the youngest of the music arts. We have a great deal of development ahead of us.

> Jerry Goldsmith, Film Composer
> Cited in *Music for the Movies*, 1997

2273. Unexplored. That's film music. It's all unexplored.

> Bernard Herrmann, Film Composer
> Speaking before the British Film Institute, 1975

2274. When you develop a song, you can always expand upon it. It's like an old friend.

> Jerry Goldsmith, Film Composer
> Cited in *Music for the Movies*, 1997

2275. By itself the screen is a pretty cold proposition.... Music is like a small flame to help warm it ...

> Aaron Copeland, Composer
> Cited in *Sounds for Silents*, 1940

2276. The soundtrack (should) tell you something about the scene that the image itself couldn't tell you. This is ... the role of music in movies.

> Leonard Rosenman, Composer
> Interview in *Film Makers on Film Making*, 1983

2277. The music is the cherry on the sunset.

> Federico Fellini
> Cited in his biography, *Fellini—A Life*, 1986

2278. Music can make (the scene) so exciting that you think they really said something, even though they didn't say a damn thing.

> Max Steiner, Film Composer
> Cited in *The Reel Tinsel*, 1970

2279. The (movie) music is the guidepost, it's the tone and the context.

> Tim Burton, Director
> Interview in *Inner Views:*
> *Filmmakers in Conversation*, 1992

2280. It's artistically liberating working with the music as an impetus to the animation.

> Sally Cruikshank, Animator
> Cited in *Moviemakers at Work*, 1987

2281. A sense of drama.

> Henry Mancini, Film Composer
> Answering, "What does it take to be a film
> composer?" cited in *Music for the Movies*

2282. The most difficult problem in music is form, and in film you already have the problem solved ... it often suggests its own rhythm and tempo.

> Jerry Goldsmith, Film Composer
> Cited in *Music for the Movies*, 1997

2283. The orchestra acts as an unseen protagonist, commenting on the action and sometimes dictating it.

> Michael Walsh
> Cited in the biography *The Hustons*, 1989

2284. The orchestra is the composer's palette. ... all of a sudden I (feel), "That's the color I want."

> Jerry Goldsmith, Composer
> Interview in *Film Makers on
> Film Making*, Vol. II., 1983

2285. I ... think in terms of the counterpoint of sound and image as opposed to the union of sound and image.

> Akira Kurosawa, Director
> Stated in his autobiography,
> *Akira Kurosawa*, 1982

2286. Everything for me is a reconstruction or deconstruction (of a preconceived music association).

> Danny Elfman, Film Composer
> Interview in *Film Score Monthly*,
> 1997, on composing for film

2287. In musical harmony the critical determinant of consonance and dissonance is expectation of movement.... Context is the determining factor.

> Norman Cazden, Film Composer
> Cited in the *Journal of Aesthetics* 4,
> "Emotions," 1945

2288. An orchestrator is a man who takes a composition and puts it into orchestra parts. An arranger ... takes a melody, puts in different harmonies ... and usually ruins it. They should all be shot.

> Max Steiner, Screen Composer
> Cited in *The Reel Tinsel*, 1970

2289. The hardest thing in scoring is to know when to start, and when to stop.... I've always tried to subordinate myself to the picture.

> Max Steiner, Film Composer
> Cited in *The Reel Tinsel*, 1970

2290. "Quiet" is an effect. And not having music is a way of scoring as well. Where the music isn't matters as much as where the music is.

> Paul Hirsch, Film Editor
> Interview in *First Cut— Conversations
> with Film Editors*, 1992

2291. What you heard was real silence ... an attentive ear can detect the thousand and one imperceptible sounds of which that silence is composed.

> Jean Cocteau
> Cited in his book, *Cocteau on the Film*, 1954

2292. Sounds are bubbles on the surface of silence.

> Trinh T. Minh-ha
> Cited in *Cinematography*, Vol. 3

2293. [A] silent image can make a lot of noise.

> Yves Yersin
> Cited in *Film Forum*, 1985

2294. With dialogue, the most effective technique is the use of silence ... nothing is as loud in films as silence.

> Bronislaw Kaper, Film Composer
> On drawing a parallel to musical scoring in
> films, as stated in *Music for the Movies*, 1997

2295. The most economical score is often the best one, just as the simplest solution is often the most effective.

> David Shire, Film Composer
> Cited in *Music for the Movies*, 1997

2296. Music in films ... must be noticed in its place ... if I hadn't made myself felt, I wouldn't have been serving the picture.

> Henry Mancini, Film Composer
> Cited in *Music for the Movies*, 1997

2297. To make a point in film you have to make your point stronger than you would in real life; I feel I can reach more people by being a little more over-the-top with the music and its feelings....

> Steven Spielberg, Director
> Interview in *Take 22:
> Moviemakers on Moviemaking*, 1984

2298. If a score is inordinately interesting— if it draws attention to itself— it has failed in its purpose.

> Alex Ross, Writer
> Written in his "Scoring for Oscar,"
> *The New Yorker*, 1998

2299. The music enters the plot directly.

> Leonard Rosenman, Composer
> Interview in *Film Makers on Film Making*, 1984

2300. Cinema music is the cinema. That's part of making the picture, not something that's put in later.

> Bernard Hermann, Film Composer
> Cited in *Overtones and Undertones.
> Reading Film Music*, 1994

2301. (I) score according to the way the character impressed me, whoever he might be. He may be a bastard....

> Max Steiner, Screen Composer
> Cited in *The Reel Tinsel*, 1970

2302. You see the hero, you state the theme, you move on....

> Danny Elfman, Film Composer
> Interviewed in *Film Score Monthly*,
> 1997, on the "Korngold" style
> model of scoring for action films

2303. You wouldn't want an elephant to be put into a bar.... He doesn't fit in a bar. If you want an elephant, put him the living room. It's the same with music.

> Max Steiner, Screen Composer
> Commenting on proper scoring, as
> cited in *The Reel Tinsel*, 1970

2304. Too often a score is used to make a point the director can't seem to make visually.

> Peter Bogdanovich, Writer-Director
> Interview in *Take 22:*
> *Moviemakers on Moviemaking*, 1984

2305. I never write (movie music) from a script ... I would have been in Forest Lawn long ago because what they can do to a script is unheard of.

> Max Steiner, Screen Composer
> Cited in *The Reel Tinsel*, 1970

2306. My attitude — to give the film what it needs ... if the picture is good, the score stands a better chance of being good.

> Max Steiner, Film Composer
> Cited in *The Reel Tinsel*, 1970

2307. Music causes the film to seem slower or faster or smoother or more disjunct in some way ... which influences your perception.

> Leonard Rosenman, Composer
> Interview in *Film Makers on Film Making*, 1984

2308. It's very important for the composer to know what music can't do. (Music) will only express majesty if what you have on the screen is majestic.

> Leonard Rosenman, Composer
> Interview in *Film Makers on Film Making*, 1984

2309. It'll play better when we add the music.

> Industry cliché
> Cited in *Making Movies*, 1995

2310. (Movie music) was like an enema in the Jewish family tradition ... "it can't hurt you."

> Leonard Rosenman, Composer
> Interviewed on the early years of film music
> in *Film Makers on Film Making*, 1983

2311. Good films have saved bad music, but even a great score never saved a bad film.

> Jerry Goldsmith, Composer
> Interview in *Film Makers on*
> *Film Making*, Vol. II, 1984

2312. The beauty of a main title is that you establish your main (musical) theme.... You plant the seed that you're going to go water later in the score.

> Danny Elfman, Film Composer
> Interview in *Film Score Monthly*, 1997

2313. I tried to have the main theme be a human theme.

> David Amran, Film Composer
> Interview in *Film Score Monthly*,
> 1998, on musical scoring

2314. I just find it really boring to reinforce what's already on the screen. It's kind of a patronizing approach, assuming the audience is rather stupid.

> Michael Danna, Film Composer
> Interview in *Film Score Monthly*,
> 1998, on musical scoring

2315. Too much film music today is mere improvisation and that is why it is of little value.

> Lukas Kendall, Editor-Publisher
> Written in his June 1998
> editorial for *Film Score Monthly*

2316. The ideal for film music is ... continuous tonal version of the story and musical illustration of the drama on the screen.

> "The American Organist"
> Stated in a 1923 edition
> of *The American Organist*

2317. A composer is always trying to bring another layer of reality to the movie. But there's also the constant of the movie and the imagery being the truths. If not it just becomes like Teflon and spits your music off the screen.

> Elliot Goldenthal, Film Composer
> Interview in *Film Score Monthly*, 1997

2318. There are a million ways of selecting music to serve as accompaniment for a picture, but there are only two ways that a good musician would choose. One is to select beautiful music ... appropriate for the scenes.... The second is to select music ... with an ear to subjugation.

> Hugo Riesenfeld, Film Composer
> Interview in *The American Organist*, 1920

2319. What we hear from the screen is not an image of the sound, but the sound itself ... there is no difference in dimension and reality between the original sound and the recorded and reproduced sound.

> Béla Balázs, Writer
> Cited in "Theory of the Film,"
> *Sound Theory — Sound Practice*, 1992

2320. If we were living in the twelfth century … the practitioners of dubbing would be burnt in the marketplace for heresy. Dubbing is equivalent to a belief in the duality of the soul.

Jean Renoir, Director
Stated in his autobiography,
My Life and Times, 1974

2321. There is no ontological difference between hearing a violin in a concert hall and hearing it on a soundtrack in a movie theater.

Gerald Mast, Writer
Cited in "Film-Cinema-Movie,"
Sound Theory—Sound Practice, 1992

2322. The suspense was done with French horns, an acre of strings, percussion to the wall, synths going berserk, and screaming guitars.

Dennis McCarthy, Film Composer
Commenting on the musical
tension element of *Letters from a
Killer* in a June, 1998,
Film Score Monthly interview

2323. They … used to say that a good score was one you didn't notice, and I … say "What the hell good is it if you don't notice it?"

Max Steiner, Film Composer
Cited in *The Reel Tinsel*, 1970

2324. My theory is that the (film) music should be felt rather than heard.

Max Steiner, Film Composer
Cited in *The Reel Tinsel*, 1970

2325. Film music makes sense only if it helps the films … the music must be secondary in importance to the story being told on the screen.

Aaron Copeland, Composer
Cited in *Sounds for Silents*, 1940

2326. If a movie played in the forest and there was no one there to watch it, would there be a soundtrack?

Stephen M. Ringler

2327. One of the most overused expressions in Hollywood is "We'll save it in the mix."

Bill Varney, Sound Re-recordist
Interview in *Moviemakers at Work*, 1987

2328. I think you have not really lived, as a sound person, until you've erased a take!

Chris Newman, Sound Recordist
Interview in *Moviemakers at Work*, 1987

2329. I don't like a single instrument even with orchestral background, because they interfere with the dialogue … one lousy clarinet can kill a scene and even the entire movie.

Max Steiner, Screen Composer
Cited in *The Reel Tinsel*, 1970

2330. Of all the noises I think music is the least annoying.

Jerome Kern
At the Academy Awards, commenting
during his Best Music award presentation

2331. There are only so many ways you can score a car chase….

Lalo Schifrin, Film Composer
Cited in *Music for the Movies*, 1997

2332. I don't like to see a man alone in the desert, dying of thirst, with the Philadelphia Orchestra behind him.

John Ford, Director
Cited in his biography, *John Ford*, 1968,
commenting on the overuse of film music

2333. If you have festive music (at the end of the picture) you are saying to the audience, "Warner Bros. congratulates the nun on quitting the convent." Is that what you want?

Fred Zinnemann
Arguing with Jack Warner on his
suggestion for upbeat music at
the end of *The Nun's Story*, 1959

2334. To write the music for *The Hunt for Red October*…. I was thinking in terms of Rachmaninoff-goes-to-sea.

Basil Poledouris, Film Composer
Cited in *Music for the Movies*, 1997

19

Special Effects

2335. Cinema itself is a special effect.
NOVA
Stated in the 1998 telecast of *Special Effects*

2336. We are synthesizing dream images....
Chris Evans, Special Effects Designer
On combining special effects
and photographed images as
cited in *Moviemakers at Work*, 1987

2337. I detest phony realism.
Billy Wilder, Director
Cited in *The Bright Side
of Billy Wilder, Primarily*, 1970

2338. I loathe tricky effects ... they are facile and obvious ... pompous effects slow up action, are boring and unpleasant, and have been mistaken for that tiresome word, "art."
Charlie Chaplin
Stated in his 1964
My Autobiography — Charlie Chaplin

2339. Call me a skeptic, but I don't believe even a jaguar can outrun a shock wave.
Roger Ebert
Stated in his 1997 *Questions
for the Movie Answer Man*

2340. The greatest effects ever produced ... are those that still manage to confound us.
Ron Fry, Actor
Stated in his co-authored, 1977,
The Saga of Special Effects

2341. A picture is not a pyramid ... it's more like a feather in a hurricane.
John P. Fulton
Cited in *The Saga of Special Effects*, 1977

2342. Natural phenomena are unpredictable; they must be made to order. Uncontrolled reality is often not filmic, usually not dramatic, and cer-tainly not dependable. Without a little gilding, reality often slips by unnoticed.
Frank P. Clark
Cited in *The Saga of Special Effects*, 1977

2343. The key to misty breath, red noses, and frosty eyebrows was so obvious it had been over-looked — lower the temperature, fool.
Frank Capra, Producer-Director
Stated in his 1971 *Frank Capra
— The Name Above the Title*

2344. One of the things movies can do strikingly is show, visually, that things are other than what they are.... It's like being delighted by a magic trick — watching one thing transform into something else.
David Mamet, Writer-Director
Interview in *Interview* magazine, 1998

2345. We're working in the film business here. The painting is not the finished artwork; the finished artwork is the image on the screen.
Chris Evans, Special Effects Designer
Cited in *Moviemakers at Work*, 1987

2346. Every fire, every explosion, every car crash we rig is a gag, and a gag is a trick, and a trick is dangerous. There's always room for a mistake.
Roy Arbogast, Special Effects Specialist
Cited in *Moviemakers at Work*, 1987

2347. [E]ven if a film is made without any attempt at tricks, they are still there.
Jean Cocteau
Stated in his 1954 *Cocteau on the Film*

2348. You're only as good as your last screw-up.
Saying in the "Special Effects"
field of filmmaking

2349. In special effects, 99% right is wrong.
Industry saying

2350. For a special effects man to be liable for everything is insane. You are in the most vulnerable spot of any job in the world ... you have to go in with a whole legal system in front of you....

Roy Arbogast, Special Effects Specialist
Referring to the danger of accidents and risk of
lawsuits if a special effect on the set goes
wrong, as cited in *Moviemakers at Work*, 1987

2351. Nothing in a film is ever real; it's all a fiction. Using (matte) paintings to fool the eye is just another aspect of that fiction.

Chris Evans, Special Effects Designer
Cited in *Moviemakers at Work*, 1987

2352. The art is predicting what will work best for a particular shot and then imposing your style onto the shot and sequence.

Dennis Muren, Visual Effects Technician
Interview in *Moviemakers at Work*, 1987

2353. The good matte artist puts aside his individual style to create an impersonal illusion.

Chris Evans, Special Effects Designer
Cited in *Moviemakers at Work*, 1987

2354. In the film business, special effects are sort of the core of the apple.

Mike Fulmer, Special Effects Miniatures
Cited in *Moviemakers at Work*, 1987

2355. Frame by frame, animation and special effects have powered the imaginations of filmmakers and audiences. The path from ink-and-paint to morphing.

Adam Rodgers, Writer
Stated in "The 100 Best Movies"
— *Newsweek Extra 2000*, 1998

2356. Artistic developments are in practice the direct outcome of technical improvements.

Jean Renoir, Director
Stated in his 1974 *Jean Renoir
— My Life and Times*

2357. In a Hollywood dictionary there is no such thing as impossible.

Liam Neeson, Actor
On visual effects, at the 1999
Academy Awards presentation

2358. With today's advanced technology we (are) able to bring "flash and fantasy" even closer together to tell a story no one believed did happen, yet reacted as if it could.

Dean Cundey, Cinematographer
Cited in *Contemporary Cinematographers:
On Their Art*, 1998

2359. The problem with all these technical advances in film is that many, many filmmakers don't see them as tools. They are only tools for telling a story or giving you an effect ... but they should be completely organic to the story.

The New York Times
On the future of films, 1997

2360. Special effects are for the benefit of the audience, not for the benefit of the actor. It is not like what you do is for the benefit of the writer.

Arnold Schwarzenegger, Actor
Cited in *The Los Angeles Times Magazine*, 1996

2361. [E]ventually, film itself will disappear and the show will be delivered as electronic data ... and displayed on a screen that will be internally illuminated.

Jonathan Erland, Special Effects Technician
Cited in *Moviemakers at Work*, 1987

2362. Even if you could create a computer model that looked just like Cary Grant, who is going to make him act?

John Lasseter, Pixar
Interview in *Los Angeles* magazine, 1997

2363. So, you want to be in pixels.

NOVA
Stated in the 1998 televised *Special Effects*

2364. I like people coming out of the screen, but I prefer they do it with their talents and not special effects.

Joan Crawford
Cited in *Bette and Joan — The Divine Feud*,
1989, against the new medium 3–D

2365. When you're telling a really fantastic story, you have to rely on something extraordinary.

Chris Evans, Special Effects Designer
Cited in *Moviemakers at Work*, 1987

2366. I wish I had gotten one of those Marky Mark prosthetic organs. Even half of Dirk Diggler's would have been fine with me.

Kevin Bacon, Actor
After being filmed full-frontal nude in the
shower, as stated in *Entertainment Weekly*, 1998

2367. John Belushi was something of a special effect himself.

Dan Aykroyd, Actor
Cited in *Inside Oscar*, 1997

20

Animation

2368. If you're watching a cartoon, you'll go into a certain mode that says, OK, this is a cartoon, I'll accept this as reality — there's a suspension of disbelief.

> Jonathan Erland, Special Effects Technician
> Interview in *Moviemakers at Work*, 1987

2369. An animated cartoon is the abstract pure madness expressed in a most natural-seeming aspect.

> Philippe Lamour, Critic
> Cited in *The New Art*

2370. Animated cartoons are the poignant reality of the unreal.

> Dorothy Graffey, Writer
> Cited in *America's Youngest Art*,
> on Disney animation

2371. The animated cartoon is a shotgun marriage between art and mechanics, with King Midas fingering the trigger.

> Ken O'Conner, Disney designer
> Stated in his lecture, "Designing Fantasia"

2372. (Animation) is the magic in seeing the impossible happen.

> Gilbert Seldes, Writer
> Cited in *Disney and Others*,
> on Disney's aesthetic urge

2373. (Disney) wanted something that lives and not just moves around.

> Eric Larson, Animator
> On the Disney design doctrine
> — an "illusion of life," as cited
> in *Character Handling*, 1938

2374. Animation enables me to give magical powers to things. In my films, I move many objects, real objects.... I use animation as a means of subversion.

> Jan Svankmajer, Animator
> Stated on the BBC2 television show *The Magic Art of Jan Svankmajer*, 1992, London

2375. Walt Disney always felt that everything you put on the page should be able to step out of that page and talk to you.

> Eric Larson, Animator
> Cited in *Character Handling*, 1938

2376. Not bound to imitating nature, (Walt Disney) distorts it as he likes: a piano is instantly turned into a grand-opera singer, a daisy into a chorus girl.

> Lewis Jacobs, Writer
> Stated in his *The Rise of American Film*, 1939

2377. The difference between Disney's lines and ... the abstractions of our "pewee Picassos" is that Disney's abstracts actually function — (they) have something significant to do and do it.

> Art Digest, 1940
> Referring to the characters in *Pinocchio*

2378. Animation should be an art. That is how I conceived it.

> Winsor McCay, Cartoonist
> Cited on the Internet Movie Database,
> 1998, from the 1911 creator of *Little Nemo*

2379. (With animation) you can appeal to the basic emotion shared by the whole of mankind — laughter.

> Shamus Culhane, Animator
> Stated in his *Animation*, 1988

2380. The first duty of the cartoon is not to picture or duplicate real action or things as they actually happen, but to give a caricature of life and action....

> Walt Disney
> In a 1935 studio memo to
> animator Don Graham

2381. Our study of the actual is not so that we may be able to accomplish the actual, but so that we may have a basis upon which to go into the fantastic, the unreal, the imaginative — and yet let it have a foundation of fact.

> Walt Disney
> In a 1935 studio memo
> to animator Don Graham

2382. (Animated artistry) are reflections of the real world in the fantastic.

> Lewis Jacobs, Writer
> Stated in his *The Rise of the American Film*, 1939

2383. I definitely feel that we cannot do the fantastic things, based on the real unless we first know the real.

> Walt Disney
> In a 1935 studio memo
> to animator Don Graham

2384. I will introduce rhythm into the concrete action of my abstract paintings ... I am creating a new visual art in time, that of coloured rhythm and of rhythmic colour.

> Leopold Survage, Animator
> Cited in *Experimental Animation*, 1976

2385. There are only two genuinely American forms of art: jazz and Walt Disney.

> News Columns, *Hollywood Citizen-News*
> Cited in a 1940 news article

2386. [T]hat for every mood there is a gesture, a pose that is the essence of the feeling translated into kinetics.

> Shamus Culhane, Animator
> In his *Animation*, 1988, on being an
> observer of the human condition

2387. [T]he emphasis on personality ... became the signature of Disney animation.

> Walt Disney, 1959
> Referring to his 1935 studio memo
> for "personality animation"

2388. "I'm not bad, I'm just drawn that way."

> Jessica Rabbit
> Animated actress, 1988,
> from the movie *Who Framed Roger Rabbit?*

2389. (Mickey Mouse) is an average young boy ... living in a small town, clean-living, fun-loving, bashful around girls, polite, and as clever as he must be for the particular story.

> Walt Disney
> His official sketch of his studio's main character, as cited in *Disney Animation*, 1991

2390. (Donald Duck) is vain, cocky, and boastful; loves to impose on other people and to heckle

them, but if the tables are turned he flies into a rage. His most likeable trait is determination ... he comes back again and again .. until either he or the opposition is in ruins....

> Disney Story Department
> Official studio character sketch, 1939

2391. "Fergy, you're a great actor.... That's why your animation is so good, because you feel. You feel what those characters feel."

> Walt Disney
> To his top artist, Norman Ferguson, considered
> the "Charlie Chaplin" of acting animation

2392. In order to "read" the emotions of a character, the audience first looks at the face, then the hands, after that, the body....

> Shamus Culhane, Animator
> Stated in his *Animation*, 1988

2393. The only time you start with the head when drawing a figure is when the person has been hanged!

> Shamus Culhane, Animator
> Stated in his *Animation*, 1988

2394. Are you trying to do something that shouldn't be attempted? Like trying to show the top of Mickey's head.

> Walt Disney
> Referring to one of his crucial 14
> Points of Animation with his staff,
> as cited in *Disney Animation*, 1991

2395. The freedom of animation is astonishing, but the physical process itself is like a truck sitting on your shoulders.

> Sally Cruikshank, Animator
> Cited in *Moviemakers at Work*, 1987

2396. People will be entertained by new visuals for only a few seconds.

> John Lasseter, Pixar
> Interview in *Los Angeles Magazine*, 1997

2397. The word Art, spelled with a capital "A," is taboo on the Disney lot, but constant study is given to works of the great masters.

> *Hollywood Citizen-News*
> Cited in a 1938 news article

2398. The audience of which you should be aware when you are animating is yourself ... let yourself without reservation be both entertainer and the entertained.

> Shamus Culhane, Animator
> In his *Animation*, 1988

2399. The rule was: if you could hold a pencil, you could animate.

Dick Huemer, Animator
Cited on the Internet Movie Database, 1998

2400. Improving your drawing is going to be a lifelong chore, without limits.

Shamus Culhane, Animator
From his *Animation*, 1988, on "draftsmanship"

2401. (Is it the) most interesting way? Would anyone other than your mother like it?

Walt Disney
Referring to one of his crucial 14
Points of Animation with his staff,
as cited in *Disney Animation*, 1991

21

Editing

2402. Editing is the only original and unique art form in film.

Vladmir Pudovkin
Cited on the Internet Movie Database, 1998

2403. Film is the combination of many different art forms. Editing is the only one that's unique to it. It's the heart of it.

Tom Lewis, Editor
Cited in *The Hollywood Reporter*, 1999

2404. No matter how pleasing it may be photographically, the material only comes to life in editing.

Tony Rose, Author
Stated in his 1972 *The Complete Book of Moviemaking*

2405. Without editing, a film is dead; with it, alive.

Vladmir Pudovkin, Director
Stated in his 1929 *Film Technique*

2406. [O]nly ... a synthesis of different separate visual images is ... endowed with filmic life....

Vladmir Pudovkin, Director
From the Eisenstein-Pudovkin theory and practice of cinema, as cited in *Lessons with Eisenstein*, 1962

2407. Film editing is an accompanying position, like a pianist accompanies a soloist.

Peter C. Frank, Film Editor
Interview in *First Cut*, 1992

2408. Editing can be subtle and evocative and surprising, but it must always be communicative, that's the bottom line.

Evan Lottman, Film Editor
Interview in *First Cut*, 1992

2409. Film editing transformed motion pictures from a recording medium to an art form. In its simplest aspect, cutting is about juxtapositions.

Ralph Rosenblum, Film Editor-Author
Stated in his co-authored 1979 *A Film Editor's Story*, on the 1902 film editing origin

2410. The art of cheating is the art of film editing, truly.

Donn Cambern, Film Editor
Interview in *First Cut*, 1992

2411. The shooting of the movie is the truth part and the editing of the movie is the lying part, the deceit part.

Paul Hirsch, Film Editor
Interview in *First Cut*, 1992

2412. Everything in filmmaking is an artifice.

Bill Pancow, Film Editor
Interview in *First Cut*, 1992

2413. Editing is the basic creative force, by power of which the soulless photographs are engineered into living, cinematographic form.

Vladmir Pudovkin
From the 1928 Eisenstein-Pudovkin theory and practice of cinema, as cited in *Lessons with Eisenstein*, 1962

2414. The ultimate storyteller is not the screenwriter, nor the director, or the actors, or the camera. It's he who holds the scissors who finally tells the tale.

Stephen M. Ringler

2415. (The editor's) job is to interpret and respect the material at hand ... respect the style, performances, composition, writing, lighting, every aspect. We are a very respectful lot!

Carol Littleton, Film Editor
Interview in *First Cut*, 1992,
on what is film editing

2416. You're writing with images, with music, with performances, you're writing with all the things … that make an emotional event.

Carol Littleton, Film Editor
Cited in *Lessons with Eisenstein*, 1962, which
translates to the English word "editing"

2417. Cinematography is, first and foremost, montage.

Sergei M. Eisenstein
Interview in *First Cut*, 1992

2418. Editing is not just controlling a flow of moments as it is an accumulation of emotions.

Sidney Levin, Film Editor
State in *Newsweek Extra 2000*,
on "The 100 Best Movies," 1998

2419. The cut itself creates another kind of movement — an emotional and psychological movement in the mind's eye.…

Martin Scorsese, Director
Interview in *First Cut*, 1992

2420. We're sort of alchemists. We put a lot of elements together, and we're hoping to make gold.

Carol Littleton, Film Editor
Interview in *Film Makers on Film Making*, 1983

2421. In French, the word is monteur, which is what it is; you're mounting the film (not editing).

Verna Fields, Editor
Interview in *First Cut*, 1992

2422. The film editor's input … is unlike beautiful photography which is apparent to the eye … film editing is much more amorphous, it's not palpable.

Barry Malkin, Film Editor
Cited in *Adventures in the Screen Trade*, 1983

2423. Editing is a process where your mind and your concept work faster than the techniques.

Dede Allen
Interview in *First Cut*, 1992

2424. Editing is a shifting of gears from being a spectator to tackling all the problems, seen or unseen.

Emily Paine, Film Editor
Cited in *Kuleshov on Film*, 1974

2425. (The film editor) coordinates and structures the pieces of film, providing compulsory and deliberate guidance of the thoughts and associations of the spectator.

V. I. Pudovkin
Interview in *First Cut*, 1992

2426. An artist is someone who stylizes life in such a way as to make truth comprehensible for those who are watching the work of art. That's how I see (the film editor).

Sidney Levin, Film Editor
Stated in his 1939 *The Rise of the American Film*

2427. Russian emphasis on editing (c. 1930s) was nearer the essence of film art than the German emphasis on camera eye and mobility (which is) a subordinate tool to the cutting process.

Lewis Jacobs, Author
Interview in *First Cut*, 1992

2428. (Every film editor) has their own little quirks … inner rhythms, their own sensibilities that become their signature in the work they do. It's like looking at two different handwritings.

Richard Marks, Film Editor
Stated in his 1974 memoir,
Don't Look at the Camera

2429. The editor can … give tempo and emphasis.… A film editor is an orchestrator.

Harry Watt, British documentary director
Interview in *First Cut*, 1992,
on the old studio system attitude

2430. Editors were: a pair of hands who existed in a state of anonymity.

Richard Marks, Film Editor
Stated in his co-authored,
1979 *A Film Editor's Story*

2431. (The film editor) inhabits an anonymous world, and various aspects of the trade conspire to keep him anonymous.

Ralph Rosenblum, Film Editor — Author
Interview in *First Cut*, 1992

2432. I'm a facilitator with a brain and a heart. I'm not a computer.

Carol Littleton, Film Editor
Cited in *Take 22: Moviemakers
on Moviemaking*, 1984

2433. Editing is … a very creative art — and a poor editor can kill you as quickly as a good one can save you.

John Badham, Director
Cited in *First Cut*, 1992

2434. You have to have a long attention span to be a good editor.

Tom Haneke, Film Editor
Interview in *First Cut*, 1992

2435. When the film is finished shooting and

everybody is gone, (film editing) is like the loneliness of the long-distance runner.

> Donn Cambern, Film Editor
> Cited in *The Bright Side of*
> *Billy Wilder, Primarily,* 1970

2436. When I am finished, there is nothing left on the cutting room floor but cigarette butts, chewing gum wrappers and tears.

> Billy Wilder, Director
> Interview in *First Cut,* 1992

2437. I can't watch (my own films). It's unbearable ... this is a cruel trick that the film gods play on the worshippers at the shrine!

> Paul Hirsch, Film Editor
> Interview in *First Cut,* 1992

2438. Dailies are unwatchable, except if you're being paid to do it, and they come out to be the movie that you are willing to pay to see!

> Paul Hirsch, Film Editor
> Referring to editing in the case of film,
> as cited in *Film Technique,* 1929

2439. In every art there must be firstly a material, and secondly a method of composing this material specially adapted to this art.

> L. Kuleshow, Director
> Stated in his 1929 *Film Technique*
> on fellow Russian director
> L. Kieleshov's view of editing

2440. The musician has sounds as material and composes them in time. The painter's materials are colour, and he combines them in space on the ... canvas.... Film work consists of pieces of film....

> Vladmir Pudovkin, Director
> Cited in *A Film Editor's Story,* 1979

2441. [T]hat the sculptor finds the statue which is waiting in the stone, applies equally to editing; the editor finds the film which is waiting hidden in the material.

> Tom Priestly, Film Editor
> Stated in his 1931 *Appreciations*

2442. Art does but consist in the removal of surplussage ... the finished work lies somewhere, according to Michelangelo's fancy, hidden in the rough-hewn block of stone.

> Walter Pater, Author
> On what to take out and still
> keep the essence, as cited in
> *The Hollywood Reporter,* 1999

2443. The essence of every picture is always there in the first cut.

> Billy Weber, Editor
> Interview in *First Cut,* 1992

2444. When I cut, I almost get into a Zen-like state, an intuition that almost occurs naturally.

> Paul Barnes, Film Editor
> Advising a new editor, Hal Ashby,
> recalled in *Directors in Action,* 1968

2445. [D]on't be afraid of the film ... you can always put it back ... and start over.

> Robert Swink, Editor
> Interview in *First Cut,* 1992, on film editing

2446. "Style" ... is not so much which techniques one uses but the degree of caring about the film.

> Gabriella Oldham, Writer

2447. Editing is essentially rewriting. It's the final rewrite.

> Carol Littleton, Film Editor
> Interview in *Moviemakers at Work,* 1987

2448. (Film editing is) the last stages of writing, really.

> Alan Heim, Film Editor
> Interview in *First Cut,* 1992

2449. Art springs from an urge to order.

> Aldous Huxley, Author
> Cited in *The Cinema as Art,* 1965

2450. My style is to communicate.

> Evan Lottman, Film Editor
> Interview in *First Cut,* 1992

2451. An editor attempts to make it better. A film, when it is edited, is redirected.

> Barry Malkin, Film Editor
> Interview in *First Cut,* 1992

2452. The development of film technique has been primarily the development of editing.

> Ernest Lindgren, Author
> Stated in his 1948 *The Art of the Film*

2453. Your first loyalty ... is to create what the director first saw as his picture.

> Anne V. Coates, Film Editor
> Interview in *First Cut,* 1992

2454. We're the director's best friend.

> Harold Kress, Film Editor
> Interview in *First Cut,* 1992, on film editors

2455. I'll climb inside the director's head if he'll let me.

> Verna Fields, Editor
> Interview in *Film Makers on Film Making,* 1983

2456. I am part of the filmmaking process ... but I am not a filmmaker.

> Tom Rolf, Film Editor
> Interview in *First Cut*, 1992

2457. There's corollary with editing which is that everyone's point of view is valid, and everyone speaks for some portion of the audience.

> Peter C. Frank, Film Editor
> Interview in *First Cut*, 1992

2458. I wish the word "editing" had never been invented ... "editing" implies correcting, and it's not.

> Verna Fields, Editor
> Interview in *Film Makers on Film Making*, 1983

2459. Film editing is getting the chaff out.... It's a question of judgment every single time. Every single frame you put through, you have to say what it is doing.

> John D. Dunning, Film Editor
> Interview in *First Cut*, 1992

2460. Nearly all editing points in narrative film are devised to set up a framework of expectations in a series of shots. The result is narrative motion.

> Steven D. Katz, Writer
> Stated in his 1991 *Film Directing Shot by Shot*

2461. The wise constructor of films knows to distill and refine ... it's a Japanese attitude about artistry. Down to the essence.

> Sidney Levin, Film Editor
> Interview in *First Cut*, 1992

2462. Use the good stuff.

> Bill Wellman, Director
> Cited in *First Cut*, 1992, when asked
> for his advice for editing his film

2463. From shit you get shit!

> Paul Falkenberg, Film Editor
> On refusing to rescue a bad film first
> cut as its proposed new editor, as
> cited in *A Film Editor's Story*, 1979

2464. Each cut is a new and fresh decision ... there's ... always something different to consider. We're building a house but none of the bricks are the same.

> Barry Malkin, Film Editor
> Interview in *First Cut*, 1992

2465. You have to say, "Screw it, all right, so it's not the greatest cut, but at least I used what I thought was best and made it play."

> Barry Malkin, Film Editor
> Interview in *First Cut*, 1992

2466. When you finish editing a picture, it's an awful problem to cut the cord. Usually they take a small team of horses and drag you out of the cutting room.

> George Sidney, Director
> Interview in *A Cut Above*, 1998

2467. Ultimately you can (edit) something forever, and at some point you say "That's it."

> Richard Marks, Film Editor
> Interview in *First Cut*, 1992

2468. Every film has its proper length, and you find that out in the editing room.

> Peter Weir, Director
> Interview in *Movieline* magazine, 1998

2469. Everyone is looking for a connection, a random connection that will make sense in a context. That's what editing is.

> Peter C. Frank, Film Editor
> Interview in *First Cut*, 1992

2470. Life is all inclusion and confusion, while art is all discrimination and selection.

> Henry James, Author
> Cited in *The Cinema as Art*, 1965

2471. The hardest thing to edit is a well-directed film ... you have screwed up if the edited version isn't better than the dailies. If you want trouble, be handed really good film.

> Sidney Levin, Film Editor
> Interview in *First Cut*, 1992

2472. You have to be alive to what's there, to the feeling on the screen, and not what's in your head about what's supposed to be there.

> Geof Bartz, Film Editor
> Interview in *First Cut*, 1992

2473. The filmed material at the moment of editing can sometimes be wiser than the author or editor.

> Sergei Eisenstein, Director
> Cited in *A Film Editor's Story*, 1979, on allow-
> ing the film to lead him in the cutting room

2474. I've always felt (as an editor) that films talk to you, and if you listen to it, it will show you its strengths.

> Donn Cambern, Film Editor
> Interview in *First Cut*, 1992

2475. You may have to admit that the film is right and that you are wrong. ... it does have a way of talking back to you.

> Elliot Silverstein, Director
> On the editing taking the film in a
> different direction than the director's
> vision, as cited in *Directors at Work*, 1970

2476. I let the film dictate to me. I let my visual eye and my editorial brain work on automatic.
Carl Kress, Film Editor
Interview in *First Cut*, 1992

2477. The story told me why to cut the picture, ... and then the picture told me how to cut the picture.
Ted Winterburn, Film Editor
Interview in *First Cut*, 1992

2478. There's an internal rhythm that comes out of the material that you have to find ... the material often tells you where to cut.
Richard Marks, Film Editor
Interview in *First Cut*, 1992

2479. Cinematographic portrayal of action enables one ... to pick out appropriate elements for accentuation ... the combination of such ... results in an editing composition — that is, the specific manner and rhythm of the author's narrative.
Vladmir Nizhny, Author
Stated in his 1962 *Lessons with Eisenstein*

2480. A good film editor allows the film to turn him on. The film should tell him what to do. His obligation is to the film, not to anybody.
Norman Jewison, Director
Interview in *Directors at Work*, 1970

2481. Cutting a film is really a matter of feeling — whatever it is, if it works, do it.
Verna Fields, Editor
Interview in *Film Makers on Film Making*, 1983

2482. A scene has its own life that mustn't be tampered with ... you're not supposed to edit unless you're supposed to edit.
Sidney Levin, Film Editor
Interview in *First Cut*, 1992

2483. My role ... is to fulfill the film's promise with what exists, not with delusion.
Sidney Levin, Film Editor
Interview in *First Cut*, 1992

2484. Life plays a great part in being an editor. You're always working with emotion. You have to open yourself to the material. You can't force film.
Alan Heim, Film Editor
Interview in *First Cut*, 1992

2485. Art is pattern informed by sensibility and emotion cultivating good form....
Herbert Reed, Author
Stated in his 1949 *The Meaning of Art*

2486. You don't want to impose onto a film a certain (editing) technique, a device, because it plays as a device. That's not style.
Donn Cambern, Film Editor
Interview in *First Cut*, 1992,
on having an editing style

2487. (Editing is more) the act of creation than the act of arrangement.
Sergei Eisenstein
Cited in *A Film Editor's Story*

2488. I can hear (visual) spaces ... how to make moments, where to leave space and where to compress space.
Tom Haneke, Film Editor
Interview in *First Cut*, 1992,
on the rhythm of editing

2489. (A film editor's) obligation's not to the director. I've never worked with an editor yet who's any good who said, "Gee, I hope he likes this."
Norman Jewison, Director
Interview in *Directors at Work*, 1970

2490. There are probably a lot of wrong ways to do things (edit), but there's no one right way.
Bill Pancow, Film Editor
Interview in *First Cut*, 1992

2491. I don't think there's any such thing as a bad film and then the editor comes in and makes it good. Editors can only work with what they have.
Bill Pancow, Film Editor
Interview in *First Cut*, 1992

2492. Don't worry, we'll fix it in the cutting room.
A popular director's prayer
Cited in *A Film Editor's Story*, 1979

2493. We don't want the audience to know it's a film.
Harold and Carl Kress, Film Editors
Interview in *First Cut*, 1992,
on quality, seamless editing

2494. The only technique of film editing ... is trying to be innocuous with it.
John D. Dunning, Film Editor
Interview in *First Cut*, 1992

2495. The best editing is the kind that is not noticed.
Jean Renoír, Director
Stated in *Jean Renoír — My Life and Times*

2496. The best cut is the one you never see.
Tom Rolf, Film Editor
Interview in *First Cut*, 1992

2497. Editing should never call attention to itself. The experience of seeing a movie should be an experience that is divorced from its technique.

Evan Lottman, Film Editor
Interview in *First Cut*, 1992

2498. I keep telling my editors, if you win an award for editing, I won't work with you anymore. Your editing shows.

Louis Malle, Director
Interview in *Reel Conversations*, 1991

2499. The work I like is the work I feel I don't do. I like to feel the film, feel the story … sort of an inner worth.

Ted Winterburn, Film Editor
Interview in *First Cut*, 1992

2500. I like the cuts I don't see. I don't want you to see the cut, I want you to feel the cut, feel the impact.

Ted Winterburn, Film Editor
Interview in *First Cut*, 1992

2501. The exact cutting points of the … shorts cannot be theoretically justified by analysis … the image is left on the screen long enough to make its point and cut at the moment the editor judges that it is made.

Karel Reisz, Author
On editing being a question of
personal judgment, as stated in
his 1998 *The Technique of Film Editing*

2502. We want to make the audience feel as though they're living in the photograph.

Ken Burns, Documentary Producer-Director
Interview in *First Cut*, 1992

2503. [M]ovement before the camera is not movement before the screen … real movement … is that obtained by the assemblage of the various strips of film.

Vladmir Pudovkin
From the Eisenstein-Pudovkin theory
and practice of cinema, as cited
in *Lessons with Eisenstein*, 1962

2504. You don't want to remind people they're looking at a movie. You want them to … be the voyeur of the story.

Tom Rolf, Film Editor
Interview in *First Cut*, 1992

2505. You're painting a picture, you're trying to involve the audience with that particular sequence, and you have to paint the picture as lucid as you can.

John D. Dunning, Film Editor
Interview in *First Cut*, 1992

2506. We play a lot with sound effects, music and voice-overs. If you view the movie as a piece of music, these become lyrics.

Billy Weber, Editor
On experimenting with the editing process,
as cited in *The Hollywood Reporter*, 1999

2507. You need to use time to the best advantage. To use the audience's mind … to be in the character….

Bill Pancow, Film Editor
Interview in *First Cut*, 1992

2508. Montage has the power of audience suggestion. I'm very keen on that method of storytelling.

Alfred Hitchcock, Director
Cited on the Internet Movie Database, 1998

2509. (Pure cinema is) complementary pieces of film put together, like notes of music to make a melody….

Alfred Hitchcock
Cited in *50 Major Film Makers*, 1975

2510. Any two pieces of film stuck together inevitably combine to create a new concept.

Sergei Eisenstein, Director
Cited on the Internet Movie Database, 1998

2511. For me, it's a totally intuitive thing…. I can't tell you why those two pieces of film really go together.

Thom Noble, Film Editor
Interview in *Moviemakers at Work*, 1987

2512. A dozen scenes can be put together in literally thousands of different combinations — but only one or two will make a story.

Frank Capra, Director
Stated in his 1971 *Frank Capra*

2513. Editing is not taking out, it's putting together.

Dede Allen, Film Editor
Cited in *Adventures in the Screen Trade*, 1983

2514. Part of what makes a great editor is what you take out, not just what you leave in.

David Lean, Director
Interview in *First Cut*, 1992

2515. Every idea is worth trying.

Anne V. Coates, Editor
On experimental editing as, as cited
in *The Hollywood Reporter*, 1999

2516. Cutting is an experiment. Unless you're

willing to try new things, you never truly serve the material.

Richard Marks, Film Editor
Interview in *First Cut*, 1992

2517. Editing is the language of the film director. Just as in living speech, so, one may say, in editing: there is a word — the piece of exposed film, the image, a phrase — the combination of these pieces.

Vladmir Pudovkin, Director
Cited in *Film as Film*, 1972

2518. I don't cut by rules. I don't really have any psychology. I just mark the film, cut it, and hope for the best.

Anne V. Coates, Film Editor
Interview in *First Cut*, 1992

2519. What happens occasionally is that this little baby — your picture — will sometimes grow two heads. You must spot that early, and one head must be chopped off immediately.

Guy Hamilton, Director
Interview in *Take 22: Moviemakers on Moviemaking*, 1984, on the first "rough cut"

2520. You'll start out with a scalpel but you've got to end up with an ax.

Bob Aldrich
Interview in *Take 22: Moviemakers on Moviemaking*, 1984

2521. (With film editing) one little push of a barge can move a huge ship.

Sidney Levin, Film Editor
Interview in *First Cut*, 1992

2522. The most important requirement for editing is objectivity. If it is not interesting, it simply isn't interesting.

Akira Kurosawa, Director
Stated in his 1982 *Akira Kurosawa — Something Like an Autobiography*

2523. It shouldn't be boring, but fast pacing doesn't make more interesting or good.

Duane Donnem, Film Editor
Interview in *Reel Conversations*, 1991

2524. Pace is not necessarily speed, pace is interest.

Robert Wise, Director, former Film Editor
Stated in his 1995 *Robert Wise: On His Films*

2525. The film assembles the elements of reality to build from them a new reality proper only to

itself; and the laws of space and time ... are, in the film, entirely altered.

Vladmir Pudovkin
Cited in *Kuleshov on Film*, 1974

2526. I learned more about (film) editing from Beethoven than from anywhere else ... the rhythmic structure ... in terms of statement of theme, development, recapitulation.

Paul Hirsch, Film Editor
Interview in *First Cut*, 1992

2527. When you take something out, it gives the film such an exhilarating pace. Once you see it out, the joy of the speed is so exhilarating that I can never put the material back.

Woody Allen
Interview in *The New York Times Magazine*, 1997

2528. That's the one thing I think never hurts a film; I mean, if you can do it faster, do it. It's a godsend. When stuff comes out, it's a mercy killing.

Woody Allen
Interview in *The New York Times Magazine*, 1997

2529. Time-saving in films is still the basic virtue. Both Eisenstein and Griffith knew it. Quick cutting and dissolving from one scene to another are the dynamics of film technique.

Charlie Chaplin
Stated in his 1964
My Autobiography — Charlie Chaplin

2530. Scenes should either echo a little of the feeling of the previous scene, then begin to take you away from it, or radically contrast with it.

Geof Bartz, Film Editor
Interview in *First Cut*, 1992

2531. You've got to have rhythm.

Verna Fields
Interview in *Film Makers on Film Making*, 1983, on film editing

2532. I cut very much by what the actors give you in their eyes ... it's something you see that works, a rhythm you have in yourself.

Anne V. Coates, Film Editor
Interview in *First Cut*, 1992

2533. The rehearsal time in theater is the equivalent to the editing time in film. You go in, and you edit and edit ... that's your rehearsal. In film, you go in and shoot ... you edit and edit — that's the rehearsal time.

Robert Altman, Director
Interview in *Inner Views: Filmmakers in Conversation*, 1992

2534. (The editor) can make a stutterer speak rapidly and a person of slow thought think quickly ... he can destroy the ... phrase (the actor) thought would make him immortal.
Josef von Sternberg
Stated in *Film Culture*, 1955

2535. However good the original idea, a joke can be made or killed in the presentation.
Karel Reisz, Author
On editing comedy sequences, as stated in his 1968 *The Technique of Film Editing*

2536. We were in the service of humor.
Tom Lewis, Editor
Referring to telling the story but letting the humor drive the editing for *The Wedding Singer*, 1998, as cited in *The Hollywood Reporter*, 1999

2537. If there's one axiom about film editing, it's that you must show what the audience wants to see at any given time.
Evan Lottman, Film Editor
Interview in *First Cut*, 1992

2538. All the time you make people look better than they are ... or if it's their worst, look their worst.
Paul Barnes, Film Editor
Interview in *First Cut*, 1992

2539. You can't create a good performance. If an actor is bad, you do the best you can, accentuating the positive, eliminating the negative.
Evan Lottman, Film Editor
Interview in *First Cut*, 1992

2540. I (try) to find a moment of each character's humanity.
Sidney Levin, Film Editor
Interview in *First Cut*, 1992

2541. (An animated feature) ... it's the reverse of live action. You edit first, then shoot the film ... you don't want to animate something that may be snipped off.
Nick Fletcher, Animated Film Editor
Cited in *The Hollywood Reporter*, 1999

2542. You are always on the person you want to be watching even if you don't know it at the time.
Stanley Kauffmann, Director
Interview in *First Cut*, 1992, on the focus of film editing in general

2543. (Choosing the best performance) tells us what we want it to tell, it moves us, it achieves the intent. How do we spotlight it?
Barry Malkin, Film Editor
Interview in *First Cut*, 1992

2544. I (try) to put in my little "tessera" in each scene, one smile, one look, one moment of compassion.
Sidney Levin, Film Editor
Interview in *First Cut*, 1992, on editing in "bright mosaic stones of expression"

2545. The truth of any moment has to be placed on screen.
Alan Heim, Film Editor
Interview in *First Cut*, 1992, on editing both drama and comedy

2546. I'm not in the (editing) room; I'm in the picture.
Carol Littleton, Film Editor
Interview in *First Cut*, 1992

2547. Being out on the set is a terribly bad idea ... you lose any objectivity you might have.
Thom Noble, Film Editor
Interview in *Moviemakers at Work*, 1987, on reviewing film only

2548. When something goes haywire with a film, try burning the first two reels.
Frank Capra, Producer-Director
Stated in his 1971 *Frank Capra*, having done so with *Lost Horizon*, 1936

2549. Carl, you've cut things in that movie that I didn't even know I shot.
Robert Wise, Director
Cited in *First Cut*, 1992, to film editor Carl Kress

2550. (David Lean) finds the most pleasure ... in the cutting room ... he likes to get the film in his fingers.
John Mills, Actor
Cited in *David Lean — A Biography*, 1996

2551. In Italy, if the (actor) says on reel number two, "I love you," it doesn't come until reel number four.
Joseph E. Levine
Interview in *Film Makers on Film Making*, 1983, on the lack of quality editing

2552. A joke can only work one way. When you've designed a visual joke, there ain't no two ways.
Jerry Lewis, Actor-Director
Cited in *Directors at Work*, 1970, on editing comedy scenes

2553. Comedy is hard. What the hell is funny…? What the hell is funny the hundred-and-fiftieth time you've seen it?

> Peter C. Frank, Film Editor
> Interview in *First Cut*, 1992

2554. "Pictures are made in the cutting room." That's nonsense. No movie editor ever put anything up on the screen that hadn't been shot.

> Sidney Lumet, Director
> Stated in his 1995 *Making Movies*

2555. When I finally photographed something, it is merely to get something to edit.

> Akira Kurosawa, Director
> Cited in *The Films of Akira Kurosawa*, 1965

2556. I improve (my films) one hundred percent (in the cutting room).

> Irving Thalberg
> To a boasting director who
> claimed 33 percent improvement, as
> cited in *Mayer and Thalberg*, 1975

22

Testing

2557. The study of film audience preferences is still a very imprecise "science," awaiting some genius who is able to make sense of the vagaries of American popular tastes. Whoever that person may be, their place in the pantheon of the motion picture industry is assured.

Bruce A. Dustin
Stated in *Current Research in Film:*
Audiences, Economics and Law, 1991

2558. (In) movies, the stakes are so high and the testing is so vital ... that the only way to deal with it (is) to embrace it.

James L. Brooks, Screenwriter-Director
Interview in *Written By*, 1998

2559. I trust (preview) testing as a tool, not as a be-all and end-all.

Lucy Fisher
Cited in *Premiere* magazine, 1998

2560. As filmmakers, we just held a mirror to the public and tried to reflect what they were feeling.

George Sidney, Director
Interview in *A Cut Above*, 1998, referring to
his films from the 1940s through the '60s

2561. We have usually worked in the past on the thesis that if we stand in the dark and throw a rock and hear a crash, we've hit the greenhouse.... It means that if you don't hear a crash, you may no longer be in the motion picture business.

C. A. Palmer
"Commercial Practices in Audience
Analysis," 1954, cited in the *Journal*
of the University Film Association

2562. The motion picture industry probably knows less about itself than any other major industry in the United States.

Eric Johnson, President, MPAA
1946

2563. Data derived from audience reaction surveys are not necessarily predictive of box-office success or a film's marketability.

"Disclaimer"
Exact words on a test audience
report, as recited in Sidney Lumet's
1995 *Making Movies*

2564. (Test screening movies) isn't natural, the audience isn't even necessarily the audience for the film — and they know they're going to be tested, so it's just a chance to be little Rex Reeds.

Barbara Hershey, Actress
Interview in *Detour* magazine, 1997

2565. We have found through many years of effort that the public cannot tell you in advance what their tastes will be.

David A. Lipton, Studio Advertising
and Publicity Executive
Cited in *Movie Business: American Film*
Industry Practice, 1972

2566. In a business in which hunches often carry more weight than demographic research, the box office record of a particular kind of film in a specific theater usually determines the releasing pattern for most future films.

David Lees, Writer
Stated in his 1981 *The Movie Business*

2567. The only prediction is that all predictions are by guess and by God until the film plays in theaters.

Old Hollywood adage
Cited in *Frank Capra*
— The Name Above the Title, 1971

2568. There's no way ... to outguess the public.

David Brown, Producer
Interview in *Film Makers on Film Making*, 1983

2569. You cannot program the human spirit ... and you cannot predict the human spirit.

Frank Capra, Director
Interview in *Film Makers on Film Making*, 1983

2570. Why don't the euphoric young semiologists who want to codify every square inch of the screen image … do a little honest audience research on what those codes really mean to various living viewers.
> Richard Dyer MacCann, Writer
> Stated in his 1976 "Film Scholarship: Dead or Alive?" *Journal of the University Film Association*

2571. I learned a little bit through test screening certain things … it's sort of manipulating yourself.
> David Lynch, Screenwriter-Director
> Interview in *Reel Conversations*, 1991

2572. If you put the audience in a lab experiment scenario, they're gonna turn into critics and … into lab animals. It doesn't help the movie.
> Tim Burton, Director
> On having a test audience dissect the film, stated in *Inner Views: Filmmakers in Conversation*, 1992

2573. In passing out (preview) cards we're asking for criticism, so we've eliminated that.
> Hal Wallis, Producer
> Interview in *Film Makers on Film Making*, 1983

2574. The urge to construct scientific explanations for art naturally turns attention away from questions of quality.
> Richard Dyer MacCann, Writer
> Stated in his 1976 "Film Scholarship: Dead or Alive?" *Journal of the University Film Association*, 1976

2575. To emasculate (the director's) vision by going through a series of market screenings — I just don't get it.
> Carol Littleton, Film Editor
> Interview in *First Cut — Conversations with Film Editors*, 1992

2576. The art world is exactly the opposite of the film world. In the movie business, a film has to "play in Peoria" to be successful. But in the art market, if it plays in Peoria, it's most definitely bad.
> John Waters, Producer-Director
> Interview in *Directors at Work*, 1970

2577. They spend millions on research and then they release it on superstition.
> Clint Eastwood
> Stated in *Clint Eastwood — A Biography*, 1996

2578. You want to open a movie at 80 percent awareness or above. Usually you're spending 80 percent of your advertising dollars in the 10 days before the opening.
> Mark Horowitz
> Interview in *The New York Times*, 1997

2579. If "Lost Horizon" can knock off those Santa Barbara snobs, I got those New York guys right in my pocket.
> Harry Cohn, President, Columbia Pictures
> His sneak preview hopes, 1936, as cited in *Frank Capra — The Name Above the Title*, 1971

2580. A movie audience is very sensitive…. I could see, hear, and "feel" the reaction to each melodrama and comedy. Boredom was registered … as clearly as laughter demonstrated pleasure.
> Adolf Zukor
> Stated in *Current Research in Film: Audiences, Economics and Law*, 1991

2581. When (Mack Sennett) laughed, the audience was going to laugh. It was a real litmus test.
> Frank Capra, Director
> On director Sennett's method of audience testing his films, cited in "Dialogue on Film," *American Film* magazine, 1978

2582. If (Mack) Sennett laughed, audiences would laugh. If Sennett didn't laugh — well, rewrite it or reshoot it.
> Dick Jones, Executive Producer
> Cited in *Frank Capra — The Name Above the Title*, 1971, referring to the Sennett comedies

2583. To profess theories about laughter is a thankless task.
> Karel Reisz, Author
> Cited in *The Technique of Film Editing*, 1968

2584. I can tell a great deal by seeing if (the audience is) fidgety and moving around, getting up to get a Coke.
> Richard Zanuck, Producer
> Interview in *Film Makers on Film Making*, 1983, on his method of testing

2585. Is this is a one-piss or a two-piss picture? If it's too long, I have to take two leaks.
> Jack Warner, Studio Head
> Explaining his method of gauging that a picture isn't too lengthy, as cited in *Clown Prince of Hollywood — The Life and Times of Jack L. Warner*, 1990

2586. You should never really overcook — when people taste it and say it's pretty good, simply ask them if they want seconds.
> Steven Spielberg, Director
> On not reworking a film that works, as stated in *Take 22: Moviemakers on Moviemaking*, 1984

2587. I knew something was wrong when they previewed the picture at a drive-in theater in Palm Springs ... in the middle of July ... at noon.

Jack Benny, Actor
On his poorly received picture, *The Horn Blows at Midnight*, as cited in *Clown Prince*, 1990

2588. What is the audience in the mood for at a particular time. No one really knows until it happens. ... you just make the film as good as you can and that's it. Put it out there and then it's up to the audience. It's their responsibility to like it or not.

Clint Eastwood
Cited in *American Cinema*, 1995

2589. The ultimate test of anything ... of painting, writing, film, is if it works. If something doesn't work, it shrieks at you.

Emile de Antonio
Stated at the 1985 New York Film Forum

2590. Is your own satisfaction the final test or must you bow to the verdict of the majority...? you can be sure of one thing: You are a better man for having made it.

Satyajit Ray, Director
On audience acceptance of your movie, as cited in *Sight and Sound*, 1957

23

Reviews

2591. "[A]bsolutely disgusting."

First known review
June, 15, 1896, in the *Chap Book—
USA of May Irwin Kiss*, 1896, cited in
Guinness—Movie Facts and Feats, 1980

2592. It is easier to bring a ready-made and arbitrarily committed set of principles to bear on a film, than to struggle to learn about the true principles of criticism. It is easier than trying to write better and better reviews knowing that you cannot succeed, that the perfect review is a chimera.

I. C. Jarvie, Author
Stated in his 1970 *Movies and Society*

2593. I am of Agee—a school of criticism considering it a conversation among moviegoers.

Judith Crist, Film Critic
Cited on the Internet Movie Database,
1998, on film critic James Agee

2594. I myself am unmoved by the more arcane versions of film scholarship in which the language of film is analyzed as if it were linguistic.

Roger Ebert, Film Critic
Interview in *Reel Conversations*, 1991

2595. In film-reviewing ... there's nothing more disastrous than trying to outguess an audience.

Arthur Knight, Film Critic
Cited in *The Reel Tinsel*, 1970

2596. The movie starts before my reactions do, and I follow my reactions to the film.

Gene Siskel, Film Critic
Cited in *The Hollywood Reporter*, 1996

2597. After a movie is finished, you can analyze it. But a work in progress is a volcano—it's like lava.

Darius Khondji
Cited in the *Los Angeles
Magazine*, 1997

2598. (Hollywood) reportage breaks down neatly into "nice pieces" and "hatchet jobs."

Mavie Brenner, Author
Cited in *Going Hollywood*, 1978

2599. (Filmmakers have) to ... know where they went wrong ... people have a tendency ... to read only the good reviews. Read the bad ones, too.

William Wyler, Director
Interview in *Directors at Work*, 1970

2600. It is intriguing and useful to listen to the sacred rhetoric of the cinema groups and intellectual critics, but very little of it gets up on the screen in the next picture.

Jerry Lewis, Producer-Director-Actor
Cited in *The Total Film Maker*, 1971

2601. To see a film once and write a review of it is an absurdity. Yet very few critics ever see a film twice or write about films from a leisurely, thoughtful perspective.

Stanley Kubrick, Director
Interview in *The New York Times*, 1976

2602. The reviews that distinguish most critics, unfortunately, are those slam-bang pieces which are easy to write and fun to write and are absolutely useless.

Stanley Kubrick, Director
Interview in *The New York Times*, 1976

2603. In our brains, we can't bury the dead. It's not like ... a play ... folds ... and be forgotten. But not a picture. That has to continue to stink.

Billy Wilder, Director
Stated in *The Bright Side
of Billy Wilder, Primarily*, 1970

2604. Movie criticism has become a cultural malady, a group case of chronic depression.

James Wolcott
Cited in *Vanity Fair*, 1997

2605. What permits the endless variety of meanings to be generated from a film are in large part the critical practices themselves....

David Bordwell, Writer
Stated in his 1989, *Making Meaning*

2606. The popular imagination may be titillated by a movie that suffers nothing but slings and arrows from the critics.

Charles S. Steinberg,
Communication Author-Professor
Cited in *Movie Business: American
Film Industry Practice*, 1972

2607. The flood of media promotion overwhelms ... the voice of a good critic....

David Densby, Writer
Stated in *The New Yorker*, 1998

2608. From the reviews, you pays your nickel for a paper and takes your choice.

Frank Capra, Director
On the common discord among critics
on a movie review, as stated in his 1971
Frank Capra—The Name Above the Title

2609. I find that reviews can hurt but not help. If everything they write about it is negative, it kills you. And if they write great things, it doesn't necessarily help you.

Woody Allen
Interview in *The New York Times Magazine*, 1997

2610. I gave up reading reviews years ago, because I found it unprofitable....

Peter O'Toole, Actor
Interview in *Playboy*, September, 1965

2611. I have nothing to learn from the critics.

Raul Julia, Actor
Interview in *Elle* magazine, 1987

2612. Whether it's painting, architecture, music, filmmaking, it takes a tough spirit to weather the critical storms, and to weather both praise and criticism. It's easy to be undone by both.

Michael Cimino, Screenwriter-Director
Interview in *Reel Conversations*, 1991

2613. If I'm entitled to be bitter about (a bad review) then I'm not entitled to be joyous about all the times I've been called wonderful....

Sidney Poitier, Actor
Interview in the *New York Times*, 1968

2614. When you've been blasted critically (on a movie), it's not just criticizing the way you write

an insurance policy ... they're getting to the very innermost part of your soul.

John Frankenheimer, Director
Stated in *John Frankenheimer—
A Conversation with
Charles Champlin*, 1995

2615. I thought unless I garnered bad reviews, I wasn't doing my job ... that great artists were always put down for taking chances, so I thought.

Nicolas Cage, Actor
Interview in *Details* magazine, 1996

2616. I never read reviews. If they're good, you get a fat head, and if they're bad, you're depressed for three weeks.

Paul Newman
Cited in the 1989 biography *Paul Newman*

2617. You cannot really make declarative statements about comedy ... the more a critic says, "Oh, I found it absolutely hilarious," the more you are damaging the film because the next person ... sits down and says, "Go ahead, be hilarious."

Judith Crist, Film Critic
Interview in *Take 22: Moviemakers
on Moviemaking*, 1984

2618. (The most review-proof genre) may be the comedy. It is very, very hard to argue someone out of a laugh, or into one.

Gene Siskel, Film Critic
Interview in *Playboy*, February, 1991

2619. Every time I review a *Friday the 13th* movie I sell tickets, because the worse I say it is, the more the audience is going to think they'll like it.

Roger Ebert, Film Critic
Interview in *Reel Conversations*, 1991

2620. No matter what they like or dislike, talented reviewers reveal themselves, like any artist.

Marlon Brando
Stated in *Conversations with Brando*, 1991

2621. We tend to exalt the works that we're emotionally and intellectually ready for. And we expect the audience to be in the same spot in their lives that we are.

Pauline Kael, Film Critic
Cited in "The 100 Best Movies,"
Newsweek Extra 2000, 1998

2622. There's nothing wrong with writing a critic ... especially to thank him for a good review.

John C. Mahoney, Critic
Cited in *Your Film Acting Career*, 1989

2623. I can quote from bad reviews; I can't remember any of the good reviews.

> Gale Anne Hurd, Producer
> Interview in the *Village View*, 1989

2624. When the reviews are good ... you don't believe them ... when they're bad ... you do believe them. What are you gonna do about it?

> Sean Penn, Actor
> Interview in *Interview* magazine, 1995

2625. I've read reviews in which the writer says, "And then Kevin Kline kisses Tom Selleck." But no, it's not me, it's the character.

> Kevin Kline, Actor
> Interview in *Playboy*, March, 1998, on
> the actor rather than the character role

2626. It's mostly the women reviewers who are attacking me.

> Barbra Streisand, Actress-Director
> Cited in *Inside Oscar*, 1996

2627. We got a very bad review from the *Village Voice*. I used it as toilet paper.

> John Schlesinger, Director
> Cited in *The Daily News*, 1998,
> on his *Midnight Cowboy*, 1969

2628. I didn't want the reviewers to say, "Well, that's a Hollywood version of what goes on in the death cell and the gas chamber."

> Robert Wise, Director
> Cited in *Robert Wise: On His Films*, 1995,
> insisting on viewing an actual execution
> prior to filming *I Want to Live*, 1958

2629. Oh, no you don't.... Not after what you did (with a negative film review).

> David Lean
> To a critic who said "hello" to him,
> recalled in the 1996 biography, *David Lean*

2630. When I die, just bury me in a Crawford-Gable picture.

> Fred Astaire
> Cited in *Mayer and Thalberg*
> *— The Make Believe Saints*, 1975

2631. After each of my movies was released, I'd read my obituary in *The Los Angeles Times*.

> Sylvester Stallone, Actor
> Cited in *The Los Angeles Times*, 1995

2632. Into this boiling lava, Federico Fellini plunged his artist's hands.

> Unknown Italian Film Critic
> Cited in *Fellini—A Life*, 1986,
> on *La Dolce Vita*, 1959

2633. I've tried to make my films into nonevents. So I like to just make the film, not read the reviews, not follow the box office, put it away and make another film.

> Woody Allen
> Interview in *The New York*
> *Times Magazine*, 1997

2634. Movies have now reached the same stage as sex: It's all technique and no feeling.

> Penelope Gilliat
> Cited in *Film Makers on Film Making*, 1983

2635. No girls, no legs, no jokes, no chance.

> An aide-de-camp of Walter Winchell
> Cited in *The Language*
> *of Show Biz—A Dictionary*

2636. "The Sound of Money."

> Pauline Kael, Critic
> Cited in *Chronicle of the Cinema*, 1995, on her
> movie review description for *The Sound of*
> *Music* in *McCalls*, for which she was fired, 1965

2637. I don't want any description of me to be accurate; I want it to be flattering.

> Orson Welles
> Cited in *Orson Welles:*
> *The Road to Xanadu*, 1996

24

Critics

2638. Throughout the ... history of the movies, the role of the critic never has been clearly defined.
Charles S. Steinberg, Communications
Author–Professor
Cited in *Movie Business*, 1972

2639. Criticism is journalism, but with a difference ... in that (critics) are expected to be reporters first and to render aesthetic judgment second.
Harris Report
Cited in *Movie Business*, 1972, on movie critics

2640. (Film critics should) take care of the facts and the values will take care of themselves.
Francis Sparshott
Stated in "Basic Film Aesthetics" in
the Mast and Cohen Anthology

2641. (Film critics) cannot make or break (a movie). They can help it or hurt it.
William Wyler, Director
Interview in *Directors at Work*, 1970

2642. The great thing criticism can do is illuminate.
Elia Kazan, Director
Interview in *Directors at Work*, 1970

2643. (The job of the film critic) is to comment on the material that provides the occasion for selling candy, pop, and popcorn.
Stanley Kauffmann, Writer
Stated in *The New Republic*, 1984

2644. It's easy to say shit is shit, and it should be said. But the real function of a critic is to see what is truly good and go bananas when he sees it.
Mel Brooks, Screenwriter-Director
Interview in *Playboy*, February, 1975

2645. I think that we are affected by critics because certain films cannot make the grade without the critics.
Richard Brooks, Writer-Director
Interview in *Directors at Work*, 1970

2646. Hollywood requires criticism to help it fix its social and cultural identity ... criticism is a necessary part of the sense-making apparatus that allows cinema to be meaningful in society.
Richard Maltby, Writer
Stated in his 1995 *Hollywood Cinema*

2647. (Cinema is) kept alive not just through systems of production, distribution and exhibition, but also through the circulation of debates which provide the cultural context in which it can flourish.
Pam Cook, Writer-Editor
Stated in her 1985 *The Cinema
Book of the British Film Institute*

2648. No such creature as the "average" reviewer exists.
T. Brown
On common background of movie critics,
as cited in *Journalism Quarterly*, 1978

2649. It is important to become a dramatic critic. It happens by accident.
George Bernard Shaw
Cited in *The Language
of Show Biz—A Dictionary*

2650. We film critics are quite unlike one another.... It can't be helped. We're working from different, or even mutually unintelligible, principles.
Arthur Knight, Film Critic
Cited in *The Reel Tinsel*, 1970

2651. More than three-fourths of those (movie critics surveyed) indicated they had completed an academic degree, albeit most with no specific training for criticism.
Charles S. Steinberg, Communications
Author–Professor
Cited in *Movie Business*, 1972,
referring to a Harris report

2652. The cinematic critic ought to take his mission in life seriously. He ought to learn all there is to be learned about his profession, cultivating a knowledge of all the other arts from which the photoplay borrows.

Frances Taylor Patterson, Writer
Stated in his 1920 *Cinema Craftsmanship*

2653. Eighty percent of film criticism comes from illiterates and deficient mentalities.

Federico Fellini
Cited in *Fellini — A Life*, 1986

2654. As if it were a duty to be bored. I mean, you're still a human being, even if you are a critic.

Pauline Kael, Critic
On walking out of "bad" movies,
stated in a 1998 *Modern Maturity* magazine

2655. Movie critics are like spotted owls.

James Wolcott
Cited in *The New Yorker*, 1998

2656. If there were no critics, show business would have to create them.

Frank Capra, Producer-Director
Stated in his 1971 *Frank Capra
— The Name Above the Title*

2657. If it weren't for guys like me, (critics) wouldn't have jobs.

Chevy Chase, Actor
Interview in *US* magazine, 1998

2658. What is important for all motion picture criticism, journalistic or academic, is that the critic functions not only to inform, but also to provide a direction-finder for the viewer.

Charles S. Steinberg, Author-Professor
Cited in *Movie Business*, 1972

2659. The greatest satisfaction a critic can have (is) to influence public opinion in support of a film that might otherwise get lost in the shuffle.

Arthur Knight, Film Critic
Cited in *The Reel Tinsel*, 1970

2660. The vast majority of people are in need of guidance in the matter of photoplays. It is no longer a question of giving them what they want. It is question of so directing their tastes that they will want what is best....

Frances Taylor Patterson, Writer
Stated in his 1920 *Cinema Craftsmanship*

2661. Film critics too often tend to write as oracles, ultimate repositories of truth to whom two questions are put: What does this film mean, and, is it any good?

I. C. Jarvie, Author
Stated in his 1970 *Movies and Society*

2662. A critic at a performance is like a eunuch in a harem: He sees it performed nightly, but cannot do it himself.

Brendan Behan
Cited in *Questions for
the Movie Answer Man*, 1997

2663. The best critics combine not only good journalism, but a sense of aesthetics and sound scholarship as well.

Charles S. Steinberg, Communications
Author–Professor
Cited in *Movie Business*, 1972

2664. The good critic has to be the ideal viewer, not the ideal director or writer or actor.

Roger Ebert, Film Critic
On critics possibly being
frustrated filmmakers, 1991,
interviewed in *Reel Conversations*

2665. I can't write, I can't act, I can't sing, I can't dance, so I'm a critic.

Steve Kmetko, Film Critic
In a June, 1988, *Playboy* interview

2666. It's the job of the filmmaker to be the best filmmaker he can be, and it's the job of the critic to be the best audience member he can be.

Gene Siskel, Film Critic
Interview in *The Hollywood Reporter*, 1996

2667. I'm a historian, I'm not a prophet. And I'm not an activist or a revolutionary. I don't want to change movies.... If I wanted to change movies, I'd go out and make them.

Andrew Sarris, Film Critic
Interview in *Reel Conversations*, 1991

2668. If you think it is so easy to be a critic, so difficult to be a poet... may I suggest you try both. You may discover why there are so few critics, so many poets.

Pauline Kael, Critic
Interview in *Modern Maturity* magazine, 1998

2669. I can be wrong. So what? That's the risk. Critics never take it.

Sidney Lumet, Director
Stated in his 1995 *Making Movies*

2670. Many are quite willing to minimize the influence of ... critics upon the size of today's audiences, few are willing to dismiss ... their salutary influence in general upon the motion picture art.

> William A. Bluem, Writer
> Cited in *Movie Business*, 1972

2671. If you had to write a criticism of a picture every day, you'd get awful sick and tired of trying to figure out what to say about it.

> Howard Hawks, Director
> Stated in his 1972 *Hawks on Hawks*

2672. I think my influence was largely in style, not substance.

> Pauline Kael, Film Critic
> Interview in *Modern Maturity* magazine,
> 1998, on influencing other movie critics

2673. I felt I had nothing new to say. Old critics tend to become tiresome....

> Pauline Kael, Film Critic
> Interview in *Modern Maturity*
> magazine, 1998, on retirement

2674. If I say yes, I'm an egotist, and if I say no, I've wasted my life.

> Pauline Kael, Film Critic
> Interview in *Modern Maturity*
> magazine, 1998, on whether or
> not her criticism has changed movies

2675. I just think that since critics have such a powerful position that if they are going to state something as fact, it damn well better be fact.

> Gale Anne Hurd, Producer
> Interview in the *Village View*, 1989

2676. It's the truth. I want to tell people the truth. I'm not out to trash movies. I'm just trying to cut through all of the hype.

> Harry Knowles, Internet Film Critic
> Cited in *The New York Times Magazine*, 1997

2677. The critic is responsible to a degree for articulating those voices dominated, displaced, or silenced by the textuality of texts ... finding and exposing things that may otherwise be hidden beneath piety, heedlessness, or routine.

> Edward Said, Scholar-Writer
> Stated in his 1983 *The World,*
> *the Text and the Critic*

2678. To many people dramatic criticism must seem like an attempt to tattoo soap bubbles.

> James Mason Brown, Writer
> Stated in his *Broadway in Review*, 1940

2679. You try to learn something from (film critics). And you very seldom do.

> William Wyler, Director
> Referring to his work as a director, 1970,
> from his interview in *Directors at Work*

2680. What critics call dirty in our (American) pictures, they call lusty in foreign films.

> Billy Wilder, Director
> Cited in the *Bright Side of*
> *Billy Wilder, Primarily*, 1970

2681. Critics used to have a unanimity of opinion. That day is gone forever ... because of different groups, different cliques, different times, different generations even, writing about films.

> Richard Brooks, Writer-Director
> Interview in *Directors at Work*, 1970

2682. There is no such thing as print criticism. There are only critics who work in print. And each one has his own voice.

> Roger Ebert, Film Critic
> Interview in *Reel Conversations*, 1991

2683. The critic's worst corruption is a desire to keep the readers happy.

> Pauline Kael, Film Critic
> Interview in *Modern Maturity* magazine, 1998

2684. A critic should not be a ventriloquist's dummy, sitting on the knee of the public and letting it put words in its mouth.

> Roger Ebert
> Stated in his 1997 *Questions*
> *for the Movie Answer Man*

2685. I find the American critics the most practical. They do not try to see too much.

> Federico Fellini
> Cited in *Fellini—A Life*, 1986

2686. You ought to save your sense of indignation for something more worthwhile.

> Anonymous Friend
> To critic Hollis Alpert, 1970,
> cited in *Fellini—A Life*

2687. The thinner the magazines, the fatter the heads of their reviewers.

> Billy Wilder, Director
> Cited in the 1970 *The Bright*
> *Side of Billy Wilder, Primarily*

2688. If that isn't a critic, I don't know what is.

> Stephen King, Author
> On obsessed Anni Wilkes (Kathy Bates),
> immobilizing her favorite writer
> (James Caan) in King's *Misery*, 1990

2689. The critic using words finds it easier to talk of these other words than of the cinematic realization of ideas.

> I. C. Jarvie, Author
> Stated in his 1970 *Movies and Society*,
> on the critic caring more for his
> own prose than the film's real substance

2690. There's not much in a critic showing off how clever he is at writing silly, supercilious gags about something he hates.

Stanley Kubrick, Director
Interview in *The New York Times*, 1976

2691. There are some people who are very ambitious young critics ... to whom it is more important that they become more famous than what they are writing about.

Richard Brooks, Writer-Director
Interview in *Directors at Work*, 1970

2692. The worst (movie critics) let their cynicism twist them beyond any recognizable connection to the experience of a general audience in a movie theater.

Jim Cameron, Producer-Director
Interview in *The Los Angeles Times*, 1998

2693. Give us a (movie critic) who respects the paying audiences who look to him or her for guidance, not lectures on how stupid they are for liking what they like.

Jim Cameron, Producer-Director
Interview in *The Los Angeles Times*, 1998

2694. (A film critic is) immodest in assuming that the truth has been revealed to "me" alone.

I. C. Jarvie, Author
Stated in his 1970 *Movies
and Society*, on reviews of films

2695. Film critics, like oracles ... pronounce their answer and there is no more to be said. The fact is that other oracles make different pronouncements.

I. C. Jarvie, Author
Stated in his 1970 *Movies and Society*

2696. Crowd reactions are precisely what the film was made for ... and no proper judgement of a motion picture can be made without the vital "third dimension" of a large audience being present.

Frank Capra
Stated in his 1971 *Frank Capra
— The Name Above the Title*

2697. The film is really built and timed for audience reaction. I can't think of anything more deadly than seeing a comedy or ... a Hitchcock thriller in an empty room.

Arthur Knight, Film Critic
Cited in *The Reel Tinsel*, 1970

2698. The good critics are on to this, that there is a special immediate experience in viewing films. A painting on the wall can be looked at for ... a half hour or the next ten days ... but a picture that's flashed on the screen is there for less than ... a second.

Arthur Knight, Film Critic
Cited in *The Reel Tinsel*, 1970

2699. It is strange how people will quite willingly accept the plethora of irrational or ambiguous factors in everyday life, yet complain bitterly when they come across them in works of art, whether novels or films....

Alain Robbe-Grillet
Cited in *Films and Filming*, 1962

2700. It's a curious thing, what happens when you expose a picture (in a press preview) to 1,500 critics, each one of whom is an idiot. Suddenly, all together, they become a genius.

Billy Wilder, Director
Cited in *The Bright Side of
Billy Wilder, Primarily*, 1970

2701. For a creative person to be criticized can be very dangerous. A creative person needs an atmosphere of approval.

Federico Fellini
Cited in *Fellini—A Life*, 1986

2702. You people ... won't be happy until I make a film in 16 millimeter and black-and-white.

David Lean
Stated in *David Lean
—A Biography*, 1996, to his critics

2703. He that is without humor among you, let him cast the first pie.

Mabel Normand, Actress-Director
Cited on the Internet Movie Database, 1998

2704. That's for taking a book that was a hit for nineteen hundred years and making a flop out of it.

Arthur Caesar
Cited in *The Zanucks of Hollywood*,
1989, after kicking Darryl F. Zanuck
for his poor production of *Noah's Ark*

2705. Critics are not why you work.

David Lynch, Screenwriter-Director
Interview in *Reel Conversations*, 1991

2706. If I depended on the critic's judgment and recognition, I'd never have gone into the motion picture business.

John Wayne, Actor
Interview in *Playboy*, May, 1971

2707. I don't accept anyone as the last word.

Andrew Sarris, Film Critic
Interview in *Reel Conversations*,
1991, on film critics

2708. It's only the best fruit the birds pick at.

Bette Davis, Actress
Cited in *Inside Oscar*, 1996

2709. Critics don't pay, you know. The people who really interest me are the paying dudes on the street.

Melvin Van Peebles, Screenwriter-Director
Interview in *Cosmopolitan*, 1972

2710. The public is the judge, and the only judge, of the popularity and success of a picture.

Ned Depinet
In his letter to Victor Ford Collins of RKO, 1949

25

Interviews

2711. (An interview) is like asking somebody to trespass on their own property.

Sean Penn, Actor
Interview in *Interview* magazine, 1991

2712. It's artificial intimacy.

Richard Gere, Actor
Interview in *US* magazine,
1990, on interviewing

2713. It's wrong. It's mis-using somebody's confidence.

Andre de Toth, Director
Interview in *Movie Maker* magazine,
1998, on asking about his personal life

2714. It makes me feel like I'm stripped down on a high school biology table with some pimply-faced sixteen year old comin' at me with a scalpel.

Sean Patrick Flanery, Actor
Interview in *Interview* magazine,
1998, on being interviewed

2715. Discussing my personal life is contrary to achieving any efficiency in doing the job (of acting).

Harrison Ford, Actor
Interview in *George* magazine, 1997

2716. There is something obscene about confessing your feelings and your sentiments for all people to view.

Marlon Brando
Stated in *Conversations with Brando*, 1991

2717. (Interviewers) are mostly conversational scavengers who sit around and wait for some slop to fall off the table. If there isn't any, they invent some.

Marlon Brando
Stated in *Conversations with Brando*, 1991

2718. I go in with an empty bucket and let the person I'm interviewing fill it.

Ben Bradlee, Former *Washington Post* Editor
Cited in *The Los Angeles Times*, 1996

2719. [I]s an interview like a picture? If it gets too long, it gets boring.

William Wyler, Director
Cited in *Directors at Work*,
1970, as a warning to a reporter

2720. The greatest celebrity hijacker in Hollywood is the phrase, "according to sources who wish to remain unidentified."

Harvey Weinstein, Co-Head,
Film Distribution Company
Cited in *Premiere* magazine, 1998

2721. [M]oney (is) the principle motivation in any interview.... I am a commodity sitting there.

Marlon Brando
Stated in *Conversations with Brando*, 1991

2722. Sometimes with interviews it's almost like trying to prove to someone that you aren't crazy when they've already decided that you are.

Barbara Hershey, Actress
Interview in *Detour* magazine, 1997

2723. Suppose you do this interview and find out that I really don't stand for anything.

Jimmy Smits, Actor
Interview in *New Woman* magazine, 1997

2724. Some interviewers look at me like, "That's the answer?" They ask, "What kind of tree do you want to be?" And I don't know.

Tom Cruise, Actor
Interview in *Vanity Fair*, 1996

2725. Why am I doing this interview...? It seemed right.... Also, I have a movie to promote, though it's never been proven that doing an interview will help.

Sean Penn, Actor
Interview in *Playboy*, November, 1991

2726. I was being interviewed by a critic of the

"cinema," which … has nothing to do with the "movies."

Joan Crawford
Cited in *Bette and Joan — The Divine Feud*, 1989

2727. There are no indiscreet questions, only indiscreet answers.

Douglas Fairbanks, Jr.
Cited in *You Must Remember This*, 1975

2728. If you need more stuff for your article, just make it up. I don't care.

Steven Spielberg
Cited in Steven *Spielberg*
— *The Unauthorized Biography*, 1996

2729. To be honest with you I'm a pathological liar, and I don't know what is and what isn't true, but if it isn't true, it should be.

Stephen King
Unknown source

2730. A Federico Fellini interview is .. a misleading game of mirrors that protects an inner reserve.

Liliana Betti, Fellini Assistant
Cited in *Fellini — A Life*, 1986

2731. If you try to probe, I'll lie to you. Seventy-five percent of what I say in interviews is false. I'm like a hen protecting her eggs.

Orson Welles
Cited in *Orson Welles: The Road to Xanadu*, 1996

2732. I don't believe in giving interviews where you say, "follow the dots."

Warren Beatty
Interview in *The Los Angeles Times Magazine*, 1998

2733. You'll find the conversation flows like glue.

Anonymous reporter on Clint Eastwood
Cited in *Clint Eastwood — A Biography*, 1996

2734. Don't ask me anything about art. I don't know anything about it.

Walt Disney
Interview in *The New York Times Magazine*, 1938

2735. Do you know the best service anyone could render to art? Destroy all biographies. Only art can explain the life of a man and not the contrary.

Orson Welles
Cited in *Orson Welles: The Road to Xanadu*, 1996

2736. It didn't mean anything at all. We called it "pan-focus" in some idiot interview — just for the fun of it.

Orson Welles
Cited in *Orson Welles: The Road to Xanadu*, 1996

2737. I'm an actor, you know, not a real cowboy.

Clint Eastwood
Cited in *Clint Eastwood — A Biography*,
1996, commenting to a reporter

2738. I've finally learned that the only way not to have people make a big deal out of your personal life is not to discuss it.

Gale Anne Hurd, Producer
Interview in *Ms.* magazine, 1989

2739. I'm not that talkative, and their job is to get me to talk.

Clint Eastwood
On Hollywood reporters, cited in
Clint Eastwood — A Biography, 1996

2740. Drawing (David) Lean out was like pulling water from a very deep well.

Denise Worrell, Reporter, *Time* magazine
Cited in *David Lean — A Biography*, 1996

2741. That's not my job.

Glenn Close, Actress
Interview in *W* magazine, 1996, on
why she doesn't give many interviews

2742. I'd rather ride down the street on a camel nude … in a snowstorm … backwards than give what is sometimes called an in-depth interview.

Warren Beatty
Superficial interview in *American Premiere*, 1992

26

Celebrity

2743. It's a long way to get into the popular consciousness.
Steve Martin, Actor
Interview in *Mirabella*, 1998

2744. It's not meant to be in human nature that somebody recognizes you who has never seen you in the flesh before.
Roger Ebert, Film Critic
Interview in *Reel Conversations*, 1991

2745. Fame is the consolation prize which is given when everything else has been sacrificed.
Marquis Busby
Cited in *The Price They Pay for Fame*

2746. Adulation is like heroin — a really terrible drug.
Sylvester Stallone, Actor
Cited in *The Los Angeles Times Calendar*, 1998

2747. Fame is like fashion, you know. You can't rely on it.
Audrey Hepburn, Actress
Interview in *Family Circle*, 1979

2748. The danger in dreams is that you just might get them.
Jon Peters, Producer
Cited in *Going Hollywood*, 1978

2749. The only way you can truly control how you're seen is by being constantly honest all the time.
Tom Hanks
Interview in *Vim & Vigor* magazine, 1996

2750. To be celebrated is nothing. To be loved is everything.
Claudette Colbert
Cited in *Vanity Fair*, 1998

2751. (There are those who) are well-known for their well-knownness.
Daniel J. Boorstin, Journalist
Cited in *Going Hollywood*, 1978

2752. Once fame happens, it doesn't unhappen.
Gus Van Sant, Director
Interview in *Premiere* magazine, 1998

2753. Celebrities have become public utilities, like sewers. They fulfill a community need.
Milan Kundera
Cited in *The Daily News*, 1998

2754. Most celebrities are basically left alone — unless they marry or have an affair or divorce. They are most interesting when they're mating.
Mike Nichols, Writer-Director
Interview in *Interview* magazine, 1998

2755. Hollywood has a way of saying, we love you, we destroy you, then we rediscover you ... and you either get resurrected or you don't.
Ali MacGraw, Actress
Cited in *Going Hollywood*, 1978

2756. Leonard Zelig (the character) is lauded, marketed and exploited; hated, forgotten, rediscovered; he is the perfect symbol for all celebrities.
Douglas Brode, Author
Cited in *Woody Allen — His Films and Career*, 1985, on the *Zelig* movie character, 1983

2757. It makes me uncomfortable when actors spout politics. I want to listen to experts. I would feel uncomfortable being a spokesperson or poster boy. I want to act.
Kevin Kline, Actor
Interview in *Playboy*, March, 1998, on not misusing his celebrity status

2758. I don't know why I'd want to be more

famous. There's something nice about the pocket that I have.

> Jeff Bridges, Actor
> Interview in *W* magazine, 1996

2759. Warren Beatty has been famous longer than he's been a person.

> Dustin Hoffman
> Cited in *The New York Times Magazine*, 1998

2760. Sure I'm famous! When I walk out of here, I guarantee you five people will speak to me before I get home....

> Laurence Fishburne, Actor
> Interview in *Vanity Fair*, 1995

2761. My celebrity is in the medium range.... I have never had my clothes torn.... It's just a kind of, heyy!

> Richard Dreyfuss, Actor
> Interview in *Esquire*, 1987

2762. If anybody gives me another box of chocolates, I'll gag.

> Tom Hanks
> Interview in *GQ* magazine, 1995

2763. I'm not Audrey Hepburn. I'm Holly Golightly or Eliza Doolittle or Sabrina.

> Audrey Hepburn, Actress
> Interview in *American Movie Classics*, 1990,
> on the public's perception of her image

2764. I'm a person, not a personality.

> Faye Dunaway, Actress
> Interview in *Detour* magazine, 1995

2765. That's the trouble. A sex symbol becomes a thing. I just hate to be a thing.

> Marilyn Monroe
> Cited in *The Century*, 1998

2766. I am an actor. That's what I do. As a matter of cultural utility, I am assigned a certain role. If I stick to that assignment, then everything's fine.

> Harrison Ford, Actor
> Interview in *George* magazine, 1997

2767. I'm an introvert. I don't want to be famous.

> George Lucas, Writer-Producer
> Cited in *Inside Oscar*, 1996

2768. I didn't want to be, "large."—I wanted to be good.

> Denzel Washington, Actor
> Interview in *The Los Angeles Times*, 1996

2769. I love being an employee.

> Drew Barrymore, Actress
> Interview in *Movieline* magazine, 1998

2770. If I'm going to say anything, I always want it to be through acting. I was never interested in fame in and of itself.

> Barbara Hershey, Actress
> Interview in *W* magazine, 1997

2771. I don't take my so-called image too seriously. That's the kiss of death for any actor.

> Sean Connery, Actor
> Interview in *Vim & Vigor* magazine, 1993

2772. I don't walk past the mirror any slower.

> Denzel Washington, Actor
> Interview in *Interview* magazine,
> 1990, on being a celebrity

2773. Your ego becomes outsized; you start actually believing the items in the newspaper that you planted about yourself.

> Binghan Ray, Studio Executive
> Cited in *GQ* magazine, 1995

2774. Either you control your ego, or your ego controls you.

> Eileen Padberg
> Cited in *Clint Eastwood—A Biography*, 1996

2775. It's when I start to think it's special that things can get out of hand.

> Samuel L. Jackson, Actor
> Interview in *LA Village View*, 1993

2776. Good evening, Hollywood phonies.

> Chevy Chase, Actor
> As host, greeting the 1987 Academy Awards
> audience, as cited in *Inside Oscar*, 1996

2777. A celebrity has a negative or an inverted sense of hearing; he can hear his name not being mentioned at forty paces.

> The Saturday Evening Post
> Cited in *Orson Welles: The Road to Xanadu*, 1996

2778. Credit you give yourself isn't worth having.

> Irving Thalberg
> Cited in *Mayer and Thalberg*
> *—The Make Believe Saints*, 1975

2779. You can be the most artistically perfect performer in the world, but the audience is like a broad—if you're indifferent, endsville.

> Frank Sinatra, Actor-Singer
> Cited in *People* magazine, 1998

2780. Make a blockbuster—you're the lion of the

cocktail circuit. Make a bomb — you buy your own drinks....

> Frank Capra, Producer-Director
> Stated in his 1971, *Frank Capra
> — The Name Above the Title*

2781. In Hollywood, you only want people with hit pictures hauling your coffin.

> Billy Wilder, Director
> Stated in *The Bright Side
> of Billy Wilder, Primarily*, 1970

2782. I think the picture a wonderful business and I will always love it, but I don't know whether it will always love me.

> Mary Pickford, Actress
> Cited in *Film Comment*, 1998

2783. Let's face it, the public can only take this good guy story about me for so long.

> Kevin Costner, Actor
> Cited in *Inside Oscar*, 1996

2784. You never see Robert De Niro's face on a watch.

> Robin Williams, Actor
> Cited in *Inside Oscar*, 1996, pointing
> out that celebrity is relative

2785. I don't want to die and have written on my tombstone: "He was a helluva actor until one day his eyes turned brown."

> Paul Newman
> Stated in his 1989
> *Paul Newman* biography

2786. If you've made a hit movie, then you get the full thirty-two-teeth display … and if you've sort of faded they say, "Are you still making movies?"

> Marlon Brando
> Stated in *Conversations with Brando*, 1991

2787. I've always had the theory that actors who beg the audience to like them … are much worse off than actors who just say, "Fuck you, if you don't like this, don't let the door hit you in the ass."

> Clint Eastwood
> Stated in *Clint Eastwood
> — A Biography*, 1996

2788. Her indifference to public opinion made her career unique.

> Alexander Walker
> Cited on the Internet Movie Database,
> 1998, on actress Greta Garbo

2789. My one regret in life is that I was not born someone else.

> Woody Allen, Writer-Director-Actor
> Cited in *Woody Allen — His Films and Career*,
> 1985, preferring anonymity to celebrity

2790. People forget me even while they're shaking hands with me.

> Woody Allen, Writer-Director-Actor
> Cited in *Woody Allen —
> His Films and Career*, 1985

2791. Maybe people do recognize me, but they're just repelled.

> Kevin Kline, Actor
> Interview in *Biography* magazine, 1998, on
> not being recognized when out in public

2792. The concept of matching the name with the face of an actor, that's what I deal with.

> Delroy Lindo, Actor
> Interview in *Vanity Fair*, 1994,
> on himself and the public

2793. If Arnold Schwarzenegger can keep his name, I can darn well keep mine.

> Renee Zellweger, Actress
> Cited in *Vanity Fair*, 1999

2794. I've gone places in a cowboy hat and shades, and people will say, "There goes Lou Gossett in the cowboy hat and shades."

> Louis Gossett, Jr., Actor
> Interview in *American Film*, 1983

2795. The (artist) who won't show his face is encroaching on holy turf. He's playing God's own trick.

> Don Delillo
> Cited in *Los Angeles Magazine*, 1995

2796. Success gives you the right to deflect all questions and criticism, directing your energy instead toward perfecting the art of gloating.

> Ron Nyswaner, Screenwriter
> Cited in *Inside Oscar*, 1996

2797. The success was so big that I lost my mind. Women, women, women.

> Carlo Ponti
> Cited in *Sophia Loren — A Biography*, 1998,
> following his first box office hit as producer

2798. He was one who was catnip to women.

> H. L. Mencken, Writer
> Cited in *Entertainment Weekly 100
> — "The 100 Greatest Movie Stars of
> All Time,"* on Rudolph Valentino

2799. Moguls? Don't like the word. It reminds me of some bad Turkish cigarettes I used to smoke.

> Jack Warner, Studio Head
> Cited in *Clown Prince of Hollywood —
> The Life and Times of Jack L.
> Warner*, 1990, on being referred to
> as the "last of the studio moguls."

2800. It's a sign of better times. More people have money to throw away on postage stamps.

Will Rogers, Actor
Cited in *The Great Movie Comedians*, 1978, on his fan mail

2801. When a soldier fighting in Vietnam writes to say he is praying for me, it's really shattering.

Sophia Loren
Stated in *Sophia Loren—A Biography*, 1998, during the 1968 news of her troubled pregnancy

2802. People seem to need to see celebrities become real: "Oh, look, they're alcoholics ... they're just like me.

Kevin Kline
Interview in *Playboy*, March, 1998

2803. When I die, Sophia (Loren) will probably show up at my funeral and get into all the photographs.

Marlon Brando
Cited in *Sophia Loren—A Biography*, 1998, complaining about her greater celebrity status

2804. The public's current preference for Donald over Mickey ... is a vote for human fallibility.

Frank Nugent, Writer

1947, on the "diabolical" Duck versus the "do-gooder" Mouse, as cited in *The New York Times Magazine*

2805. Remember, it was an actor who shot Lincoln.

Popular saying among Agents
Cited in *The Language of Show Biz—A Dictionary*

2806. There are three and a half billion people at this moment living, breathing on this planet. I can guarantee you right now very few are thinking about you.

Anthony Hopkins, Actor
Cited in *Movieline* magazine, 1998, on thinking you're a celebrity

2807. If you have something to hide, then hide it.

Warren Beatty, Actor-Writer-Director
Cited in *Vanity Fair*, 1999

2808. It's almost impossible to live a myth ... to be a celebrity is not healthy.

Jon Voight, Actor
Interview in *US* magazine, 1983

27

Stardom

2809. One of the greatest stars that ever lived was Rin Tin Tin ... so there can't be too much of a trick to it.

> Robert Mitchum, Actor
> Cited in *Big Reel*, 1997

2810. A star doesn't do anything really well, but looks good doing it. A celebrity doesn't do anything at all, but looks great not doing it.

> *People* magazine
> 1998

2811. You cannot combine being a movie star with not being a movie star.

> Martin Amis, Columnist
> Stated in *New Yorker* magazine, 1995

2812. The public makes the stars.

> Irving Thalberg
> Cited in *Mayer and Thalberg*
> — *The Make Believe Saints*, 1975

2813. The star represents something that belongs to people. They are happy to see that in close-up: They can criticize it.

> Jean-Luc Godard, Director
> Cited in *Film Forum*, 1985

2814. You evolve, or you don't evolve, in front of millions of people. You evolve in front of dads then in front of their children.

> Kevin Costner
> Cited in *Clint Eastwood—A Biography*, 1996

2815. How did the world exist before there were movie stars? Whom did people think about during sex? Whom did the Dalai Lama hang out with?

> Libby Gelman-Waxner, Writer
> Cited in "The 100 Best Movies"
> — *Newsweek Extra 2000*, 1998

2816. To be a star you have to have a certain edge.

> Sir Laurence Olivier, Actor
> Cited in *Screen Acting*, 1986

2817. Movie stars are like models perfected: They're interactive Vogue layouts.

> Libby Gelman-Waxner, Writer
> Cited in "The 100 Best Movies"
> — *Newsweek Extra 2000*, 1998

2818. To have "It," the fortunate possessor must have that strange magnetism.... "It" is a purely virile quality, belonging to a strong character ... but beauty is unnecessary. Conceit or self-consciousness destroys "It" immediately.

> James Robert Parish
> Stated in his 1972 *The Paramount Pretties*

2819. They became stars because of their very difference. They don't match the crowd at all ... They don't even come close to it.... Some have it, some don't.

> Sydney Guilaroff
> Cited in *American Cinema*, 1995

2820. He's just somebody that you really want to sit and look at. I thought that really summed up what makes a movie star. There are so many people I don't want to sit and look at.

> Oliver Stone, Director
> Interview in *Premiere* magazine, 1998

2821. A star has two things an actor doesn't have: charisma and the ability to sell tickets.

> Ned Tanen
> Cited in *Nicolas Kent—Naked Hollywood*, 1991

2822. It's the work that matters.

> Lillian Gish
> Cited in *George Cukor—A Double Life*, 1991

2823. If you look at yourself as a star, you've already lost something in the portrayal of any human being.

> Gene Hackman, Actor
> Interview in *The New York Times Magazine*, 1989

2824. I'm an actor, not a star. Stars are people who live in Hollywood and have heart-shaped swimming pools.

Al Pacino, Actor
Cited in *Inside Oscar*, 1996

2825. I wanted to be known as an actress, not necessarily as a star, although that would be frosting on the cake.

Bette Davis, Actress
Cited in *Bette and Joan
— The Divine Feud*, 1989

2826. (Humphrey Bogart) regarded the somewhat gaudy figure of Bogart, the star, with amused cynicism; Bogart, the actor, he held in deep respect.

John Huston, Director
Cited in *Entertainment Weekly 100*,
"The 100 Greatest Movie
Stars of All Time," 1997

2827. Olivia de Havilland was a star long before she became a great actress.

Elsa Maxwell
Cited in *Inside Oscar*, 1996

2828. (Woody Allen) is not concerned with fame, stardom, money — only work.

Charles Joffe, Agent
Cited in *Woody Allen
— His Films and Career*, 1985

2829. Once you become a "star" people come to you instead of the role and you cease to act.

Morgan Freeman
Recited by Darrell I. Hope
in *Venice* magazine, 1995

2830. In your heart of hearts you know perfectly well that movie stars aren't artists.... A prostitute can capture a moment!

Marlon Brando
Stated in *Conversations with Brando*, 1991

2831. It is said that no star is a heroine to her makeup artist.

Richard Corliss, Journalist
Cited in *Time* magazine, 1997

2832. You're only big in other people's eyes.

David Lynch, Screenwriter — Director
Cited in *Reel Conversations*, 1991

2833. I may be one of the big actors, but I'm the smallest one in the room.

Richard Gere, Actor
Interview in *US* magazine, 1997

2834. We grow our idols slowly. We also grow them big.

Ty Burr
Stated in *Entertainment Weekly 100*,
"The 100 Greatest Movie Stars
of All Time," 1997, on movie stars

2835. If we were a primitive society, movie stars would be gods.

Sydney Pollack
Cited in *American Cinema*, 1995

2836. There are lots of false idols being bowed to in Hollywood today.

James L. Brooks
Cited in *Time* magazine, 1997

2837. Stars are not important. You have to be General MacArthur to achieve fame.

Joan Crawford, Actress
Cited in *Bette and Joan
— The Divine Feud*, 1989

2838. Film stars to me were always six feet four, had perfect teeth and could do handstands on Malibu Beach ... and didn't need glasses.

Michael Caine, Actor
Interview in *Take 22: Moviemakers
on Moviemaking*, 1984

2839. They used to relate to (Jimmy Stewart) as though he was a movie star, then they'd realize he was one of the boys.

Walter Matthau, Actor
Cited in *Entertainment Weekly 100*, "The 100
Greatest Movie Stars of All Time," 1997

2840. I'm not going to wear jewelry anymore. I'll wear my children's arms around my neck.

Sophia Loren
Following the theft of her jewelry during a
promotional visit to New York City, as stated in her 1998 *Sophia Loren — A Biography*

2841. You became a prisoner of your image. It's a gold-plated cell, but it's still a cell.

Rick Nicita
Cited in *American Cinema*, 1995

2842. Fame is a demon. It's "I want." You want to be something. Another whole being gets created in fame ... once you set up that star structure most of your energy goes into maintaining it.

Nick Nolte, Actor
Interview in *Playboy*, 1999

2843. It blows a lot harder at the top of the mountain.

Kevin Costner
Cited in *Premiere* magazine, 1998

2844. The air is mighty thin at the top of the mountain.

Angela Bassett, Actress
Interview in *New Yorker* magazine, 1996

2845. No matter what I do, I always end up on page one.

Jean Harlow, Actress
Cited in *Vanity Fair*, 1990

2846. In every field of human endeavor, he that is first must perpetually live in the white light of publicity.

Theodore MacManus, Essayist
Writing on "The Penalty of Leadership,"
as cited in *US* magazine, 1993

2847. Best table. Best chair. Best glass. Best fork. Best napkin!

Roberto Benigni,
Actor-Writer-Director-Producer
Reply to a CBS *60 Minutes* reporter
when asked if his new stardom gets
him the best table in restaurants, 1999

2848. Jean (Harlow) had all the sensitivity necessary to be a star, but she lacked one of the qualifications for surviving stardom ... enough ego.

Anita Loos
Stated in her 1977 *Anita Loos — Cast of Thousands*, on the 1937 death of Harlow

2849. I can't ... look in the mirror and say "I'm a famous actress" and expect that to get me through the day.

Audrey Hepburn, Actress
Interview in *Family Circle*, 1979

2850. The trouble with Clint (Eastwood) is that he doesn't know he's a movie star.

Burt Reynolds
Cited in *Clint Eastwood — A Biography*, 1996

2851. (Clint Eastwood) is the last demonstration of what star glamour used to mean.

David Thompson
Cited in *Clint Eastwood — A Biography*, 1996

2852. I don't think Paul Newman really thinks he's Paul Newman in his head.

William Goldman
Cited in the 1989 biography *Paul Newman*

2853. I always knew that I could be a star for the audience that didn't relate to John Wayne or Al Pacino.

Richard Dreyfuss, Actor
Interview in *The New York Times Magazine*, 1978

2854. More people had seen me than saw Napoleon, Lincoln or Cleopatra.

Mae West, Actress
Cited in *The Great Movie Comedians*, 1978, on her movie viewers

2855. I don't know what (being) a star means. Of course, for me, it's something I look at through a telescope and claim I've been there....

Shirley MacLaine
Cited in *The Hollywood Reporter*, 1998

2856. You asked for Joan Crawford. You got Joan Crawford. And Joan Crawford always comes first on the marquee.

Joan Crawford, Actress
Cited in *Bette and Joan
— The Divine Feud*, 1989

2857. You cannot give second billing to the Queen of England — or to me.

Bette Davis
On demanding her name be before
Errol Flynn's on the movie *Essex
and Elizabeth*, as cited in *Bette
and Joan — The Divine Feud*, 1989

2858. Lay it on. Don't be timid. Flynn may be a star outside but here he is only a slave.

Michael Curtiz, Director
On a whipping scene of Errol Flynn,
as cited in *Warner Bros.*, 1975

2859. When you get to be a star you stop being a supplicant.

Richard Dreyfuss, Actor
Interview in *Close Up*, 1978

2860. The studio was looking for stars and my star was not lit.

Michael Pressman
Interview in *DGA* magazine, 1997

2861. Somebody can be an accidental star ... but if a star has staying power, generally speaking, they're talented.

Michael Eisner
Cited in *American Cinema*, 1995

2862. We are like boxers, one never knows how much longer one has.

Clint Eastwood
Stated in *Clint Eastwood — A Biography*, 1996

2863. Ask ... kids now who Humphrey Bogart or Clark Gable was. "Didn't he play for the Yankees?"

Marlon Brando
Stated in *Conversations with Brando*, 1991

2864. To be anointed a brand-new star, you're not really allowed to have a past.
> Paul Thomas Anderson, Director
> Cited in *Premiere* magazine, 1998

2865. I played a star part the very first time I walked on stage and I've been working my way down ever since.
> Orson Welles
> Cited in *Orson Welles: The Road to Xanadu*, 1996

2866. I plummeted to stardom.
> Dustin Hoffman, Actor
> Interview in *The Sunday Times*, London, 1993

2867. The tragedy of fame? The tragedy is when no one shows up....
> Frank Sinatra, Actor-Singer
> Cited in *People* magazine, 1998

2868. There ain't never a horse that couldn't be rode — there ain't never a rider who couldn't be throwed.
> Gary Cooper, Actor
> Reciting an old cowboy saying to express his
> attitude on stardom, as cited on the 1998
> televised A&E *Biography*, "Gary Cooper"

2869. Success is fine.... There's nothing that says you are more holy if you are poor and destitute.
> Richard Gere, Actor
> Cited in *US* magazine, 1997

2870. Fame is the by-product. It's not an end in itself. It's the thing you learn to put up with.
> Jim Carrey, Actor
> Interview in *Movieline* magazine, 1998

2871. Fame is funny. It's more fun trying to get it than it is to have it.
> Barbra Streisand
> Interview in *All About Barbra*, 1987

2872. Once you are a superstar, there are two choices open to you: You can become a bore or a monster.
> Joyce Haber, Columnist
> Stated in *Calendar*, 1969

2873. Until you're known in my profession as a monster, you're not a star.
> Bette Davis
> Cited in *Entertainment Weekly 100*, "The 100
> Greatest Movie Stars of All Times," 1997

2874. Stars ... are like ducks: Their plumage is waterproof. One may pour buckets of water over them and they come out perfectly dry.
> Jean Renoir, Director
> Stated in his 1974 *Jean Renoir — My Life
> and Times*, explaining his mistrust of stars

2875. All stars learn how to cultivate one very important asset in their career: a very short memory. They remember only what they want to remember.
> George Cukor, Director
> Cited in *Bette and Joan — The Divine Feud*, 1989

2876. The star's face must always be seen, even if it's midnight in a tunnel.
> Louis B. Mayer, Studio Head
> Referring to onscreen presence, as cited in
> *Fred Zinnemann — An Autobiography*, 1992

2877. A director's face is not the same wattage as a movie star's.
> Lawrence Grobel, Biographer
> Stated in his 1989 *The Hustons*

2878. People always say what makes a movie star is the way the light hits a person's face, but I think it's something that the camera records about the light inside....
> Chloe Webb, Actress
> Interview in *GQ* magazine, 1994

2879. In Hollywood, they like you until you're standing on a pedestal.
> Yul Brynner, Actor
> Cited in *Inside Oscar*, 1996

2880. Hollywood is a strange place. One day you're on a billboard, the next day you're on a milk carton.
> Mario van Peebles, Actor-Director
> Interview in *A Cut Above*, 1998

2881. I'm popular with the public, but that doesn't make me popular at the country club.
> Clint Eastwood
> Cited in *Clint Eastwood — A Biography*,
> 1996, referring to many years
> not winning an Academy Award

2882. When a man's work becomes the standard for the whole world, it also becomes a target for the shafts of the envious few.
> Theodore MacManus, Essayist
> Writing on "The Penalty of Leadership,"
> as cited in *US* magazine, 1993

28

Awards

2883. The Oscar Award has to do with American civilization, as it is and wants to see itself.

Vincent Canby
Interview in *Variety*, 1998

2884. In the mythology of cinema, Oscar is the supreme prize.

Federico Fellini, Director
Cited in *Inside Oscar*, 1996,
upon winning his fourth Oscar

2885. The Oscar seemed to have been confused with the Nobel Peace Prize.

Janet Maslin
Cited in *Inside Oscar*, 1996

2886. The Academy Award is the Nobel Prize of motion pictures.

Leroy Johnston, 1935
Cited in *Inside Oscar*, 1996

2887. (Winning an Oscar is) kind of like winning an Olympic medal because it's so identifiable. Only in the Olympics you win it because you're the best.

Al Pacino, Actor
Interview in *Playboy*, December, 1996

2888. Nice show, a big show, but I don't know if the prizes are right.

Federico Fellini
On the Academy Awards ceremony
where he won an Oscar for *La Strada*,
1954, cited in *Fellini—A Life*, 1986

2889. Every year in Barcelona they give awards for poetry. The third prize is a silver rose. The second prize is a gold one. The first prize ... is a real rose.

Peter Bogdanovich, Director
1971, cited in *Behind the Oscar*, 1993

2890. If you have no hope of getting one, they're despised. But if you have, they're very important.

David Lean
Cited in *David Lean
—A Biography*, 1996, on the Oscars

2891. Sometimes the best award you get is the fact that you get to make the picture at all.

Martin Scorsese, Director
Interview in *The Future of the Movies*, 1991

2892. As for me, prizes are nothing. My prize is my work.

Katherine Hepburn, Actress
Cited in *Inside Oscar*, 1996

2893. Act well the part, there all the glory lies.

Rawley Farnsworth
High school drama teacher's advice
to his student, Tom Hanks,
as cited in *Inside Oscar*, 1996

2894. It might mean I'd get more scripts without other actors' coffee stains on them.

Michael Caine, Actor
On practical importance of his
possibly winning an Oscar, 1996,
as cited in *Inside Oscar*, 1996

2895. I don't care if we're nominated for best morons.

Matt Damon, Actor-Screenwriter
Interview in *Entertainment Weekly*, 1998,
on his pending Oscar nominations, 1997

2896. No extraneous factors should be allowed to color your (voting) consideration of excellence. The Academy, the film industry and the world must trust your judgement.

The Governors of the Board
Of the Academy of Motion Pictures in an
official statement to its award voting members

2897. Institutions aren't the best judges of a work of art, just like the Académie des Beaux-Arts rejected the Impressionists.

Robert Solo, Producer
Cited in *Behind the Oscar*, 1993

2898. Critics have more right than the academy to

pick the Oscars ... we have one important advantage over the people who now vote: We've seen all the movies.

> Gene Siskel, Film Critic
> Interview in *Playboy*, June, 1984

2899. Whether Hollywood likes it or not, the voter casts his ballot emotionally, not critically.

> Henry Rogers
> Cited in *Behind the Oscar*, 1993,
> on the annual Academy Awards

2900. No one should have a chance to see so much desire, so much need for a prize, so much pain when not given it.

> Glenda Jackson
> Best Actress, 1970 and 1973, Academy
> Awards, as cited in *Behind the Oscar*, 1993

2901. The Academy is essentially a trade union.... The awards are the awards of any union in any company town, a vote for jobs — and hits provide jobs, flops don't.

> Jean Gregory Dunne, Screenwriter

2902. Why, he looks just like my Uncle Oscar!

> Margaret Herrick, Academy Librarian, 1931
> Unwittingly coining the official
> name for the award statuette, as
> cited in *Chronicle of the Cinema*, 1995

2903. A perfect symbol of the picture business; a powerful athletic body clutching a gleaming sword, with half of his head, that part which held the brains, completely sliced off.

> Francis Marion, Scriptwriter
> Cited in *Chronicle of the Cinema*,
> 1995, in describing the Oscar figurine

2904. The Oscar is not Jewish, you can tell.

> Marty Feldman, Actor
> As presenter at the 1977 Academy Awards
> ceremonies, cited in *Inside Oscar*, 1996

2905. (Oscar) has no genitalia and he's holding a sword.

> Dustin Hoffman, Actor
> Upon examining his award, 1980,
> as cited in *Behind the Oscar*, 1993

2906. [T]hey're nothing but bookends with a sneer.

> Bob Hope
> Cited in *Inside Oscar*, 1996,
> describing the Oscar statuette

2907. Isn't it beautiful and shiny, Mr. Disney?

> Shirley Temple, Child Actress, 1938
> Age 10, upon presenting an Oscar to Walt
> Disney, as cited in *Inside Oscar*, 1996

2908. (Oscar:) The tail that wags the Academy.

> Charles Champlin, Entertainment Editor
> In *The Los Angeles Times*, quoted
> in *Behind the Oscar*, 1993

2909. But — Academy, thy name is capricious.

> Frank Capra, Producer-Director
> Stated in his *Frank Capra — The Name
> Above the Title*, 1971, on the
> Academy Awards being without
> a consistent criteria for selection

2910. The tendency is for important films to win over popcorn entertainment ... history is more weighty than popcorn.

> Steven Spielberg, Director
> On his Academy Award for
> Best Picture, *Schindler's List*, 1994,
> as cited in *Behind the Oscar*, 1993

2911. As much as I love the Oscar night pageantry, it's a silly bingo game. It's like five names in a hat, and one gets pulled out.

> Jodie Foster, Actress
> Cited in *Behind the Oscar*, 1993,
> on the Academy Awards

2912. The only honest way to find the best actor would be to let everybody play Hamlet.

> Unknown

2913. (The Oscars) are the apex of our dream world. That's what we put aside as what it is to be beautiful and loved.

> Jon Voight, Actor
> Interview in *Rolling Stone*, 1979

2914. If you're nominated for an Oscar and you don't win, after a week it's pretty much forgotten. And if you do win, after two weeks it's pretty much forgotten.

> Hollywood saying

2915. (The Academy Awards) is enjoyable in the way that bobbing for apples is enjoyable. You can't take the game seriously.

> Warren Beatty
> Cited in *Behind the Oscar*, 1993

2916. I envy boys who get the Technical Awards. They don't have to get nervously drunk before.

> Donald Ogden Stewart
> Speaking at the 1940 Academy Awards
> in reference to the non-televised
> awards portion of the Oscar presentation

2917. The Oscars are some sort of masturbatory

fantasy. People think: An Academy Award — now if I get a parking ticket I don't have to pay it.

Elliot Gould, Actor
Cited in *Behind the Oscar*, 1993, as
commented at the 1970 Oscar ceremonies

2918. It was just a small group getting together for a pat on the back.

Janet Gaynor
First winner, Academy Awards, Best Actress,
1928, cited in *Behind the Oscar*, 1993

2919. Awards are nice, but I'd much rather have a job.

Jane Darwell, Actress
Comment to reporters following the
Oscar win for Best Supporting
Actress, 1940 in *The Grapes of Wrath*,
lamenting her lack of work since that film

2920. We want to thank all of you for watching us congratulate ourselves tonight.

Warren Beatty, Actor
Cited in *Behind the Oscar*, 1993,
speaking at the 1976 Academy Awards

2921. I'm kind of nebulous about this whole awards thing.... You're in contests you haven't willingly joined.

Samuel L. Jackson, Actor
Interview in *Detour* magazine, 1995

2922. [H]onors beget honors. Once you get honored, somebody says, "We might as well honor him too."

Carl Reiner, Writer-Actor
Upon being honored at the 1999 Santa
Barbara Film Festival, his third
honor in two months, as cited
in the *Santa Barbara News-Press*, 1999

2923. It is what it is. Besides, it's much more fun to bitch about it and look at the clothes.

Pauline Kael, Critic
Cited in *Modern Maturity* magazine, 1998,
on how to improve the Academy Awards

2924. They should have an (Oscar) award for the fastest left-handed standby painter (of) ... sets.

Marlon Brando
Interview in *Conversations with Brando*,
1991, on how he finds awards "ridiculous"

2925. I think the Academy (Awards) ought to set aside a special award for Ingrid Bergman every year whether she makes a picture or not.

Cary Grant, Actor
Her frequent co-star, as cited in
Ingrid Bergman — My Story, 1989

2926. You'll go to the Academy Awards or you'll never hear the end of it from me.

Bing Crosby's mother
To son, Bing, upon him being nominated
for an Oscar for his role in *Going
My Way*, 1944, cited in *Inside Oscar*, 1996

2927. Bette Davis drops in at these affairs every year for a cup of coffee and another Oscar.

Bob Hope
Cited in *Inside Oscar*, 1996, as a presenter
at the 1941 Academy Awards ceremony

2928. When you play crazy ladies you always walk away with the honors.

Joan Crawford, Actress
Cited in *Bette & Joan — The Divine Feud*, 1989

2929. The members of the Academy often give Oscars to young women for a first sensational part. But men have to win their spurs.

David Lean, Director
Cited in *European Travel and Life*, 1990

2930. It couldn't have happened to an older guy.

George Burns, Actor
Cited in *Chronicle of the Cinema*, 1995,
upon winning an Oscar at age 80, 1976, as
Best Supporting Actor in *The Sunshine Boys*

2931. As Joan Crawford once said, "I'll show ya a pair of Golden Globes."

Bette Midler, Actress
Cited in *Inside Oscar*, 1996

2932. I'm sorry. I can't come any further so I'll have to ask Mr. Disney to accept my (Oscar) prize for me.

Mickey Mouse
Speaking from a cartoon on screen at the
1932 Academy Awards

2933. I came home and there was "Oscar" in a tutu. It happened that the Barbie things fit perfectly.

Kevin Kline, Actor
Interview in *Playboy*, March, 1998, on what
his small daughter did with his Oscar

2934. Moral: Don't make the best picture you ever made in the year that someone makes *Gone with the Wind*.

Frank Capra, Producer-Director
of *Mr. Smith Goes to Washington*,
upon winning only one
Oscar to *GWTW*'s 10 Oscars, 1940

2935. Winning an Oscar at Poverty Row (Columbia Pictures) would be as easy as telling the sex of a fly.

> Frank Capra, Director
> Stated in 1929 in his *Frank Capra
> — The Name Above the Title*, 1971

2936. You see, people have to know you're acting.

> Cary Grant, Actor
> On why he never won an Oscar, as cited in
> *Bob Hope — Don't Shoot, It's Only Me*, 1990

2937. Now I'll have to demonstrate that I'm a good actor.

> Roberto Benigni, Actor
> Upon receiving the 1999 SAG
> Best Actor award for *Life Is Beautiful*

2938. It's not good enough to win an Oscar. Suppose next time I make a stinker. I'm worrying about that now.

> Sam Goldwyn, Studio Head-Producer
> Cited in *Inside Oscar*, 1996

2939. It's so much fun being nominated — everyone is a winner. And then — there are four losers.

> Liv Ullman, Actress
> Cited in *Inside Oscar*, 1996

2940. The terrible thing is, somebody has to win.

> Judith Dench, Actress
> Upon receiving the 1999 Oscar
> for Best Supporting Actress

2941. This isn't sour grapes with me because I didn't grow any grapes last year. I didn't even sow a wild oat.

> W. C. Fields, Actor
> Complaining that comedians weren't
> nominated for acting awards,
> as cited in *Inside Oscar*, 1996

2942. I mean: It's not bad winning it.

> Robert De Niro, Actor
> Cited in *Going Hollywood*, 1978,
> upon winning his first Oscar, 1975

2943. It's nice, but it would have meant more forty years ago. I would have tried different things in the movie business.

> Jack Palance
> Upon winning the Academy Award
> for Best Supporting Actor, 1992,
> as cited in *Behind the Oscar*, 1993

2944. I thought it was a typo.

> Woody Allen, Director
> Cited in *Inside Oscar*, 1996, upon being
> nominated for Best Director,
> 1984, by the Academy

2945. Up until now, the Oscar I knew was on Sesame Street or the Odd Couple.

> Kim Basinger, Actress
> Acceptance speech, upon
> winning an Oscar, 1997

2946. Actually, it should be much higher. I was robbed fifteen times.

> Billy Wilder, Producer-
> Director-Screenwriter
> On having a .286 career Oscar
> winning average with 6 for 21 nominations,
> 1970, cited in *The Bright
> Side of Billy Wilder, Primarily*

2947. You just can't allow any organization to be the one to put the "Good Housekeeping Seal" or the USDA stamp or to deem your work worthwhile.

> Spike Lee, Director
> Interview in *Fade In* magazine, 1998

2948. (Receiving an award) doesn't make a film any better or any less of a film than what it really is.

> Norman Jewison, Director
> Interview in *Directors at Work*, 1970

2949. An Oscar is a wonderful thing to have, of course, but it doesn't convince you of anything about yourself. You have to keep accomplishing.

> Sidney Poitier, Actor
> Interview in *The Saturday Evening Post*, 1964

2950. The (Academy) awards mean nothing to the kind of pictures that get made next year. It never spills over....

> Bruce Beresford, Director
> Cited in *Behind the Oscar*, 1993

2951. The way to survive an Oscar is never to try to win another one. (Winners) spend the rest of their lives turning down scripts while searching for the great role to win another one.

> Humphrey Bogart, Actor
> Cited in *Behind the Oscar*, 1993

2952. Quentin Tarantino told me it would be really cool if I screamed out "fuck" at the Academy Awards if I lost.

> Nicolas Cage, Actor
> Interview in *Playboy*, September, 1996

2953. You can't eat awards — nor, more to the point, drink 'em.

> John Wayne, Actor
> Cited in *Behind the Oscar*, 1993

2954. I hate getting the award for "life achieve-ment." I'd rather it be for half a life.

Dustin Hoffman, Actor
Interview in *Variety*, 1997, at
the 1996 Venice Film Festival
to accept such an award

2955. When you die, the newspaper obituaries will say, "The Academy Award-winning _____ died today."

Walter Matthau, Actor
Commenting on the additional
benefit to winning an Oscar,
as cited in *Behind the Oscar*, 1993

29

Careers

2956. A publicity man can't do anything for you. The only thing that counts is your own merit in a performance.

Spencer Tracy, Actor
Interview in the *San Francisco Sunday Examiner and Chronicle*, 1967

2957. If I'm not controlling my image, then who is?

Arnold Schwarzenegger, Actor
Cited in the *Los Angeles Times Magazine*, 1996

2958. In my Anglo-Saxon upbringing … you don't fuss about yourself and you don't make a spectacle of yourself. All of which I've earned a living doing.

Audrey Hepburn, Actress
Interview in *American Movie Classics*, 1990

2959. The public wants you the way they found you.

Sylvester Stallone, Actor
On his mistake in doing comedy instead of action-drama, as cited in the *Los Angeles Times—Calendar*, 1998

2960. We should respect the art in us, not us in the art.

Ving Rhames, Actor
Cited in *US* magazine, 1998

2961. Making movies is an exercise in self-exploration.

Shirley MacLaine
Acceptance speech, for the Cecil B. DeMille award at the 1998 Golden Globe ceremonies

2962. I started by working for people who don't buy into trends and the superficial. That's how I continue to work.

Alfre Woodard, Actress
Interview in *People* magazine, 1987

2963. You can't wait around at Schwab's in a tight sweater anymore, and hope somebody will discover you.

Robert Townsend, Actor-Director
On actresses taking control of their career moves, as stated in a 1987 *L.A. Style* magazine interview

2964. In this industry you're either on the rise or falling — there's no standing still.

David Westberg, Agent
Cited in *Your Film Acting Career*, 1989

2965. Okay. I can't get into the Guild without a job, and I can't get a job without the Guild. They're not going to screw my head up. I'm going to beat them at this.

An unknown actress
Cited in *Your Film Acting Career*, 1989

2966. You cry when you're not working because you want to work more. Then, when you work too much you cry…. So, you may as well cry and work.

Jimmy Smits, Actor
Interview in the *Los Angeles Herald Examiner*, 1989

2967. That's the role of an artist…. The artist exhibits or the artist can't survive.

Peter O'Toole, Actor
Cited in *GQ* magazine, 1981

2968. There are three acts in a star's life: "Yes, Sir," "F —- you," and "I just want to do good work and live a good life."

Hollywood saying
Cited in the *Los Angeles Times Calendar*, 1998

2969. Before I take on a client, I look for three things: talent, guts and imagination.

Barbara Best, Publicist
Cited in *Your Film Acting Career*, 1989, referring to actors

2970. In Hollywood, everybody is more or less a journeyman.

> Arthur Knight, Film Critic
> Cited in *The Reel Tinsel*, 1970

2971. You feel so disposable at times. I'm working in the most expendable industry known to man. After ... years in Hollywood, I still feel I'm here on a day pass.

> Sean Patrick Flanery, Actor
> Interview in *Interview* magazine, 1998

2972. I got fired for many years for doing a lot of the things that I'm now getting accolades for.

> Robert Altman, Director
> Interview in *Directors in Action*, 1968

2973. Hollywood is littered with the bodies of the sons and daughters of the famous who didn't make it.

> Michael Douglas, Actor-Producer
> Interview in *Vanity Fair*, 1995

2974. People say how did you get in at the top? Because no one would let me in at the bottom.

> Melvin van Peebles, Screenwriter-Director
> Interview in the *Los Angeles Times Calendar*, 1968

2975. I'm already hearing young black filmmakers referred to as the next John Singleton.... I'm still trying to be the next John Singleton.

> John Singleton, Director
> Interview in *People* magazine, 1991, at 25 years of age

2976. There are a dozen girls I know who can sing better, dance better and act better. I can do a little of all three and I suppose that's why I get by.

> Betty Grable, Actress
> Cited in *The Technicolor Years*, 1980

2977. I'm not Blockbuster Boy. I would feel untrue to myself, untrue to the people who appreciate the choices I've made. For me, the career thing has to be a little purer, more organic.

> Johnny Depp, Actor
> Interview in *Biography* magazine, 1998

2978. The cinema allows you this double game of telling a story, and while telling it, living it yourself as an adventure, and with extraordinary people in each realm.

> Federico Fellini
> Stated in *Fellini—A Life*, 1986

2979. You tolerate me! You really tolerate me!

> Sean Penn, Actor
> Independent Spirit Award, comment of acceptance, Best Actor, 1996

2980. Hell! Why, he'll be makin' Westerns a couple a years after he's dead.

> Pat Ford
> Son of director John Ford, who made more Westerns than any other director, as cited in *John Ford*, 1968

2981. (I don't) want to achieve immortality through art, but through not dying.

> Woody Allen, Director
> Cited in *Woody Allen—His Films and Career*, 1985, on his films making him immortal

2982. These days I like my orange juice shaken, not stirred.

> Sean Connery, Actor
> Commenting on his senior status as an actor, in *Vanity Fair*, 1999

2983. I fantasize playing guard for the Knicks. If I had my life to live over again, I'd rather be a black basketball player.

> Woody Allen, Writer-Director
> Cited in *Woody Allen—His Films and Career*, 1985

2984. I took a loveable character and used him to make a place for Sidney Poitier, for Sammy Davis, for Lena Horn.

> Stepin Fetchit, Actor
> Interview in *The Chicago Sunday America*, 1968, on himself

2985. The one advantage I have is that if you're looking for a Chris Walken type, you have to get Chris Walken. I have a place. I own it. This means I can work for a long time.

> Christopher Walken, Actor
> Interview in *Details* magazine, 1993

2986. I'm trying to grow up a little bit and be able to take off the red nose and floppy shoes when I need to.

> Chris Farley, Actor-Comedian
> Cited in *Entertainment Yearbook*, 1998

2987. If you asked me if I'm the luckiest guy on earth, the answer is, "Yep."

> Gary Cooper, Actor
> Cited in the televised A & E *Biography*, "Gary Cooper," 1998

2988. I've had many people tell me that they remember certain little things I did in pictures. I think it's wonderful to have been able to give people little pieces of time they can remember.

> James Stewart, Actor
> Stated in *The Life of James Stewart: Pieces of Time*, 1997

2989. I will always be known in movie history as the man who brought Arnold Schwarzenegger to his knees.

Danny DeVito, Actor
Interview in *Cable Choice* magazine,
1989, commenting on how they got
both heads in the same frame in *Twins*

2990. My first ambition was to be a painter and live in Europe.

Robert Redford
Cited in *The New York Times Magazine*, 1997

2991. Whether you make a million dollars or two dollars, people remember you for the work.

Danny Glover, Actor
Cited in *US* magazine, 1984

2992. When you call yourself a production designer, you get more money.

Harry Horner, Production Designer
Cited in *Film Makers on Film Making*,
1983, as opposed to an art director

2993. Today I'm Jack L. Warner. Tomorrow I'll just be another rich Jew.

Jack Warner, Producer
Cited in *Clown Prince of Hollywood*,
1990, on his last day as owner and
head of Warner Bros. Studio

2994. It's a shame he wasn't born rich, because he would have had so much fun.

Ruth Eastwood, Clint Eastwood's mother
Cited in *Clint Eastwood
— A Biography*, 1996

2995. Have "screw you" money.

Barry Shear, Producer-Director
Cited in *Your Film Acting Career*,
1989, advising actors to have the
financial means to be selective

2996. Be sure you can afford to be an actor.

Vikki Bandlow, Theatrical Agent
Cited in *Your Film Acting Career*, 1989

2997. I don't see any reason to take a 1,000 percent cut in wages.

Michael Caine, Actor
Stated in *Take 22: Moviemakers on
Moviemaking*, 1984, on not wanting
to leave screen acting for stage acting

2998. Betty's like any average American girl who makes a million a year.

Mother of Betty Grable
Cited in *The Technicolor Years*, 1980

2999. I thought I was ... with a group of artists.

All you want to talk about is money. I think you're getting near graduation time.

Kirk Douglas
Cited in *Film Makers on Film
Making*, Vol. II, 1983, speaking to a
group of American Film Institute students

3000. Financially. Period.

Sean Penn, Actor
Interview in *Interview* magazine,
1995, on why he acts

3001. You will confer with generals ... dine ... with kings, and ... sleep with titled women. All of this you will do while being dead broke. That's what being a director is.

John Huston
Stated in *The Hustons*, 1989

3002. Directing is everything — it's the difference between being a chess player and a chess pawn.

Burt Reynolds, Actor-Director
Interview in *Take 22: Moviemakers
on Moviemaking*, 1984

3003. They taught me three words ... "Camera" ... "Action" ... and "Cut." That's the secret. You get those three words ... and you're a director.

Allan Dwan, Director
Cited in *Bright Lights*, 1979

3004. I never planned to become a director. The fates and a combination of luck — good and bad — were responsible.

Ida Lupino, Director-Actress
Interview in *Action!* magazine, 1967

3005. [H]aving done both, I tell you that directing is a pleasure and writing is a drag.

Billy Wilder, Writer-Director
Interview in *Film Makers
on Film Making*, 1983

3006. [D]on't get mad, don't argue until you become a director.

John Huston
Cited in *The Hustons*, 1989

3007. It is possible to be called a Director in modern-day filmmaking and not know anything, except maybe the producer.

Haskell Wexler, Cinematographer
Interview in *Film Makers
on Film Making*, 1983

3008. Film lovers are sick people. I don't know if once one becomes a director one is cured.

François Truffaut, Director
Stated in *Film Makers on Film Making*, 1983

3009. Please, you directors, don't think that the art director is just a carpenter.

Harry Horner, Production Designer
Cited in *Film Makers on Film Making*, 1983

3010. It is a recorded fact that no one dropped a sandbag on me at any time during the last three pictures which I have directed.

Ida Lupino, Actress-Producer-Director
Interview in *The Los Angeles Evening Herald & Express*, 1950, when asked if she had experienced any resistance as a female director

3011. The industry's cinematographers are, as a class, perhaps the most invaluable and yet generally underrated men in Hollywood.

John Huston
Stated in 1941, as cited in *The Hustons*, 1989

3012. You have to have a colossal stockpile of faith in yourself to do this job ... feeling like you aren't exactly God's gift to cinematography, you are left with only one resource — yourself.

Tom Ackerman, Cinematographer
Interview in *Contemporary Cinematographers: On Their Art*, 1998

3013. As long as your career is guided by the close-up, you are largely dictated to by your physiognomy.

Paul Schrader, Director

3014. [I]t is the actors who are in front of the camera, and who have the most at stake personally ... you can have a nom de plume as a writer or as a director.... But it's pretty hard to have a face de plume.

Warren Beatty
Interview in *American Premiere*, 1992

3015. If I'd looked like Robert Redford I probably wouldn't have become an actor.

Dustin Hoffman
Interview in *Time Out, London*, 1993

3016. I was lucky that I happened to be at the bottom of the barrel at that time. I was inexpensive....

Elliot Silverstein, Director
Interview in *Directors at Work*, 1970, on getting his first directing job, for *Cat Ballou*, 1966

3017. I am a wife-made man. Sylvia has a fine head on my shoulders.

Danny Kaye, Actor
Cited in *Reader's Digest*, 1988, on his manager wife, Sylvia Fine

3018. I learned my craft while no one was looking.

Sharon Stone
Cited in *The New York Times Magazine*, 1997

3019. I've done better and I've done worse, but in the final analysis, it was better than not doing anything at all.

Paul Newman
Cited in *Paul Newman*, 1989, referring to his acting career

3020. What got me up there on stage and out there in the bullring wasn't a lack of nerves, it was an absolutely perfect lack of ambition. I saw no glorious future for myself in either episode.

Orson Welles
Cited in *Orson Welles: The Road to Xanadu*, 1996

3021. My success need not be analyzed beyond saying that it was the result of ... remarkable ... timing and good luck ... I was in my career almost on a pass.

Sidney Poitier, Actor
Interview in *Essence* magazine, 1981

3022. It sure beats working.

Robert Mitchum, Actor
Cited in *Life* magazine, 1998, on his motivation to be an actor

3023. Time will turn you into a hag if you don't show the bitch who's boss.

Mae West, Actress
Cited in *Detour* magazine, 1995

3024. A dancer starts losing out after 21 because while he's learning his art form his anatomy's going downhill.

Gene Kelly, Actor
Cited in *Los Angeles*, 1972

3025. Other artists are envied by dancers to be truthful, because we have a much shorter life. The legs go.

Gene Kelly, Actor-Dancer
Cited in *Cue* magazine, 1976

3026. [A] lot of child stars don't make it (because) it's hard to see someone as cute and then to all of the sudden see them as having depth ... I was just lucky that, when I was little, nobody thought I was cute.

Christina Ricci, Actress
Cited in *Vanity Fair*, 1999

3027. And on that awful day when someone says,

"You're not pretty, you're no good," think of me and don't give up!

> Ruth Gordon, Actress-Screenwriter
> Cited in *Reel Women*, 1991

3028. In this business, success is determined by longevity. It doesn't matter if you're young and you're doing a movie right now.

> John Singleton, Director
> Interview in *People* magazine, 1991

3029. I'm not afraid of time. I'm afraid of a lack of time.

> Catherine Deneuve, Actress
> Cited in the *Santa Barbara News-Press*,
> 1998, at age 54, upon receiving
> a career achievement award

3030. Everything is momentary. You do a good picture, great; you do a lousy one, nobody wants you. That's why you have to have a husband, children, and antique furniture.

> Barbra Streisand
> Stated in *All About Barbra*, 1987

3031. "To surgery."

> John Huston
> On what he attributed his longevity to,
> c. 1985, as cited in *The Hustons*, 1989

3032. I've made 48 films of which only five were good … I will never make another, and I will never visit a plastic surgeon.

> Brigitte Bardot, Actress
> Upon retiring at 39, as cited in
> *Chronicle of the Cinema*, 1995

3033. Fish don't applaud.

> Bob Hope
> When asked why he didn't retire
> and go fishing, as cited in *Bob Hope
> —Don't Shoot, It's Only Me*, 1990

3034. Include me out.

> Sam Goldwyn
> His suggestion for his epitaph, as
> cited in *You Must Remember This*, 1975

3035. You have to fail—that's part of being an actor, being really bad so you can see where the good stuff is.

> Minnie Driver, Actress
> Interview in *Biography* magazine, 1998

3036. … Chicken one day, feathers the next.

> Frank Capra, Director
> Stated in *Frank Capra—The
> Name Above the Title*, 1971,
> describing comedy screen actors' fame

3037. When I make a picture … I live in a dimension in which I am absolved, taken by life. My crises begins when the picture finishes … God, wife, women, taxes.

> Federico Fellini
> Cited in *Fellini—A Life*, 1986

3038. If you have wounds that are bleeding, I don't think acting will ever get them to stop.

> Rebecca De Mornay, Actress
> Interview in *Interview* magazine, 1993

3039. It's funny, I don't know which is worse, the fear of failure or the fear of success.

> Barbra Streisand
> Stated in *All About Barbra*, 1987

3040. Oh, I liked (acting) beforehand—all the preparation—and I liked it afterward, if it went well. But the thing itself is scary!

> Audrey Hepburn, Actress
> Interview in *Parade* magazine, 1989

3041. I suppose I made it look easy but, gee whiz, did I work and worry.

> Fred Astaire, Actor-Dancer
> Cited in *Chronicle of the Cinema*, 1995

3042. I'd rather die of overwork than be bored to death by inactivity.

> Irving Thalberg
> Cited in *Anita Loos—Cast of Thousands*, 1977

3043. If I don't amuse myself, making movies is an awful job.

> Federico Fellini
> Cited in *Fellini—A Life*, 1986

3044. Being an actor is hard. So many people want your job.

> Christopher Walken, Actor
> Interview in *Playboy*, September 1997

3045. Because it's not fun. It's work doing a play.

> Warren Beatty, Actor
> Cited in *The New York Times Magazine*,
> 1998, when asked why he doesn't do plays

3046. When I accept a picture … I wall myself up. It's like accepting a prison term.

> Montgomery Clift, Actor
> Cited in *The Citizen News*, 1960

3047. The only difference between me and other actors is that I've been in jail more.

> Robert Mitchum, Actor
> Cited in *Big Reel*, 1997

3048. You're put on the earth somehow to be some sort of channel of expression.

Barbra Streisand
Stated in *All About Barbra*, 1987,
on choosing to be an actress

3049. If I have any artistic ability at all, (acting) is my medium of expression, and the public must accept me for that.

Rudolph Valentino, Actor
Stated in his 1929 *My Private Diary*

3050. I can only be understood through my films.

Federico Fellini
Cited in *Fellini — A Life*, 1986

3051. It all boils down to scratching your name in the bark of a tree ... I was here.

Mel Brooks, Screenwriter-Director
Interview in *Playboy*, February 1975

3052. There is only so much time you have in a lifetime.

Arnold Schwarzenegger, Actor
Interview in *Interview* magazine, 1991

3053. Get a good education first. Everything feeds into it.

Faye Dunaway, Actress
Cited in *Drama-Logue* magazine, 1997

3054. If you don't go off and experience life, you'll soon have nothing left to contribute to your art.

John Travolta, Actor
Interview in *Playboy*, March 1996

3055. Most dancers, like most violinists or football players or high-wire acts, spend a lot of their lives perfecting one thing....

Gene Kelly, Actor-Dancer
Cited in *Los Angeles*, 1972

3056. In the work is the experience, and in that experience is the reward.

Harvey Keitel, Actor
Interview in *Playboy*, November 1995

3057. Whenever I buy popcorn, it goes right on my expense account at the *Chicago Tribune*. That's part of my arrangement ... it's an occupational hazard.

Gene Siskel, Film Critic
Interview in *Playboy*, June 1984

3058. My whole life has been movies and religion. That's it. Nothing else.

Martin Scorsese
Interview in *The New Yorker*, 1997

3059. Alfred Hitchcock has throughout his career experimented with the possibilities of cinema.

Donald Spoto, Author
Stated in his *The Art of Alfred Hitchcock*, 1975

3060. The thing that's so frightening to hear is that someone's a video-shelf actor.

Matthew Modine
Cited in *The New York Times Magazine*, 1997

3061. How lucky it is to be an actor — join SAG and see the world.

Sigourney Weaver
Cited in *Premiere* magazine, 1998,
referring to the Screen Actors Guild

3062. I'm just going to sign up with a Japanese team and sit on the bench and wait for Kurosawa to break his leg.

Billy Wilder, Director
Interview in *Film Makers on Film Making*, 1983, on maybe not retiring

3063. (I) very probably will retire, like Secretariat, to stud.

Billy Wilder
Interview in *Film Makers on Film Making*, 1983, on doing one more film

3064. You just have to grab a bigger racket and rush the net.

Helen Hunt, Actress
Cited in *Time* magazine, 1997, on handling both a career and parenting

3065. You have to constantly try to keep in check why it is you're doing what you're doing and not let inertia carry you forward.

Ethan Hawke, Actor
Cited in *Premiere* magazine, 1998

3066. While it may not be possible to train people to make films, it is possible to create a climate in which people can learn to make films.

George Stevens, Jr., Founding Director of
the American Film Institute
Interview in *Film Makers on Film Making*, Vol. II, 1983

3067. I have a good career as a hired hand.

Robert Duvall, Actor

3068. I baby-sat for three generations. I'm very proud of that.

Lucille Ball
Cited in *Time* magazine, 1998,
on character roles in hit movies

3069. Nobody understands my pictures — I don't understand them myself.

Ingmar Bergman, Director
Interview in *Film Makers on Film Making*, 1983

3070. My talent for my work, but my genius for my life.

Oscar Wilde
Interview in *Film Makers on Film Making*, 1983, on his first five films

3071. I want my sons to surpass me because that's a form of immortality.

Kirk Douglas
Cited in *The Hustons*, 1989

3072. The "little girl" made me. I wasn't waiting for the "little girl" to kill me.

Mary Pickford
Cited in *Hollywood Dynasties*, 1984

3073. I've made a career of playing sons of bitches.

Kirk Douglas
On retiring from movies at age 40, as cited in *Entertainment Weekly 100*, "The 100 Greatest Movie Stars of All Time," 1997

3074. I don't want to be a "Hey, you!" all my life. I want people to call me mister.

Kirk Douglas
Cited in *Entertainment Weekly 100*, "The 100 Greatest Movie Stars of All Time," 1997

3075. You're going to kill [Clark Gable]. You get him at the end of a rope, fighting those horses, and that's going to be the end of him.

Robert Mitchum
Comment to John Huston on Gable's final picture, *The Misfits*, c. 1959, as cited in *The Hustons*, 1989

3076. I was a worshipper of the foolhardy and the melodramatic....

Charlie Chaplin
Cited in *Entertainment Weekly 100*, 1997

3077. What makes him think a middle-aged movie actor who's played with a chimp could have a future in politics?

Charlie Chaplin, commenting on Ronald Reagan in his 1964 *My Autobiography — Charlie Chaplin*

3078. You have talent, but it is necessary to first learn how to ruin it.

Jean Renoir, Director
On Clint Eastwood running for mayor, as cited in *Entertainment Weekly 100*, "The 100 Greatest Movie Stars of All Time," 1997

3079. It took him twenty years to become an overnight success.

Anonymous
Often used explanation for previously unknown success, as cited in *The Language of Show Biz*

3080. Each month Stanley Kubrick isn't making a film is a loss to everybody.

Sidney Lumet, Director
To screenwriter François Giroud, as cited in *Chronicle of the Cinema*, 1995

3081. I'm happy — at times — making films. I'm certainly unhappy not making films.

Stanley Kubrick, Director
Cited in *Kubrick — Inside A Film Artist's Maze*, 1982

3082. I play John Wayne in every picture regardless of the character, and I've been doing all right, haven't I?

John Wayne, Actor
Cited in *Kubrick — Inside A Film Artist's Maze*, 1982

3083. The next one is always my favorite.

Hal Wallis, Producer
Cited in *Chronicle of the Cinema*, 1995

3084. Movies are binary. They're either zero or they're one. It either works or it does not work and there's nothing you can do about it. Except make another one.

Robert Zemekis
Interview in *Film Makers on Film Making*, 1983, on which of his films was his favorite

3085. So many film students are film illiterate.

Woody Allen
Cited in *The New York Times Magazine*, 1997

3086. I'm making films for 40 years from now.

Quentin Tarantino
Cited in *The New York Times Magazine*, 1997

3087. You're only one movie away from being there.

Tom Hanks
Cited in *The New York Times Magazine*, 1997, referring to that career breakthrough opportunity

3088. If Brian (De Palma) hadn't become a director, he'd have been an assassin.

Undisclosed friend
Cited in *Premiere* magazine, 1998

3089. If it is any comfort, I was fired from the biggest picture ever made.
George Cukor, initial director of
Gone with the Wind
Cited in *George Cukor — A Double Life*, 1991

3090. Everything I have I owe to spaghetti.
Sophia Loren
Stated in *Sophia Loren — A Biography*, 1998

3091. I've done everything that I wanted to do.... Regret only makes wrinkles.
Sophia Loren
Stated in *Sophia Loren — A Biography*, 1998

3092. My films are all one long book to me, y'know, my secret craft — it's all autobiography.
Jack Nicholson
Cited in *Jack's Life
— A Biography*, 1994

3093. (In the) production unit, the cameraman is the only ... free soul — because you don't see the results ... of his work 'til the rushes are viewed twenty-four hours later.
Gregg Toland
Cited in *Orson Welles:
The Road to Xanadu*, 1996

3094. I envy painters because they can paint every day for all their lives.
Federico Fellini
Cited in *Fellini — A Life*, 1986

3095. "Where are you?" always precedes "How are you?" in Hollywood.
Samuel Marx
Cited in *Mayer and Thalberg
— The Make Believe Saints*, 1975

3096. I can't make stars as fast as L. B. (Mayer) can fire them.
Irving Thalberg, MGM
Cited in *Mayer and Thalberg
— The Make Believe Saints*, 1975

3097. We have no blacklist. But I'll see that he is taken off it.
Irving Thalberg
Cited in *Mayer and Thalberg
— The Make Believe Saints*,
1975, on director George Cukor

3098. I was marinated in poetry and to learn right at the beginning a sense of awe, wonder and delight.
Orson Welles
Cited in *Orson Wells: The Road to Xanadu*,
1996, on the performing arts

3099. Don't call me back until you're not ready.
Michael Curtiz, Director
Cited in *The Clown Prince of Hollywood*,
1990, to Jack Warner upon quitting work at
Warner Bros.

3100. (The making of animal pictures) is not in keeping with the policy that has been adopted by us for talking pictures, very obviously ... because dogs can't talk.
Warner Bros.
Recited in *The Clown Prince of
Hollywood*, 1990, as a formal letter
to "Rin Tin Tin" firing him, 1929

3101. [E]verybody in the world wants to be a filmmaker. How can I be egotistical enough to turn down the opportunity.
Woody Allen
Cited in *Woody Allen
— His Films and Career*, 1985

3102. In fifty years, it will all be disintegrating in the cans.
Alfred Hitchcock, Director
To someone suggesting he would achieve
lasting immortality through his films

3103. I tried for the classics and fell on my face.
Paul Newman
Cited in *Paul Newman*, 1989

3104. "I'm returning to the stage to refine my craft." That's what the Hollywood actors always say.... No one leaves movies for the stage unless they can't get work.
Bette Davis, Actress
Cited in *Bette and Joan
— The Divine Feud*, 1989

3105. The truth is nobody discovered (Ingrid Bergman). Nobody launched her. She discovered herself.
Gustav Molander, Swedish actor
Cited in *Ingrid Bergman — My Story*, 1980

3106. George (Burns) certainly knew how to wait for the right script.
Bob Hope
On Burns going from 1938 to 1975 with no movie
role, until winning an Oscar in *The Sunshine Boys*

3107. I've had more help in my career than a starlet with a stuck zipper.
Bob Hope
Stated in *Bob Hope —
Don't Shoot, It's Only Me*, 1990

3108. What I've learned is that there are several

different definitions of the word "actor." In New York theater it's what will make the literature work; in Hollywood, it's what sells.

> Beth Holmes, Casting Director
> Cited in *Your Film Acting Career*, 1989

3109. I created my own standard of fun ... no director ever taught me a thing ... I had no precedent, nothing to imitate.

> Mabel Normand, Actress-Director
> Pioneer of silent screen comedy
> Cited in *Classic Film Collector*, "Madcap,
> the Story of Mabel Normand," 1970

3110. Role models are crucial. If you're a woman filmmaker or black or Hispanic or whatever ... there's an inclination to think, "Yes, I can," if someone preceded you.

> Donna Deitch, Director
> Cited in *Reel Women*, 1991

3111. Quit kid — you'll never top it.

> Billy Rose, Director
> Cited in *Take 22: Moviemakers
> on Moviemaking*, 1984, friend to
> 27-year-old Orson Welles, after
> he directed *Citizen Kane*, 1941

3112. For the first few years I was working, I didn't know what an actor was; I only knew what a star was.... I thought it was all about glamour and being a diva.

> Maggie Cheung, Actress, China, 1929
> As cited in *Interview* magazine, 1998

3113. Well, there's about 50 of them that are tied.

> John Wayne, Actor
> Interview in *Playboy*, May, 1971, when
> asked which was his worst film

3114. You were either between pictures or on suspension.

> Ida Lupino, Actress-Director
> In *Los Angeles Times*, 1966, on what motivated her to move from acting to directing

3115. I want to be a bigger star than Burt Reynolds.

> Arnold Schwarzenegger, Actor
> Comment upon arriving in Hollywood
> for the first time, as cited in the
> *Los Angeles Times Magazine*, 1996

3116. A (screenwriting) career comes from having something to say.

> Bruce Joel Rubin, Screenwriter
> Interview in *Creative Screenwriting*, 1998

3117. Throughout Chaplin's career, the actor/tramp/comedian has been asking the audience to "love me."

> Robert Warshaw
> Cited in *The Immediate Experience*, 1971

3118. Being a writer is a perfect job for a high school dropout — I have homework for the rest of my life.

> Carrie Fisher, Screenwriter–Script
> Doctor, and a high school dropout
> Interview in *Creative Screenwriting*, 1988

3119. When an actor is not playing a part, he's not 100 percent whole.

> Paul Mazursky, Director
> Interview in *US* magazine, 1988

3120. Life's on the wire. The rest is just waiting.

> The Flying Wallendas, Family high-wire act
> Cited in *Rolling Stone*, 1996

3121. I had to work twice as hard and be twice as good and twice as on time ... to get this far.

> Wesley Snipes, Actor
> Interview in *Movieline* magazine, 1998

3122. A lot of times, as a black filmmaker, I feel like I'm in the Special Olympics.

> Robert Townsend, Actor-Director
> Interview in *Vogue* magazine, 1991

3123. I never saw it as a choice between career and family. Acting is making a living. Acting is not a life.

> Denzel Washington, Actor
> Interview in *USA Weekend*, 1998

3124. Not to suck!

> Chris Rock, Actor-Comedian
> Replying to a reporter asking
> what his career goal was

3125. This thing we call "failure" is not the falling down, but the staying down.

> Mary Pickford, Actress
> Cited in *The Wit and Wisdom
> of Women*, 1993

3126. I never learned how to spell regret.

> Joan Crawford
> Cited in *American Cinema*, 1995

3127. I didn't have a color chip on my shoulder. It never occurred to me that I couldn't (produce films) because of my color, if I had the talent.

> Mario van Peebles,
> Producer-Director-Actor
> Interview in *The Daily Breeze*, 1998

3128. They said if I could tap dance, maybe they could place me.
> Melvin van Peebles, Screenwriter-Director
> On his first entry to Hollywood, as
> cited in *The Foreign Cinema*, 1968

3129. I'm happiest when I'm up to my ears in actors.
> William Beaudine, Director
> Interview in *TV Guide*, 1963

3130. Last year I was a broke, unheard of film-maker. Now I'm a broke, heard-of filmmaker.
> Christopher Cherot, Screenwriter-Actor-
> Director, 1998
> Interview in *Premiere* magazine, 1998

3131. I wish someday someone would pass a law in Hollywood: Whoever takes drugs, or even doesn't show up on time, they're not allowed to work.
> Avi Lerner, Producer
> Cited in *The New Yorker*, 1998

3132. The unholy alliance of animation is: You are called upon to be an artist — but on the other hand, you are called upon to be a zombie factory worker.
> Tim Burton, Animator-Director
> Interview in *Inner Views:*
> *Filmmakers in Conversation*,
> 1992, recalling his work at Disney

3133. You can be a drunkard and get over it, but you can make a picture and you never get over it.
> Allan Dwan, Director
> Cited in *The Valley News*, 1979

3134. With an American actor, becoming an actor is rather like a lady becoming a nun ... with an English actor, it's like becoming a plumber.
> Michael Caine, Actor
> Interview in *Take 22:*
> *Moviemakers on Moviemaking*, 1984

3135. Before you become an actor, anywhere, you become an out-of-work actor.... So wherever you go, all actors are basically the same.
> Michael Caine, Actor
> Interview in *Take 22:*
> *Moviemakers on Moviemaking*, 1984

3136. Each actor is responsible for his own career and I invite you to assume that responsibility. It's your career. It's your business.
> Roz Tilman, Personal Manager
> Cited in *Your Film Acting Career*, 1989

3137. The more an actor knows about films, the

more he realizes his helplessness, the more he therefore will seek to control the selection of story, director, cameraman, as well as that process of ultimate demolition known as editing.
> Josef Von Sternberg
> Cited in *A Film Editor's Story*, 1979

3138. As an agent, it's easy. You are who you represent.
> Ed Limato, Agent
> Interview in *Vanity Fair*, 1999

3139. Changing agents is like changing chairs on the deck of the Titanic.
> Old Hollywood saying
> Cited in *Your Film Acting Career*, 1989

3140. But it is only work that satisfies.
> Bette Davis, Actress
> Cited in *Bette and Joan — The*
> *Divine Feud*, 1989, when asked about sex

3141. The strength of a talented individual lies in his ability to continue to create.
> Barry J. Weitz, Talent Agent
> Cited in *Movie Business:*
> *American Film Industry Practice*, 1972

3142. Change only comes by doing things you're afraid of.
> Sylvester Stallone, Actor
> Cited in the *Los Angeles Times Calendar*, 1995

3143. Why do I do it? Because of the fire.
> Norman Lloyd, Actor-Director-Producer
> On why he is in "Entertainment,"
> as cited in *Vanity Fair*, 1999

3144. I've always had a very strong connection with my own gut instincts and if I ever lose that, I'll stop making movies.
> Steven Spielberg
> Interview in *Premiere* magazine, 1998

3145. I feel that where I've gone today has been mostly based on instinct, animal instinct.
> Clint Eastwood
> Cited in *Clint Eastwood — A Biography*, 1996

3146. There is nothing connected with the staging of a motion picture that a woman cannot do as easily as a man, and there is no reason why she cannot completely master every technicality of the art.
> Alice Guy Blachè, First
> director of a narrative film
> Stated in the 1914 *Moving Picture World*,
> "Woman's Place in Photoplay Production"

3147. The producer must be a prophet and a general, a diplomat and a peacemaker, a miser and a spendthrift. He must have vision tempered by hindsight, daring governed by caution, the patience of a saint and the iron of a Cromwell....

Jesse Lasky
Stated in the 1937 *The Producer Makes a Plan — We Make the Movies*

3148. Women (in the movie industry) are finally making certain breakthroughs. What time will tell now is how many women will pursue nontraditional roles as careers (camera assistants, drivers, grips, electricians, etc.).

Kathleen Kennedy, Studio Executive
Interview in *The Hollywood Reporter*, 1992

3149. When I get to the point where I think almost everyone will have forgotten me, then I make the next movie.

Warren Beatty
Cited in *American Premiere*, 1992

3150. I don't like going to bad movies. And I sure as hell don't like making them.

Tom Cruise, Actor
Interview in *Vanity Fair*, 1996

3151. When you are a young developing artist, the first tenet is iconoclasm. And you just have to tear down what was before in order to start something new.

Steve Martin
Interview in *The Observer — London*, 1995

3152. I've had some of the most incredible parts for an actress of any hue.

Angela Bassett
Interview in *The Los Angeles News*, 1995

3153. I made it in New York, boys, so I can certainly make it here.

Mae West
Cited in *Going Hollywood*, 1978, to the press corps upon arriving in Hollywood, c. 1933

3154. Unfortunately the MGM studio was no longer the symbol of glamour and grandeur; nor was I.

Bette Davis, Actress
Cited in *Bette and Joan — The Divine Feud*, 1989, upon joining the studio in 1954

3155. The name of the game is always your next picture.

Joan Crawford, Actress
Cited in *Bette and Joan — The Divine Feud*, 1989

3156. You don't have to do "issues" pictures to be worthwhile. Entertainment is one of the great values of mankind.

Sally Field
Interview in *Playboy*, March 1986

3157. I was tricked into acting by a nun at school.

Alfre Woodard, Actress
Interview in the *Los Angeles Herald-Examiner*, 1977

3158. Only French singers don't have regrets.

Peter O'Toole, Actor
Cited in *US* magazine, 1989

30

Peers and Personas

3159. Charlie Chaplin is the patron saint of laughter.

Sophia Loren
Cited in *Sophia Loren—A Biography*, 1998

3160. I am just a little nickel comedian trying to make people laugh.

Charlie Chaplin, Actor-Director
Cited in Internet Movie Database, 1988

3161. Instead of a funny man, he is a man of humorous imagination … a consummate actor.… He's a part of humour.

Max Eastman
On Charlie Chaplin, cited in *Chaplin*, 1974

3162. (Charlie Chaplin's) power is to stand for a sort of concentrated essence of the common man.…

George Orwell
Cited in *Entertainment Weekly—100*, 1998

3163. The sonofabitch is a ballet dancer.

W. C. Fields
Cited in *Entertainment Weekly 100*, 1998, on Charlie Chaplin

3164. Charlie means more to me than the idea of God.

François Truffaut
On Charlie Chaplin, as cited in
Entertainment Weekly 100, 1998

3165. The lyric poet of the silent screen.

Marion Meade, Biographer
On Buster Keaton, as cited in
Entertainment Weekly 100, 1998

3166. How can a man in slap shoes and a flat hat be considered a genius?

Buster Keaton, Producer-Director-Actor
Cited in Internet Movie
Database, 1988, about himself

3167. Claudette Colbert is the best thing we've gotten from France since the Statue of Liberty.

Gregory Peck

3168. Greta Garbo was all about a sense of mysterious possibilities. You could look into her eyes and believe you were seeing the wisdom of the ages.

Michael Gross, Author
Cited in *People* magazine, 1995

3169. A nice Italian man who liked to work on cars.

Myrana Loy, Actress
Cited in *Newsweek* magazine,
1987, remembering Rudolph Valentino

3170. None of us thought we were making anything but entertainment for the moment. Only Ernst Lubitsch knew we were making art.

John Ford, Director
Cited in *John Ford*, 1975,
on fellow director Ernst Lubitsch

3171. To me, great people are always simple and Ernst (Lubitsch) was the simplest man I ever knew. He had no flaw in his greatness, no chichi, no false vanity. On the set he had a greatness of his art, but no "artiness."

Jeanette MacDonald, Actress, 1948
Cited in the Internet Movie Database, 1988

3172. When (Harry Cohn) decided to back you, he'd back you to the hilt – even if he'd rather see the hilt sticking out of your back.

Frank Capra, Producer-Director
Stated in his *Frank Capra*, 1971

3173. Pictures were made for him. The theater was too little.

Allan Dwan, Director
Cited in *Time* magazine, 1996,
on Douglas Fairbanks, Sr.

3174. (Douglas Fairbanks, Sr.) will always be remembered for winning the fight, the girl and the glory.
David Hochman
Cited in *Entertainment Weekly 100*, 1998

3175. (John) Barrymore was one of the very few who had that divine madness without which a great artist cannot work or live.
Greta Garbo, Actress
Cited in *Behind the Oscar*, 1993

3176. It just goes to show, give the public what it wants and they'll show up.
Billy Wilder, Screenwriter-Director
Commenting on the SRO crowd at Louis B.
Mayer's funeral, as cited in *Inside Oscar*, 1996

3177. Bette Davis taught Hollywood to follow an actress instead of the actress following the camera, and she's probably the best movie actress there's ever been.
Elaine Stritch
Cited in *Entertainment Weekly 100*, 1998

3178. I know I've been a perfect bitch. But I couldn't help myself.
Bette Davis
To Vincent Sherman, as
cited in *Premiere* magazine, 1998

3179. The nearer the camera, the more tender and yielding she became. The camera saw, I suspect, a side of her that no flesh and blood lover ever saw.
George Cukor, Director
Cited in *Entertainment Weekly 100*, 1998, on Joan Crawford

3180. You would have to be momentarily deranged to ever consider rewriting Joe Mankiewicz.
Katherine Reback, Screenwriter
Cited in *Creative Screenwriting* magazine

3181. No one was more unreal or stylized ... yet there is no moment when he is not true.
Orson Welles, Actor-Director
On James Cagney, as cited
in *Entertainment Weekly 100*, 1998

3182. He is an actor's star. He is a people's star. His quality is clear and direct. Ask a question – get an answer. No pause.
Katharine Hepburn, Actress
Cited in *Entertainment Weekly 100*, 1998, on Spencer Tracy

3183. Spence is the best we have, because you don't see the mechanism at work.
Humphrey Bogart, Actor
Cited in *Boxoffice* magazine, 1995, on actor Spencer Tracy

3184. (Humphrey) Bogart's a helluva nice guy until 11:30 p.m. After that, he thinks he's Bogart.
Dave Chasen, Restaurateur
(Cited in *Entertainment Weekly 100*, 1998)

3185. There are women and there are women – and then there is Katie. There are actresses and actresses — then there is Hepburn.
Frank Capra, Producer-Director
Stated in his 1971 *Frank Capra*

3186. Don't ask me how (Shirley Temple) does it. You've heard of chess champions at 8 and violin virtuosos at 10? Well, she's Ethel Barrymore at 6.
Adolphe Menjou
Cited in *Entertainment Weekly 100*, 1998

3187. When Stepin Fetchit speaks: It's what molasses would sound like if it talked.
The New Yorker, 1990

3188. Groucho Marx would be funny in still photographs.
Otis Ferguson, Film Critic
Cited in a 1935 *New Republic* review

3189. (Jean-Luc Godard) is the analytical conscience of the modern cinema.
Andrew Sarris
Cited in *Time* magazine, 1997

3190. (Jean) Renoir could make a wardrobe act.
Lulu Wattier, Theatrical Agent
Cited in *Jean Renoir — My Life and Times*, 1974, on the French director

3191. Maybe there really wasn't an America, maybe it was only Frank Capra.
John Cassavettes, Screenwriter-Actor-Director
Cited in *American Visions*, 1977

3192. Everything about me is a contradiction, and so is everything about everybody else. We are made out of oppositions; we live between two poles.
Orson Welles
Cited in *Orson Welles: The Road to Xanadu*, 1996

3193. Vivien Leigh was a porcelain broach.
Cindy Adams, Writer
Cited in *People* magazine, 1995

3194. If we are not like Jimmy Stewart, we would like to be.
Charlton Heston
Cited in the A & E *Biography*, "Jimmy Stewart," 1998

3195. I told him to forget the camera was there. That was all he needed.

> Spencer Tracy, Actor
> Cited in *Architectural Digest*, 1998,
> on actor Jimmy Stewart, 1935,
> on the set of his first film

3196. Everyone wants to be Cary Grant. Even I would like to be Cary Grant.

> Cary Grant, Actor
> Cited in A & E *Biography*, "Cary Grant," 1998

3197. A megaphone has been to John Ford what the chisel was to Michelangelo: his life, his passion, his cross.

> Frank Capra, Producer-Director
> Stated in *Frank Capra*, 1971

3198. Take everything you've heard, everything you've ever heard — and multiply it about a hundred times — and you still won't have a picture of John Ford.

> James Stewart, Actor
> Cited in *John Ford*, 1968

3199. John Ford, John Ford and John Ford.

> Orson Welles, Actor-Director
> Cited in *John Ford*, 1975, when asked
> which directors he most admired

3200. His supreme achievement may have been in inventing John Wayne.

> Charlton Heston, Actor
> Cited in A & E *Biography*, "John
> Wayne," 1998, on actor John Wayne

3201. He is at his best precisely when he is being what we have come to call "John Wayne."

> Peter Bogdanovich, Director
> Cited in the Internet Movie Data base, 1998

3202. He gave the whole world the image of what an American should be.

> Elizabeth Taylor, Actress
> Cited in *Entertainment Weekly
> 100*, 1998, on John Wayne

3203. In his face we saw the courage we wished in ourselves.

> Peter Graves, Actor
> Cited in A & E *Biography*,
> "Gary Cooper," 1998, on Gary Cooper

3204. Every woman who knew him fell in love.

> Ingrid Bergman, Actress
> Cited in A & E *Biography*,
> "Gary Cooper," 1998, on Gary Cooper

3205. About me being the "silent man" type …

my theory is simply … unless I know what I'm talking about, I keep my mouth shut….

> Gary Cooper, Actor
> Interview in *Silver Screen* magazine, 1941

3206. The difference with the great people is, they leave you with more than you showed up with and Ruth Gordon was one of those greats.

> Bud Cort
> Cited in *Premiere* magazine, 1998

3207. To have (George) Cukor directing your script was emblematic of your importance, like having Vuitton luggage or that table at Ciro's.

> Donald Stewart
> Cited in *George Cukor — A Double Life*, 1991

3208. I mean it kindly. In a way, George Cukor was the first great female director of Hollywood.

> Joseph L. Mankiewicz
> Cited in *George Cukor — A Double Life*, 1991

3209. One Huston is bad enough, but two are murder.

> Humphrey Bogart
> On John and Walter Huston,
> as cited in *The Hustons*, 1989

3210. Deep down, I'm pretty superficial.

> Ava Gardner
> Cited in *The Hustons*, 1989

3211. There's a reason (Sammy Davis, Jr.) has been called the world's greatest entertainer for the last 40 years … he's the most talented.

> Liza Minnelli, Actress
> Interview in *Variety*, 1989

3212. Lunching with Ingrid (Bergman) is like sitting down to an hour or so of conversation with an intelligent orchid.

> Thornton Delaharty
> Cited in *Ingrid Bergman*, 1980

3213. What do dancers think of Fred Astaire? It's no secret. We hate him. His perfection is an absurdity, and that's hard to face.

> Mikhail Baryshnikov, Dancer
> Cited in *Entertainment Weekly 100*, 1998

3214. (Fred Astaire) seems like a celluloid phantom, a trick of light…. Look closely, though, and you'll see a working definition of grace.

> Ty Burr, Senior Writer, *Entertainment Weekly*
> Cited in *Entertainment Weekly 100*, 1998

3215. I'm even an enigma to myself.

> Red Skelton, Actor–Screen Comedian
> Cited in *The Great Movie Comedians*, 1978

3216. Danny Kaye is a lot of person. He's a group photo.

Vin Scully
Cited in *Ford Times*, 1982

3217. (As director) on the set they all call me mother … not "that mother," just plain "mother…." [I]f somebody on the set should call me "Ida" or "Miss Lupino" I wouldn't know what to do.

Ida Lupino, Producer-Director-Actress
Interview in *Action!* magazine, 1967

3218. (I am) the poor man's Bette Davis.

Ida Lupino, Actress
Cited in the *Los Angeles Times*, 1995

3219. When acting is as good as he does it, you don't see it.

John Huston, Director
Cited in *Big Reel* magazine,
1997, on actor Robert Mitchum

3220. I look like a shark with a broken nose.

Robert Mitchum, Actor
Cited in *Big Reel* magazine, 1997

3221. The beauty of that man. He's so still. He's moving and yet he's not moving.

Lee Marvin, Actor
Cited in *Entertainment Yearbook*,
1998, on Robert Mitchum, actor

3222. Sophia Loren didn't walk into the room, she swept in. I never saw so much woman coming at me in my entire life.

William Holden
Cited in *Sophia Loren — A Biography*, 1998

3223. Sophia (Loren) doesn't bother about looks. She's interested in acting.

Carol Reed, Director
Cited in *Sophia Loren — A Biography*, 1998

3224. If I was as beautiful as you, I wouldn't have to open my mouth.

Barbra Streisand
To Sophia Loren, as cited in
Sophia Loren — A Biography, 1998

3225. You should have been sculpted in chocolate truffles so the world could devour you.

Noel Coward
Cited in *Sophia Loren — A
Biography*, 1998, to Sophia Loren

3226. I am not a sexy pot.

Sophia Loren, Actress
Cited in *Inside Oscar*, 1996,
responding to the compliment

3227. (Alfred Hitchcock) is the only director whose movies are sold on his name alone….

Peter Bogdanovich
Cited in *50 Major Film Makers*, 1975

3228. I learned more from film acting in three months with (Federico) Fellini than I'd learned in all the movies I'd made before then.

Anthony Quinn
Cited in *Fellini — A Life*,
1986, on *La Strada*, 1954

3229. This filmmaker is incapable of a stillborn frame, his pictures celebrate what they criticize.

Richard Corliss
Cited in *Fellini — A Life*,
1986, on Federico Fellini

3230. With Roberto Rossellini it is possible to make a movie with the same direct complicity and rapport with which a writer writes or a painter paints.

Federico Fellini
Cited in *Fellini — A Life*, 1986

3231. (Robert Flaherty's) films were travelogues to places that never were.

Richard Barsam
Stated in his 1992 *The Non-Fictional
Film*, on his documentaries

3232. In (Akira) Kurosawa's hands, even Shakespeare spoke Japanese.

Carmela Ciurarh, Writer
Referring to his 1957 *Throne of Blood —
Macbeth* and the 1985 *Ran — King Lear*,
as cited in *Entertainment '99 Yearbook*

3233. (Stanley Kubrick) made movies with the language of dreams.

Roberto Benigni, Actor-Director
Memorializing him at the 1999 SAG
awards ceremony on the day of his death

3234. I would never have believed that my passion for cinematography would one day exceed the limits of Platonic love.

Sergei Eisenstein
Cited in *A Film Editor's Story*, 1979

3235. (Robert) Flaherty's films are not just moving pictures. They are experiences…. Flaherty is a country, which having once seen never forgets.

Arthur Calder-Marshall
Stated in his 1966 *The Innocent Eye*,
on his documentaries

3236. (Charlton Heston) is an axiom of the cinema.

French Critic
Cited in *Film Makers on Film Making*, 1983

3237. (Marilyn Monroe) was able to convey carnality through innocence in a way that still remains a complete mystery.

Roger Ebert, Film Critic
Interview in *Reel Conversations*, 1991

3238. To put it bluntly, I seem to be a whole superstructure without a foundation.

Marilyn Monroe, Actress
Cited in the Internet Movie Database, 1998

3239. (Jack Lemmon's) genius was so riveting that I would often come in on my days off just to watch him cast his comic spell before the camera.

Shirley MacLaine, Actress
Cited in *Entertainment Weekly 100*, 1998

3240. He brings his own lights.

Unknown
Cited in *California* magazine,
1990, on Laurence Olivier

3241. (Laurence Olivier) will put himself out on a limb. In fact, he'll put himself out on a twig of a tree.

Anthony Hopkins, Actor
Cited in *Entertainment Weekly 100*, 1998

3242. (Walt Disney) must be seen as a major architect of modern American culture.

Steven Walts, Writer
Cited in *The Magic Kingdom* epilogue

3243. (Walt Disney is) a first rate artist who lives somewhere near the human center and knows innumerable truths that cannot be taught.

William R. Weaver, Writer
Stated in the *Chicagoan*, 1930

3244. Leonard da Disney.

Mark Van Doran, Writer
Referring to Walt Disney, the artist, as
cited in *Nation* magazine, 1938

3245. I don't even like apple pie.

Doris Day, Actress
On her "All-American image,"
as cited in *TV Guide*

3246. I knew Doris Day before she was a virgin.

Oscar Levant
Cited in *Entertainment Weekly 100*, 1998

3247. (James Dean) was the first guerilla artist ever to work in the movies.

Dennis Hopper, Actor
Interview in *Los Angeles Magazine*, 1996

3248. With Jimmy Dean, we understood for the first time what an actor is: A guy who put his back to the camera and mumbled.

Dusan Makavejev
Cited in *Film Forum*, 1985

3249. She was built like an apartment house with balconies.

John Huston
On Gina Lollibrigida, as cited
in *The Hustons*, 1989

3250. Celluloid loved (Marilyn) Monroe.

Billy Wilder

3251. (Jessica Lange) is one of the few actors who can really play a character with a secret. You always feel there is something else going on.

Des McAnuff, Director
Interview in the *Los Angeles Times*, 1998

3252. They say Woody Allen got something from the Marx Brothers. He didn't. He is an original. The best. The funniest.

Groucho Marx, Actor
Cited in *Entertainment Weekly 100*, 1998

3253. (Sylvester Stallone) thinks of the body as art.

John Travolta, Actor
Interview in *Playboy*, March 1996

3254. Steve Martin is like the Jack Nicklaus of comedy.

Rick Moranis, Actor
Cited in *The New York Times Magazine*, 1992

3255. Jimmy's not a ham. He's the whole pig.

Actor Jim Carrey's father
Cited in *Entertainment '99 Yearbook*

3256. Bad publicity pales in the glow of her extraordinary genius.

Rex Reed
Cited in *Women's Wear Daily*,
on Barbra Streisand

3257. I'm an ecktress.

Barbra Streisand
Cited in *Vanity Fair*, 1995, comment
before turning professional

3258. I think Jack Nicholson has very many aspects of the character to play. With Jack — I still don't know if he's so smart or so crazy.

Milos Forman, Director
Interview in *Film Forum*, 1985

3259. When you're with Sean (Connery), you learn pretty quickly what your own place in the galaxy is – and it pales.
Kevin Costner, Actor
Cited in *Entertainment Weekly 100*, 1998

3260. (Marlon Brando) has always transcended the techniques he was taught.
Bette Davis, Actress
Cited in *Conversations with Brando*, 1991

3261. [T]he only genius I ever met in the field of acting.
Elia Kazan, Director
Cited in *Conversations with Brando*, 1991,
on Marlon Brando

3262. Mr. Eastwood's talent is his style, unhurried and self-assured, that of a man who goes through life looking down at other men's bald spots.
Vincent Canby, Critic
Cited in *Clint Eastwood—A Biography*, 1996

3263. He's not an exclamation point – he's a question mark.
Saul Rubinek
On Clint Eastwood, as cited in
Clint Eastwood—A Biography, 1996

3264. Zen and the art of control.
Tom Stern
On Clint Eastwood, as cited in
Clint Eastwood—A Biography, 1996

3265. There's a rebel lying deep in my soul.
Clint Eastwood
Cited in *Clint Eastwood—A Biography*, 1996

3266. If a movie camera could be a political weapon, then Haskell Wexler is Hollywood's great cinematic agitator.
David Geffner, Writer
Cited in *Movie Maker* magazine, 1998

3267. (Neil Simon) is the most successful playwright on the planet. More so even than William Shakespeare. I'm not saying he's better than Shakespeare. Just more successful.
Walter Matthau, Actor
Interview in *Take 22:
Moviemakers on Moviemaking*, 1984

3268. I am and forever will be devastated by the gift of Audrey Hepburn before my camera. However you define the encounter of the sexes, she wins.
Richard Avedon
Interview in *Interview* magazine, 1990

3269. Audrey (Hepburn) is like a good tennis player. She is unpredictable, interesting, and varies her shots.
Humphrey Bogart, Actor
Interview in *American Movie Classics*,
1990, on his co-star actress

3270. She could have dirt on her nose and still be gorgeous. It was her own personality that penetrated.
Rebecca Moses
Cited in *Interview* magazine,
1990, on Audrey Hepburn

3271. I taught her to cuss; she taught me to dress.
Shirley MacLaine
Cited in *The Hollywood Reporter*,
1998, on Audrey Hepburn

3272. Her silhouette marked an epoque.
Azzdine Alada
Cited in *Interview* magazine,
1990, on Audrey Hepburn

3273. Vanessa Redgrave never seemed to be acting; like Spencer Tracy, she was just there.
Fred Zinnemann, Director
Stated in his 1992 *Fred
Zinnemann*, on filming Vanessa

3274. My other child.
Clint Eastwood
On Burt Reynolds, as cited in
Clint Eastwood—A Biography, 1996

3275. If God had designed a perfect acting machine, it would be pretty close to Jodie Foster.
Jon Amiel, Director
Cited in *Entertainment Weekly 100*, 1998

3276. (Tom Cruise) does it for sport. He does it for craft. He does it for art. He does it for life.
Jeffrey Katzenberg
Interview in *Vanity Fair*, 1994, on Cruise's acting

3277. He has charisma that needs exercising.
Oliver Stone, Director
Cited in *Tom Cruise
—Unauthorized*, 1997, on Tom Cruise

3278. Robin Williams ... can be brilliant in comedy, drama, and whatever else he gets his mind around.
Sam Shepard, Actor-Director
Cited in *Entertainment Weekly*, 1998

3279. Robin (Williams) embodies everything about the child inside of us.
Steven Spielberg, Director
Cited in *Entertainment Weekly 100*, 1998

3280. I've directed a lot of great actors, but Tony's simply the best. He'll risk everything for you. Every time.

> Oliver Stone, Director
> Cited in *Entertainment Weekly 100*, 1998
> on Anthony Hopkins

3281. Sam doesn't fly, so we drive everywhere.

> Jessica Lange, Actress
> Cited in *Vanity Fair*, 1988, on her actor
> husband, Sam Shepard, who played ace
> pilot Chuck Yeager in *The Right Stuff*, 1983

3282. One of the great things about Roman Polanski is that he strives to be understood.

> Robert Towne
> As a director, as cited in *Film Makers
> on Film Making*, Vol. II, 1983

3283. When Sally Field says f––, it doesn't count.

> Gary Lucchesi, Studio Executive
> Cited in *People* magazine, 1991

3284. Do you realize you just spent a year of your life making shit?! Any director in Hollywood could have made that and you're better than them. You have something honest to say.

> John Cassavetes
> Cited in the *Fade In* magazine, 1997,
> to Martin Scorsese on *Boxcar Bertha*

3285. The suburban kid who would rather film his toy trains than play with them.

> Roger Ebert, Film Critic
> Cited in Internet Movie Database,
> 1998, on Steven Spielberg

3286. I was Steven Spielberg — once.

> Billy Wilder
> Cited in *Steven Spielberg
> — The Unauthorized Biography*, 1996

3287. I'm not a funny guy.

> Steven Spielberg
> Cited in *Steven Spielberg
> — The Unauthorized Biography*, 1996

3288. Spielberg is B–movie literate. One day, Spielberg will be known as the greatest second-unit director in America.

> Peter Benchley, Author of *Jaws*
> Cited in *Steven Spielberg
> — The Unauthorized Biography*, 1996

3289. Arnold Schwarzenegger is a self-made myth, someone who has invented himself and stayed in control of himself.

> Emma Thompson, Actress
> Cited in *Entertainment Weekly 100*, 1998

3290. If Arnold hadn't existed, we would have had to build him.

> John Milius, Director of *Conan the Barbarian*
> Cited in *Entertainment Weekly 100*, 1998

3291. John (Travolta) has got this physicality; his entrances and exits become the character. Audiences go crazy just watching this man walk up a flight of stairs.

> Barry Sonnenfeld, Director
> Cited in *The Hollywood Reporter*, 1996

3292. Johnny has an uncanny ability to actually inhabit another person; to live, breathe and become rather than play that person.

> Kelly Preston, Actress
> Cited in the *Los Angeles Times*,
> 1998, on husband John Travolta

3293. John Travolta is somewhere between Cary Grant and Shirley Temple ... maybe there's a Cagney–Mickey Rooney quality, only taller.

> Turteltaub, Director
> Cited in *The Hollywood Reporter*, 1996

3294. Danny DeVito is a human grenade who's just had his pin pulled.

> Film Critic
> Cited in *Time Out—London*, 1990

3295. What Toshiro Mifune is to Akira Kurosawa, Ice Cube is to me.

> John Singleton, Screenwriter-Director
> Cited in *Inside Oscar*, 1996

3296. Seamless and effortless. Preternaturally gifted without a trace of how it happens. He is couture.

> Ashley Judd, Actress
> Cited in *Entertainment Weekly*,
> 1998, on actor Morgan Freeman

3297. He's an incredible presence. You can't not watch him.

> Amy Heckerling, Director
> Cited in *Entertainment Weekly*,
> 1998, on actor Sean Penn

3298. (Kevin Kline) appreciates the deliciousness of acting. He'll get everything you can possibly throw at him and come back at you with more.

> Sigourney Weaver, Actress
> Cited in *Entertainment Weekly*, 1998

3299. There's an incredible innate sexiness, but there's also great depth. She's deeper than [the] Mariana Trench.

> Robin Williams, Actor
> Cited in *Entertainment Weekly*,
> 1998, on actress Susan Sarandon

3300. People sometimes get complacent about actors that are so good, mostly because they're consistent. (John Malkovich) always shines.

Clint Eastwood, Actor-Director
Cited in *Entertainment Weekly*, 1998

3301. That walk, those hands, that head — it all makes him seem inhabited.

Paul Schrader, Director
Cited in *Details* magazine,
1993, on Christopher Walken

3302. It's not about being sexy. It's … about being powerful.

Richard Gere, Actor
Cited in *USA Weekend*, 1996, on himself

3303. Whatever that mysterious electrochemical process is that makes the camera fall in love with someone, Denzel Washington's got more of it than any one person should have.

Freddie Fields
Cited in *California*, 1979

3304. He's so pure and honest and artistic, it's a little like Don Quixote walking through Hollywood.

Garry Marshall, Director
Interview in *GQ* magazine,
1992, on actor Al Pacino

3305. In his acting, his instrument is himself, his emotional nakedness.

Sidney Lumet, Director
Interview in *Venice* magazine, 1992
on actor Al Pacino

3306. He's compressed carbon, like a diamond.

Jeff Goldblum, Actor
Cited in *LA Village View*, 1994,
on actor Laurence Fishburne

3307. You don't direct him. You just sit there getting lucky.

Nora Ephron, Director
Cited in *Biography*, 1998, on Tom Hanks

3308. Tom would have made a terrific soldier. He's a common man with an uncommon talent.

Dale Dye, Retired Captain, U. S. Marine Corps
Cited in *Entertainment Weekly*,
1998, on Tom Hanks

3309. The great thing about (Tom Hanks) is that the world can see (his) star even in the daytime.

Steven Spielberg
Cited in *The Hollywood Reporter*, 1995

3310. Tom Hanks must be fundamentally a good person, or he is an even better actor than we think.

Roger Ebert
Interview in *Playboy*, 1994

3311. (Ving Rhames) is one of those actors that brings the level up of whoever he's working with. Things go better with Ving.

George Clooney, Actor
Cited in *US* magazine, 1998

3312. (Nicholas Cage) doesn't just pick up a wedge of cheese. He wants to know the history. He wants to know exactly who made the cheese.

Jim Carrey, Actor
Cited in *Vanity Fair*, 1996

3313. (Gene Siskel) is the world's baldest critic.

Roger Ebert, Critic
Cited in *Los Angeles Times*, 1986

3314. (Roger Ebert) is the world's largest film critic.

Gene Siskel, Critic
Cited in *People* magazine, 1984

3315. (Roger Ebert) is the second-best film critic in Chicago.

Gene Siskel, Critic
Cited in *People* magazine, 1984

3316. I don't know why he insists on doing it. Lassie has feelings, too, you know.

Rudd B. Weatherwax, Owner of Lassie
Cited in *TV Guide*, 1963, complaining
that director William Beaudine
calls her "the meat-hound"

3317. I think he should be called Mickey Mouse.

Lilly Disney, wife of creator Walt
Cited in *Disney's Art of Animation*, 1991

3318. Mickey Mouse has a touch of Fred Astaire … Charlie Chaplin, and … Douglas Fairbanks.

Walt Disney
Cited in *Disney's Art of Animation*, 1991,
describing his acting animation flexibility

3319. Miss Piggy is a prima donna, and her reputation proceeds her, I'm afraid, just like her snout.

Kermit the Frog, Actor
Cited in *TV Guide*, 1996

3320. It was great working with (Frank Oz) who's been a Muppeteer all these years, although I did draw the line at him putting his fist up my ass.

Marc Shaiman, Film Composer
Cited in *Film Score Monthly*, 1997

31

Montage

3321. (A film censor) is someone who even sees three meanings in a double-entendre.

Unknown
Cited in the 1998 *Handbook
of American Film Genres*

3322. I am not going to spend my life sitting in movie-set offices and saying, I gotta take out one "shit" and one "screw." This is crazy.

Jack Valenti, President
of the Producer's Association
On not having to be the enforcer of
the censorship code for movies, resulting
in the "Ratings System," cited in
Clown Prince of Hollywood, 1990

3323. Film melts the door marked "forbidden."

Brian Gysin
Cited in *Cinematograph*, Vol. 5

3324. (Avoid) any licentious or suggestive nudity — in fact or in silhouette; and any lecherous notice thereof by other characters in the picture.

MPPDA
Number Two on the production code list of
"Don'ts," 1927, as cited in *American
Cinema*, 1995

3325. (Avoid) pointed profanity — by either title or lip — this includes words "God," "Lord," "Jesus," "Christ," "hell," "damn," "Gawd," and every other profane and vulgar expression, however it may be spelled.

MPPDA
Number One on the production code
list of "Don'ts," 1927, as cited in
American Cinema, 1995

3326. Is democracy so feeble that it can be subverted merely by a look or a line, an inflection, a gesture?

Humphrey Bogart, Actor
1947, on certain people's concern about
the possible "Russianization of movies,"
as cited in *City Boys*, 1992

3327. Bullshit!

Mel Brooks, Screenwriter-Director
On being accused of vulgarity in his pictures,
as stated in his 1975 *Playboy* interview

3328. That was a first for black people. The Negro boy was written and performed as an educated person. This caused a great deal of joy among Negroes.

Bette Davis
Referring to *In This Our Lives*, 1942, as cited
in *Bette and Joan — The Divine Feud*, 1989

3329. When I first walked onto the 20th Century–Fox lot, I was there with the shoeshine boy, (the) only two blacks there.

Sidney Poitier
Cited in *Film Makers on Film
Making*, 1983, referring to 1950

3330. To make a film about racism Hollywood uses the buddy movie.

Gavin Smith, Writer
Cited in *Film Comment* magazine, 1988

3331. The lower down the economic scales and the deeper into the ghetto the story is set, the more likely the studio will feel it just doesn't know that world, and the more freedom the (black) filmmaker will be allowed.

Melvin van Peebles, Screenwriter-Director
Interview in *Los Angeles Times*, 1996

3332. The '70s were a great period for blacks in the movies. We got a chance to smile and not cover our mouths.

Pam Grier, Actress
Cited in *Premiere* magazine, 1998

3333. Well, you know, I can have an Oscar in one hand and still not be able to flag a cab with the other.

Denzel Washington, Actor
Interview in *GQ* magazine, 1991

3334. Let's have at least one executive. Not two,

three, four; let's have one executive who can green light a picture.

Spike Lee, Director
Interview in *Fade In* magazine, 1998

3335. I'm a black actor, but I don't do movies about the tragedy of being black…. I just do movies about what my character is going through….

Eddie Murphy, Actor
Cited in *Time Out* magazine, 1996

3336. Not one (black American actor) has ever been seriously challenged to deliver the best that is in him.

James Baldwin, Writer
Cited in *The Devil Finds* Work, 1975

3337. ("B" movie directors are) like Mack trucks. They don't wait for the time, the money or the actors — they just go.

Kathryn Bigelow, Writer-Director
Interview in *People* magazine, 1991

3338. What is art for the goose is not art for the gander.

Walt Disney
Arguing how can anyone say who an artist is, as stated in a 1938 *The New York Times Magazine* interview

3339. It is easier to copy than to think, hence fashion.

Wallace Stevens

3340. You can make films or you can cultivate a garden. If your film or your garden is a good one it means … you are entitled to consider yourself an artist.

Jean Renoir, Director
Stated in his 1974, *Jean Renoir — My Life and Times*

3341. If you have something worthwhile to say, dress it in the glittering robes of entertainment and you will find a ready made market … without entertainment no propaganda film is worth a dime.

Darryl F. Zanuck, Studio Head
His address to The Writer's Congress in Los Angeles, 1943

3342. Real life frees the imagination, and then places it in a straitjacket.

Somerset Maugham
Cited in *David Lean — A Biography*, 1996

3343. Nobody sets the stage…. Who knows what

style is…? I see something that is good, and I say, "That is good." I do not see it in terms of style.

Stanley Kramer, Producer-Director
Stated in *Directors at Work*, 1970

3344. To copy a genius is to admit one is not a genius.

Douglas Brode, Author
On those who try to emulate Federico Fellini, as cited in *Woody Allen*, 1985

3345. Everyone in the cast and crew was male but me, and there was no carrying on … this is a profession — not the oldest profession.

Rita Hayworth, Actress
Interview in *Headliner* magazine, 1977

3346. When a film set is harmonious … it's like a microcosm of a really good society.

Sean Connery, Actor
Cited in *The Lucas Film Fan Club* magazine, 1989

3347. For me every picture should be a love affair. I have to fall in love with the script and with everyone I'm working with; otherwise the picture doesn't jell.

Rita Hayworth, Actress
Cited in *Headliner* magazine, 1977

3348. The Disney operation is a psychiatrist's heaven because none of the patients are dangerous.

Arthur Miller
Cited in the *Birmingham News-Age Herald*, 1938

3349. See the water tower? Whose name is on it?

Jack Warner, Head of Warner Bros. Studio
When arguing with an employee, as cited in *Clown Prince of Hollywood*, 1990

3350. The only star at MGM is Leo the Lion.

Eddie Mannix, Producer, MGM
Sign on his desk, as cited in *Frank Capra*, 1971

3351. I hear you're having fun on the set. This must stop!

Jack Warner, Studio Chief
Cited in *The Warner Bros.*, 1975, to director Howard Hawks

3352. I have a concept I'm thinking of turning into an idea.

Woody Allen, Screenwriter-Director
Interview in *Rolling Stone* magazine, 1995

3353. Independent films are the most important things in our country…. They're the lifeblood of the filmmaking industry. They set the new standards ... the trends and they have the wildest ideas and the most interesting stories.

Sam Raimi

3354. The indie movement exists as a perpetual promise — a slippery Sundance of dreams — and not as an achieved body of great work.

David Densby, Writer
Stated in *The New Yorker*, 1998

3355. All distribution and decision-making power is in the hands of the conglomerates, and the word "independent" when applied to a producer is nothing but a genuflective misnomer.

William Fadiman
Cited in *Hollywood Now*, 1972

3356. If "Hollywood is like high school with money," the independent film world is like high school without money.

Sherman Alexie, Screenwriter
Cited in *Creative Screenwriting* magazine, 1998

3357. I've sold everything I had to make this film — washing machine, bed, everything I didn't need.

Peter Tong, Gobsmacked
Cited in *Variety*, 1998

3358. I've shot six independents now ... which may explain a few of those odd behavioral patterns of mine.

Mark Petersen, Cinematographer
Cited in *Movie Maker* magazine

3359. [A]fter a while you learn to ignore all impediments. To survive as a free agent in this world you have to maintain certain fictions.

Terrence Malick, Producer-Director
Cited in *After Dark*, 1974, on
being an independent producer

3360. There's no chair with your name on it. You're working as a team to make it, so you really learn how films are made.

Sharon Stone
On independent films, as cited in
The New York Times Magazine, 1997

3361. I do know the difference between a big movie and a small movie: sacrifices and attitude.

Lawrence Godon
Cited in *The New York Times Magazine*, 1997

3362. An independent film is not necessarily a bunch of people running around Soho dressed in black making a movie for $25,000. It's simply a film that stays free as long as possible to be what ever it wants to be.

Robert Redford
Cited in *The New York Times Magazine*, 1997

3363. Independents can no longer be mistaken for a farm team for the majors....

Janet Maslin
Cited in *The New York Times Magazine*, 1997

3364. I really don't care for all those gritty independent films about ordinary people ... and normal-looking actors. Excuse me, but if I want reality, I'll just leave the movie theater.

Libby Gelman-Waxner, Writer
Cited in *Newsweek Extra 2000*,
"The 100 Best Movies," 1998

3365. Attending film festivals is as much fun as walking down the street with a revolver in my mouth.

Paul Newman
Stated in *Paul Newman*, 1989

3366. (The Austin, Texas) film festival is the only festival I know that starts out by saying the film will not be shown here without the writer.

Robin Swicord, Screenwriter
Cited in *Movie Maker* magazine, 1998

3367. Entourages are born to dislike everything.

Jennings Lang
Cited in *Clint Eastwood — A Biography*, 1996

3368. [N]aturally the picture will be filmed through a thin slice of Roquefort cheese. If you make a picture for a film festival, you have to throw out anything that smacks of professional moviemaking.

Billy Wilder, Director
Stated in *The Bright Side of
Billy Wilder, Primarily*, 1970

3369. So let's provide an exhibition. I simply wanted to get the movies seen.

Robert Redford
On the genesis of Sundance, as stated in
The New York Times Magazine, 1997

3370. Film festivals and New York cocktail parties, they both have the same atmosphere, with all those people who come and talk, talk, talk.

Federico Fellini
Stated in *Fellini — A Life*, 1986

3371. [M]ost film festivals are not about supporting independent cinema, they're about PR and politics.

Mark Petersen, Cinematographer
Cited in *Movie Maker* magazine

3372. Pick your enemies carefully — or you'll never make it in this town.

Rona Barrett, Critic
Cited in *Going Hollywood*, 1978, on Hollywood

3373. (Hollywood has) a lot of destructive competitiveness ... just do the work and insulate yourself from the undercurrent of low-level malevolence.

Stanley Kubrick, Director
Cited in *Kubrick — Inside a
Film Artist's Maze*, 1982

3374. Failure's growth if you don't let it castrate you. Try again....

Myles Connolly, Writer
To Frank Capra upon on his first feature
film flop, as cited in *Frank Capra*, 1971

3375. Producers supply vision, augment vision, and direct vision. We (agents) navigate between art and commerce.

Paula Wagner, Agent
Cited in *People* magazine, 1991

3376. I've done my part for motion pictures. I've stopped making them.

Liberace
Cited in *Inside Oscar*, 1996

3377. "Early to bed, early to rise, work like hell and advertise."

Mario van Peebles, Director-Actor
Cited in *People* magazine, 1994, quoting the
only professional advice given him by his father

3378. Don't do it the way I showed you — do it the way I mean it.

Michael Curtiz, Director
To his cast, as cited in *Liberty* magazine, 1948

3379. By the time I was your age, I was fifteen.

Michael Curtiz, Director
Scolding a child star, as cited in *American
Movie Classics* magazine, 1996

3380. The next time I send a damn fool for something, I'll go myself.

Michael Curtiz, Director
To a crew member, as cited in *American
Movie Classics* magazine, 1996

3381. I want a movie with belly laughs. I don't want to spend time forcing a plot.

Woody Allen, Director
Cited in *Woody Allen
— His Films and Career*, 1985

3382. Between Jackie Chan's broken English and Chris Tucker's Ebonics, no one is going to understand a word of this movie. We'll end up being nominated for "Best Foreign Language Film."

Brett Ratner, Director
Cited in *Premiere* magazine, 1998

3383. If you think this picture's no good, I'll put on a beard and say it was made in Germany, and then you'll call it art.

Will Rogers, Actor
Cited in *The Saga of Special Effects*,
1977, on *The Roping Fool*

3384. What seems to make them more adult than ours is that we don't understand the dialogue.

Billy Wilder, Director
On comparing the subject matter of European
movies with that of Hollywood's, as cited in
The Bright Side of Billy Wilder, Primarily, 1970

3385. One has to fill out. A good painting, a good novel or a good opera makes its subject burst at the seams.

Auguste Renoir, Painter
As recalled by his film director son, Jean
Renoir, in his 1974 autobiography, *Jean Renoir*

3386. The realism of the cinema follows directly from its photographic nature.... The cinema can be emptied of all reality save one — the reality of space.

Andrè Bazin
Stated in *What Is Cinema*, 1971

3387. I've never gone in for the creaking door type of suspense. To me, murder by a babbling brook drenched in sunshine is more interesting.

Alfred Hitchcock
Interview in *The Saturday Evening Post*, 1957

3388. Show me a great actor, and I'll show you a busy husband; show me a great actress, and you've seen the devil.

W. C. Fields, Actor
Cited in *Bette and Joan — The Divine Feud*, 1989

3389. One of an artist's duties is to feed himself. It's hard to be creative on an empty stomach.

Kevin Kline, Actor
Interview in *Playboy*, 1988

3390. (Being a producer) doesn't interest me as a function. It interests me as a control.

Stanley Kramer, Producer-Director
Stated in *Directors at Work*, 1970

3391. I don't profess any beliefs.

Dino De Laurentis, Film producer of *The Bible*
Cited in *The Hustons*, 1989

3392. It's more like my two and one-half.
Woody Allen, Screenwriter-Director-Actor
Cited in *Chronicle of the Cinema*, 1995,
upon his *Annie Hall* compared to 8½

3393. Parents love best the child that is lame.
Akira Kurosawa, Director
That his own favorite film production
was the critics' least favorite, as stated
in *Show Business Illustrated*, 1962

3394. In show business, tampering with sacred
cows sometimes yields cream....
Frank Capra, Producer-Director
Stated in his *Frank Capra*, 1971,
on breaking studio tradition

3395. Your job is to protect Shakespeare from us.
Irving Thalberg, Producer
Upon hiring Dr. William Strunk, Jr.,
a professor from Cornell University,
as cited in *Fred Zinneman
—An Autobiography*, 1992

3396. That awful moment of truth, the "sneak"
preview ... the most excruciating ... hours in the
entire process of movie making ... like putting
one's child up for public auction.
Fred Zinnemann, Director
Cited in his 1992 *Fred Zinneman
—An Autobiography*

3397. Cinema grub is like a big lump of mashed
potatoes, a mutable prop for the director's vision.
Doris Weisberg, N.Y. University
Cited in *The New York Times*, 1997

3398. Food (in cinema) has been both plot and
motive. It has been both grand and sumptuous,
poignant and dreary, sexy and scary.
Molly O'Neill
Cited in *The New York Times Magazine*, 1997

3399. Book vs. film is as false a contrast as trash
book vs. good book. The lack of one does not
channel people to the other.
I. C. Jarvis
Stated in his 1970, *Movies and Society*

3400. Frankly, I like the book better.
Billy Wilder, Director
Commenting on a documentary of Hitler's rise
to power, called *Mein Kampf*, cited in *The
Bright Side of Billy Wilder, Primarily*, 1970

3401. Such a bitchin movie, figured it would be
a good book.
Amy Heckerling, Director
Cited in *Vanity* Fair, 1996

3402. Looking to the Academy for representation
was like trying to get laid in your mother's house.
Somebody was always in the parlor watching.
Dorothy Parker
Cited in *Inside Oscar*, 1996

3403. Agents are the Catch–22 of the movie business. Everybody starting out desperately needs one
and nobody starting out can possibly get one.
William Goldman, Author
Stated in his 1983 *Adventures in the Screen Trade*

3404. (The talent) agents are diplomats, negotia-
tors, salesmen, friends, and a very real part of the
performer's life....
Barry J. Weitz, Talent Agent
Cited in *Movie Business: American
Film Industry Practice*, 1972

3405. There's something very asexual about being
an agent.
Sue Mengers, Hollywood Agent
Cited in *Going Hollywood*, 1978

3406. (Hollywood) is not America at all, but it is
all America.
Ross Wills, Writer
Cited in *Southern California*, 1973

3407. (Hollywood) is America in flight from itself.
Carey McWilliams, Writer
Stated in her 1973 *Southern California*

3408. You can't explain Hollywood. There isn't
any such place.
Rachel Field, Writer
Cited in *Southern California*

Bibliography

A & E *Biography,* "Cary Grant," 1998 telecast.

A & E *Biography,* "Clark Gable," 1998 telecast.

A & E *Biography,* "Jimmy Stewart," 1998 telecast.

A & E *Biography,* "John Wayne," 1998 telecast.

Ach'ow Magazine, "60 Years in Film," July-Aug., 1969.

Acting for the Camera, by Tony Barr. New York: Harper Perennial, 1997.

Acting in the Cinema, by James Naremore. Berkeley: University of California Press, pg. 70, 1988.

Acting Is Everything, by Judy Kerr. Hollywood: September Publishing, 1981.

Action! Magazine, May–June, 1967.

Adventure, Mystery and Romance, by John G. Cawelti. Chicago: University of Chicago Press, 1976.

Adventures in the Screen Trade, by William Goldman. New York: Warner Books, p. 37, 1982.

After Dark, June 1974.

Akira Kurosawa — Something Like an Autobiography, by Akira Kurosawa. New York: Random House, 1982.

All About Barbra, No. 9, p. 22; No. 11, p. 19. 1987.

AMC: American Movie Classics Magazine, July, 1990; May 1996; November 1996.

America in the Movies by Michael Wood. New York: Basic Books, 1975, pp. 17–18.

The American Cinema — Directors and Direction, by Andrew Sorris. New York: Dutton, 1968.

American Cinema: One Hundred Years of Film Making by Jeanine Basinger. New York: Kuzzoli International Publications, 1995; pp. 18, 21, 23, 25, 28, 31, 48, 49, 65, 71, 75, 83, 87, 106, 150.

American Cinematography, February 1997.

American Film Genres by Stuart A. Kaminsky. Chicago: Nelson-Hall, 1984; p. 7.

American Film Magazine, "Dialogue on Film," October 1978, Frank Capra, p. 40; December 1998, Martha Coolidge, p. 16; October 1987, Karen Arthur, p. 113.

American Film Magazine, March, 1979, p. 46; August 1985; August 1990; Sept.-Oct., 1991, p. 21; April, 1993.

American Film, September-Oct., 1991, p. 18.

American Films Now, by James Monaco. New York: New American Library, 1979, p. 280.

The American Organist Journal, 1920, Vol. 3, No. 5, pp. 171–173; 1921, Vol. 4, No. 1, pp. 25, 26; 1923, Vol. 6, No. 4, p. 234; 1927, Vol. 10, No. 5, p. 130.

American Premiere Magazine, "The Role of the Film Commissioners," March, 1982, pp. 11–16.

American Premiere, June 11, 1992, p. 9, 11, 14, 16, 188.

American Visions, by Louis Block. Cinema Texas Program notes. Block, 1977, p. 75.

America's Youngest Art, p. 337.

AMPAS meeting in 1989 regarding the previous 25 years.

Anatomy of the Movies, by David McGillivray. New York: Macmillan, 1981.

Animation from Script to Screen, by Shamus Culliane. New York: St. Martin's Press, 1988, pp. 147, 150, 152, 160, 161, 181.

Animation Magazine, May, 1998, p. 4.

Anita Loos — Cast of Thousands by Anita Loos. New York: Grosset & Dunlap, 1977.

AP Newsfeature Wire, September 26, 1965.

Apparatus, by Jean-Louis Baudry. New York: Tanam Press, 1981, p. 54.

Architectural Digest, "Pinocchio, "February 15, 1940, p. 13; April 1994, p. 142; April, 1998, p. 187.

The Art and Craft of Cinematography, 1987.

Art Direction for Film and Video by Robert Olson. Boston: Focal Press, 1993.

The Art Director — Behind the Screen by William Cameron Menzies. New York: Dodge, 1938.

The Art of Alfred Hitchcock: 50 Years of His Motion Pictures by Donald Spoto. New York: Hopkins and Blake, 1975.

The Art of the Art Director: The Blue Book of the Screen. Hollywood, 1923.

The Art of the Film by Ernest Lindgren. London: George Allen & Unwin, 1948.

Artrage Autumn, 1989, p. 15.

Association of Motion Picture Producers.

Attaché Magazine, November 1997.

Bartlett's Book of Familiar Quotations, by John Bartlett and Justan Kaplan. New York: Little, Brown, 1992, p. 985–A, 984–B.

Basic Dimensions for a General Psychological Theory by A. Mehrabian. Cambridge, Mass: Oelgeschlager Gunn & Hain Publishers, 1980.

Basic Film Aesthetics in the Mast and Cohen Anthology.

Behind the Oscar — The Secret History of the Academy Awards, by Anthony Holden. Plume, 1994.

Bernard Shaw on Cinema.

Bette & Joan — The Divine Feud by Shaun Considine. New York: E.P. Dutton, 1989.

Beverly Hills Magazine, October 13, 1983.

Big Reel Magazine, August 1997, p. 114, 115.

Biography Magazine, March, 1998; May, 1998; July 1998, p. 32, 60, 93, 97.

Birmingham News-Age Herald, December 4, 1938, "Mickey Mouse's Home Is Like a College," by George Nagel.

The Black Path of Fear by Cornell Woolrick. New York: Ballantine Books, 1982.

Blockbuster Video Magazine, June, 1991.

Bob Hope — Don't Shoot, It's Only Me with Melville Shavelson. New York: G.P. Putnam's Sons, 1990.

The Boston Sunday Globe, February 23, 1997.

Box Office, December, 1995, pp. 10, 11, 14; May, 1995, p. 8; February, 1998, p. 24.

Brentwood Magazine, Winter, 1997.

Bright Lights, 1979, No. 8.

The Bright Side of Billy Wilder, Primarily, by Tom Wood. New York: Doubleday & Co., 1970.

British Film Institute talk by Bernard Herrmann, 1975.

Broadway In Review, 1940.

Business Week, 1998.

Buzz Magazine, February, 1994, pp. 46, 47.

Cable Choice Magazine, January 1989, p. 19.

The Cable Guide, September 1990, p. 32.

Cahiers du Cinéma, July 1956, XI, No. 61, pp. 10–19.

California Magazine, September, 1990, p. 79.

California, 1979.

The Camera Smart Actor by Richard Brestoff. New Hampshire: A. Smith and Kraus Books, 1994.

CBS — *60 Minutes.*

The Century by Peter Jennings. New York: Doubleday, 1998.

Chaplin by Roger Manuell. Boston: Little Brown & Co., 1974.

Character Handling by Ham Luske. October 6, 1938.

The Chicago Sunday America, July 28, 1968.

The Chicago Sunday Tribune, 1949.

Chicago Tribune, Hedda Hopper column, May 9, 1948.

Chicagoan, May 10, 1930.

The Christian Science Monitor, April 1987.

Chronicles of the Cinema, New York: D. K. Publishers, 1994, 1995, 1998.

The Cinema as Art, by Ralph Stevenson and Jean R. DeBrix. United Kingdom: Harmonsworth; Penguin, 1965.

The Cinema Book London: British Film Institute, 1985, p. v.

Cinema Craftsmanship by Frances Taylor Patterson. New York: Harcourt, Brace and Howe, 1920, p. 150.

Cinematograph, 1988, Vol. 3, p. 65.

Cinematographe, February, 1982.

Cinematographers on the Art and Craft of Cinematog-

raphy by Anna Kate Sterling. New York: Scarecrow Press, 1987.

Cinematography, Vol. 3, 1988, p. 65.

The Citizen News, 1960.

Citizen News, November 16, 1960; March 2, 1962.

City Boys. Princeton, NJ: Princeton University Press, 1992, p. 195.

Classic Film Collector, Spring-Summer, 1970, "Madcap, The Story of Mabel Normand," by Sam Peeples, p. 24.

Clint Eastwood — A Biography by Richard Schickel. New York: Alfred A. Knopf, 1996.

Close Up, 1978.

Clown Prince of Hollywood — The Life and Times of Jack L. Warner by Bob Thomas. New York: McGraw Hill Publishing, 1990.

Cocteau on the Film by Jean Cocteau and André Fraigneau. London: Dobson, 1954.

The Collected Works of Paddy Chayefsky. New York: Applause Books, 1995.

Collier's, May 3, 1924, pp. 7, 28; January 29, 1938.

The Complete Book of Moviemaking by Tony Rose. New York: Morgan & Morgan, 1972.

Contemporary Cinematographers: On Their Art by Pauline Rogers. Boston: Focal Press, 1998.

Conversations with Brando by Lawrence Grobel. NY: Hyperion, 1991.

Cosmopolitan, September 1972.

The Costume Designer's Handbook by Rosemary Ingham & Liz Covery. Portsmouth, NH: Heinemann Educational Books, Inc., 1992.

Creative Screenplay Magazine, May 1.

Creative Screenwriting Magazine, July/August, 1998.

Creative Writing magazine.

Cue Magazine, September 18, 1976; March 16, 1979.

CUE New York, 1979.

Current Research In Film: Audiences, Economics and Law, Vol. 5, by Bruce A. Austin, Editor. New Jersey: Ablex Publishing, 1991, Vol. 2, p. 214.

A Cut Above: Directors in Action, by Bob Thomas. Indianapolis: Merrill, 1973.

D. W. Griffith: His Life and Work, by Robert Henderson. New York: Oxford University Press, 1972.

The Daily Breeze, March 31, 1991.

Dark Cinema by Jon Tuska. Westport, CT: Greenwood Press, 1984.

The Dark Side of the Screen: Film Noir, by Foster Hirsch. San Diego: A. S. Barnes, 1981.

David Lean — A Biography, by Kevin Brownlow. New York: St. Martin's Press, 1996.

Deeds Rather Than Words, by Walt Disney, in "There's Always A Solution File."

Delsorte System of Expression, by Genevieve Stebbins, New York: Edgar S. Werner, 1902.

Department of State: File 840–4061, MP-3.25. 46.

De Sica — Miracle In Milan by Vittorio De Sica. New York: The Orion Press, 1968.

Designing Fantasia.

Designing for Films by Edward Carrick. New York:

The Studio Publications, 1949.

Details Magazine, December 1993; June 1996, p. 90.

Detour Magazine, March 1995, pp. 36, 39; May 1995, pp. 3, 5; February 1997, pp. 1, 42.

The Devil and Susan Seidelman, by Louise Bernikow, 1990, p. 111.

The Devil Finds Work: An Essay, by James Baldwin. New York: Dial Press, 1976.

DGA Magazine, February 1997.

The Dial Magazine, August 1981, p. 15.

Directing—Learn from the Masters, by Tay Garnett. Lanham, MD: The Scarecrow Press, 1996.

Directors in Action—50 Film Directors Talk About Their Craft, by Michael Sting. Los Angeles: Lone Eagle, 1968.

Directors at Work, by Bernard R. Kantor, Irwin R. Blacker, Anne Kramer. New York: Funk & Wagnalls, 1970.

Directors Guild of America News, November 1979.

Disney and Others, p. 172.

Disney Animation—The Illusion of Life, by Frank Thomas and Ollie Johnston. New York: Abbeville Press, 1991, pp. 125, 551–553.

Disney Story Department, Reference Manual, June 20, 1939, pp. 1–2.

Disney's Art of Animation, by Bob Thomas. New York: Welcome Enterprises, 1991, p. 18.

Documentary Explorations, by G. Roy Levin. New York: Doubleday, 1971, pp. 135, 234, 235.

Don't Look at the Camera, by Harry Watt. New York: St. Martin's Press, 1974.

Drama-Logue Magazine, October 20, 1983, p. 17; May 1, 1986; March 28, 1991, p. 6; May 30, 1991, p. 4; June 26, 1997, p. 5.

Dreams for Sale, by Andrzej Wajda. London: Harrap, 1989, p. 19.

Early Women Directors, by Anthony Slide. New York: A. S. Barnes, 1977, p. 103.

Edinburg Film Festival, 1974.

Elle Magazine, November 1987.

The Encyclopedia of Film, edited by James Monaco. New York: Perigee, 1991.

Entertainment Weekly 100, Special Edition—"The 100 Greatest Movie Stars of All Time," on Rudolph Valentino, 1997.

Entertainment Weekly, June 10, 1994; January 16, 1998; February 20, 1998; March, 1998; April, 10, 1998; August 7, 1998.

Entertainment World, March 6, 1970, p. 9.

Entertainment Yearbook, 1998, Special Edition.

Entertainment Yearbook, 1999.

Ernst Lubitsch: A Critical Study.

Esquire Magazine, October 10, 1978; November 1987; September 1992; September 1995, p. 140; February 1996, p. 77; December 1996, p. 93–94; August 1998, p. 126.

Essence Magazine, 1981.

Esthétique et Psychologie du Cinéma: The Aesthetics and Psychology of the Cinema, by Jean Mitry. Bloomington: Indiana University Press, 1990, p. 100.

"Ethical Issues," in the 1986 study of the film industry.

Ethical Issues Study on the film industry, 1986.

European Travel & Life, September 1990, p. 62.

Experimental Animation, by R. Russett and C. Starr. New York: Da Capo, 1976, p. 36.

The Face of the Century—100 Years of Make-up and Style, by Kate de Castelbajoc. New York: Rizzoli, 1995.

Fade In: Magazine, Winter 1997–98; Spring 1998.

Family Circle, June 26, 1979.

Fashion in Film, by Regine and Peter W. Engelmeier. Munich, Germany and New York: Prestel-Verlag, 1990.

Fellini—A Life, by Hollis Alpert. Collier Macmillan Canada, Inc., 1986.

The Fierce Imagination of Luis Buñuel, by Michael Wood. Great Film Directors, 1978.

50 Major Film Makers, edited by Peter Cowie. New Jersey: A. S. Barnes & Co, 1995.

Film Architecture—Set Designs, 1996.

Film as Film, "Understanding and Judging the Movies," by V. F. Perkins. Harmondsworth: Penguin, 1972, pp. 156–157.

Film Buff, February 1976.

Film Comment Magazine, July 1978, pp. 25–32; November-December 1988, p. 30; January-February 1997; March 4, 1998.

Film Culture Magazine, Winter 1955; Summer 1961, pp. 66–67; Spring 1962, pp. 45–61.

Film Design, by Peter Von Arx. New York: Van Nostrand Reinhold Co., 1983.

Film Design by Terence St. John Marner. London: The Tantivy Press, 1974.

Film Directing Shot by Shot, by Steven D. Katz. Los Angeles: Michael Wilse Productions, 1991, p. 147.

The Film Encyclopedia. Putnam's Sons, 1979.

Film Forum by Elena Oumano. New York: St. Martin's Press, 1985, pp. 37, 83, 84, 87, 91, 97, 100, 102, 106, 108, 110, 121, 123, 133, 135, 136, 137, 142, 144, 148, 154, 286, 292, 326.

Film Makers on Film Making, Vols. I and II, edited by Joseph McBride. Los Angeles: J. P. Tarder, Inc., 1983, pp. 40, 52, 82, 83, 84, 86, 87, 117, 118.

Film Score Monthly, June 1997, p. 21, 22, 24; July 1997, pp. 13–15; August 1997; October 1997; January 1998; February 1998; June 1998, pp. 2, 16, 17, 19.

Film Technique by V. I. Pudovkin. London: G. Newnes, 1933.

Film Theory and Criticism by Robert Warshaw, 3rd edition, "Movie Chronicle: The Westerner." New York: Oxford University Press. 1985, pp. 438, 439, 449.

Film Theory and Criticism by Gerald Mast and Marshall Cohen. New York: Oxford University Press, 1985.

Film: An Anthology, Daniel Talbot, editor. Berkeley: University of California Press, 1975, pp. 29, 30.

The Film: A Psychological Study by Hugo Münsterberg. New York: Dover, 1970, p. 31.

Filmmakers and Financing by Louise Levison. Boston: Focal Press, 1994.

Filmmusik, by Hans-Christian Schmidt. Basel: Baren-reiter Kassel, 1982, p. 16–18.

Films and Filming Magazine, January 1961, pp. 13, 38; June 1961, pp. 7, 41; February 1962; March 1962.

Films in Review Magazine, January 1980, p. 6.

The Films of Akira Kurosawa, by Donald Richie. Berkeley: University of California Press, 1965.

Films of the Golden Age Magazine, Spring 1998, William Hare, pp. 30, 38.

First Cut— Conversations with Film Editors, by Gabriella Oldham. Los Angeles: University of California Press, 1992.

For Marx. New York: Random House, 1970, pp. 25, 211, 212.

For Vitaphone Talking Pictures, 1927.

Ford Times, March, 1982.

The Foreign Cinema, July 12, 1968, Vol. 1, No. 5.

France Observateur, 1958.

Frank Capra— The Name Above the Title: An Autobiography, by Frank Capra. New York: The Macmillan Co., 1971.

Fred Zinnemann— An Autobiography: A Life In The Movies, by Robert Stewart. New York: Charles Scribner's Sons, 1992.

Funny Business: The Craft of Comedy Writing, bv Sol Saks. Lone Eagle, 1985.

The Future of the Movies, interviews by Roger Ebert and Gene Siskel. Kansas City: Andrews and McNeal, 1991.

The Gangster as Tragic Hero.

George Cukor— A Double Life: A Bio of the Gentleman Director, by Patrick McGilligan. New York: St. Martin's Press, 1991.

George Magazine, August 1997; March 1998.

Going Hollywood, by Marie Brenner. New York: Delacorte Press, 1978.

Going Steady, by Pauline Kael. Boston: Little, Brown, 1970, pp. 104, 105, 113, 114.

GQ Magazine, September 1983, p. 344–346; July 1989, p. 129–130; June 1995, p. 167; October 1995, p. 181–183; January 1994, p. 74; April 1981, p. 193; June 1992, p. 160; September 1992, p. 280; October 1985; February 1991, p. 72.

Great Film Directors— A Critical Anthology, edited by Leo Brandy and Morris Dickstein. New York: Oxford University Press, 1978.

The Great Movie Comedians by Leonard Matlin. New York: Crown, 1978.

The Green Book Magazine, April 1914, pp. 556–562.

Growing Up In Hollywood, by Robert Parrish. London: Bodley Head, 1976, p. 209.

Guardian, October 3, 1991, p. 28, Robert Leedham's column.

Guinness— Movie Facts and Feats, A Guinness Record Book, by Patrick Robertson. New York: Sterling Publishing Co., 1980.

Handbook of American Film Genres, edited by Wes D. Gehring. Westport, Connecticut: Greenwood Press, 1988.

Harper's Bazaar, 1946; December 1996.

Hawks on Hawks, by Joseph McBride. Los Angeles: University of California Press, 1982.

Headliner Magazine, 1977, p. 92.

Hello Magazine UK, c. 1989.

Heroes of the Silver Screen, by Richard Schickel. New York: Galahad Books, 1982.

Hitchcock, by Francois Truffaut. New York: Simon and Schuster, 1983.

Hollywood— The Pioneers, by John Kobal and Kevin Brownlow. New York: Alfred A. Knopf, 1979.

Hollywood and History— Costume Design in Film by Edward Morder. Thames and Hudson: L. A. County Museum of Art, 1987.

Hollywood Cinema, by Richard Maltby. Cambridge, Massachusetts: Blackwell, 1995, p. 189.

Hollywood Citizen-News, February 28, 1938; February 19, 1940.

Hollywood Director: The Career of Mitchell Leisen, by David Chierichetti. New York: Curtis Books, 1973.

Hollywood Dynasties, by Stephen Farber and Marc Green. New York: Delilah Communications, Ltd., 1984.

Hollywood Genres, by Thomas Schotz. New York: Random House, 1981.

Hollywood in a Suitcase— Sammy Davis, Jr., by William Marrow. New York: Morrow, 1980.

Hollywood Looks at Its Audience: A Report of Film Audience Research, by Leo A. Handel. Urbana: University of Illinois Press, 1950.

Hollywood Now, by William Fadiman. New York: Liveright, 1972, pp. 153, 154.

Hollywood Reporter, December 12, 1995; December 8, 1992; February 20, 1939; September 10, 1996; November 25, 1996; September 24, 1997; December 10, 1996.

The Hollywood Reporter, June 11, 1968; December 2, 1992; March 6, 1996; December 10, 1996; December 9, 1997; March 21, 1996, p. 5–15; January 19, 1998; March 8, 1995.

Hollywood Studio Magazine, September 1985. From the collection of Brian O'Dowd.

Hollywood, the Dream Factory: An Anthropologist Looks at the Moviemakers, by Hortense Powdermaker. Boston: Little, Brown, 1950, pp. 71–72.

"Hollywood's Pattern of Sameness," 1946.

How to Read a Film, by James Monocao. New York: Oxford University Press, 1981.

"How the Hell Do You Survive in Hollywood?" Winter, 1997/98.

The Hustons, by Lawrence Grabel. New York: Charles Scribner's Sons, 1989.

The Illustrated History of the Camera, by Michael Auer. New York Graphic Society. Boston: Little, Brown & Co., 1975.

The Imaginary Signifier, by Christian Metz. Bloomington: Indiana University Press, 1982, p. 8.

The Immediate Experience, "The Gangster as Tragic Hero," by Robert Warshow. New York: Atheneum, 1971, p. 113.

The Independent on Sunday, London, February 25, 1996.

Ingrid Bergman—My Story, by Ingrid Bergman and Alan Burgess. New York: Delacorte Press, 1980.

Inner Views: Filmmakers in Conversation, by David Breskin. New York: Da Capo Press, 1992.

The Innocent Eye: The Life of Robert J. Flaherty, by Arthur Calder-Marshall. New York: Harcourt Brace Jovanovich, 1966, p. 229.

Inside Oscar: The Unofficial History of the Academy Awards, 10th Anniversary Edition, by Mason Wiley and Darnien Bona. New York: Ballantine Books, 1996.

Internet Movie Database, Ltd., "Film 100," 1998, www.imdb.com.

Interview Magazine, October 1995; July 1990, p. 72; April 1998; February 1991; September 1991, p. 96; June 1993; November 1, 1980; March 1993, p. 14; March 1990; November 1995; August 1990, p. 97, 101; August 1989.

Interviews with Film Directors. Indianapolis: Bobbs-Merrill, 1967.

An Introduction to Film Studies, edited by Jill Nelmes. London: Routledge, 1996.

Jack Nicholson—"Jack's Life"—A Biography, by Patrick McGilligan. New York: W. W. Norton & Co., 1994.

James Hillier column, 1977.

Jean Renoir—My Life and My Films. New York: Wm. Collins Sons & Co. Ltd., and Atheneum Publishers, Inc.

John Ford—The Man and His Films, by Tag Gallagher. Berkeley: University of California Press, 1986.

John Ford, by Joseph McBride and Michael Wilmington. New York: Da Capo.

John Ford, by Peter Bogdanovich. Berkeley: University of California Press, 1968.

John Frankenheimer—A Conversation with Charles Champlin, 1995.

John Wayne's America: The Politics of Celebrity, by George Wills. New York: Simon & Schuster, 1997.

Journal of Aesthetics 4, "Emotions," 1945.

Journal of Marketing, with Marjorie Fiske, January 1947, pp. 273, 280.

Journal of Social Psychology, No. 48, p. 272–271.

Journal of the University Film Association, "Commercial Practices in Audience Analysis," 1954; "Film Scholarship: Dead or Alive?"

Journal of the University Film Association, Spring 1954, p. 9; Winter 1976, p. 5.

Journalism Quarterly, Spring 1978, p. 35.

KCET Magazine, February 1988.

Kubrick—Inside a Film Artist's Maze, by Thomas Allen Nelson. Bloomington: Indiana University Press, 1982.

Kuleshov On Film. Berkeley: University of California Press, 1982.

L.A. Style, April 1987, p. 112.

LA Village View, February 12, 1993, p. 11; November 18, 1994, p. 34; July 21, 1995.

The Language of Show Biz—A Dictionary. Chicago: The Dramatic Publishing Co.

Laughing Matters, by Larry Gilbert. New York: Random House, 1998.

Lears, January 1990.

Lessons with Eisenstein, by Vladmir Nizhniy. London: G. Allen & Unwin, 1962.

Letter to Victor Ford Collins, August 3, 1949, File 2—RKO.

Lew Hunter's Screenwriting 434, by Lew Hunter. New York: Perigee, 1993.

Liberty Magazine, January 1, 1948, p. 28.

A Life in the Movies, by Michal Powell. Heinemann, London, 1986.

Life Magazine, March 1992, p. 52, 54; January 1998.

The Life of James Stewart: Pieces of Time, by Gary Fishgall. A Lisa Drew Book/Scribner.

Living Images, by Stanley Kauffmann. New York: Harper & Row, 1971, p. 122.

Look Magazine.

The Los Angeles Daily News, October 15, 1995.

The Los Angeles Evening Herald & Express, August 31, 1950.

Los Angeles Examiner, March 24, 1950.

Los Angeles Express, October 22, 1972.

Los Angeles Herald Examiner, August 31, 1977; March 26, 1989, p. 13.

Los Angeles Magazine, December 1995; April 1996; June 16, 1996; March 1997, April 1998.

Los Angeles Style Magazine 1991.

Los Angeles Style, July, 1991; September 1991, p. 162.

The Los Angeles Times, October 26, 1989; January 8, 1996; May 14, 1995; June 29, 1965; June 16, 1996; March 28, 1998; June 5, 1977, p. 43; May 19, 1966; August 31, 1997; December 6, 1990; January 5, 1986; August 11, 1996; April 1996; June 19, 1998; October 25, 1968; January 23, 1992; January 1, 1995; January 5, 1997; May 4, 1991.

The Los Angeles Times—Calendar, July 7, 1996; May 14, 1998; Jan 27, 1991, p. 3; December 19, 1993; December 18, 1994, p. 87; May 14, 1995; May 19, 1968; July 7, 1991, p. 5; August 18, 1991; March 29, 1992, p. 29; November 16, 1997; April 17, 1989; April 5, 1998.

The Los Angeles Times Magazine, August 4, 1991; March 1997; May 3, 1998; June 16, 1996; February 4, 1996; March 20, 1994; January 11, 1998.

Los Angeles View, September 29, 1995, p. 17.

Los Angeles Village View, November 18, 1994, p. 34.

Los Angeles, 1972, p. 45.

The Lucas Film Fan Club Magazine, Fall 1989, No. 9, p. 5.

The Magic Art of Jan Svankmajer, June 1992, London, BBC2.

The Magic Kingdom, by Steven Walts. New York: Houghton Mifflin Co, 1997, p. 453.

Make-up Artist Magazine, August-September 1997, p. 34; February-March 1998, pp. 55, 62; April-May 1998, pp. 19, 48; June-July 1998, pp. 20, 26.

Making Meaning, by David Bordwell. Cambridge, MA: Harvard University Press, 1989, p. 245.

Making Movies, by Sidney Lumet. New York: Alfred A. Knopf, 1995.

A Man with a Camera, by Nestor Almendraz. New York: Ferrar-Straus & Giroux, 1984.

Max Factor's Hollywood, Glamour-Movies-Makeup, by Fred E. Basten and Paul Kaufman. W. Quay Hayes Publisher, 1995.

Maybe Maybe Not— Second Thoughts on a Secret Life, by Robert Fulghum. New York: Random House, 1993.

Mayer and Thalberg— The Make Believe Saints, by Samuel Marx. New York: Random House, 1995.

McCalls Magazine, "The Documentary Film," August 1939, p. 171.

McCormick Foundation, "Ethical Issues in the Film Industry" study, 1986, pp. 225, 236.

The Meaning of Art.

MGM press release, 1940, AMPAS library.

Mirabella, January 11, 1998.

Modern Maturity Magazine, March-April, 1998.

Monthly Bulletin of the Society of Motion Picture Art Directors, March 1951.

The Morning Telegraph, December 24, 1922; September 9, 1923; January 27, 1924.

Motion Picture Association of America Archive, New York 1930, AMPP Code File, pp. 138–139.

Motion Picture Association, "The Motion Picture As A Business," given April, 1928, Archive. New York.

Motion Picture Classic, by Kenneth MacGowan, March 1919.

Motion Picture Export Associations 1953–54 Annual Report.

Motion Picture Magazine, Aline Carter, "Muse of the Reel," March 1921.

Motion Picture Marketing and Distribution by Fred Goldberg. Boston: Focal Press, 1991.

Moveline Magazine, April 1998; May 1998; June 1998; August 1998, p. 63, 76, 78, 85.

The Movie Business, by David Lees. New York: Vintage Books, 1981, p. 117.

Movie Business: American Film Industry Practice, edited by A. William Bluem and Jason E. Squire. New York: Hastings House, 1972.

Movie Classic 8, "Do Movies Influence the Paris Designers," by Laura Bloyney, June 1935.

Movie Maker Magazine, April 1998, p. 76; July 1998, No. 29, Vol. 5.

The Movie World of Roger Corman, J. Philip di Franco, editor; New York and London: Chelsea House, 1979.

Moviegoer Magazine, February 1986, p. 11.

Moviemakers at Work by David Chell, Microsoft Press, 1987, pp. 41, 49, 68, 294, 320.

Movies and Money, by Janet Wasko. Temple University, New Jersey: Ablex Publishing Corp., 1982.

Movies and Society, by I. C. Jarvie. New York: Basic Books, 1970.

Movies as Mass Communications. Beverly Hills: Sage, 1980, p. 27.

Moving Picture Weekly, "The Dual Personality of Cleo Madison," 1916, p. 25.

Moving Picture World, by John F. Barry, "Women's Place in Photoplay Production," July 11, 1914, p. 40.

MPPDA, Motion Picture Producers, Directors Association, Production Code Preamble, 1930.

Mrs. Fiske: Her Views on Actors, Acting and the Problems of Production, New York: Century City Co., 1917.

Ms. Magazine, September 1989; January 1976, p. 112.

Music for Silent Films by Gillian B. Anderson. Washington, D.C. Library of Congress, 1988.

Music for the Movies by Tony Thomas. Los Angeles: Silman-James Press.

My Autobiography— Charles Chaplin. London: The Bodley Head, Ltd., 1964.

My Private Diary, by Rudolph Valentino. Chicago: Occult, 1929.

Naked Hollywood, by Nicolas Kent. London: BBC Books, 1991, p. 79, 121.

Nation Magazine, January 22, 1938.

National Film Society lecture by John C. Tibbetts, "Introduction to the Photoplay," April 10, 1929.

New American Cine. "A Rose is a Rose," p. 125.

The New American Cinema, John Lewis, editor. Durham, NC: Duke University Press, 1998.

New Republic, "A Night at the Opera" review, December 11, 1935, p. 130.

The New Republic, March 26, 1984, p. 24.

The New Wave, by Peter Graham. New York: Doubleday, 1968, p. 18.

New Woman Magazine, October 1997, p. 130.

New York Film Forum.

New York Herald Tribune, "Femine Director Depends On Reason, Discards Instuition," June 26, 1932, p. vii, 6.

The New York Times, May 5, 1946, "Breaking Hollywood's Pattern of Sameness," by Frank Capra; October 23, 1977, Sec. 2, p. 17; August 30, 1981; November 10, 1968, p. D-15; January 11, 1976, p. D-13; April 21, 1991; June 26, 1983, Sec. 2, pp. 1, 17; August 6, 1967; January 1, 1984, Sec. 2, p. 11; June 22, 1990; January 24, 1975, p. 54; January 11, 1998.

The New York Times Magazine, May 24, 1992; July 10, 1938, p. 5, by S. J. Woolf, "Walt Disney"; November 16, 1997; May 10, 1998, p. 24; January 15, 1978, p. 16; May 31, 1992, p. 44.

The New Yorker, March 16, 1998, p. 79; April 6, 1998; March 19, 1989; February 20, 1995, p. 212; April 29, 1996, p. 136; May 11, 1998, p. 107; March 9, 1998, "Scoring For The Oscars," pp. 82, 83; December 8, 1997; May 16, 1998; February 5, 1990.

Newsweek Extra 2000, "100 Best Movies" list from the American Film Institute, "A Century On Screen," 1998.

Newsweek Magazine, March 30, 1970; November 9, 1987; April 26, 1993.

The Non-Fiction Film, by Richard Barsam. Bloomington: Indiana University Press, 1992, p. 53.

Nostalgia Isn't What It Used to Be, by Simone Signoret. New York: Harper and Row, 1978.

Novels into Film, by George Bluestone. Baltimore: John Hopkins Press, 1957.

The Observer—London, August 6, 1995.

Ohio Film Bureau, "Feature Film Making In Ohio," March 10, 1983.

On Method Acting, by Edward Dwight Easty, 1966.

On the History of Film Style, by David Boldwell. Cambridge, MA: Harvard University Press, 1997.

The Orange County Register Show, October 25, 1994.

Orange County Register—SHOW, 1994.

Orson Welles: The Road to Xanadu, by Simon Callous. New York: Viking Penguin, 1996.

Overtones and Undertones: Reading Film Music, by Royal S. Brown. Berkeley: University of California Press, 1994.

Parade Magazine, March 5, 1989, p. 4; August 30, 1998.

The Parade's Gone By, by Kevin Brownlow. New York: Ballantine Books, 1969, p. 155.

The Paramount Pretties, by James Robert Parish. New Rochell, New York: Arlington House, 1972, p. 65.

Paul Newman, by Elenva Oumano. New York: St. Martin's Press, 1989.

PBS telecast, 1998.

Pearson's Magazine, August 1915.

Penguin Film Review, January 1948, pp. 22–29.

People Magazine, June 1, 1998, p. 54; October 4, 1982; December 18, 1989, p. 121; September 28, 1987; December 30, 1991; June 19, 1989; Spring 1991; August 20, 1984; May 8, 1995, p. 192; July 8, 1991, p. 57; March 7, 1994.

Photoplay, "Miracle Men at Work to Make You Lovelier," February 1917; July 1939, p. 26.

Photoplay, Frances Deuton, 1917.

Picture Personalities, by Richard de Cordova. Urbana: University of Illinois Press, 1990, p. 13.

The Plain Dealer, March 2, 1978.

Playboy Magazine, March 1998; February 1975; September 1965, p. 94; February 1991, p. 70; June 1984, pp. 129, 178, 180; November 1991, p. 64; May 1971; June 1988; March 1986, p. 57; September 1993, p. 169; March 1996, p. 146, 147; September 1997, p. 52; March 1992; January 1993, p. 70; April 1995, p. 134; November 1995; December 1996; September 1996, p. 142; December 1994, p. 150; April 1998; January 1991.

Played By Ear, by Father Daniel A. Lord. Chicago: Loyola University Press, 1955, p. 273.

Political and Economic Planning, London, 1952, p. 205.

Post-War American Films: The Gangster Film.

Power 50 Magazine, December 12, 1995.

Premiere Magazine, January 1998; March 1998; May 1998; July 1998.

The Price They Pay for Fame.

The Producer Makes a Plan—We Make the Movies, by Jesse Lasky. New York: Norton, 1937, pp. 1–5.

Production Design Magazine, December 1951, p. 14.

Pulse Magazine, July 1996, p. 53.

Quarterly Review of Film Studies, "The Film Viewer as Consumer," by J. Allen, No. 5, Fall 1980, pp. 481–499.

Questions for the Movie Answer Man by Roger Ebert. Kansas City: Andrew-McNeil, 1997.

Raul Walsh. Edinburg Film Festival, 1974, p. 43.

Raymond Chandler In Hollywood, by Al Clark. Proteous Publishing, 1983.

Reader's Digest, June 1988.

Reel Conversations, by George Hickenlooper. New York: Carol, 1991.

The Reel Tinsel, by Bernard Rosenberg and Harry Silverstein. New York: Macmillan, 1970.

Reel Women—Pioneers of the Cinema, 1896 to the Present, by Ally Acker. New York: Continuum, 1991.

The Rise and Fall of British Documentary, by E. Sussex. Los Angeles: University of California Press, 1976, p. 52.

The Rise of the American Film, by Lewis Jacobs. New York, 1939, pp. 502, 503, 504.

Robert Wise: On His Films, by Sergio Leeman. Los Angeles: Silman-James Press, 1995.

Rochester Democrat Chronicle, July 19, 1936.

Rolling Stone Magazine, May 31, 1979; November 28, 1982; June 11, 1992, p. 19; September 7, 1995; October 17, 1996; September 7, 1998.

The Saga of Special Effects, by Ron Fry and Pamela Fourzon. New Jersey: Prentice Hall, 1977.

The San Francisco Examiner & Chronicle, 1967.

San Francisco Film Festival, 1975.

San Francisco Sunday Examiner and Chronicle, June 11, 1967, Sec. 4, p. 4.

Santa Barbara Film Festival, Screenwriters Panel, 1997.

Santa Barbara News-Press, February 22, 1998; March 3, 1998; March 6, 1998; March 12, 1998; March 14, 1998; May 19, 1998; October 30, 1998; December 8, 1998, p. D-7.

Saturday Evening Post, 1957.

The Saturday Evening Post, July 27, 1957, pp. 36–37, 71–73; June 20, 1964.

Screen Acting, by Brian Adams. Sydney, Australia: Image Book Co., 1986.

Screen Acting, by Helen Klamph. New York: Falk, 1922, p. 181.

Screen Actor Magazine, May-June, 1968, p. 10.

Screen Actor, Fall 1986, p. 17.

Screen International, December 6, 1980; February 9, 1996.

Screenwriters on Screenwriting, by Joel Engel. New York: Hyperion, 1995.

Script Magazine, Vol. 4, No. 2.

Sets in Motion. Art Direction and Film Narrative by Charles Affron and Mirella Jona Affron. New Jersey: Rutgers University, 1995.

Show Business Illustrated, April 1962.

Sight and Sound, September 1934; Autumn 1946; Spring 1957, pp. 203–205.

Silver Screen Magazine, July 1941.

Sophia Loren—A Biography, by Warren G. Harris. New York: Simon and Schuster, 1998.

Sound Theory—Sound Practice, "Film—Cinema Movie" by Rick Altman. New York: Routledge, 1992, p. 65.

Sound Theory—Sound Practice, "Theory of the Film," by Rick Altman. New York: Routledge, 1992.

Sounds for Silents, by Charles Hofmann. New York: DBS Publication, 1970.

Southern California, by Carey McWilliams. Santa Barbara, CA: Peregrine Smith, Inc., 1973, pp. 330–342.

Sports Illustrated, 1986.

The Stanislavsky Heritage. New York University Press, 1965, p. 261.

Stanley Kubrick—A Biography, by Vincent La Brutto. New York: Donald I. Fine, 1997.

Steven Spielberg—The Unauthorized Biography by John Baxter. New York: HarperCollins, 1996.

Study on the film industry, 1986.

Suddenly Doors Open Up, by Gerald Moore, p. 201.

The Sunday Times, London, April 11, 1993, p. 6, 7.

Take 22: Moviemakers on Moviemaking. New York: Viking Penguin, 1984.

Talking Pictures, by Barrett C. Kiesling. Richmond, VA: Johnson, 1937, p. 2.

The Technicolor Years, by Fred E. Basten. New Jersey: A. S. Barnes and Co., 1980.

The Technique of Film Editing, by Karen Reisz and Gavin Miller for the British Film Academy. New York: Hastings House, 1968.

The Technique of Screenplay Writing by Eugene Vale. New York: Grosset and Dunlap, 1973, p. 63.

Terra Magazine, "The Man of a Thousand Faces," March-April 1996.

Theatre Arts Monthly, October 1937.

Theory of Film, by Siegfried Kracauer. New York: Oxford University Press, 1971, p. 90–91.

They Went Thataway, by Michael Wilmington. San Francisco: Mercury House, 1994.

Thinking in Pictures: The Making of the Movie, Matewan. Boston: Houghton Mifflin, 1987.

Thumbnail Sketches, by Dick Huemer, p. 38.

Time Magazine, December 15, 1997; August 4, 1997; January 1998; August 11, 1997, p. 72, 71; August 25, 1997; June 17, 1996; May 1, 1996.

Time Out London, February 14, 1990; February 24, 1993, p. 23; August 14, 1993, p. 17; March 27, 1996.

Time Out Magazine, August 28, 1996, p. 22.

The Today Show—NBC.

Toledo, Ohio Times, "Introducing Donald Duck—Fighting Professor," by John Stanley, Octo. 20, 1937.

Tom Cruise—Unauthorized, by Wensley Clarkson. Hasting House, 1997.

The Total Film Maker. London: Vision Press, 1971, p. 157.

The Tribune Chronicle. Warren, Ohio, December 1, 1981, p. B-8.

True and False, Heresy and Common Sense for the Actor, by David Mamet. New York: Pantheon Books, 1997.

True Magazine, November 1947.

TV Guide, December 21–27, 1963; March 16–22, 1996, p. 32; December 6–12, 1996.

Twentieth Century's Fox: Darryl F. Zanuck and the Culture of Hollywood, by George F. Custen. Basic Books, 1997.

UPI wire service story, c. October 30, 1950.

US Magazine, January 1993, p. 25–28; May 1993, p. 62; April 25, 1983; December 1997, p. 66; April 30, 1990; June 27, 1998; November 5, 1984; August 22, 1988; March 6, 1989, p. 56; July 1998, p. 79; November 1991, p. 50; August 1996, p. 48.

USA Weekend, January 9–11, 1998, p. 4–5; March 29, 1996, p. 8.

The Valley News, June 22, 1979.

The Valley Vantage, June 9, 1994, p. 10.

Vanity Fair, April 1997; January 1998; December 1995, p. 174; May 1994, p. 94; July 1990, p. 60; June 1996, p. 134; January 1995; October 1995; June 1993, p. 144; September 1995, p. 202; October 1988, p. 189; October 1994; July 1996, p. 76; January 1994; April 1996.

Variety Daily, May 2, 1991; June 3, 1992.

Variety, February 28, 1998; May 12, 1982; February 7, 1997; September 9, 1997; January 7, 1997, p. 46; January 10, 1998; May 24, 1989, p. 9; January 18, 1998; November 18, 1981, pp. 5, 32.

Variety's On Production, Vol. 5, No. 10, November 1996.

Venice Magazine, February 1995, p. 28–29; February 1993, p. 38; January-February 1996, p. 29, 31; September 1992, p. 37; November 1997, p. 45; August 1991, p. 28; June 1998.

The Village View, July 21–27, 1989; August 16, 1991, p. 9; March 23, 1990; January 18, 1990, p. 17.

The Village Voice, June 14, 1976.

Vim & Vigor Magazine, Winter 1993, p. 17; Summer 1996, p. 19–20.

Vogue, March 1964; March 1991, p. 256; February 1990, p. 200.

Voices in the Mirror.

W Magazine, March 1996, p. 166; November 1996, p. 4; January 1997, p 124.

The Wall Street Journal, August 23, 1994; June 18, 1997.

Walt Disney Interview, 1959.

Walt Disney Studio, Memo to Don Graham, December 23, 1935.

Warner Brothers by Charles Higham. New York: Charles Scribner's Sons, 1975.

Webster's Dictionary of Quotations, 1998.

What an Art Director Does: An Introduction to Motion Picture Design, by Ward Preston. Los Angeles: Silman-James Press, 1994.

"What I Believe" Forum, October, 1930.

What Is Cinema, Vol. II., "The Western: or The American Film Par Excellence." Berkeley: University of California Press, 1971.

What Is Cinema? Or the American Film Par Excellence, by André Bazin. Berkeley: University of California Press, 1971, p. 108.

When the Shooting Stops, the Cutting Process Begins: A Film Editor's Story, by Ralph Rosenblum and Robert Karen. New York: Viking, 1979.

The White Album, by Joan Didion. Harmondsworth: Penguin, 1981, p. 162.

Will Rogers: His Wife's Story. Norman: University of Oklahoma Press, 1941, p. 147.

Wisconsin Law Review, with Ray Bates and Peter Herman, 1970, pp. 791–838.

The Wit and Wisdom of Women. Philadelphia: Running Press, 1993, p. 69.

Women Film Directors, An International Bio-Critical Dictionary, by Gwendolyn Audrey Foster. Westport, CT: Greenwood Press, 1995.

Women In Motion Pictures, 1991.

Women's Wear Daily.

Woody Allen — His Films and Career, by Douglas Brode. New Jersey: Citadel Press, 1985.

The Word In a Frame, by Leo Braudy. New York: Anchor Press, 1976.

The World, the Text and the Critic, by Edward Said. Cambridge MA: Harvard University Press, 1983, p. 53.

The Writer's Congress in Los Angeles, 1943.

Writer's Congress, Los Angeles, October 1943, Roger Manuel address, "Films and the Second World War." New York: Dell, 1974, p. 203.

Written By Magazine, Writers Guild of America, January 1997; March 1998.

You Must Remember This, by Walter Wagner. New York: G. P. Putnam's Sons, 1975.

Your Film Acting Career, by M. K. Lewis and Rosemary Lewis. Santa Monica, CA: Gorham House Publishing, 1989.

The Zanucks of Hollywood, by Marlys J. Harris. New York: Crown, 1989.

Source Names and Movie Titles Index

Keywords Index